Transgender Communication Studies

Transgender Communication Studies

Histories, Trends, and Trajectories

Edited by
Leland G. Spencer and Jamie C. Capuzza

LEXINGTON BOOKS
Lanham • Boulder • New York • London

Published by Lexington Books
An imprint of The Rowman & Littlefield Publishing Group, Inc.
4501 Forbes Boulevard, Suite 200, Lanham, Maryland 20706
www.rowman.com

Unit A, Whitacre Mews, 26-34 Stannary Street, London SE11 4AB

British Library Cataloguing in Publication Information Available

Library of Congress Cataloging-in-Publication Data

Transgender communication studies : histories, trends, and trajectories / edited by Jamie C. Capuzza
and Leland G. Spencer.
pages cm.
Includes bibliographical references and index.
ISBN 978-1-4985-0005-0 (cloth : alk. paper)—ISBN 978-1-4985-0006-7 (electronic)
1. Transgenderism. 2. Transgenderism on television. 3. Transgender people--Identity. 4. Interpersonal communication. I. Capuzza, Jamie C., editor. II. Spencer, Leland G., editor.
HQ77.9.T7154 2015
306.76'8--dc23
2014047128
ISBN 978-1-4985-0007-4 (pbk : alk. paper)

∞ ™ The paper used in this publication meets the minimum requirements of American
National Standard for Information Sciences Permanence of Paper for Printed Library
Materials, ANSI/NISO Z39.48-1992.

Printed in the United States of America

Contents

Contents

II: Media

6 News: What's in a Name? Transgender Identity, Metareporting,
  and the Misgendering of Chelsea Manning   93
  Jamie C. Capuzza

7 Television: The Provisional Acknowledgment of Identity
  Claims in Televised Documentary   111
  E. Tristan Booth

8 Film: Becoming One of the Girls/Guys: Distancing Transgender
  Representations in Popular Film Comedies   127
  Lucy J. Miller

9 Visual Communication: From Abomination to Indifference: A
  Visual Analysis of Transgender Stereotypes in the Media   143
  Paul Martin Lester

10 Social Media: Fleshy Metamorphosis: Temporal Pedagogies of
  Transsexual Counterpublics   155
  Joshua Trey Barnett

III: Public and Rhetorical Communication

11 Language: Traversing the Transcape: A Brief Historical
  Etymology of Trans* Terminology   173
  Mary Alice Adams

12 Religious Discourse: Coming Out, Bringing Out: God's Love,
  Transgender Identity, and Difference   187
  Leland G. Spencer IV

13 Legal Discourse: The Trans-Exclusive Archives of U.S. Capital
  Punishment Rhetoric   199
  Peter Odell Campbell and Cory Holding

14 Public Memory: Historical Trans-cription: Struggling with
  Memory in *Paris Is Burning*   217
  Thomas R. Dunn

References   233

Index   261

About the Contributors   275

Acknowledgments

Like any project, this book emerged neither *ex nihilo* nor entirely and exclusively from the meritorious efforts of our collaboration. We owe our intellectual communities a profound debt of gratitude for their contributions to our lives and to this work. This collection would not exist, of course, without the generative thinking, hard work, and determined effort of our contributors. While we've both heard horror stories about the hassles of doing an edited collection, we feel fortunate to regard those tales as mostly mythical in our experience with this volume. Our authors did excellent work and happily and punctually revised to make it even better. We're thankful and proud of the result.

We appreciate the tirelessness, promptness, and enthusiasm of Alison Pavan and Emily Frazzette at Lexington Books. They've answered many questions and helped us tremendously along the way. We thank Karen Teal for going above and beyond her responsibilities to draft an initial version of the volume's reference list and we thank Joshua Hamburg for his assistance finalizing the references.

Leland: I thank many faculty colleagues, administrators, and support staff at Miami University not only for intellectual generosity but also for practical assistance at every step of this project. Everyone should have as supportive and creative a department director as Louise Davis. Departmental colleagues Michelle Abraham, Michelle Buchberger, Caryn Neumann, Madhu Sinha, and especially Jeff Kuznekoff have listened tirelessly as I've talked about this project. Deans Cathy Bishop-Clark and Moira Casey and my faculty mentor Theresa Kulbaga have offered support and advice from the project's inception. Whitney Womack Smith encouraged me to apply for internal funds and explained how. G Patterson lent both ear and expertise as I struggled through a challenging part of writing the introduction. I'm particularly grateful for the many members of the faculty who attended my campus seminar talk based on the book's introduction and shared inspiring observations and questions. I couldn't survive without expert administrative support from Amy Depew. The indefatigable staff of Miami's libraries deserves more thanks than words can ever convey. I gratefully acknowledge Jim Oris and Vanessa Gordon in Miami University's Office for the Advancement of Research & Scholarship and the Committee on Faculty Research for a grant that defrayed costs associated with this project.

Beyond Miami University, I thank many friends and family members too numerous to list for their ongoing support and longsuffering patience with my enthusiasm for my work. Joshua Trey Barnett and Mary Alice Adams read initial drafts of my content chapter and provided invaluable feedback. I've admired Jamie Capuzza since I took her Introduction to Communication class at Mount Union in 2004; working alongside her on this project has been an absolute delight. Finally, I thank Jason Rutledge and our beloved miniature schnauzers Tobi and Bruiser; they love me even when I work too late and leave piles of books and articles all over the house.

Jamie: Working on this project was made even more meaningful for me because it provided an opportunity to work with Leland. I can still remember exactly where he sat (the front row, of course) in that Introduction to Communication course. I am proud of this book, but I am just as proud that our relationship matured from student and teacher to professional colleagues and that Leland will continue to make important contributions to the field during what I am sure will be an illustrious career.

I thank Jodi Kirk for her willingness to share both her intellect and her heart; her friendship, concern for social justice, and humanity both grounded and inspired me to pursue the book contract. I thank my partner, Ben Ghiloni, for his everlasting patience and encouragement during this project. Your idealism, adventurous spirit, open-mindedness and devotion have made the last 25 years better than I could have imagined and have made me a better person.

Introduction

Centering Transgender Studies and Gender Identity in Communication Scholarship

Leland G. Spencer IV

Checking my Facebook newsfeed on a quick break from preparing for classes to begin in August 2014, I read with delight that the city of Cincinnati had recently approved the addition of transgender surgery benefits to the municipal health insurance package. *Cincinnati Enquirer* journalist Sharon Coolidge (2014) reported that the change would make the city a more desirable employer and would likely earn Cincinnati a perfect score on the Human Rights Campaign Municipality Index. Cincinnati's change in policy followed a similar shift by the U.S. Department of Health and Human Services in May 2014. Coolidge's laudatory article noted that Cincinnati joins San Francisco, Seattle, Berkley, and Portland as well as private employers Procter & Gamble and US Bank in providing transgender inclusive health coverage; the article further framed this development as one in an ongoing arc of Cincinnati's efforts to become more inclusive of lesbian, gay, bisexual, and transgender (LGBT) people (2014).

Transgender Communication Studies: Histories, Trends, and Trajectories aims, in part, to do the same kind of work for the field of communication. This collection, the first of its kind in the communication discipline, asks students and scholars of communication to think seriously and thoroughly about gender identity on its own terms. The "T" too often tacked onto the end of "LGBT" demands a spot at the center of communicative and rhetorical analyses. The earliest communication research ostensibly about LGBT lives focused primarily on gay men, but scholarship about transgender lives has grown substantially in the last few years. The steady growth of scholarship about transgender communication has brought us to a critical juncture in the field where we must assess past research and plot a clear vision for the future. The specific goals of this book include synthesizing existing research from across varied communication sub-disciplines, making original contributions to transgender scholarship in communication studies, and proposing appropriate future research agendas for students and scholars of transgender communication.

In this introduction, I begin by considering definitional possibilities. Then I offer overall observations about communication scholarship centered on transgender lives, including the development of the field to the point where a collection such as this can and should emerge. I then explain guidelines we as editors invited all of this collection's contributors to follow for consistency throughout the volume but also as a natural extension of our axiological commitments; we hope our readers share the ethical commitments that underlie our expectations of this collection's contributors and apply the same principles in their own scholarship. Finally, I preview the organization of the book's chapters.

Before proceeding to a definitional explication, I want to acknowledge the joy of editing this volume collaboratively with Jamie Capuzza. While I drafted this introductory chapter, readers will notice frequent references throughout to "we editors." I invoke the first person plural with Jamie's blessing to explain reflexively and consciously the choices we made throughout the process of proposing and editing this collection. I introduce us both in more detail below.

DEFINITIONS: WHAT CAN TRANSGENDER MEAN?

Nearly every book or article about transgender lives—whether from within or beyond the communication discipline—begins with a discussion of the definition of transgender. Beginning with definitions makes sense regardless of a work's topic. Indeed, readers expect scholarly monographs, edited collections, and textbooks to start by explaining the terms and concepts that inform and shape the work ahead. Paradoxically, advanced study in an area necessarily complicates the assumptions and terminology otherwise regarded as basic in the field. In transgender studies (within and beyond communication), the work of definition always vexes. Most articles begin with definitions but also with reflections on the difficulty and contingency of defining "transgender."

I will not repeat excellent arguments made in other places, but I echo both the need for and impossibility of defining this work's central terms. The need confronts us: for this collection to have coherence, we must know what its most important terms mean. The impossibility haunts us: among scholars, students, activists, practitioners, service providers, media producers, the general public, and countless others, wide varieties of opinions and uses for "transgender" (and several related terms) circulate. Some differences in use seem subtle or inconsequential; others encourage, offend, or inspire heated debate. As I proceed, I do so with reflexive humility, constantly aware of the need for and the impossibility of definition. I recognize and ask readers to understand that universal agreement about terminology eludes us all, but such a challenge need not frustrate our attempts to learn and understand. Instead, we should embrace the range of possibilities these terms offer us. Rather than asking what *transgender* means, we might ask, "What can it mean?"

Of the many articles and books I have read that attempt to address the question of definition, nearly all of the most recent works cite Susan Stryker's definition from her 2008 book *Transgender History*:

> Because "transgender" is a word that has come into widespread use only in the past couple of decades, its meanings are still under construction. I use it in this book to refer to people who move away from the gender they were assigned at birth, people who cross over (trans-) the boundaries constructed by their culture to define and contain gender. Some people move away from their birth-assigned gender because they feel strongly that they properly belong to another gender in which it would be better for them to live; others want to strike out toward some new location, some space not yet clearly defined or concretely occupied; still others simply feel the need to get away from the conventional expectations bound up with the gender that was initially put upon them. In any case, it is the movement across a socially imposed boundary away from an unchosen starting place—rather than any particular destination or mode of transition—that best characterizes the concept of "transgender" that I want to develop here. (2008, p. 1)

Stryker's definition underscores the performative character of *transgender*. Rather than a static identity classification or political label, *transgender*, for Stryker, describes a subject-in-movement. Not quite a verb and certainly not a noun, *transgender* remains an adjective in Stryker's use—but not one that relies on rigidity or fixed identity.

In addition to citations to Stryker, another theme that emerges in definitions treats *transgender* as an umbrella term for any gender expression, identity, or presentation that varies from what we might understand as normative. The umbrella metaphor figures cross-dressing, transsexuality, trans (by itself or as a prefix to any number of more specific terms), trans* (with an asterisks to represent a multiplicity of identities), genderqueer, and other terms as subcategories of *transgender*. If the umbrella metaphor holds, the relationship between *transgender* and any other term might analogize to that of a square and a rectangle. Just as all squares are rectangles (but not all rectangles are squares), so are all persons who identify as transsexual transgender (though not all transgender folks are transsexual). The coherence of the umbrella metaphor finds itself quickly in crisis, though. What about a person who identifies as genderqueer because s/he believes the concept of *transgender* relies on a system of gender and sex binaries that s/he rejects? S/he might then identify as specifically genderqueer—and decidedly *not* transgender. (Astute readers will note that even my choice of both gendered pronouns in the awkward "s/he" in the previous sentence reveals the challenges of genderqueer identities for the politics of naming and language use more broadly.)

Complications and exceptions abound and will productively demand our attention in classroom and conference discussions as well as the pages of academic books and journals for some time to come. At least some chapters in this collection contribute to and confound the ongoing construction of meaning (or possible meanings) in even seemingly basic terminology. For that reason, we have made the decision as editors not to insist on a closed, firm, or unyielding definition of *transgender* or any related term. Many authors in this collection explain the terms they use and justify those terms' appropriateness for the arguments in their chapters. Many authors stick with *transgender* and use it consistently with Stryker or as an umbrella term as described above. Other authors prefer more specific terms like trans (by itself), transman and transwoman, or transsexual. As editors, we pushed authors to strive for internal clarity within each chapter; we have eschewed the temptation to sacrifice authors' academic freedom and intentional, precise language choice on an altar of volume-wide terminological uniformity. Before I discuss other considerations that guided the assembly of this volume, I turn to the developments within communication studies that make a collection such as this possible.

THE EMERGENCE OF TRANSGENDER
STUDIES IN COMMUNICATION

In their profoundly useful history of research on human identity and diversity in communication studies, Karma R. Chávez and Cindy L. Griffin (2012) noted that very few essays about transgender people or featuring transgender perspectives appeared in communication journals before 2004. Borrowing their approach to surveying the field, in preparing to edit this collection, I conducted an extensive search of journals in our field (including all the journals affiliated with the International Communication Association, the National Communication Association, and the four regional associations in the United States as well as particularly relevant niche journals like *Feminist Media Studies* and *Women's Studies in Communication* and other top tier journals in the field such as *Rhetoric & Public Affairs* and *Rhetoric Society Quarterly*). My initial search yielded approximately 40 articles once I eliminated articles where the word *transgender* appeared once or twice but did not feature prominently in the article's argument or contribution. Shortly after my initial search, the new journal *QED: A Journal in GLBTQ Worldmaking*, edited by communication scholars Charles Morris and Thomas Nakayama, published a special issue on Chelsea Manning, so I read those articles as well. I also considered edited collections in LGBTQ communication, looking especially for chapters that focused on transgender lives or gender identity and occasionally followed citations to articles published by communication scholars in journals outside the discipline. Following the generic conventions of "state of the art" articles (see, for example, Condit, Lynch, & Winderman, 2012; Dow & Condit, 2005), I organize the articles reviewed in defined categories (in this case, the organizational scheme for the book—human communication, media, and rhetoric and public communication); then, within each category, I offer general themes of research findings and then share an example or two I found notable.

As I discuss in greater detail in the next section, many articles that use the acronyms LGBT or LGBTQ could more accurately use LGB or even the phrase "lesbian and gay." However, some articles that use the full acronym reflect carefully about the relationship between gender identity and sexuality. For example, Meyer (2004) analyzed the tensions between three LGBT student groups on a university campus. Not surprisingly, she found that the most radical of the three groups wanted to raise awareness and education about the experiences of transgender students; this goal ruffled feathers among the groups more focused on LGB assimilation. In another article related to education, McGrath (2013) offered a class activity that explains gender, sex, gender identity, and sexuality but focuses primarily on gender identity. Dixon and Dougherty's (2014) article on the workplace experiences of LGBTQ employees found that transgender employees may experience their workplaces as safe places to come out as gay or lesbian, but not as transgender. Calling for future research about this tension, they ask: "how does a gay-friendly workplace come to also be a transgender-friendly workplace?" (2013, p. 17). Even while I call for more research on transgender lives in particular and gender identity at the center of the analysis, I celebrate studies where the "T" appears at the end of the acronym *and matters* in the arguments presented.

Within sub-disciplines primarily concerned with human communication (in this collection understood to include at least health, organizational, interpersonal, family, and intercultural communication), a few studies have focused exclusively on transgender people. Health communication scholars have studied safer sex communication among transgender adults (Kosenko, 2010, 2011) and the efficacy of health-related Web sites targeted for transgender audiences (Horvath, Iantaffi, Grey, & Bockting, 2012). Although their study about an educational film about HIV/AIDS also addresses gay and bisexual men, Ramirez-Valles, Kuhns, and Manjarrez (2014) laudably wrote reflexively about the process that resulted in their decision to include a transwoman's story in the film as well:

> Some participants were conflicted about the inclusion of a transgender woman character in the film. They felt that the topic was too complicated to include in the film, because of the conflation of sexuality and gender identity. Others, however, noted that transgender women's experiences of discrimination overlap with those of gay men. (p. 4)

In this case, the authors acknowledged openly why they made a decision that some people might understand as conflating sexuality and gender identity. Within the context of their work (reducing the stigma related to living with HIV/AIDS), they found that transwomen and gay and bisexual men share similar experiences.

The *Journal of International and Intercultural Communication* became the first National Communication Association journal to devote an entire special issue specifically to queer and trans concerns in 2013 when Karma Chávez guest edited "Out of Bounds? Queer Intercultural Communication." Before that issue, very few intercultural communication articles considered queer theory, and, according to Chávez's (2013) introduction to the issue, no intercultural communication articles or book chapters in major collections focused on trans lives. The special issue featured articles and a dialogue among scholars about intersections of culture and gender identity (Aiello et al., 2013; Johnson, 2013; Yep, 2013).

In interpersonal and family communication, studies have focused primarily on transgender people's coming out processes. Meyer (2003) argued that coming out research focused on lesbians and gay men does not adequately account for the experiences of transgender people. Nuru (2014) found that transgender individuals navigate internal and relational tensions as they come out and manage their own identities as well as their identities in relationship with romantic partners and family members. On the other side the relationship equation, Norwood (2012, 2013a) has studied families' reactions to their loved ones' coming out experiences and found that family members often describe their loved ones' transitions as an experience of loss or grief. Alegría and Ballard-Reisch (2012) studied the impact of one partner's transition experience on couples' romantic relationships; they found that effective communication strategies on the part of both people in such couples can ameliorate the challenges associated with the transition.

Compared to human communication, more scholarship in media studies addresses transgender lives. In this volume, we define media studies to include news media, television studies, film studies, visual communication, and new/social media. Scholars studying mainstream news coverage of gender non-conformity (including stories about transgender people, but not exclusively so) have repeatedly found that news media discourses work in multiple ways to reify strict gender binaries and discipline transgender identities (Barker-Plummer, 2013; Cloud, 2014; Sloop, 2000, 2004). Film and television studies scholars have analyzed narrative movies and shows that depict transgender characters (Cavalcante, 2013; Cooper, 2002) as well as reality television's portrayal of transgender individuals and gender non-conformity (Booth, 2011; Patton & Snyder-Yuly, 2012). In my analysis of *The Little Mermaid*, I contend that scholars interested in gender identity might extend Doty's (1993) and Slagle's (2003) theorizations of a queer critical lens by reading films not ostensibly about gender identity through a transgender lens (Spencer, 2014).

Compared to studies of news discourse, film, and television, fewer studies appear in communication journals that explore transgender people and visual communication or new/social media. Landau's (2012) analysis of audiences' interactions with photographs of Thomas Beatie (popularly dubbed "the pregnant man") revealed that at least some audiences used the photograph as an opportunity to raise important questions: "it is progressive that the conversation that occurred in the interaction with at least one digital photograph resulted in a deliberation of science related issues about gender, sex, and reproductive biology" (p. 197). Emily Cram's (2012) visual rhetorical analysis explored the role of images in constructing transgender identities and enacting political agency and citizenship in contexts of juridical violence. Scholars of new and social media have analyzed online activism campaigns (Rawson, 2014; Sundén, 2001; Wight, 2014) and the role of online communities in the construction of self at the intersection of gender identity and (dis)ability (Jack, 2012).

Within rhetoric and public communication (herein, language, religious communication, legal rhetoric, and public memory studies), most scholars have focused on transgender activists. For example, Eric Darnell Pritchard's (2009) case study explored the literacy activism of black Southern transgender woman Ella Mosley. Other activism research has focused on genderqueer identities as a site for community building (Barnett & Johnson, 2013), the gender-radical possibilities of online cyberfeminism (Sundén, 2001), and the postmodern rhetorical strategies at work in popular trans-activist discourse (Hundley & Rodriguez, 2009).

Scholars working in the area of legal rhetoric often write from an activist critical perspective (regardless of whether activism is the object of their analyses). For example, Morris and Nakayama (2014) offer an enthusiastically activist rationale for devoting an issue of *QED* to Chelsea Manning. Similar impulses inform and inspire the contributions to that issue, including Sara

McKinnon's (2014) interview with activist Nathan Fuller as well as more traditional academic essays that illuminate the role of the state's violent legal interventions on Manning's body and life (Bean, 2014; Spade & Willse, 2014). Beyond the *QED* issue on Manning, activist impulses clearly undergird Magnet and Rodgers's (2012) analysis of airport surveillance as a form of policing that inflects harm on gender non-conforming bodies, Chávez's (2010) case study of transwoman and Customs and Immigration Enforcement detainee Victoria Arellano's death, West's (2010, 2013) work on trans and disability activists' collaborative bathroom accessibility advocacy, and Ilyasova's (2009) critique of arguments about the Employee Non-Discrimination Act (see also, West, 2013). Readers will find that several contributors to this volume write from an activist perspective both with respect to their topics and to their views on the future of transgender studies in communication.

As later respective chapters in this volume explain, little research on transgender lives and gender identity in communication books and journals has addressed religious rhetoric, language (on its own terms), and public memory. Sloop's (2007) rhetorical-historical account of Lucy Lobdell's life stands out a notable exception in the latter sub-discipline. And though this volume does not explicitly include a chapter from the perspective of a performance studies scholar, a few articles attest to generative possibilities in the future of performance studies for offering new ways of understanding or imagining transgender lives and creatively complicating how we all think about gender identity in art, literature, music, and theatre (Bokser, 2010; Cavanagh, 2013; Fox, 2010).

Although I approached this review with a somewhat systematic methodology, I do not claim to have cited every relevant article in the field; my approach especially meant I missed a lot of work published by communication scholars in books and journals outside the field. As Chávez (2013) noted in her editor's introduction to the aforementioned special issue, many scholars working on queer or transgender projects have found communication journals difficult or impenetrable as outlets for their work. Nevertheless, I contend that a pattern emerges across the studies I reviewed and cited: a majority of them have appeared since 2010. I hesitate to call this trend an influx or a proliferation, but I feel confident using the word *emergence*. As an emerging area of interest in the field of communication, transgender studies now stands not only in relationship to feminist studies and LGBQ studies but also as an area of interest in its own right. Jamie and I see this volume as a logical next step in the emergence of transgender studies in communication. We feel encouraged that Lexington openly sought out this book and enthusiastically championed its development as additional evidence in support of the volume's timeliness. Further, we hope the calls for future research throughout the collection contribute and lead to a true influx or proliferation of scholarship in the field focused especially on transgender lives and gender identity *qua* gender identity.

TRANSGENDER STUDIES IN COMMUNICATION: HERE AND BEYOND

Now that we have considered the development in the field of communication that paves a way for a collection like this, I want to offer a brief account of the guidelines we as editors asked contributors to follow as they prepared their chapters. We strove to respect individual academic freedom while also working toward a coherent, consistent book that reflects an inclusive, humanist, and dignity-affirming axiology. While the structural guidelines we offered are specific to this book, our expectations about language use and the ethical principles that underlay our approach may (and ought to, in my judgment) apply to future research about transgender lives (from within and beyond the communication discipline).

In terms of structure, we began this project by identifying leading transgender and cisgender scholars in the field who had some research, teaching, or service experience related to intersections between transgender studies and various sub-disciplines within communication. We asked each author or team of authors to include in their chapters, at minimum: a review of the literature on transgender lives in their sub-discipline, an original argument that makes a contribution to the field, and suggestions for future research on transgender lives in their sub-discipline. As we saw in the foregoing section, literature reviews often proved difficult as work within the field of communication studies has seldom focused exclusively on trans folks, especially in some sub-disciplines. Therefore, many literature reviews include several citations from outside the communication discipline; rather than a limitation of this collection, we see this variety as an invitation for communication students and scholars to bring our particular training, theoretical sensibilities, and methodological sophistication to the variety of research questions that await us. We defined "original argument" capaciously, such that authors could submit theoretical, empirical, or rhetorical/critical chapters. We hope the research directives in each chapter will encourage and inspire our students and colleagues to produce robust, astute, and timely research with and about transgender people.

Beyond structure, we offered some general guidelines to authors that we hope our readers will embrace in their own writing as well. With respect to language use, we asked authors first and foremost to use the language their research participants or subjects used. Names, pronouns, and identity labels should come from the person or people the research describes; researchers should not impose them. For this reason, readers may discover plural pronouns (they, their) used to describe individuals. As I stated above, this also explains why some chapters invoke different terms as more central to their argument than others (sometimes *transgender*, sometimes *transsexual*, and so on). We asked authors to use *transgender* as an adjective without an *–ed* suffix and to avoid using *transgender* as a noun.

The acronyms LGB, LGBT, and LGBTQ (lesbian, gay, bisexual, transgender, queer/questioning) appear in some places throughout the book. Authors have put the letters in a consistent order at our request, but this collection offers an important departure from much of the field's use of these acronyms, particularly the latter two. As I searched for relevant articles to include in the previous section, I found that using the search term *transgender* returned several results, but in a vast majority of those cases, the word appeared in the articles only once: on the first use of the acronyms LGBT or LGBTQ where style manuals require authors to spell out the acronym. The words "gay" or "lesbian" often appeared several more times in the articles. As much as I share the political sensibilities of West's (2014) call for solidarity between social justice advocates concerned with sexuality and those focused on gender identity, I regret that so much scholarship in our field (and countless others) conflates trans folks' experiences with lesbians', gay men's, and bisexual persons' experiences—even when study samples include no or precious few trans-identified research participants. I reviewed a well-written qualitative study several months ago. The author had interviewed family members of lesbians and gay men, but the author used the acronym LGBT throughout the essay. When I read the revised version of the essay, I felt pleased to learn that the editor and author agreed with my advice in the original review: *There is nothing wrong with an article about lesbians and gay men, but it should not claim to be about bisexual and transgender people as well, so just use the phrase "lesbians and gay men."* We asked the same of authors in this collection, and I believe all the contributors have thought carefully about when to use which acronym.

As a corollary to this advice, I hope this whole collection encourages students and scholars of communication to recognize a *relationship between* rather than an *amalgamation of* sexual orientation and gender identity. Yes, homophobia and transphobia share connections in the matrix of what bell hooks (2000) called a white supremacist capitalist patriarchy. But, as many chapters in this collection remind us (again), lesbian, gay, and bisexual persons who identify as cisgender (a term discussed in more detail below) enjoy many privileges as a result of that identification—especially upper class, white, highly educated gay men who always seem to benefit the most from legislative "victories" and other so-called markers of progress (the ubiquitous banner of marriage equality stands out as a recent and prominent example). As students and scholars of communication, then, we must stop conflating gender identity and sexual orientation and consequently treating transgender people, gay men, lesbians, and bisexual persons as interchangeable.

We felt strongly as editors that identities matter, and that includes marginalized identities as well as identities of privilege. Therefore, we wanted to name cisgender privilege and address it explicitly. Certain authors also invoke cisnormativity, analogous with respect to gender identity to the relationship between heteronormativity and sexual orientation. Just as men have gender, white people have race, and U.S. Americans have nationality, so cisgender persons have gender identity. By actively naming cisgender privilege and social structures of cisnormativity, we resist defining transgender persons as Other and everyone else as normal.

I recognize in making this choice that we invoke a term not without its own problems. As A. Finn Enke wrote: "'cisgender' has long been associated with a kind of stasis, based on the Latin root 'cis-,' which prefixes things that stay put or do not change property" (2012, p. 61). As such, and especially because *cisgender* and *transgender* often circulate as opposing poles in a binary, Enke lamented, the term *cisgender* relies on assumptions of gender stability—something transgender, queer, and feminist scholars and activists have long resisted. Furthermore, *cisgender* demands visibility by transgender folks: if everyone identifies (or gets identified as) cisgender until proven otherwise, transgender people inherit an obligation to come out.

While I cannot aver to solve the many problems Enke introduced, I maintain the importance and power inherent in naming *all* identities. Further, I contend that the term cisnormativity draws attention to the assumptive normativity of *cis* and critiques it. On the question of binaries, I suspect we might understand transgender and cisgender as points on a continuum—not as polar opposites, but as categories that represent more or less movement within or across systems of gender identity complexity. While these responses only partially account for Enke's critiques, particularly about the gender ambiguity even within some cisgender identities, I suggest that terminological ambiguity and contingency haunt all work on human identity and diversity. Just as *transgender* invites multiple meanings and interpretations, so does *cisgender*. Activists and academics alike benefit from seeing these terms (and others) as perpetually open, never calcified, and certainly not indicative of stability in an absolute sense. Furthermore, many of Enke's concerns about *cisgender* apply to other identity labels as well. Terms' meanings come in part from their difference in contrast to other terms. This limitation—if we call it that—is one of language, not of *cisgender* in particular.

A LOOK AHEAD

Especially in light of Enke's critiques, I acknowledge as I prepare to preview the organization of this volume that Jamie and I approached editing this volume with humility and some measure of trepidation. We both identify as cisgender allies to our transgender friends, colleagues, and students. We share research, teaching, and service interests and experience in the intersections of human identity and gender diversity. I identify as a white, gay man. Jamie identifies as white, heterosexual woman. We both experience class and educational privilege as well as professional privilege within the academy. Jamie is a tenured professor, and I am an assistant professor in a tenure-track position. We did not ask our contributors how they identify, though we know that some contributors identify as transgender. Because we know some of the contributors personally, we feel comfortable acknowledging that this collection likely over-represents white cisgender scholars from the United States. We celebrate the richness of these contributions and the diversity of our contributors, even while we recognize that greater diversity of gender identities, nationalities, and racial and ethnic identities would be ideal.

From the outset, we envisioned this project as comprehensive and thoroughly intra-disciplinary. We intentionally sought contributors who hold communication degrees and work in communication departments (or hold joint or affiliate appointments therein). We both have training as feminist rhetorical critics, though we each see ourselves as communication generalists, particularly in our teaching. As instructors at small universities, we find ourselves teaching content informed by social scientific and media and cultural studies research in our field as much or more than work that draws on our more humanistic specialties. Reflecting our broad interest and investment in the discipline, we designed a collection that includes research from social scientific perspectives on human communication (health, organizational, family, interpersonal, and intercultural), media studies (news, television, visual, new/social media, and film), and public and rhetorical communication (religion, legal, language, and public memory). We recognize that any attempt to organize sub-disciplines in our field ultimately falters when scrutinized too closely, but this arrangement of sections with loose boundaries seems to reflect at least some departments' and degree programs' divisions of the field. Of course, we invite readers to engage the book in whatever way makes the most sense for individual courses or research programs. Each chapter stands on its own, and readers who explore the whole book or multiple chapters will find fruitful overlaps throughout.

The first section, focused on human communication, begins with Kami Kosenko, Lance Rintamaki, and Kathleen Maness's chapter about transgender patients' positive healthcare experiences. Kosenko, Rintamaki, and Maness reveal several communicative strategies healthcare providers can use to reverse the trend of discrimination and mistreatment many trans folks experience in physicians' offices and hospitals. Next, Jenny Dixon shares the workplace experiences of several transgender employees. She reminds us of the importance and limitations of non-discrimination policies that include gender identity. matthew heinz examines how the social and communicative needs of transmen on Vancouver Island changed during the course of the transitioning process. He finds that relational uncertainty contributed to perceptions of social isolation on the part of transmen. Kristen Norwood and Pam Lannutti's qualitative study of the family members of transgender individuals offers helpful conclusions for families and loved ones of transgender persons for reducing the stress and anxiety family members often experience when someone transitions. Finally, Gust Yep, Sage Russo, and Jace Allen offer a model for classifying and assessing communication between people of different gender identities within the same culture or across cultures. The authors identify and discuss implications of "transing" communication in intercultural contexts both within and across research domains.

In the media section, Jamie Capuzza's analysis of news coverage of Chelsea Manning examined the role of metareporting in regulating transgender identity. Tristan Booth's rhetorical criticism of several televisual documentaries about sex reassignment surgery reveals that television producers seem to rely more on visual cues than on individuals' self-identification when deciding how to construct these narratives. Booth argues that these documentaries are in tension with the actual self-identifications of transsexual men and women they attempt to represent. Paul Martin Lester wrote the visual communication chapter, exploring various visual transgender stereotypes commonly found in both television and film. Joshua Trey Barnett's chapter about the blog *Gender Outlaw* argues that the photographic evidence on the blog offers a temporal pedagogy that presents transitioning as evolutionary rather than instantaneous. Finally, Lucy Miller's chapter analyzes crossdressing in eight feature films. Narratives about cross-dressing, in Miller's view, inform how dominant audiences understand and perceive trans people. Unfortunately, cinematic representations reify cisnormativity rather than challenging or subverting gender binaries.

The rhetoric and public communication section begins with Mary Alice Adams's chapter on language. Adams explains the etymological development of terminology related to gender identity. My chapter about the potential for overlap between religious communication and transgender communication scholarship follows next. After I analyze the coming out sermon of the Rev. David Weekley, I suggest that students and scholars of religious communication and transgender communication ought to come out with Weekley by emerging from our closets that often presume the incompatibility of religious and transgender identities. Peter Campbell and Cory Holding's chapter on legal rhetoric examines gender identity on death row. Campbell and Holding suggest that statistics underestimate the violence of the prison industrial complex on trans lives and bodies and offer a challenge to scholars of legal rhetoric to conduct their work in a way that challenges regimes of statist violence. Finally, Tom Dunn explores the possibilities and critiques the limitations of understanding *Paris Is Burning* as a work of transgender public memory.

CONCLUSION

We hope these 14 chapters represent a turning point in our field toward more intentional and reflexive attention to gender identity and transgender lives. We expect readers will find this collection useful for teaching, learning, researching, acting, serving, and—most important—living. And we realize this collection could have included many more chapters. For that work, we look to our readers: take from this volume not just what we argue in each chapter, but inspiration to continue the project of thinking critically about gender identity and transgender lives from within the vocabularies and methodologies of communication studies.

I

Human Communication

Chapter One

Health Communication

Patient-Centered Comunication: The Experiences of Transgender Adults

Kami Kosenko, Lance Rintamaki, and Kathleen Maness

The transgender community is a diverse group comprised of transsexuals, cross-dressers, and genderqueer individuals, among others (Bockting, Robinson, Benner, & Scheltema, 2004). Population estimates, which tend to focus on the prevalence of transsexuality, fail to capture this diversity; as such, we know little about the size or makeup of the transgender community (Rosser, Oakes, Bockting, & Miner, 2007). Much more is known about the challenges faced by community members. Transgender individuals' efforts to cross or, in some cases, transcend the gender binary are met with hostility by those invested in enforcing gender norms (Lombardi, Wilchins, Priesing, & Malouf, 2001). This gender policing comes in various forms, ranging from discrimination to violent victimization, and manifests in myriad contexts, including employment and health care settings (Nemoto, Bodeker, & Iwamoto, 2011). For example, in one large-scale study of transgender adults, 37% of the sample had experienced employment discrimination, 55% had endured verbal abuse and harassment, and 26% had been physically assaulted (Lombardi et al., 2001). Clements-Nolle, Marx, and Katz (2006) documented equally high rates of gender-based discrimination and violent victimization in a sample of 392 male-to-female (MTF) and 123 female-to-male (FTM) transsexuals. Sexual assault of transgender individuals is also disturbingly common, with some studies reporting rates as high as 86% (Wyss, 2004). In light of these and other study findings, Stotzer (2009) concluded that transgender individuals are likely to "experience multiple acts of violence and intolerance on a daily basis" (p. 177).

Gender policing undermines the health and wellbeing of transgender individuals in numerous ways and, thus, represents a pressing concern for health communication scholars and practitioners. Depression and suicide are more common in the transgender community than in the general population (Nuttbrock et al., 2010), and studies of transgender youth and adults report high rates of anxiety, tobacco and illicit drug use, and unsafe sexual encounters (Brennan et al., 2012; Horvath, Iantaffi, Grey, & Bockting, 2012). Unprotected insertive and receptive sex and involvement in commercial sex work increase some transgender individuals' risks of contracting and spreading HIV/AIDS and other sexually transmitted infections (Bockting, Robinson, & Rosser, 1998). In fact, studies suggest that HIV prevalence in the transgender community is equal to or greater than that of other high-risk groups (Lombardi, 2001). Although few studies in health communication or related disciplines have tested or demonstrated a direct relationship between transphobia and mental and physical health outcomes, several researchers contend that stigma and discrimination underlie elevated rates of substance abuse, mental health disorders, and HIV/AIDS in the transgender community (Clements-Nolle et al., 2006).

Transgender individuals face additional challenges when seeking care for these and other health issues. A small but growing literature documents a disturbing trend of providers mistreating transgender patients (Bockting et al., 2004). For example, in the National Transgender Discrimination Survey (Grant, Mottet, & Tanis, 2010), completed by over 7000 transgender adults, 19% described being denied care because of their transgender status, and 30% reported being harassed or abused by a health care provider. In addition, 28% delayed or avoided care when sick or injured due to prior experiences with discrimination in health settings. In a large-scale qualitative study, Kosenko and colleagues (2013) found that transphobia in health care contexts takes many forms. For example, participants described being denied services, given substandard care, forced into psychiatric treatment, and subjected to insensitive comments and questions and verbal abuse. This mistreatment of transgender individuals has been documented in various health care settings, including HIV/AIDS care and substance abuse treatment facilities (Bockting et al., 1998; Lombardi, 2001). These studies, when coupled with those documenting a lack of provider knowledge of and education on transgender health issues, indicate that many transgender individuals are not receiving quality care (Grant et al., 2010).

Recognizing the unique health care needs and experiences of transgender individuals, several organizations, including the American College of Physicians, have called for additional research and provider training to promote culturally sensitive and appropriate treatment of transgender patients, otherwise known as "trans-positive patient care" (Beagan et al., 2013). Some organizations, such as the American Medical and Psychiatric Associations, also have established rules governing the treatment of transgender patients (Byne et al., 2012); however, neither these rules nor the calls for additional research and training offer providers specific guidance regarding behaviors to perform or avoid when interacting with transgender individuals (Lombardi, 2001). In addition, the extant literature, with its emphasis on mistreatment of transgender patients in health care settings, offers few examples of trans-positive patient care for providers to emulate. As such, we know little about what constitutes culturally sensitive and appropriate care of transgender patients.

Health communication scholars, although well equipped for studying and remedying patient-provider communication issues, have yet to explore the transgender patient experience. In fact, only a handful of articles in communication journals (e.g., Kosenko, 2010, 2011; Ramirez-Valles, Kuhns, & Manjarrez, 2014; Redfern & Sinclair, 2014) even mention transgender health. Kosenko (2010, 2011) interviewed self-identified transgender adults about their definitions of and experiences with safer sex and safer sex negotiation and found that the negotiation process was complicated by the multiple, often conflicting, meanings ascribed to sexual safety by transgender community members. Redfern and Sinclair (2014) reviewed the literature on communication and structural barriers to transgender health care in order to identify ways to improve access and the quality of care, and Ramirez-Valles et al. (2014) explored the potential for a film, featuring a transgender woman coping with social rejection and substance abuse, to educate viewers and reduce the stigma associated with transitioning. Pilot tests suggested that the film was moderately successful in changing viewer attitudes toward the transgender community. These articles represent the extent of the extant transgender health communication literature. Although this inattention to transgender health issues is discouraging, it does represent an opportunity for health communication scholars to learn more about patient-provider communication, in general, and the transgender patient experience, in particular. As Redfern and Sinclair (2014) explained, "Meeting the health care needs of the growing population of transgender people may require many practitioners to acquire new communication skills, knowledge, and attitudes as well as bolster their awareness and receptivity to the transgender population" (p. 25). Identifying and learning how to cultivate these new communication skills are tasks best suited for health communication scholars.

Although scholars in communication and related disciplines have yet to examine or articulate what counts as trans-positive patient care, the considerable body of work on patient-centered communication can inform studies of this kind. Patient-centered communication, or PCC, is widely recognized as beneficial to both patient and provider (Wanzer, Booth-Butterfield, & Gruber, 2004). In fact, high quality provider-patient communication has been linked to an array of positive outcomes, including higher satisfaction, fewer malpractice claims, greater adherence, less decisional regret, and improved physical and mental health (e.g., Brown et al., 2010; Levinson, Roter, Mullooly, Dull, & Frankel, 1997; Step, Rose, Albert, Cheruvu, & Siminoff, 2009; Stewart, 1995; Venetis, Robinson, Turkiewicz, & Allen, 2009). Not surprisingly, various medical organizations, including the Institute of Medicine and the American College of Physicians, have issued reports focused on the importance of patient-centeredness in health care delivery (Roter & Hall, 2011). Although PCC is widely studied and advocated, we lack a consensus definition of the term. Conceptual definitions of patient-centered communication are broad and varied, with some describing PCC as a communication style, others depicting it as a clinical technique, and still others portraying it as a medical philosophy akin to the biopsychosocial medical model (Roter & Hall, 2011; Slatore et al., 2012). Epstein and Street (2007) offered the most specifics in their definition of the term. They associated PCC with four key processes:

> eliciting, understanding, and validating the patient's perspective; understanding the patient within his or her own psychological and social context; reaching a shared understanding of the patient's problem and its treatment; and, helping a patient share power by offering him or her meaningful involvement in choices related to his or her health. (p. 2)

The authors also provided examples of patient-centered provider behaviors, including maintaining eye contact, leaning forward, nodding, avoiding patient interruptions, validating patient emotions, using language free from jargon, and checking patient understanding (among others).

Researchers have developed various coding schemes to measure and assess these behaviors. For example, del Piccolo and colleagues' (2008) Verona Patient-Centered Communication Evaluation scale (VR-COPE) involves the observation and assessment of nine aspects of patient-provider interaction. Stewart and colleagues' (1995) Measuring Patient-Centered Communication scale (MPCC) focuses on three aspects of patient-centered communication—seeking common ground, trying to understand the patient's perspective, and treating the whole patient (and not just his or her injured parts). As with the VR-COPE, the MPCC requires coders to observe patient-provider interactions and to determine which, if any, aspect of PCC occurred. Although shown to be reliable and valid, these coding schemes do not capture the patient's perspective, which, some have argued, is the "only perspective that matters when assessing patient-centeredness" (Clayton, Latimer, Dunn, & Haas, 2011, p. 300). Epstein and colleagues (2005) echoed Clayton et al.'s argument, adding that observer ratings of patient-provider interaction "fail to distinguish what is said from what the patient hears" (p. 1517). Scales completed by patients instead of trained coders can provide some insight into the patient's perspective, but, as McCormack and colleagues (2011) argued, these scales provide little information about the specific provider behaviors that led to the patient's perceptions. Taken together, these critiques suggest that a qualitative approach, focused on patient perceptions of specific provider behaviors, would add to our understanding of PCC and its underlying processes. Given the need for research on trans-positive patient care and the potential for a qualitative approach to enhance our understanding of PCC, we designed a qualitative study to explore transgender individuals' experiences with and perceptions of patient-centered communication.

METHODS

We collected the data for this study in 2010 as part of a needs assessment of transgender adults. In June of that year, we began recruitment efforts, which entailed developing a Web site with a link to an online questionnaire, posting links to the site and the questionnaire on online bulletin boards and in discussion forums, and mailing study announcements to lesbian, gay, bisexual, and transgender (LGBT) organizations across the United States. Study announcements described the purpose of the project, listed researcher contact information, included a link to the Web site, and mentioned that participants would have the option of entering a raffle for a $50 gift card. Interested parties were directed to the online questionnaire created and hosted on Qualtrics.com.

The questionnaire began with a consent form, which participants were encouraged to print for their records. Those who consented to participate provided an electronic signature and advanced to the first set of survey questions; those who did not consent to participate were thanked for their time and consideration. Participants were asked if they had experienced any positive interactions with health care providers. An affirmative response led to a series of open-ended questions about a particularly salient positive interaction with a health care provider. Participants were asked to describe the encounter, including specific behaviors performed by the provider and the setting in which the interaction took place. Although participants were asked to think of one specific interaction when answering these questions, we gave them the opportunity to describe up to three different positive experiences. The questionnaire ended with a series of demographic and health history questions. After submitting their responses, participants were thanked for their involvement and given the opportunity to provide contact information and be entered in a raffle.

Grounded theory (Strauss & Corbin, 1990) informed our approach to data collection and analysis. For example, concurrent data collection and analysis, recommended by grounded theorists, helped us identify emerging themes and determine when saturation, the point at which additional data fail to yield additional insights, had been reached. Data were analyzed via the constant comparative method, an approach to qualitative data analysis associated with grounded theory. This approach involves inductive category development through the identification and comparison of units of meaning or themes (Maykut & Morehouse, 1994). Through open, axial, and selective coding processes, themes are compared and grouped into like categories. We began with open coding, a process by which "data are broken down into discrete parts, closely examined, and compared for similarities and differences" (Corbin & Strauss, 2008, p. 62). During open coding, each member of the research team read survey responses to identify and categorize positive provider behaviors and practices. After this independent review of the data, the coders met to construct an exhaustive list of the positive provider behaviors reported by transgender participants. Axial coding entailed identifying the linkages between and the dimensions of the categories identified during open coding (Maykut & Morehouse, 1994). After completing this second independent review of the data, the coders met to compare findings and construct a category system. Coders returned to the data once more to complete selective coding, which involved assessing the system's exhaustiveness and developing labels for core categories (Strauss & Corbin, 1990). The result of this multi-stage analytic procedure was an exhaustive but not mutually exclusive category system describing the kinds of behaviors and practices performed by providers and deemed positive by transgender patients.

RESULTS

Sample Characteristics

One hundred fifty-two self-identified transgender adults who hailed from 40 different U.S. states and two foreign countries participated in the study. Over 80% of the sample identified as non-Hispanic White, with Native Americans (5.9%), Asian Americans (5.4%), African Americans (3.9%), and Latinos/ Latinas (3.9%) comprising the rest of the sample. The mean age of these individuals was 39.4 years (SD = 15.5 years; range = 18–74 years), and the majority (79.6%) reported having health insurance. Participants described being employed full-time (30.3%) or part-time (12.5%). The remainder of the sample were full-time students (21.1%), unemployed (11.2%), self-employed (4.6%), on disability (6.5%), or retired (5.9%). Participants represented a broad subset of the transgender community, with 59.2% identifying as transsexuals, 14.5% as genderqueer, 9.2% as cross-dressers, 6.6% as intersex, 6.6% as androgynous, and 3.9% as part of a third gender.[1]

Patient Perceptions of Positive Interactions with Providers

Despite the diversity of the transgender community, in general, and this sample, in particular, participants' descriptions of their positive experiences with providers bore marked similarities. Based on these descriptions, we identified seven behaviors performed by providers and deemed trans-positive by participants: communicating sensitivity to gender issues, admitting ignorance, having a good bedside manner, curing the disease (and not the patient), protecting patient privacy, advocating for transgender health, and treating all patients equally.

Communicating Sensitivity to Gender Issues

Given the centrality of gender and sex to transgendering, it is no surprise that transgender patients preferred providers who seemed sensitive to these issues. Communicating sensitivity to gender issues entailed using pronouns and terms of address that matched the patient's gender presentation, referring to the patient by his or her chosen (as opposed to given) name, and asking if unsure of the correct terms. Participant 14 stated,

> It starts with the front office personnel. Even if they can obviously tell that one is trans, they should still have enough respect to use proper pronouns and ask if the person has a preferred name to be used when a nurse calls out for them in the waiting room.

Participant 30 added, "If you're unsure of what pronouns or name to use, ask politely. Make note of gender identity/preferred name in records so we don't have to go through the explanations each time we visit." Participant 91 gave an example of how one clinic handled this issue: "At the clinic I go to, they go out of their way to be trans-friendly to the point of having separate fields for sex and gender in their signup sheets, with more options than just male or female."

Participants also stressed the importance of being sensitive to transitioning bodies by using patients' preferred terms for their body parts and recognizing patients' varying levels of comfort with their bodies. Participant 31 provided one such example:

> Be sensitive to some of the language. For instance, a trans man who has not had chest reconstructive surgery may not like to have his chest referred to as "breasts" or his genitalia referred to as a "vagina." Use neutral language or the language the patient uses to describe his body.

As participant 54 explained,

Pay attention to what language they're using for their body parts, and echo it back. Ask permission before touching them anywhere. This is true in general for health care but especially among people who might be super dysphoric about certain body parts. Just be respectful.

Admitting Ignorance

Participants recognized that not all providers were comfortable with or knowledgeable about transgender individuals and their health needs. Transgender patients encouraged these providers to be honest with themselves and their patients about personal biases or knowledge deficits. Participant 34 suggested, "If you don't know, admit that you don't know but promise to do your research and follow-up on that promise." This sentiment was echoed by participant 23: "Partner with me in my healthcare by being willing to research and learn[,] given the unknowns related to trans-health." Most participants encouraged providers to educate themselves on trans-health issues. For example, participant 63 said, "Educate yourselves. It's very stressful for us to carry the burden of dual roles of patient and educator." Some participants urged providers who lacked the necessary comfort with and knowledge of trans-health to refer transgender patients elsewhere. As participant 115 explained, "It's ok if you're not an expert or not comfortable. Just make referrals to someone who is." Participant 85 added:

> Study their needs and learn about trans patients. If you do not know or do not have the experience, then do not use the trans person as a learning tool. Make references to those professionals that do know trans persons' needs and how to treat them.

Having a Good Bedside Manner

Transgender patients described providers who were honest, open, and nonjudgmental as having a good bedside manner. As participant 51 succinctly stated, "Be open, welcoming, and affirming." Listening, being gentle during exams and procedures, and acting comfortable around transgender patients also were deemed important by participants. For example, participant 79 advised, "Accept the patient. Listen to the history and be supportive/empathetic. Don't fear sitting close to the patient. Be gentle during physical exams. Care for the patient." Participant 12 concurred:

> Being in the hospital or going to the doctor is already scary and uncomfortable . . . Don't forget to be friendly and smile and ask how your patient is doing. Give professional and adequate care and tell your residents to do so no matter what type of person they are treating. If there is a group of residents learning and are all huddled around one patient, please treat the patient like they exist and are a real person. Let the person know your [sic] going to touch/do/poke whatever before you do it and ask if it's okay.

Controlling negative or surprised reactions was also an important part of having a good bedside manner. As participant 36 explained, "The number one thing I tell healthcare providers to do in regards to trans patients is to not show a reaction." Participant 124 elaborated: "I feel that all they really need to do is not act like my feminine appearance is unusual. They don't need to go out of their way to do anything; they should just not act surprised that I'm male." Participant 60 offered another tip: "Remember that many trans people are very uncomfortable with their bodies, so be extra careful not to look disgusted." Participant 14 added, "If they feel the need to giggle, leave the area so that we don't have to hear them." Some patients indicated that, if providers are unwilling or unable to control their reactions, then they should find another provider who is. Participant 57 suggested, "If the doctor or nurse is not comfortable with the transgender individual, it would likely be best if s/he found another doctor or nurse to take her/his place."

Curing the Disease, Not the Patient

Participants recounted negative interactions with providers who treated transgender patients as diseased. These providers focused on curing patients of transgendering rather than curing diseases in transgender patients. Participants argued that, to avoid stigmatizing and medicalizing transgender patients, providers should focus on the health issue at hand, ask only medically relevant questions, and not make assumptions about the patient's health history or problems. Participant 74 offered an example: "When I told them I was trans, they asked appropriate, relevant questions to my health care. They did not ask me about my sexuality and/or sexual activities, which weren't medically relevant. That made me feel more comfortable." Participant 105 added:

> Ask questions relevant to the reason that the patient is there. If you realize that you might need to ask more invasive questions relating to the person's transition, state why you need to ask those questions (i.e., that it might be medically relevant in this situation-- otherwise you wouldn't be asking these questions).

Participants also preferred that providers ask questions rather than make assumptions. As participant 140 stated,

> I understand that knowing someone's birth sex may be needed to diagnose a medical problem. If it is, then learn how to ask questions politely, and do not make assumptions about anything. It's better to feel awkward asking questions than to assume.

Protecting Patient Privacy

Several participants stressed the importance of discretion in the health care setting and encouraged providers to be mindful of transgender individuals' unique privacy concerns. Being outed was one such concern. Participant 55 explained, "Give us privacy. Only people who take care of the transgender patient need to know his/her status, especially if he/she is 'stealth' or not out about being transgender." For trans men, the gynecologist's office was seen as particularly threatening to one's identity; however, one participant described a particularly positive experience with a gynecology practice. Participant 38 recounted, "They scheduled my appointment at a time when no others would be sitting in the waiting area and took me right back to the exam room so I wouldn't risk being called when others were around. They made every effort to make me more comfortable about the whole thing." The potential for privacy violations in hospital common areas, such as waiting rooms, was also noted by participant 14 who explained:

> If they have a need to discuss a gender-specific topic concerning a treatment or other application when in the presence of other patients, kindly ask us to a private area for the discussion and don't ask in front of a complete stranger.

Transgender patients offered other suggestions for privacy management. For example, participant 55 suggested, "If possible, a single room for hospitalized transgender patients would be ideal to prevent harassment or uncomfortable situations with patients in the same room."

Advocating for Transgender Health

One other way in which providers can demonstrate comfort with and knowledge of transgender individuals and their health concerns is to act as an advocate for transgender individuals. Advocating for transgender health entailed becoming involved in and showing support for the transgender community. Participant 23 offered the following suggestions: "Display a non-discrimination policy that includes Gender Identity. Display materials from LGBT health awareness week. Sponsor a trans-support group. Do community talks with trans people about healthcare. Volunteer to work in trans clinics." Participant 7 recommended that providers:

> advocate for transgender patients with insurance agencies to ensure that care will be covered. Oftentimes, strong advocacy from a treating doctor/surgeon is successful in securing coverage for transgender peoples' care. Specific ways that doctors can help include submitting insurance claims for the patient, providing strong evidence of medical need with those claims, considering use of alternative diagnosis and procedural codes that are more likely to result in claim approval, and working with patients to file appeals after initial rejections.

Treating All Patients Equally

Above all, transgender individuals wanted to be shown the same courtesy and respect given to other patients. As participant 10 explained,

> Treat a transgender individual no differently than anyone else. Talk to him or her like a person, not like he or she is only transgender. The label makes trans folk seem like objects rather than real human beings, and if that wall is just removed, from any setting, people will feel respected and at ease.

Participant 23 added, "Treat my difference like any part of human diversity, not like a freak show." As participant 58 succinctly put it: "They should treat a trans patient as they treat every other patient—kindly." Taken together, these data indicate that transgender patients prefer providers who advocate for transgender health, treat the disease (but not treat the patient as diseased), have a good bedside manner, admit ignorance, treat patients equally, protect patient privacy, and communicate sensitivity to gender issues.

CONCLUSION

Although research suggests that medical interactions are fraught with complications for transgender individuals (e.g., Bockting et al., 1998; Grant et al., 2010; Kosenko et al., 2013), this study accentuates the positive health care experiences of transgender community members. Our analysis of transgender patient accounts of positive interactions in health care settings suggests that provider communication contributes to transgender patient satisfaction. In particular, providers who communicated sensitivity to gender issues, protected patient privacy, treated patients equally, focused on curing the disease as opposed to curing the patient, admitted ignorance, had a good bedside manner, and advocated for transgender health were deemed supportive by transgender patients. Possible explanations for and implications of these findings are described more fully below.

Despite resolutions and policy statements from leading medical organizations encouraging trans-positive patient care (Byne et al., 2012), little is known about what constitutes culturally relevant and appropriate care for this population. This study provides insight into the patient's perspective on trans-positive care and offers providers specific advice for working with transgender patients. This advice can and should be incorporated into the curricula for medical schools and other provider training programs—most of which currently fail to provide adequate instruction in lesbian, gay, bisexual, and transgender health (Obedin-Maliver et al., 2011). These findings also underscore the importance of communication skills and cultural sensitivity training for health care providers. Despite research linking patient-centered communication to important patient outcomes, such as satisfaction and malpractice claims (Roter & Hall, 2006), medical schools devote little time and attention to communication skills training, and continuing education programs, with their focus on the biomedical aspects of care, provide few opportunities for developing and honing these skills (Celega & Broz, 2012). Similarly, cultural sensitivity is given short shrift in medical education (Flores, Gee, & Kastner, 2000). Increased attention to transgender health, communication, and culture in provider education programs is the first step toward creating a more inclusive and supportive health care environment for transgender patients.

Patient accounts of providers' efforts to cure them of transgendering may be a byproduct of institutionalized transphobia. The inclusion of gender identity disorder (GID) in the *Diagnostic and Statistical Manual for Mental Disorders, Fourth Edition* (*DSM-IV*) generated considerable controversy and drew criticism from transgender advocates who claimed that the diagnostic label pathologized gender variance and institutionalized transphobia. Some worried that that the inclusion of GID in the *DSM-IV* gave credence to the idea that transgender individuals could be "cured" of their "sickness" (Bradford & Meston, 2011), but others cautioned that removing GID from the *DSM-IV* could negatively affect insurance coverage and access to care (Lev, 2005). In an effort to reduce the stigmatizing effects of a GID diagnosis, the authors of the recently released fifth edition of the *Manual* replaced GID with gender dysphoria; however, findings from this study suggest that, for some, the damage has already been done. Participants described encounters with providers who pathologized trans-patients and focused their efforts on curing the patient of his or her transgender status instead of curing the patient of disease. Whether these providers were willing accomplices to or unwitting tools of institutional stigma, their actions point to problems with how gender identity issues are understood and treated by health professionals. Although the efforts to revise the *DSM* and reduce the stigma surrounding gender variance are laudable, continued study of the gender dysphoria diagnosis and its impact on the lived experiences of transgender individuals is necessary to determine if the *DSM* revisions have had their intended effect.

In addition to these practical applications, study findings suggest potentially fruitful avenues for future health communication research. For example, some transgender patients implored providers to admit their ignorance, an idea that runs counter to those voiced by participants in studies of provider expressions of uncertainty (e.g., Ogden et al., 2002; Sheer & Cline, 1995). Past research in this area indicated that many patients (and even some practitioners) preferred that providers speak in no uncertain terms about diagnoses and prognoses, as not to exacerbate the uncertainty and anxiety inherent to the illness experience (Blanch, Hall, Roter, & Frankel, 2009; Johnson, Levenkron, Suchman, & Manchester, 1988). Given that the only certainty in medicine is the presence of uncertainty (Blanch et al., 2009), Katz (1984) and others have argued that the best way for providers to manage uncertainty is to be aware of it and to disclose it to patients. Some, however, have questioned how patients will respond to such disclosures and have called for additional research on the subject (Ogden et al., 2002). Although this study was not designed to test patient responses to provider expressions of doubt or uncertainty, study findings indicate that transgender patients may welcome a more honest and uncertain dialogue with their providers. More work in this area is needed to determine if other patient populations share this perspective.

Study findings concerning the importance of a good bedside manner also have implications for health communication research and practice. Participants preferred providers who were warm, open, gentle, affirming, professional, and welcoming—all of which are considered nonverbal immediacy cues. Nonverbal immediacy has received little attention from health communication scholars, but it has been the subject of several studies in instructional and interpersonal communication (Siminoff & Step, 2011; Witt, Wheeless, & Allen, 2004). Research on instructor immediacy cues underscores its importance for teachers and students alike. For example, instructor immediacy has been linked to students' willingness to talk in class (Sidelinger, 2010), intentions to persist in college (Witt, Schrodt, Wheeless, & Bryand, 2014), cognitive and affective learning outcomes (Witt & Wheeless, 2001), perceptions of instructor credibility (McCroskey, Valencic, & Richmond, 2004), and evaluations of teacher effectiveness (McCroskey et al., 1995). Interpersonal scholars have linked immediacy to important relational perceptions and outcomes, such as dominance, intimacy, comfort, liking, and satisfaction (Siminoff & Step, 2011). Taken together, these studies suggest that nonverbal immediacy may play an equally important role in the patient-provider relationship; however, further research is needed to understand the form and effects of nonverbal immediacy in health care contexts.

Although this study offers specific guidance for health care professionals and provider training programs, it places the onus on providers for fostering and maintaining supportive relationships with transgender patients. For providers, various factors, including time, money, and energy, might serve as disincentives or barriers to creating these kinds of relationships and taking on new and unfamiliar roles, such as acting as a community advocate and activist. Given that providers will differ in their willingness and ability to enact these roles and behaviors, transgender patients might be best served by acting as their own advocates. A growing body of literature attends to the promise and pitfalls of patient self-advocacy (Wiltshire, Cronin, Sarto, & Brown, 2006); however, its frequency, forms, and functions have yet to be explored in this specific patient population. The available literature indicates that active patients are more satisfied with and likely to adhere to treatment regimens, score higher on quality of life measures, and experience less pain and distress following medical visits than passive patients (Martin et al., 2011). Despite these benefits of patient activism and advocacy, not all patients desire an active role, and not all providers respond favorably to patients' attempts at self-advocacy (Wiltshire et al., 2006). As such, additional research is needed to determine if self-advocacy will prove to be a boon or a bust for transgender patients.

Participant comments also have implications for the study of patient-centered communication. For example, transgender individuals pointed to particular provider behaviors as well as aspects of the health care environment that contributed to their evaluations of that provider and setting as trans-positive. These findings are consistent with holistic perspectives on patient-centered communication, which paint PCC as a byproduct of an effective tripartite relationship between provider, patient, and the health care environment. The Institute of Medicine, for example, asserts that providers, patients, and health care delivery systems all contribute to patient-centered care and communication (Epstein et al., 2005). These perspectives suggest that patient-centeredness is contextually bound and that patients use context cues in their evaluations of providers and health care environments (McWilliam & Freeman, 2006). Findings from this study support these assertions and point to specific aspects of the health care environment that communicate trans-positivity. For instance, participant comments indicated that providers could communicate trans-positivity by displaying a non-discrimination policy that included gender identity and/or LGBT-friendly reading materials in their offices. Many participants suggested that providers make changes to sex and gender questions on intake forms, another aspect of the health care environment. Although participants recognized and responded to these contextual cues, patient-centered aspects of the health care environment are rarely discussed in the PCC literature. Most coding schemes only focus on the provider's behavior and, thus, give little insight into the environment in which these behaviors are performed and interpreted (McCormack et al., 2011). More context-specific or context-dependent measures are needed to capture the full range of ways in which providers and health care systems can demonstrate patient-centeredness.

Study limitations also warrant consideration. The hidden nature of this population and the lack of reliable estimates of its size precluded the use of random sampling techniques (Rosser et al., 2007), which would have produced a more representative sample. As a result, certain participant characteristics, such as access to health insurance, are over-represented in this sample. Furthermore, qualitative methods, though well suited to generating thick descriptions of behavior in context, are not designed to produce generalizable data. As such, these findings might not represent the perspectives and experiences of all transgender individuals. Better representation in future studies of transgender patient perspectives will require innovative and sophisticated approaches to recruitment and sampling. Despite these limitations, this study captured the voices of a group that has been silenced and marginalized. It also offered specific examples of behaviors for providers to emulate when working with transgender patients. We hope these findings give fodder to further discussion of and education on transgender treatment in health care settings.

NOTE

1. The study was open to anyone 18 or older who could read and write in English and who self-identified as transgender. Although some question whether intersex is covered by the transgender umbrella, some intersex individuals chose to participate in this study.

Chapter Two

Organizational Communication

The Workplace Socialization of Gender Identity:
A Phenomenological Exploration of
Being Transgender at Work

Jenny Dixon

Company stakeholders are increasingly aware of the benefits of implementing nondiscrimination policies (HRC, 2014a). Policies ensuring the equal treatment of all employees help boost productivity, strengthen the image of the workplace, and help companies to recruit the best and brightest (Sheridan, 2009). However, the presence of workplace policies does not guarantee protection. An organizational communication lens is employed in this chapter to explore policies as rhetorical artifacts and as social constructions. Studying the lived experience of being transgender at work affords an opportunity to examine the integrity of nondiscrimination policies with the hope of discovering ways to make policies better.

Nondiscrimination policies with reference to gender identity and expression (henceforth *gender identity policies*) can encompass hiring procedures, availability of health benefits, restroom use, and workplace bullying. Gender identity policies occur frequently in the form of assuring equal consideration when hiring new employees. Capital One, Costco, and IBM are just a few companies to have formal pledges to equal opportunity employment for transgender applicants (HRC, 2014b). In some instances, gender identity policies include the granting of gender-affirmative healthcare (e.g., hormone replacement therapy, gender affirmative surgery, etc.) to transgender employees and health benefits for transgender employees' spouses. Gender identity policies can also ascribe rights including allowing transgender employees to use the restroom of their choosing and providing an environment that is free of gender-related bullying.

As companies touting nondiscrimination policies continue to increase (HRC, 2014a), so do mechanisms for determining whether a workplace meets the needs of a diverse workforce. The Corporate Equality Index is a benchmarking tool, developed by the Human Rights Campaign, for recognizing companies with policies from which gay, lesbian, and transgender employees benefit. In 2013, 304 businesses won a top score, including over 60% of Fortune 500 companies—a dramatic spike from the 13 achieving a perfect score in 2002, when the index was first introduced (HRC, 2014a). However, it is important to note that this composite score combines gender identity policies and sexual orientation nondiscrimination policies. A cursory look at the index's report shows the former lagging consistently behind.

Gender identity policies strive to protect organization members who are transgender, or embody a gender other than one signified by the sex usually assigned at birth. Similarly, sexual orientation policies seek to protect employees who are gay, lesbian, or bisexual. According to the Corporate Equality Index, 91% of Fortune 500 Companies have a sexual orientation nondiscrimination policy, whereas only 61% have a gender identity-related policy. This is an improvement from 2008, when 88% of Fortunate 500 companies had policies protecting sexual orientation and only 25% protected gender identity. This consistent delay suggests a workplace may enjoy a reputation of being "LGBT Friendly," while the unique needs of transgender employees fall short. The disparity of gender identity policies in relation to sexual orientation policies may present some unique ambiguities for transgender adults seeking an inclusive work environment. In addition to determining whether policies exist, transgender employees may have an added burden of discovering what purpose they actually serve.

Viewed from an organizational communication perspective, gender identity policies can be considered a rhetorical tool, and an opportunity for a communicated development of meaning. Used as a rhetorical tool, gender identity policies can create and maintain an image for the organization. A report by the Williams Institute found that the foremost reason the top 50 Fortune 500 companies adopted diversity policies was to recruit and retain employees (Sears & Mallory, 2011). Another popular reason is to allow the company to benefit from a diverse customer base. These reasons suggest that such policies project an image of the company to potential employees and customers. Of course, the image projected and the actual workplace climate do not always align.

Another way that policies can be examined through a communication lens is by considering ways in which they are communicated into being. For example, the Williams Institute reports another motivation for having policies is that policies foster employee productivity. Disharmony in the workplace takes away from productivity as employees are distracted from their work and time is taken to try to remedy unfavorable situations. However, the reasoning that policies unequivocally lend to productivity is flawed: Whether policies are effective depends largely on communication *about* policies. Just as employees may elect not to take paternity leave for fear of speculation that time off is being used for activities other than childcare (Kirby & Krone, 2002), gender identity policies may not actually protect employees because the policies are not taken seriously by management, coworkers, or other stakeholders. Policies can be communicatively constructed as an essential precursor to a harmonious workplace climate, or as an empty and dismissible bullet point in a handbook. Transgender working adults often have the daunting and ongoing task of determining which is the case.

Employees can make these determinations and other decisions during the socialization process. Socialization has been defined as "the process by which an individual acquires the social knowledge and skills necessary to assume an organizational role" (Van Maanen & Shein, 1979, p. 211). Though recent socialization research has focused on coming to understand task-based expectations (Madlock & Chory, 2014) and the unique experiences of socialization in volunteer organizations (Kramer, 2011), much is gained from using the socialization process as a heuristic map for exploring gender norms and expectations (Allen, 2000). For the purpose of studying policies for transgender employees, the socialization process is assumed to consist of organizational anticipatory socialization (Kramer, 2010), encounter (Feldman, 1981), metamorphosis (Jablin, 1982), and exit (Jablin, 2001). This stage model will be employed in the results section of this chapter as a heuristic tool for exploring the role of gender identity policies for transgender employees during the process of organizational socialization.

This chapter explores how transgender working adults consider gender identity policies as they become socialized into a new work environment. Using organizational socialization as a guiding framework, the remainder of this chapter (a) reports on the lived experience of coming to understand the gendered norms of a workplace, in relation to polices, from the perspective of transgender working adults, and (b) provides recommendations for curating better practices for ensuring the legitimacy of gender identity policies. As explained later in this chapter, the disparity between the existence of workplace policy and its potential can function as a prompt for introducing practical workplace initiatives as well as opportunities for future organizational communication research.

METHODS

The present study is part of a larger project exploring gender identity and sexual orientation in the workplace. Qualitative interviews were conducted with ten individuals self-identified as transgender, transsexual, or gender-queer. Participation was limited to adults aged eighteen or older and who work or have worked outside the home. Participants were recruited through word of mouth, listserv advertisements, informal dissemination of information at community events, and online social sites such as Facebook. Interview locations included conference rooms in libraries, coffee shops, restaurants, and participants' homes. Participant recruitment continued until phenomenological saturation (Denker, 2009) was achieved. Upon completing the transcription process, the author engaged in a close textual analysis of the data.

Thematic Analysis

Analysis of the transcribed interviews took place with the hope of locating cogent and informative themes. Van Manen (1990) explained that themes relate to the notion of what is being studied by (a) getting at the notion of the object of study, (b) giving shape to otherwise shapeless concepts, (c) describing the content of the notion, and (d) functioning as a reduction of the notion. Applying each characteristic of a theme, the present study used thematic analysis to get at the notion of the lived experience of organizational socialization for transgender employees in relation to gender identity policies.

For the present study, thematic aspects of regulation, gender identity, and workplace socialization were isolated using a selective approach in which interview transcripts were examined, line-by-line, in an effort to extrapolate meaning from every sentence or sentence cluster (van Manen, 1990). Guided by van Manen (1990), selective analysis developed over three stages. First, upon completing the transcription process, I engaged in a cold reading of the interviews, making notes for each interview as initial themes began to emerge. Initial themes were determined in relation to the purpose of the study. For example "the restroom issue" was an initial theme because of its connection to transgender concerns about coworkers' expectations in relation to workplace policies that may or may not have been in place. It was in these initial notes that I began coining terms to potentially describe the lived experience of being transgender in relation to gender identity policies.

Second, themes were marked with sticky notes and gained complexity as the stages of analysis commenced. For example, in the initial wave of coding, a very simple color scheme was used: Restroom use was beige, bullying was red, transition within the workplace (e.g., new management) was orange and using policies to determine whether one would accept a position was pink.

As more nuanced characteristics of the codes emerged, other colors were posted next to the original colors to indicate an added dimension had been determined. For example, a part of the data that included bullying and was marked with a red sticky note was also marked with a mauve sticky note if it contained bullying as a prompt for leaving a workplace. Additionally, memoing (Charmaz, 2006) was used to record thoughts and emerging themes during analysis. It was in these initial notes that potential themes emerged to describe the role of gender identity policies for transgender employees.

The third and final stage of analysis provided a more sophisticated approach to the themes, resulting in a more nuanced understanding of participants' lived experience. Analysis continued after drafts of results were initially crafted. In the final analysis, I approached the data with the themes created in the second stage of analysis in mind. This resulted in a more detailed theme development. For example, the transitions affecting the interpretation of policies were initially limited to those occurring in the workplace (e.g., new management, change in work schedule, etc.). Further analysis of the data in relation to transitions revealed that changes in employees' personal lives (e.g., marriage, undergoing gender affirmative surgery, etc.) also prompted a change in understanding of policies. The themes formed a coherent picture of being transgender at work and the role of policies within this phenomenon.

RESULTS

The central finding of this study was that determining whether a workplace is transgender-friendly was an ongoing process in which interpretations of gender identity policies play a primary role. To illustrate this process of information seeking in relation to workplace policies, the socialization model is used to report the results of this study. All participant names used throughout this chapter are pseudonyms.

Anticipating Workplace Membership

The organizational anticipatory stage marks the time from learning that one will enter a new workplace (e.g., getting a job offer) to the moments before encountering said space (Kramer, 2010). Participants responded to prompts such as, *Describe any concerns related to gender identity when you first learned you got a new job.* The interviews illuminated varying degrees of concern about gender role expectations when anticipating organizational entry. Cisgender newcomers anticipate their entry into a new workspace with trepidation regarding catching on to task-based expectations and successfully balancing work and non-work obligations. In addition to these and other concerns, transgender newcomers anticipate joining a new workplace uncertain of what restroom to use, the extent to which gender issues are openly discussed, and—in some cases—whether the newcomer will need to conform to gender expectations. Participants discussed considering the presence of gender identity policies as a hint that a workplace would be gender inclusive. This speaks to the efficacy of using policies as a rhetorical tool to recruit employees. However, two factors emerged illustrating policies as a less than foolproof means of determining gender culture. Specifically, participants recounted shortcomings in the emphasis placed on policies during new employee training sessions, as well as the capacity for policies to exist only as a symbolic gesture.

Diversity training sessions are enlightening opportunities for determining not only whether nondiscrimination policies exist, but also how opinion-leaders (i.e., those leading the training session) feel about the policies in place. If a training session leader discusses nondiscrimination with a dismissive tone, new workplace members may rightly question the legitimacy of the policies. Similarly, an inability to discuss transgender issues in an informed manner can hint to the lack of open discussion about gender inclusivity. Mo, a grocer, believed that "most people don't have any language to discuss trans issues." Similarly, Ieuan, a fiction writer, discussed attending a training session in which it was apparent that the members of the organization "did not understand their own social justice objectives." Communicating about policies in a way that is disconnected from the current needs of transgender employees makes for a powerful foreshadowing of the organization's gender culture.

Where present, policies during the anticipatory socialization stage emerged as a real or speculated recruitment tool. This tool could either serve as an explicit means of allowing potential employees to know they are welcome or as a ploy for branding the company as inclusive, regardless of the actual work environment. Though many participants were pleased with the inclusion of policies and policies' explication during the training sessions, some participants saw policies as "token gesture[s]," available in word but not in deed. Mary, a store clerk, discussed "an executive order on the books banning discrimination" however "there [was] no specific protection for people who are trans." In some instances, transgender newcomers were pleased with the gender identity policies supported by the organization, until their first day of work.

Encounter

Organizational entry is a time of learning what insiders consider to be "normal" behavior (Feldman, 1981). Participants responded to interview questions such as, *Tell me about any assumptions you had about being transgender at work; in what ways (if any) were those assumptions confirmed or disconfirmed?* The encounter stage may be a particularly tenuous time for transgender newcomers because messages conveyed at the anticipatory stage do not hold true once the newcomer has entered the day-to-day norms of the workplace. More poignantly, the encounter phase holds the potential to expose communicatively constructed gender norms that are different from non-discrimination policies introduced in the anticipatory stage.

The encounter phase may mark a point of hypervisibility in the workplace, as coworkers consider transgender identity to be a source of spectacle and a prompt for inquiry (Dixon & Dougherty, 2014). Also, the encounter stage marks a time of reconciling personal norms with the norms of the workplace. For transgender employees who do not conform to a dichotomous gender structure, considerations such as which restroom to use inevitably surface. Mo explained:

> When I was very genderqueer, I didn't know which bathroom to go into to be comfortable. Or, more importantly for everyone else, being comfortable. And [for] somebody [to] not try and attack me or go tell the manager I was in the wrong bathroom.

Unfortunately, Mo's uncertainty regarding which restroom to use is not unique. Organizations are showing increasing advocacy for unisex or "family" restrooms that employees of any gender are allowed to use. Additionally, more and more organizations are establishing explicit rules stating employees should use the restroom that most readily aligns with their preferred gender (Sheridan, 2009). However, most workplaces are wrought with ambiguity. Despite gender identity policies realized at the anticipatory stage of socialization, uncertainties persist in the encounter stage, such as what questions coworkers will ask, what restroom to use, and whether bullying, including physical violence, will be tolerated. Many of these uncertainties remain even after the newcomer has become an experienced member of the company.

Metamorphosis

Metamorphosis begins when newcomers feel they are seasoned members of an organization (Kramer, 2010). As fully integrated organization members, employees are assumed to have an understanding of workplace norms. Given this presumed understanding, one might assume that making sense of gender identity policies would no longer be necessary. However, there are many ways in which new insight about gender identity policies can be gleaned after the employee is no longer a newcomer. Specifically, organizational changes and personal changes prompt new communication about policies. *Organizational changes* include changes to workplace policies or changes in personnel responsible for enforcing policies. *Personal changes*, in contrast, can be seen as changes in one's personal life that prompt explicit use of policies.

The socialization literature has explored many of the changes that can occur during one's time in an organization, including promotion (Kramer & Noland, 1999), changes in leadership (Ballinger & Schoorman, 2007), transfer (Kramer, 1995), and coping with being a surviving member during a reduction in force (Casey, Miller, & Johnson, 1997). To explore gender-related concerns during these changes, participants were given prompts such as, *Talk about a time when you went through a transition within an organization; in what ways (if any) did rules about gender expression change during this time?* Organizational changes prompting a reevaluation of gender identity policies occurred as transgender employees discuss organizational turnover and ascending to leadership positions.

The gender norms of a workplace depend largely on the communicated sensibilities of individual organization members. When membership changes, renegotiations of the gendered nature of the workplace must occur. Returning to what several participants referred to as "the restroom issue," transgender employees often find that when new employees enter a workplace, particularly new authority figures, there is sometimes cause to reconsider which restroom to use. In some cases, transgender employees are expected (and sometimes explicitly asked) to re-calibrate their gender performance to accommodate binary notions of gender despite policies designed to eliminate such expectations. Here "the restroom issue" is a communication issue in that the gravity of selecting a restroom to use, and the stigma of using a restroom deemed inappropriate by coworkers, is a communicated construction. The discussion section of this chapter provides recommendations for productive communication about this issue.

In some instances, organizational changes allowed for more inclusive workplaces. When a transgender employee is promoted to a leadership position, that person may have an opportunity to influence communication about gender identity policies. Transgender employees in leadership positions can set the tone for an inclusive work environment. As one participant explained: "[Other members of the company] were actually less intimidated to talk to me, you know, like if they had something sort of different going on. It was like 'well, you're definitely not gonna judge me.'" Despite the potential for advocacy for transgender employees in leadership positions, it is important to understand employees in these positions may actively choose not to advocate for gender identity nondiscrimination out of concern that they will be drawing attention to their gender identity and away from their professional qualifications.

Just as organizational changes affect communication about gender identity policies, personal changes do so as well. The most prominent personal change to influence perceptions of policies is undergoing gender transition.

Though many transgender working adults consider gender identity policies beginning at the anticipatory stage of socialization, some only begin to think about policies when they make the decision to undergo gender transition. As one participant explained, policies play a large role in whether gender affirmative surgeries take place: "Our insurance doesn't regard any sort of transition or gender-affirmative procedures to be. . . . They feel like it's all optional, therefore they won't pay for any of it. The whole structure is not great." Several participants talked about postponing, or even ruling out, gender affirmative surgery because it was not covered on health insurance policies. If an employee is capable of affording gender affirmative surgery, the personal change will undoubtedly test the integrity of policies at the workplace, as well as the way uncertainty about gender identity is managed. Interestingly, some transgender employees find they transition into gender conformity (e.g., becoming a man in a male-dominated occupation) (Schilt, 2010). In these instances, gender identity policies become less prevalent as institutional memory of the employees' previous gender eventually fades.

Exit

The exit stage is divided conceptually into two parts: *voluntary exit* and *involuntary exit* (Kramer, 2010). Whether one's exit from an organization is voluntary or involuntary is sometimes difficult to determine. For example, none of the participants were fired explicitly because of gender identity, so we could reasonably conclude that involuntary exit did not occur. However, when participants discussed having no choice but to leave the organization, characterizing the decision a voluntary exit hardly seems appropriate.

Transgender employees sometimes leave their workplaces because the communicated understandings of gender identity policies prove flawed or no longer valid. Put another way, participants reach a conclusion that their workplaces are unsafe. To explore how faults in gender identity policies serve as an impetus for embarking on the exit stage of socialization, participants were asked questions such as, *Describe a time (if any) when you left an organization because you felt mistreated because of your gender identity.* Some participants left organizations because the consequences of staying and fighting injustice were deemed too costly. Others left because an assumed explicit support structure—such as the support of zero-tolerance policies—did not actually serve its intended purpose.

Many participants voiced concern about the possibility of getting fired because of gender identity. Josie, a truck driver, explained that her biggest concern at a previous workplace was the possibility of being fired for being transgender. When I asked her if this had ever happened, she relayed a story that included the following:

[W]hen I first transitioned, they wanted me to have an escort to the rest-room . . . because some of the women there were uncomfortable with having this used-to-be-a-guy coming into the bathroom. But that was supposed to go away after a month or two and it did, but then we changed human resource managers a couple of times and then for some inexplicable reason, it came back. And from that point onward, it just felt I was being discriminated against. But . . . until [the state I lived in] amended its human rights statute, it was perfectly legal to do so against me because trans people were not specifi-cally covered. [That state] finally changed that and at that point, it started being insidious little ways to see if they could piss me off enough for me to stomp out of the company. But eventually, we parted on terms that basically said, okay, we're not going to sue each other because that would have been . . . it would have been ugly. And . . . I wouldn't have been able to work again. So . . . that was what I did . . . and we finally agreed to part company, and we did.

The assumption that a lawsuit "would have been ugly" and "drawn out" made leaving the organization seem like the better option. Josie remained keenly aware of the rights of transgender people throughout her time with the firm. When her rights were nonetheless violated through "insidious little ways" to get her to "stomp out of the company," she determined that policies would not protect her from discrimination. With this information, she de-cided to leave the firm.

Interestingly, Josie's situation builds from the previous section in which participants faced uncertainty about identity policies despite being fully so-cialized members of the workplace. For example, the "bathroom issue" went from not being a problem to being an issue based on changes in staffing in the human recourses department. This transition no doubt changed the way Josie looked at gender identity in the workplace, and the way she viewed the integrity of workplace policies in general.

Though Josie left the firm because the protections she thought were in place proved ineffective, Mo also left because the zero-tolerance policies he thought would protect him did not:

[A coworker] admitted in the interview that he threatened to kill me, but he just said "Ah, but I was joking." I was like "Okay, let's say 99% chance . . . he was joking. One percent chance I'm a sitting duck and it's late night, huge warehouse, or he follows me home and I get killed, I don't get a second chance." . . . I was like "Why should I have to live with that 1% chance?" I was like, "Aren't you supposed to provide me with a harassment-free workplace?" [My boss was] like, "Well, we are. We've talked to him about the harassment and, he knows that there will be consequences if he does it again." I said "Well, how is that keeping with your zero tolerance policy?"

As the quotation describes, Mo's manager did not seem interested in upholding the store's "zero tolerance" policies. Mo left the large retail store because the policies he thought would protect him did not.

DISCUSSION

There is alarming potential for disconnection between the promise of gender identity nondiscrimination policies and the lived experience of being transgender in the workplace. The anticipatory stage presents an opportunity for transgender newcomers to determine whether a company has gender identity policies and begin to discern clues as to whether the organization's culture aligns with the stated worth of the policies. Encountering the workplace is a revealing time for transgender employees as assumptions gathered from the anticipatory stage are confirmed or disconfirmed. The organizational and personal changes occurring during the metamorphosis stage shed light on how transgender employees are never really finished negotiating gender identity. Finally, disparities in policies and workplace culture can prompt transgender employees to leave an organization in search of a more accepting place to work. Existing research coupled with the socialization experiences shared by the ten participants who contributed to this chapter suggest opportunities for workplaces to ensure better gender identity equality, as well as future directions for scholars interested in gendered workplace norms.

Recommendations for Workplaces

Although many workplaces have adopted transgender nondiscrimination policies, it is possible that harassment, gossip, hurtful jokes, unsuitable comments, and exclusion may still occur (Sheridan, 2009). There are several measures that workplaces can take to encourage workplace culture to align with policies. First, a growing trend in many workplaces is to develop committees charged with the continual assessment of nondiscrimination policies. Policy stewardship can make strides to ensure policies are used, honored, and kept up to date. Of course, it is important the committee charged with ensuring the legitimacy of gender identity policies maintain legitimacy itself. Measures to safeguard the integrity of the committee include inviting various organizational stakeholders to be represented and integrating the work of the committee into an existing battery of assessment. Among the tasks this committee should perform is the development and close evaluation of diversity training curriculum. Many companies elect to hire an outside diversity consultant to direct or run diversity training sessions (Sheridan, 2009). In this case, the committee charged with assessing gender identity policies should actively vet possible consultants to ensure they meld with the ideal inclusive workplace culture.

A second recommendation for workplaces addresses what is referred to in the literature and in research interviews as the "restroom issue" (Sheridan, 2009). Many new employees worry about making a "rookie mistake," such as forgetting a coworker's name or parking in a reserved parking place. Knowing which restroom to use is generally taken for granted. However, negotiating what restroom to use is a common issue for transgender working adults, especially those who have not "gone stealth" (Schilt, 2010) and are able to pass as male or female. Why is this an ongoing problem? Currah (2008) astutely asserts that though much has been done to conceptually separate sex from gender, very little has been done to distinguish gender identity from sex. Indeed, misunderstandings and faulty attributions of what it means to be transgender can result in transgender employees actively seeking to avoid the label of pervert. Strategies for dealing with the restroom issue include making available more unisex restrooms and asserting that everyone should use the restroom that most closely aligns with the gender to which they affiliate (Sheridan, 2009).

Finally, when a coworker files a complaint against a transgender employee, extra care should be taken to ensure equality and fairness in arriving at an appropriate resolution. Several participants discussed being required to change shifts or use a different restroom to accommodate a disgruntled coworker. This pattern shows a striking resemblance to the phenomenon of victim blaming unearthed in sexual harassment research (Jensen & Gutek, 1982). In these instances, employees who had been sexually harassed were assigned different shifts or relocated to a different location, while those accused of sexual harassment remained undisrupted. Workplaces should invite any employees who are upset with a transgender employee's restroom choice to locate another restroom (Sheridan, 2009). Similarly, if a transgender employee is found to be the victim of workplace bullying, the bully should be the inconvenienced party.

Recommendations for Organizational Communication Research

Organizational communication research has illustrated the problematic disparity between policies and organizational culture (Dixon & Dougherty, 2014; Kirby & Krone, 2002). This study made an admittedly broad and sweeping examination of the use of policies as transgender employees are introduced to, become enmeshed in, and exit from a workplace. Future organizational communication research should examine each of the stages of the socialization model more carefully. First, an analysis of gender (as well as sexual) harassment prevention training sessions can pinpoint ways in which policies are (de)legitimized through its introduction to new and existing workplace members. Research triangulating a critical analysis of training curriculum with qualitative interviews of employees' impressions of the training sessions could yield insightful information about how instructor communication during diversity training sessions can be improved.

Second, it is important to demystify what it means to be transgender. As many participants explained, coworkers are not always aware of what it means to be transgender, often conflating it with sexual deviance. Longitudinal studies could explore ways in which the meaning of nondiscrimination policies changes for a transitioning employee. Schilt (2010) discussed the transient nature of gender (non)conformity for transitioning employees. A better understanding of the lived experience of transitioning gender in the workplace will serve as an invaluable tool for developing and improving social justice initiatives.

Finally, case studies should investigate companies earning 100% on the Corporate Equality Index, soliciting the workplace experiences of transgender employees. The worth of such a study would be twofold: If transgender employees report workplace satisfaction, communication prompting this satisfaction should be identified so that other organizations can adopt similar practices. In the event transgender employees are not as satisfied with their workplace climate as their company's score might suggest, work can be done to understand ways in which the needs of gay and lesbian employees may be distinguishable from transgender employees. On this same point, future research in workplace bullying may benefit from featuring transgender perspectives in particular.

CONCLUSION

This project studied the lived experience of discerning gender identity workplace norms in relation to nondiscrimination policies. It is clear a disparity exists between nondiscrimination policies and workplace culture. This study looks at an aspect of the workplace that is ever-present, and yet startlingly unexamined in the discipline of organizational communication. Using the socialization model as a theoretical framework, organizational communication scholars should continue to explore the disparity between policies and culture in the workplace with the goal of helping to create more inclusive workspaces.

Chapter Three

Interpersonal Communication

Trans Interpersonal Support Needs

matthew heinz

While increasing public visibility and greater social acceptance are creating more welcoming social landscapes for many trans people in North America, the tangible boundaries of loneliness and social isolation remain in place for now. This chapter explores the emotional and social support needs voiced by trans individuals living on Vancouver Island, British Columbia, to illustrate the applied and theoretical potential of emerging studies in interpersonal trans communication scholarship.

Estimated percentages of representation in populations indicate that trans people constitute a numerical minority, even if one takes into account that estimates of trans presence are increasing across the globe (Winter & Conway, 2011). More trans people are seeking medical system assistance (e.g., Reed et al., 2009; Spack et al., 2012), and more trans people are identifying at earlier ages (Brill & Pepper, 2008). Estimates of trans representation in the U.S. population vary between 0.3% (Gates, 2011) and 3% (Burdge, 2007).

In British Columbia, the central source of information for trans people exists in the form of the Transgender Health Program of Vancouver Coastal Health in Vancouver. The program recently renamed itself to "Transgender Health Information Program" to emphasize that it does not have the resources to provide counseling, medical, or social support. Vancouver is located on the mainland of British Columbia, and not easily reachable for residents of Vancouver Island, which is home to Victoria, the capital of British Columbia.

Much trans research focuses on urban populations, and much of it focuses on U.S. populations (e.g., Kenagy, 2005; Sperber, Landers, & Lawrence, 2005; Xavier, Bobbin, Singer, & Budd, 2005). While research on transgenderism and transsexuality occurs across the globe (De Cuypere et al., 2007; Reed, Rhodes, Schofield, & Wylie, 2009; Winter & Conway, 2011), communication foci are just now beginning to emerge. Canada is no exception. While research and scholarship on trans-related issues have benefitted from the establishment of the Canadian Professional Association for Transgender Health, a national affiliate of the World Professional Association for Transgender Health, much communication research in Canada focuses on media and policy; explorations of identity and culture from interpersonal communication studies perspectives are less common. A group of researchers in Ontario recently conducted the first large-scale Canadian Transgender Health Needs Assessment, which focused on health dimensions, and while it included measures of social determinants of health, communication needs were not singled out (Bauer, Boyce, Coleman, Kaay, Scanlon, & Travers, 2010).

Once barely visible and subsumed within lesbian, gay, bisexual, transgender, and queer (LGBTQ) scholarship, trans communication is emerging as a viable and vital field of study within communication studies. This trend appears driven, much like the gay, lesbian, and bisexual publishing trend years ago, by actual population trends, increasing and increasingly positive media representation (Alegria, 2011) as well as representation of trans-identified scholars in higher education. However, it appears premature to speak of a consistent body of scholarship or theoretical development since the range of articles and books on trans communication is quite diverse. Trans communication scholarship appears to be in an early stage, drawing from highly variant and often contradictory theoretical frameworks and epistemologies, and integrating trans experiences into prior communication scholarship in a somewhat incidental manner. Kosenko (2010, 2011) has begun a steady line of research on sexual communication among trans individuals; Hancock and Helenius (2012) studied male-to-female transgender voice and communication therapy; Norwood (2012) examined online family communication processes surrounding transgender identity; and Yep (2013) examined the intersections of queer and transgender studies and intercultural communication with a focus on the body. Interpersonal communication processes have been studied less frequently among trans populations, although it would seem that this body of knowledge has much to offer. Interpersonal communication core concepts are often embedded (but not articulated) in trans needs assessments (e.g., Bauer, Hammond, Travers, Kaay, Hohenadel, & Boyce, 2009; Sperber, Landers, & Lawrence, 2005; Xavier, Bobbin, Singer, & Budd, 2005); they would seem to lie at the core of many experiences identified in such needs assessments since they likely play a primary role in the everyday experiences of trans people.

Research involving trans people consistently points to strong emotional and support needs, regardless of whether that research approaches trans experiences via analyses of media portrayals (e.g., Sjöberg, 2012), interviews and surveys involving trans people (e.g., Beemyn & Rankin, 2011; Budge, Katz-Wise, Tebbe, Howard, Schneider, & Rodriguez, 2013), health-related research (Kimmel, Rose, & David, 2006), large-scale surveys of trans-identified populations (Grant et al., 2011), or human rights-based analyses (Davy, 2011). An acute awareness of social isolation and the related need for emotional and social support are also reflected in news stories (e.g., Labossiere, 2007), online blogs and Web sites maintained by trans people (e.g., http://tranifesto.com/), educational literature (e.g., Brill & Pepper, 2008) and the by now numerous autobiographical accounts (e.g., Bono, 2011). It would therefore seem appropriate for trans communication studies to be recognized as an area of study in its own right. Interpersonal communication scholars, for example, could begin studying the experiences of trans people in a systematic manner, offer specific recommendations, and provide intellectual and social leadership designed to improve the lives of trans people and their families.

One theoretical framework within interpersonal communication studies that might be of particular relevance to trans communication studies is the relational turbulence model as conceptualized by Solomon and Knobloch (2004), Knobloch and Theiss (2010), and McLaren, Solomon, and Priem (2012). I illustrate the potential applicability of this framework in this chapter. One of the most recent applications of the relational turbulence model appears in the work of Nagy and Theiss (2013), who studied relationship dynamics in married, heterosexual couples who have entered the empty-nest phase of their relationship. Their application builds on preceding uses of the model to explain relationship dynamics experienced by couples entering a more involved relationship stage (Solomon & Knobloch, 2004), managing infertility (Steuber & Solomon, 2008) or illness (Knobloch & Knobloch-Fedders, 2010; Weber & Solomon, 2008), and returning from military deployment (Knobloch & Theiss, 2012).

In a nutshell, the model suggests that relationship transitions interfere with "the normative behaviors and routines that partners are accustomed to and give rise to heightened relational uncertainty and interference from partners. *Relational turbulence* arises in response to changing relational norms and is manifest in intensified reactions to relationship circumstances" (Nagy & Theiss, 2013, p. 281). To the best of my knowledge, this framework has not been applied to interpersonal relationships affected by an individual's gender transition, although its central assumptions would appear to be highly applicable to such circumstances. Beyond addressing some of the immediate needs of trans people and their families, communication research in this area could also influence a broader social reengagement with notions of sex and gender that may not be as fossilized within society as it may appear at first glance. Finally, the results of studying trans interpersonal communication from a relational turbulence model perspective could lead to a deeper understanding of concepts already approached by relational turbulence model scholars, for example, the concept of hurt (McLaren, Solomon, & Priem, 2012).

EMPIRICAL ACCOUNTS: VANCOUVER ISLAND FINDINGS

In this chapter, I explore the emotional and social support needs of trans people from a communication perspective. I base my exploration on recent interviews with trans people (Heinz, 2014a; Heinz, 2014b), survey data (Heinz & McFarlane, 2013), and online discourse analysis (Heinz, 2012). My applied research goal was to identify the primary needs of trans people on Vancouver Island via a community-guided approach. My theoretical research goal was to use a small-scale empirical study to examine the potential of communication scholarship to improve the lives of trans people and their families and to contribute to the purposive building of trans communication scholarship. Consistent with the definitions offered by Iantaffi and Bockting (2011, para.16), I use the term *transmasculine* as a shared referent for "transgender people who were assigned female at birth and now identify as male or masculine;" I use the term *transfeminine* as a shared referent for "transgender people who were assigned male at birth and now identify as female or feminine."

Over a two-year period, 54 participants completed a survey, and 40 participants (most of whom had completed the survey) participated in interviews. For the purpose of this study, trans was defined as a descriptor for those who identify as transgender, transsexual, or transitioned, and all participants identified with the label "trans" if defined as such. Survey participants ranged in age from 18 to 68 with a mean age of 40. Fifty-two percent had been assigned to the female sex at birth and 48% to the male sex. Of the participants, 43% identified on the transmasculine spectrum, 39% identified on the transfeminine spectrum, and 18% identified as transgender/bi-gender/ mixed gender or genderqueer only. The majority of survey participants (85%) had family doctors and health care coverage (96%) through the British Columbia provincial health care plan. The participants' responses reflected a sense of belonging to a small sexual minority and a sense of being one of few other trans people on the island. While some participants in this study had extensive networks of trans-identified people, many said they only knew a handful of other trans people. Protecting confidentiality while allowing the study to reveal the details that validate lived experience (van Manen, 1990) was therefore a concern, so I chose not to describe participants via profiles or biographical sketches.

A community advisory board guided the study. Participants were recruited through health providers, community members, LGBTQ support organizations, word-of-mouth, and social media. The surveys were analyzed by calculation of descriptive statistics. Some but not all interviews were audio-recorded, and notes were taken throughout. Interviews were transcribed shortly after the conversations and participants were offered a copy of the findings as they would become available later on. The interview data were analyzed via standard inductive thematic analysis (Lindlof & Taylor, 2002), in which the transcripts and notes were read multiple times to identify recurrent themes. This chapter focuses on the thematic analysis of the interviews but draws on some of the survey results to provide further context. Excerpts from the interviews were chosen on the basis of representativeness of the theme. Participants were asked two main questions: (1) *If you were asked to express in one sentence or phrase what it is like to be transperson on Vancouver Island, what would come to mind?*, and (2) *Are your everyday interactions with people here affected by the fact that you are a transperson? If so, how?*

LONELINESS AND SOCIAL ISOLATION

It was surprising how fast the experience of isolation and loneliness emerged as the defining theme, both in terms of prominence and in terms of conceptual consistency and clarity. Although the study had not been designed specifically to explore notions of loneliness, social isolation, or social exclusion, the ubiquitous nature of this theme was evident from the interview and survey responses. Ten interview participants answered the first question with one of the following one-word answers: *Isolated, Isolating, Lonely,* or *Lost,* while others provided longer answers largely describing the same phenomenon. Living in the Vancouver Island region, these trans people said they find themselves cut off from community, whether trans community, LGBTQ community, or social community in general. They tended to experience themselves as lost when it comes to finding resources or information. The participants varied on specific aspects of community belonging but it clearly emerged from the data that having a strong trans community was important to the participants. Most participants did not feel strongly connected to a trans community, whether that community was defined as local island trans community, mainland British Columbia trans community, online trans community, or international trans community. Participants varied to which degrees they saw their lack of belonging as a function of individual choices or preferences, unavailability of a community, or lack of access to existing communities. Loneliness, then, emerged as the major theme across the interviews in this study. Four sub-themes each speak to aspects of loneliness: the difficulty in locating other trans people on the island ("Till We Find One Another"), the challenges in finding social support even within trans communities ("I Give Up"), the micro-stressors of living trans ("Stressful and Nerve-wracking"), and the lack of physical go-to spaces ("No Place to Go"). The potential of further examining these findings in future research from a relational turbulence model perspective is highlighted.

"Till We Find One Another"

The first sub-theme articulated by participants could be described, in their words, as "Till We Find One Another." It characterizes isolation as the perceived and/or real distance from other trans people. A participant said: "The surprising part is how many transgender people I have met on the island, especially Nanaimo and north. We all have a common feeling of being isolated and alone till we find one another." Another participant offered the following observation:

> What I haven't found here is a support group. One person tried to set one up, but there were differences in approaches on what the group should be like. . . . A lot of people I've met on the Internet are shy, not trusting, they have been scared off by past experiences. . . . For me that's the big thing. A support group—all the stuff that comes up—fashion, taking the next step forward, being able to talk about your experiences, being able to understand and be understood.

Many participants shared that their social belonging needs are not adequately met, even when they have supportive friends, employers, or family members. While such support is vital, the need to relate to others who share the experience of being trans is also important, they said. One transmasculine participant said he is not getting sufficient access to a trans community or even a queer community:

> I feel really isolated here, and it's not for lack of trying. There was more of a community in Ottawa. Maybe it's a function of the numbers. . . . In Ottawa, we used to do something monthly—just being social, hanging out with other men, having real conversations. There, we had guys of all different ages—such a range of experiences. It would be nice to talk about things from a trans perspective, not just about trans issues. That would also make it easier to find, try out, and model different kinds of masculinity.

Another participant stated: "There seems to be nothing here other than the trans group I attend, and that group contains nobody with whom I feel real rapport." The lack of a community increases the sense of being alone in a cisnormative society, as one participant explained:

> People on the street all perceive me differently. Some see me as a woman, some don't. In a city that's mostly gendernormative if not heteronormative,

it's the feeling of being on the edge, not part of it. Living in stealth, passing—these are real for me. There are no resources and only a very small supportive community. I have very little contact with people my own age.

This experience of social isolation appeared quite specific and seemed to be experienced as both a function of the physical reality of living on an island and the social reality of not fitting into social and cultural understandings of gender and sex. In the survey responses (see Heinz & McFarlane, 2013), the majority described their sense of belonging to the "island trans community," the "mainland trans community," the "international trans community," and the "online trans community" as somewhat or very weak. At the same time, most reported that being connected to a strong trans community was important to them (Heinz & McFarlane, 2013). One participant said his social support system had decreased drastically since transitioning:

It's getting smaller. I barely had enough to begin with. Since I've done this, I've become more alone. We can't turn it back. My support system has been completely diminished. We pay a big price with human relationships. There's not enough support for people in our age group—middle-aged people. I fell through the cracks a lot. We don't talk about middle-aged people, people who are parents, who don't drink or do drugs.

This sense of lack of a peer trans community was echoed by another participant, who said: "Are there any 'normal'—I hate to use the word 'normal'—trans people out there? People who are interested in playing Wii and parenting?" A different participant also voiced a similar need:

I have a huge desire to go to trans community events but not to the things that are happening. I would like non-drinking, more family-friendly, not parties. Recreational activities. Not support groups but social/community events. I went to one support group but that was not a good scene. It was a mess, really.

One participant said there is a need for social trans-inclusive events: "There are the gay bars but I'm too old for those. What else is there?" One participant said he was "just a hetero person who wanted kids" before his transition. Now he finds it difficult to maintain family relationships or social connections with people who used to know him. "That's one of the hardest parts of it all. I'm stealth. I have no community," he commented. While experiences and impressions of isolation came up for many participants, they appeared to be a function of individual circumstances as much as of geographical location and the loneliness that may come with a gender identity minority status. A participant who had begun his transition eight years ago said he was not seen as a transperson and does not experience direct transphobia: "I'm getting indirect transphobia. I'm marked visible as a racialized person. Being a transperson in Victoria for me is very tied to living in fear of the city." A participant who lived in a rural community said he had offered his name up as a contact for trans people because "there is absolutely nothing out there for people who think they're trans—so they can talk to someone face to face. I did that in response to meeting other trans people who are coming in suicidal without proper info or care. It's just not there." Location plays a role, too, he noted: "It's so isolated here. I think people either go to live on little islands where they're completely isolated on their farmstead or go back into the big city."

Several participants observed that while they felt alone, they were aware that they were not taking any active steps to address this sense of isolation. One participant said he felt isolated "maybe because of the lack of interactions. I avoid interacting." Another participant said he does not always "feel like educating others." "It would be great to be able to have a contact person—a resource person, phone community support that is readily accessible," he added. People outside of the trans community are not aware of his needs, he said. "That's probably me not really expressing what my needs are. If I'm approached a certain way, I just shut down."

As these participants' responses reveal, the relational turbulence model offers a promising theoretical foundation for explorations of the changes affecting interpersonal relationships between transitioning individuals and their family members and non-trans friends. McLaren, Solomon, and Priem (2012) explored the value of the relational turbulence model to understanding the experience of hurt. They proposed to incorporate judgments of dominance and disaffiliation as an explanatory link to people's experiences of hurt. The sudden changes in social roles that transitioning individuals experience almost invariably bring about relational disaffiliation as previous roles as daughters or sons, fathers or mothers, brothers or sisters are destabilized. The need to locate "one another" speaks to the need to engage in communication with other individuals who are familiar and perhaps comfortable with the uncertainty transitioning causes and could be examined as a desire to stabilize and affiliate at a time when most or all existing relationships are subject to varying degrees of destabilization and disaffiliation.

"I Give Up"

A second sub-theme was that for some, attitudes within the trans community on the island had furthered isolation rather than fostered contact. A participant who identifies as trans and lives in their felt gender, which is bi-gender, provided the following account of attending an event sponsored by a Victoria-based trans activist organization with their spouse. This participant expressed frustration that members of the trans community could read their gender identity only as pre-transition ("haven't hit the wall yet") or as ally ("glad you're supportive"):

That day I felt really sick. People just didn't get why I was there. They looked at me and saw this femmy lesbian and it was sort of like "oh, you haven't hit the wall yet" or "glad you're supportive." I've hit the wall for 16 years now and I'm not really either male or female. I wanted to be frank but I felt really isolated within the trans community there. I felt "I give up. I surrender."

Another participant who used to be involved in the trans community has purposefully shifted to looking for support outside of it:

I did look to the trans community for support. I no longer do so. I got burned out and also no longer need it. I am concerned about the lack of peer support. There are people who have such a need for connectedness and emotional support. There's a profound sense of loneliness among transpeople. Those who offer support may be the ones most needing support. That need sometimes manifests itself in poor social skills, personality disorders (which may stem from earlier trauma and/or intense isolation), and poor boundary issues. . . . I have provided peer support to hundreds of transpeople over the years. I'm aware that there is a powerful need for non-stigmatized social services, counselors, employment assistance, and so on. But there is also an incredible sense of entitlement in the trans community. The things that have been most hurtful to me came from my own (trans) community.

For a few of the participants, the inclusion of trans outreach in lesbian, gay, bisexual, and queer (LGBQ) communities is counterproductive. One participant noted that LGBQ programs should include gay, lesbian, and bisexual trans people only, and that he would not be comfortable walking into a gay community center:

I don't want to be out as trans. Sometimes people put me into the queer category and I really don't want that. I identify with straight people. I don't think we have that much in common with queer people. The goals of transsexualism and genderqueer are opposite to me. I feel uncomfortable being a straight guy in a gay setting.

Another participant offered that she did not want to attend events sponsored as part of an LGBTQ event because she does not identify as lesbian or bisexual. Other participants noted that there is strength in numbers and that accessing services and support via LGBQ organizations would be better than not accessing services and support at all. Participants who identified as genderqueer, queer, lesbian, gay, or bisexual were appreciative of inclusion in LGBTQ efforts but noted that "trans" cannot just function as an obligatory add-on and that the specific needs of trans people are often not met by the services offered by so-called LGBTQ groups.

The at times tenuous relationship between trans individuals and a larger trans community could also benefit from an analysis based in the relational turbulence model. Knobloch and Solomon (2003) suggested that future studies of relationships and conversations between romantic partners should evaluate specific message properties that can reveal relationship conceptualizations. It is plausible that trans people's conceptualizations of their relationships to other trans people, a trans community at large, or an LGBTQ community might be driven by interpersonal communication needs originating from relational turbulence.

"Stressful and Nerve-wracking"

A third sub-theme centered on the ways in which simply being trans affects one's everyday interactions. One participant said she felt separate from everyone around her: "It's practically impossible to fit in with other groups." Another participant noted that she feels isolated by others' indirect responses: "Walking here, I heard people talking behind my back. You can see people talking about you. I think it's a bit more accepted now than in the past, but definitely a major obstacle." Another participant described her life on Vancouver Island as "stressful and nerve-wracking":

> Even when I'm going to buy a salad at [a local grocery store] I get looks every day, 20 times a day. But my life is pretty good all things considered. You feel like people are interacting with you very differently, which makes it very difficult.

For many, the inability to escape gender paradigms creates isolating experiences at work, at play, and in public in general. One participant stated:

> Pretty much everything is affected by the fact that I'm a transperson. At work, I work with the public. Often, there's confusion about my gender, which causes lots of awkwardness. . . . I play competitive Scrabble, which is pretty awesome. But I found out two days later that some refer to me as female and some as male. A few get hostile because they get embarrassed. It doesn't bother me; they just need to get over it.

For those who can be read as the gender they identify with, the invisibility of being trans creates another type of psychological distance. A participant remarked:

> I'm pretty invisible as a transperson. However, that brings its own challenges. Do I tell them? Or do I not tell them? If I don't tell them, that creates a distance. Sometimes it's easier when people know. For example, in doctor's offices, you have to tell the whole story when you go in.

Interactions do not have to be negative to be remarkable to participants; it appears to be the cumulative impact of the degree to which interactions are affected that furthers the sense of isolation. A participant shared that her everyday interactions are positively affected by being a trans person:

> Most people have been really showing a genuine effort to interact with me once they know I'm trans, especially people who have known me before I came out as trans. I've learned to look like a biological female. If I'm in heels, it's easier to walk like a woman. I still walk too much like a man. I still get called "sir" depending on what angle someone looks at me. I get into quite a bit of trouble in the women's washroom. . . . Confusion is pretty frequent and marks my interactions. The more I learn to look like a woman, the more people think "I'm normal" which is ironic.

Many participants noted that their response to the level of stress caused by ordinary interactions is withdrawal or avoidance. "I avoid interaction," one participant said. Another participant offered: "It takes too much work to deal with people that way. I'm so tired of it all. When new people pop up, I don't want to educate them. If they're cool with it, great."

However, at the same time, several participants observed the opposite trend, stating that identifying as trans or transitioning had encouraged communication with others. Most everyday interactions are affected by the fact that he is trans, a participant said, but in mostly positive ways. Another participant also said interactions with others are positively influenced because being out as trans helps create awareness and reduces stigma. A third participant also said transitioning has had positive effects in regard to relationship with others:

> It makes me feel less cagy than before. I can be me. I can do things and feel comfortable doing them . . . . Most importantly, my career, which will deal with human rights and justice. I didn't feel like I could do that before, at least not with as much vigor.

A participant who was looking forward to beginning physical transition at the time of the interview voiced a similar perspective:

> I used to be paralyzed by agoraphobia. Now, I won't let me hold me back. My family knows I have no insecurity now. When I feel like I need to go home, I go out of my way to approach people now. Instead of curling into a little ball, I get bigger now.

One participant said being trans sometimes was an advantage in the queer community "because of being both female and identifying as male."

The relational turbulence model could shed further light on participants' experiences of being trans as stressful and nerve-wracking. Minority health literature continually points to the cumulative effects of micro-stressors. In the context of the study of romantic relationships, Solomon and Knobloch

(2004) documented that individuals experiencing relational uncertainty are subject to magnified positive and negative impressions. If the experience of relational uncertainty among romantic partners translates to the experience of relational uncertainty in other interpersonal relationships, then the heightened perception of irritations as threatening to one's relationship could play a role in this dynamic. Conversely, the strengthened interpersonal relationships trans individuals often speak of after having transitioned with the support of family, friends, or romantic others could perhaps also be explained by the relational uncertainty model.

"No Place to Go"

The fourth sub-theme informing the experience of being trans on Vancouver Island pertains to the physical reality of distance from the services available in the Vancouver metro area. Time off from work, travel time, and the expenses of ferry transportation and accommodations in Vancouver make it impossible for most of the participants to access resources available there. These are typical island problems (Royle, 2001). One participant noted: "Vancouver had everything. There are no resources here for recovery from addiction for trans people." A participant who has provided support to community members for 15 years offered:

> Being transgender on Vancouver Island has been a wild ride. A ride of intense support at times to a dearth of anything resembling care. . . . We need a designated Trans Health Program on Vancouver Island with outreach workers that can connect with people where they are at in their communities. Even the most privileged of us have trouble keeping ourselves afloat sometimes.

Vancouver Island needs trans spaces "where people can be together and build community," another participant observed. Cisgender partners or family members also experienced the lack of a go-to person or space. The parent of a young participant said he was frustrated by the lack of availability of resources for parents who do not know how to support their trans children, or where to find support for themselves as they are coming to terms with their children's transition. The same applies to cisgender partners of trans participants. A participant said more than finding someone to talk to her herself, she would like to ensure that her wife has someone to talk to:

> She often has questions and concerns and she doesn't know where to go. There is no place for her to go. I admire her patience. I try to immerse her in the trans community so she knows I'm not the only person but the trans community is not that accepting.

Almost all participants spoke to the lack of resources on the island compared to the multitude of services available in the metro Vancouver area on the mainland, such as trans-friendly LGBT support groups, trans peer discussion groups, dedicated clinics, trans-friendly substance abuse rehabilitation programs, social and cultural events for trans audiences, or drop-in groups.

DISCUSSION

The participants in this study described their lives as characterized, at least in part, by loneliness. The theme of loneliness, along with perceptions of social isolation, was reflected in the participants' narratives even though they generally reported positive attitudes toward self; many spoke of support of family, friends, and employers during transition (although for some, transitioning led to complete break-downs of relationships with family members or significant others). Most of the participants spoke to the positive experiences of transitioning or being a trans person on Vancouver Island, characterizing Victoria in particular as tolerant, supportive, and accepting. In this context, it is important to acknowledge the limitation that participants were drawn from a convenience sample. Participants from groups previously identified as particularly victimized, such as sex trade workers, prison inmates, or people experiencing homelessness (Holman & Goldberg, 2006), were not widely represented. Many participants acknowledged that their positive experience of living on the island might not be representative; however, it was clear that for these participants, Vancouver Island was generally considered a desirable location. Participants described themselves as strong, persistent, and accepting of their own gender diversity. While these self-portrayals may apply only to the participants in this study, they are consistent with more recent findings in which trans people reject pathologizing discourses and describe positive transition experiences (Greatheart, 2010) and the emergence of more frequent, and positive, media portrayals (Alegria, 2011). One participant said she feels personally supported but "[t]here still remains a sense of isolation societally reflected in part by a lack of knowledge within the medical profession, and misdirected discussions about sexuality of transgendered people." Outside the realm of communication studies, loneliness and isolation have been consistently identified as an aspect of trans experiences (e.g., Beemyn & Rankin, 2011; Brill & Pepper, 2008; Ekins & King, 2006; Lev, 2013; Girshick, 2008; Valerio, 2006). In turn, loneliness and isolation have been linked to poor health (Distel, Rebollo-Mesa, Abdellaoui, Derom, Willemsen, Cacioppo, et al., 2010; Rosedale, 2007; Segrin, 2012). However, while research on trans populations and trans autobiographical accounts agree that feeling alone, lonely, socially isolated, or socially excluded are frequently part of trans lives, there is no agreement among scholars as to what exactly constitutes loneliness or social isolation. In the context of providing nursing care to breast cancer survivors, Rosedale (2007) presents one of the most wide-ranging reviews of scholarly treatments of the concept of loneliness by summarizing popular, religious, philosophical, psychological, and nursing perspectives. This range of approaches extends from loneliness as an essential part of the human condition and a "chance to reflect, ask oneself why, and discover, envision, and invent one's future" (p. 202) to loneliness as "perceived dissatisfaction between the actual and desired satisfaction with one's social relationships" (p. 204).

Relational Uncertainty

Trans individuals, regardless of how much support they receive in identifying as trans or transitioning, lose the familiar guideposts of interpersonal relationships as all of their relationships become estranged. Estrangement does not necessarily mean that a relationship comes to an end or is negatively affected; it can simply refer to the changed nature of the relationship resulting from one relational member's gender transition. While their family members, friends, and coworkers also need to adjust the guidepost of their relationship with the trans person, the impact of this estrangement of familiar relationships is compounded for trans people since the nature of all of their relationships changes, often in a fairly compressed time period. This is where the relational turbulence model offers a promising theoretical framework for further exploration. Its key construct, *relational uncertainty*, is defined as "the degree of confidence people have in their perceptions of involvement within interpersonal relationships" (Solomon & Knobloch, 2004, p. 797). According to Solomon and Knobloch, relational uncertainty is an umbrella construct that consists of three interrelated sources of ambiguity: *self-uncertainty*, *partner uncertainty*, and *relationship uncertainty* (2004, p. 797). Identifying as trans and socially or physically transitioning inevitably reflect and enact each of these sources of uncertainty across one's interpersonal relationships, be they romantic, familial, friendly, or collegial in nature. Solomon and Knobloch argued: "relational uncertainty may be quite limited in *nonintimate* associations because normative role expectations . . . and scripts for relationship initiation . . . provide relatively concrete schemas for making sense of the relationship" (p. 797). In the context of gender transition, however, normative role expectations and scripts for relationship initiation not only fail to provide concrete sense-making schemas, they also clash with the sense-making schemas that grounded one's interpersonal relationships.

A second area of exploration within the relational turbulence model might focus on the concept of interdependence. As McLaren, Solomon, and Priem (2012) suggested, "[i]nterdependent partners have the ability to both hinder and help each other in achieving their everyday goals" (p. 952). For a trans individual, it is vital that one's gender identity and/or gender expression are acknowledged and respected in a safe manner. The significance of adjusting pronouns in everyday speech, for example, and the perceived or real communicative intent of adjusting, not adjusting, sometimes adjusting, or apologizing for not adjusting could be understood as *partner interference* or *partner facilitation* (p. 952). In relational turbulence model studies, uncertainty about feeling understood and lack (or perception of lack) of social support have been identified as sources of relational uncertainty, which cause stress in couples' relationships (e.g., Steuber & Solomon, 2008; Weber & Solomon, 2008). It would seem likely that similar underlying principles would apply to other interpersonal relationships in which gender role and sex perception are initially perceived to be stable referents. Such work should not frame research on relationships affected by gender transition as a studies that "focus on the dark side of relational transitions" (Nagy & Theiss, 2013, p. 296); rather, such work should focus on the model's value in identifying and predicting turbulence as "*polarized* reactions to interpersonal events" (Nagy & Theiss, 2013, p. 297). This model might be helpful in explaining the charged intensity of interpersonal communication in relationships affected by gender transition; in return, studying interpersonal relationships affected by gender transition might make an important contribution by extending the model.

Social Belonging

In this study, participants described, without being prompted to do so, how their social and communicative needs changed over the course of their transitions or over the course of outing their trans identities. For those who had lost family support from parents, siblings, spouses/partners, or children, isolation was often painful. Others said they felt supported by family members and friends. One participant said: "If I need help I have many to ask and draw wisdom from." Another participant also assessed his level of social support as very good: "My dad is still trying to stop calling me sweetheart. I call him sweetheart, too."

Another participant said his most urgent needs are social and mental health and a support network: "I'm isolated. It's a very small community here. I miss a feeling of belonging to a community. Access to counseling would be amazing. . . . I tried going to a counselor once but I had to pay for it. It's too expensive. The counselor wanted me to come back every week but I spent all my spare cash for the month on that one session."

Trans individuals who seek a medical explanation for their feelings and identity processes or who seek to transition physically will rely to some degree on medical experts. Given the relational implications of openly identifying as trans, medical care providers may play a pivotal role beyond providing medical diagnosis, recommending treatment options, or offering counseling support. Trans individuals may expect providers to be available to listen, to provide expert guidance on alternative ways of living as a trans-identified person, to prescribe hormones or endorsement for surgeries, or simply, but fundamentally, to ensure trans people that they are not alone. However, patient-provider interactions may not always live up to such expectations. A participant who identifies as genderqueer offered the following comment: "I have a lovely GP [General Practitioner] but I can't have an open conversation with him. I wish there was more training for GPs. He talks about my breasts as if I'm a woman but I don't feel that way about my breasts."

CONCLUSION

Communication scholarship would seem well positioned to unravel some of the complex interactions that lead to stress, discomfort, and loneliness in trans people's lives, but it appears to have been underutilized in this regard. Heinrich and Gullone (2006) argued that loneliness is "a crucial marker of social relationship deficits" (p. 695) and that researchers should pay renewed attention to the construct. They suggested that research aimed at "preventing and alleviating the harmful consequences of severe and persistent loneliness are long overdue" (p. 712). For trans people, it may be a question of to which degree loneliness may be a natural correlate of identifying as trans or transitioning and to which degree it may be a harmful effect of social discrimination and exclusion. For interpersonal communication scholars working with trans people, it may be a question of identifying interpersonal communication dynamics that work best to counter real or perceived social isolation.

Dialectical Struggles

In addition to the relational turbulence model, other interpersonal communication theories and models also offer much promise. Norwood (2012) presented her findings on family communication as an initial exploration of discourses surrounding transgender identity in families. In a similar vein, this study offers a glimpse into the experience of loneliness that appears to be shared by many trans people, including the participants in this study. Loss of the ability to validate the meaning of one's gendered life through the guideposts of one's interpersonal relationships may, arguably, affect trans people even more strongly because ultimately, validation of their trans identities remains an internal process. Norwood further argued that "interview data would be beneficial for analyzing not just the presence of meaning-making struggles, but the roots of the struggles, that is, the meaning systems that are at play that bring about the experience of a transgender person as present and absent, or as the same and different" (p. 90). Norwood identified several dialectical struggles in online postings of family members in regard to transgender identity: Presence vs. Absence, Sameness vs. Difference, and Self vs. Other. While Norwood analyzed these dialectical tensions in regard to sex, gender, identity and family roles, it is also apparent that isolation and loneliness would be embedded in notions of presence and absence and boundaries between self and others. This suggests the merits of a deeper exploration of the linkages between loneliness and isolation and trans health, with a particular focus on communication dynamics that may create perceptions of loneliness and isolation or that may mitigate such experiences.

Bylund, Peterson, and Cameron (2012) provided a detailed overview of interpersonal communication theories which have received much scholarly attention within communication studies textbooks, but which are rarely applied to provider-patient encounters. They suggested, "many interpersonal communication theories remain overlooked and have been applied only sparingly to healthcare communication" (p. 261). The theories reviewed (goals-plans-action theory, uncertainty theories, action assembly theory, communication accommodation theory, speech codes theory, social penetration theory, and communication privacy management) all offer themselves to application in trans communication processes. Other interpersonal communication theories that would appear of relevance to trans communication dynamics include relational framing theory, imagined interaction theory, and attribution theory.

One next step for interpersonal communication scholars could be a complex, multi-faceted exploration of the trans experience of isolation and loneliness. The interviews conducted for this study show a remarkable range in idiosyncratic manifestations of isolation and loneliness (cf., Kanai, Bahrami, Duchaine, Janik, Banissy, & Rees, 2012), which also merits a line of inquiry. For some participants, the experience of social isolation was quite specific and experienced as both a function of the physical reality of living on an island and the social reality of not fitting into social and cultural understandings of gender and sex. One participant said he has an amazing partner and "on a day to day basis, life is awesome." His family is "not so supportive" but he maintains contact with them. While he is involved in a number of communities, they are "all very mainstream and can't relate":

> People are nice and love me but they are not on the same page as me. I can't talk about trans topics with them. People who are not in crisis mode—who just get together once a month or so—that would be great. . . . I'm queer. Very queer. The vast majority of people in my life are straight. People make many assumptions. None of it harms me but it's wearing and contributes to feeling isolated.

The psychological distance between trans-identified and cisgender people can affect trans people's everyday interactions, leading to discomfort or withdrawal from interactions. A participant observed:

> I'm really working on not reinforcing the gender binary system by not taking issue with female referents. It would be nice though . . . It's not the end of the world but when I get my blood work done, for other conditions, the people at the lab often call me by my legal name or refer to me as "Ms." A little way of accommodating would make a big difference. We need better ways to navigate the medical system.

Another participant said most people are "ignorant, but I don't mean that in a mean sense. I mean it in a realistic sense. Ignorance is rampant, even among my coworkers."

It is important to keep in mind that most participants consciously and intentionally questioned popular and scholarly narratives of victimization and pathology. Those who felt very positive about their transition experiences were quick to express their awareness that their experience would not be mirrored by those in marginalized positions and that a generational shift has occurred, making it easier for trans people to identify publicly today. This tension of balancing communicative needs with the need to construct positive self-representation should be further explored. These communicative needs are urgent because trans populations are affected by high levels of suicidal ideation and attempts (Chamberland & Saewyc, 2011; Grant et al., 2011; Kenagy, 2005; Scanlon, Travers, Coleman, Bauer, & Boyce, 2010; Xavier & Simmons, 2000). However, recent research suggests that suicide attempt rates are lower for trans people whose family ties remained strong during and post transition (Alpert Reyes, 2014), creating a sound rationale for interpersonal communication studies on strengthening family ties during and post transition.

Finally, the island location that provides the geographical context for this study needs to be kept in mind. Royle (2001) offered the following description of island isolation: "an island sits alone, any person wishing to visit must make a dedicated and unusual journey over water; they must leave the mainland, the familiar, and venture to the remote insular world" (p. 11). This also rings true of trans experiences. Arriving at living in our felt gender requires a dedicated and unusual journey; we must leave the mainland of familiar gender classification and sex designation, and we venture to the remote insular world of a self-understanding that is difficult to share.

Chapter Four

Family Communication

Families' Experiences with Transgender Identity and Transition: A Family Stress Perspective

Kristen M. Norwood and Pamela J. Lannutti

The communication that occurs amongst family members is foundational for the development of individuals' communication skills and influences the quality of relationships inside and outside the family. Recently, scholars who study communication in families have called for an expansion of research to address diverse family configurations, issues, and identities (Foster, 2008; Galvin, 2006). These calls have been partially answered in that communication scholars have begun to look at issues faced by lesbian, gay, bisexual, and transgender (LGBT) individuals and their families. However, the bulk of the communication literature focuses on those who identify as "LGB" and less on those who identify as "T." Willoughby, Doty, and Malik (2008) described family discoveries of LGB identities as stressful and having the potential to change family roles, dynamics, and boundaries as well as to test family belief systems. Not surprisingly, parental and other familial reactions to an LGB member's coming out have important outcomes for the LGB individual as well as the larger family system (Willoughby, Doty, & Malik, 2008). Despite possible similarities in experiences, gender identity and sexual orientation are quite distinct and likely function differently in families.

While there is a growing body of research examining communication, transgender identity, and families, more research is needed to better understand what happens when a transgender family member's identity is disclosed or discovered. In this chapter, we explore three issues related to the experience of transgender identity as a family stressor: First, we outline family members' reactions to the "coming out" of transgender relatives or

51

partners. Next, we describe how family members perceived a disclosure or discovery of transgender identity as more monumental than one of LGB sexual orientation. Finally, we highlight factors that were significant in family members' adjustments to their relatives' or partners' transitions. We hope to contribute to the fields of family communication and transgender studies.

FAMILY STRESS AND STRESSORS

Family stressors are events that generate change in family systems (McCubbin et al., 1980). These incidences can be normative (e.g., having children) or non-normative (e.g., a member's incarceration). As Boss (1988) explained, "With change comes disturbance, pressure—what we call stress" (p. 12). Boss (1992) later explained, "change does not automatically lead to negative stress—*strain, hassle,* or *crisis* . . . nor does it automatically lead to positive stress. Change is, however, by its very nature a disturbance in the status quo and thereby, at minimum, neutrally stressful" (p. 114). Therefore, stressors can be experienced by family members negatively, positively, or both, but at base they require adjustment to change. Several factors influence a family's experience with stress including the meaning that is constructed for the stressor, the family's store of resources, and the number of stressors the family endures at a time. Boss (1992) argued that the framing of the stressor is most significant among these factors. For stressors where stigma is involved, it is especially important for family members' well-being as well as their acceptance of the member who is stigmatized (Lazarus & Folkman, 1984).

One such family stressor is sexual orientation. Researchers have shown parental responses to the disclosure of a gay, lesbian, or bisexual child to include offerings of acceptance, feelings of grief, tolerance, rejection, and calling into question family values and beliefs (Willoughby, Malik, & Lindahl, 2006). More accepting and supportive attitudes correspond to family members' beliefs that LGB sexual orientation is not a choice (Altemeyer, 2001). The body of research on families' experiences with transgender identity suggests it operates in similar ways; however, it is worth exploring potentially important differences.

FAMILY STRESS AND COMMUNICATION
SURROUNDING TRANSGENDER IDENTITY

Family communication surrounding transgender issues is unique, complex, and stressful. "Coming out" as transgender to a family member often marks the beginning of a transgender person's and family's transition process. Family members, including partners, often must change the way they conceptualize the transgender person's gender identity, the pronouns and name used to refer to the transgender person, and even the ways in which they relate to that person (Norwood, 2012; Whitley, 2013; Zamboni, 2006). Even if the transgender relative or partner chooses not to transition their sex category from female to male or male to female, the family experiences stress as they reconceptualize the relative or partner as transgender.

While research suggests that social support is an important influence on the well-being of transgender individuals (Bockting, Benner, & Coleman, 2009), support from family members is not always available, especially at the time of transition. Some family members are instantly supportive of their transgender relative or partner and adjust to the transition without much difficulty; however, others struggle with making sense of transgender identity, accepting their transgender loved one, or adjusting to the changes that often occur during the transition process (Grossman, D'Augelli, Howell, & Hubbard, 2005; Israel, 2006; Norwood, 2013a, 2013b). For partners and spouses of transgender persons, a primary struggle is the relational uncertainty and the adjustments they must make in expectations of relational intimacy, relationship routines, and public presentation of the transgender partner and the relationship (Alegria, 2010; Hines, 2006).

Norwood (2013b) connected family members' support of their relatives and partners to the meanings they constructed for transgender identity. Some family members constructed transgender identity as a medical condition, others regarded it as a natural nuance in gender identity, and a few believed it is a lifestyle choice. Those who constructed transgender identity as a medical condition were wary of stigma but supported their relatives (although not always immediately) and firmly defended the family against potential critics. Those who constructed it as gender nuance said that there is nothing wrong with their family member, but with the culture that restricts gender expression. These participants adjusted well to transition and were wholly supportive. Finally, those who saw transgender identity as a lifestyle choice condemned it and did not fully support family members.

Family members' conceptualization of the transgender person's identity in light of transition is another meaning-making issue that is important to the experience of this stressor. As Zamboni (2006, p. 175) noted, transgender identity "Touches on fundamental aspects of identity with regard to gender and sexuality—and challenges one's notion of these concepts." Pearlman (2006) examined the experiences of mothers of people who transitioned from female to male and found that they underwent a process of reconciliation, which involved feelings of loss and devastation. These participants were aided in their perceptual shift of seeing their daughters as sons by key turning points in the transition processes, such as male physical presentation. Norwood (2013a) has likened the experience of a family member transitioning to a kind of living death for some. Most of her participants reported feeling as if a family member had been lost to some extent, although the person still remained. This ambiguous loss is connected to the symbolic contradiction of male and female identities and of pre- and post-transition identities, which were sometimes seen as distinct persons. Norwood found that some family members were better able to cope with or largely avoid feelings of grief by constructing the transgender person as the same person throughout transition.

These studies suggest that communication is integral to families' adjustment, but more questions need to be asked and answered in order to generate a more complete picture of the transgender family experience. In this chapter we posed the following:

RQ1: Besides grief, what reactions do family members have to the disclosure or discovery of a relative or partner's transgender identity?

RQ2: How do family members perceive transgender identity as compared to LGB identities?

RQ3: What factors surrounding disclosure and transition ease or exacerbate stress related to a family member's transition?

METHODOLOGY

The first author collected data for this chapter as part of a larger study exploring family members' experiences with a relative or partner's transgender identity and transition. She completed 37 telephone interviews, ranging from 36 to 102 minutes long, with those who consider themselves family of transgender persons. While the primary focus of interviews was participants' struggle with loss, several other issues emerged as significant to their experiences, three of which are the subject of the present analysis.

Participant Recruitment

Participants were recruited via transgender support Web sites, emails to transgender persons and significant others of transgender persons, friends, family, and allies support groups, and snowball sampling. Participants self-identified as family and included 19 mothers, five fathers, four siblings, three adult children, one former and two current spouses, and three current partners of transgender persons who had begun a transition process. Five males and 32 females ranging in age from 18 to 70 years participated in the study. Two identified as Hispanic, one as Asian American and 34 as Caucasian. Nineteen participants' family members were described as female-to-male (FTM), meaning they were genetically female with a male gender identity. Sixteen were described as male-to-female (MTF), meaning they were genetically male with a female gender identity. Two participants described their relative or partner as genetically female and as having made transitional changes (e.g., hormone therapy), but as not necessarily male-identified. The youngest transgender relative discussed was 6 years old and the oldest was over 60.

Data Collection and Analysis

The first author asked participants to tell their stories and then asked follow-up questions to delve into certain topics. She began preliminary thematic analysis after interview number four. She reached theoretical saturation (Lindlof & Taylor, 2002) at interview 28, but collected additional data in order to ensure validity of analysis. She continued the analysis as she transcribed the interviews, replacing names with pseudonyms in the process.

We approached the present analysis from a family stress perspective and focused on issues relevant to family members' adjustment. We used the constant comparative method (Strauss & Corbin, 1998) to identify and refine themes that spoke to the research questions. For example, participants commonly reported that they either noticed signs of the family member's gender variation before disclosure or did not, which made their adjustment to the disclosure and transition easier or more difficult, respectively. These types of comments cohered into initial themes which were eventually refined into a category labeled *foreseen-unforeseen* with regard to the disclosure of a transgender identity.

FINDINGS

Our analysis yielded significant insights into family members' experiences of stress related to transgender identity. We discovered themes regarding reactions to disclosure or discovery of transgender identity, to the magnitude of transgender identity as a stressor compared to LGB identities, and to factors that influence family members' adjustment to the stress of transition.

Disclosure or Discovery of Transgender Identity

Many participants began their stories at the moment they learned of their relative's or partner's transgender identity, and others discussed it later in the interview. While their reactions ranged from immediate acceptance, and even advocacy, to anger and denial, the most common reactions can be characterized as something in between. Themes related to felt emotion were *shock, confusion, sadness, concern for the transgender person,* and *relief,* and themes related to action were *information-seeking* and *support-seeking*. It is nearly impossible to parse out the illustration of themes due to their interconnectedness in participants' narratives; therefore we present them in an interwoven manner.

Several participants indicated that they felt some degree of *shock*, surprise, or disbelief upon learning of their family members' transgender identities, whether the revelation came via the transgender person's disclosure or through a more indirect discovery of the transgender identity. Patty (interview #9), the sister of an MTF transgender person said:

> Okay, so growing up I had an older brother and then before my junior year of high school we sat down and we had a talk . . . she told me that she was not really my brother anymore that she was deciding to transition to become a woman. And that was kind of shocking to me because I'd spent my entire childhood wanting to be like my older brother. Um, you know, we played Teenage Mutant Ninja Turtles and He-man together growing up, so kind of a big shock to me, but I mean, I didn't really have a problem with it, but it was just very strange to know that my brother wasn't my brother anymore.

Even though Patty was accepting of her sibling, she still felt shock upon the disclosure. Often, participants' feelings of shock were accompanied by feelings of *confusion* or a lack of understanding of transgender identity. Alaina (interview #1), the spouse of an MTF transgender person, described experiencing shock and confusion, along with anger. In response to the former she engaged in *information-seeking* behaviors. She said:

> I didn't understand it at all . . . when he said, like, "Hi, I'm transgender" I'm picturing some guy in bright pink lipstick looking pretty horrible and, you know, just playing dress up, pretty much. . . . I didn't know where to go and we had probably a very, very long rough patch where I was just so confused because I didn't understand anything and I had to do research to at least try to understand, in a way.

The same was true for Roxy (interview #21), mother of an FTM transgender child, who relayed feeling shocked and uninformed about transgender identity upon her teenager's disclosure:

> . . . he came out to us in November of 2004, we were in terrible shock. I mean, we didn't even know what trans was, really. I thought it was like cross-dressing or something . . . When he came out as *needing* to be a boy, *needing* to transition, after overcoming the sort of shock and bewilderment and a lot of grieving and fear, I, in particular, in the family started to do a lot of research.

For some, shock was connected to having never noticed signs of gender variance before disclosure or discovery of the transgender identity. For many, shock seemed closely connected to a lack of understanding. Interestingly, some participants referred to an image or idea they had of what it means to be transgender. Patty's shock seems connected to an image of her sibling as a traditionally masculine boy and big brother and, presumably, someone she would not imagine would struggle with gender issues. Alaina described picturing transition as someone dressing in hyper-feminine drag, rather than the subtle female identity to which her spouse transitioned. This stereotypical idea of an MTF transgender person seemed to add to the jolt Alaina felt upon disclosure. Finally, Roxy indicated that she assumed transgender identity was the same as cross-dressing, which she seems to frame as less serious. It may be that having little or the wrong idea about transgender identity exacerbates the disturbance and, therefore, the stress that some family members experience upon disclosure or discovery.

Uncertainty seemed to be a common thread in participants' experiences of finding out about a loved one's transgender identity. Most participants immediately sought information to remedy uncertainty, either from Web sites, books, support groups, physicians, or even academic and medical journals, which was indicated as helpful for coping. However, even for Evelyn (interview #15) who had a great deal of interaction with transgender people in her job, *the experience of her (adult) child coming out* as MTF was traumatic. When asked if having worked with transgender persons made her child's coming out easier she replied:

> Oh I was completely confused and completely overwhelmed and I was devastated. It was so hard to think about . . . it's one thing to have somebody else's child be transgender or some friend say, "Hi, I'm transgender,"—that's fine, but when it's your own child you've given birth to and nursed and raised and called Steven. There were on many, many levels it was difficult, confusing.

Perhaps even a familiarity with transgender identity cannot prepare a parent for the experience of having a transgender child. Evelyn indicated that much of her emotional reaction involved feelings of loss and grief, but that she felt sadness and concern for her child as well.

Sadness was another common emotional reaction for family members. While it is certainly connected to a sense of ambiguous loss, articulated elsewhere (Norwood, 2013a), it also seemed connected to concern for the transgender person. Participants described feeling intense sadness in realizing that the transgender loved one had been struggling with very serious, negative feelings and in anticipating their transgender relative or partner's future. Evelyn finished her description of her reaction by saying:

> I was actually hoping that she wouldn't go through with it [transitioning] . . . I was so worried about her, I was worried about all the things you worry about, whether she'd be accepted, whether she'd be happy, whether people would be mean to her . . . I went home that night and I cried for an hour . . . I remember just crying and crying and crying and just letting it all hang out.

Claire (interview #23), a mother of an FTM transgender child, described her reaction, which captures both sadness and concern. She said:

> I cried for about a couple days. Like maybe 4 or 5 days, I cried almost constantly . . . I was devastated that my kid was gonna have to go through this. That's what, that was like, "Oh my god, what is this poor child gonna have to endure throughout his lifetime?"

The theme of concern was most common among parents of transgender children or adults, but was not exclusive to them. Liz (interview #36), the spouse of an MTF transgender person, described her reaction to her spouse's disclosure:

> I was very worried, now I have never really been worried about me—I'm a tough cookie, but I was concerned about how family and friends would take it and how we would fit into their world, whether they would accept us anymore, because I was not gonna leave Beth in favor of anyone.

Liz's concern for her spouse centered on family acceptance, which was a concern mentioned by several other participants as well.

Whether their emotional reactions included shock, grief, sadness, or fear, many family members sought support. Support-seeking served as a way of getting information from others who had similar experiences, but also as a way of feeling less alone in the experience. Ellie (interview #12), mother to an FTM son, was determined to find support. She said:

> After we came back [from the therapist's office] I said, "I need a support group." This is really something I need help with because I wanted to understand, I mean there was surgery involved, hormones or testosterone, and uh, I just needed to know more so I called PFLAG and I told them I had a transgendered son and I'm looking for support and I think the gal said, "well I think I've heard of that [transgender]—what is it?"

Upon learning there was no group in existence nearby, Ellie started her own support group. Nora (interview #28), mother of a young FTM transgender child, had better luck finding the support she needed to feel some sense of validation and guidance. She said:

> It still took us as parents a little while to wrap our heads around it. . . . We got in contact with a couple of organizations, TYFA [Trans Youth Family Allies] being one of them, and they helped us in the initial stages of, "You're not alone. This is normal. There's other people out there." And we didn't think we were alone, we just needed some guidance. "Okay, we're not crazy, she's not crazy. Ok, well it's not *she* anymore, it's a *he*." And trying to learn how to transition *with* him.

Organizations like TYFA were instrumental in helping families to cope with this stressor and seemed especially vital for families with young transgender children.

Although most of the emotional reactions discussed so far center on some form of distress, there was one that differed significantly. For those who had watched their loved ones struggle for some time without knowing what was wrong, namely, parents, the reaction to disclosure or discovery was actually *relief*. For Karrie (interview #20), mother of an FTM teen, her son's disclosure was the answer she'd been looking for:

> I don't know where I fit into the normal parent reaction, but for me it was just like an "Oh!" moment—"This explains a lot." . . . I've used the analogy of the pieces of the puzzle falling into place. So many times I've used that and that's the way it was because you could tell in Toby's life that things just didn't quite fit. And then when he told me that he was trans, it's like, "I can see that now."

Karrie seemed to differ from others who experienced uncertainty upon discovery or disclosure. She seemed to feel *more* certain once she had a label to help make sense of her child's identity.

Carter (interview #16), father of an FTM transgender teen, described feeling both relief and concern:

> There was this relief of having a label to put on a problem we'd been struggling with for many years. So, there was that part of it. But um, there was also concern or worry for our child's well-being, how our child would be viewed and perceived by the rest of society. For me, there were financial worries because I realized quickly that the therapy here is very expensive for people who are transitioning.

Carter's reaction, like many others', was characterized by multiple and mixed feelings.

In discussions of disclosure or discovery, participants commonly reported that before their relatives or partners came out as transgender, they had come out as gay, lesbian, or bisexual. Participants also commonly reported that they had *assumed* that the relative's gender variance meant that he or she was gay, lesbian, or bisexual. They believed these to be different experiences than finding out about a family member's transgender identity.

Transgender Identity vs. Gay, Lesbian, or Bisexual Orientation

Participants who compared or who were asked to compare transgender identity to an LGB sexual orientation indicated that having a family member come out as gay, lesbian, or bisexual was or would have been an easier pill to swallow. The most common reasons given for this were that LGB orientations are *more accepted* or *less stigmatized, less confusing,* and *more easily*

kept private than transgender identities. Furthermore, family members reported that there was or would be *greater adjustment in reconceptualizing
the person's identity* in the matter of transgender identity vs. LGB orientations. For example, Bianca (interview #11), the mother of an MTF transgender person, said: "I have said a number of times, 'I'd trade gay in a minute!' . . . I think it's more common and more acceptable in society." Ann
(interview #35), mother of an MTF child, also talked about stigma and the
observable changes that come with transition as part of why she perceived
transgender identity to be harder for families. When asked if it would have
been easier if her child identified as gay rather than transgender, she explained:

> Yeah, I think so because that's something that's more easily hidden. A gay
> child doesn't have a name change or a pronoun change or a visible change.
> There was a period of time where I thought about my child being gay and I
> thought, "Oh god, I hope that's not true." But then when this came out—most
> of the parents at PFLAG are parents of gay and lesbian children and they
> would talk about their angst and their difficulty and I'd be sitting there saying,
> "Oh, please, you don't know. You don't have a clue how embarrassing and
> difficult it can be." Gay and lesbian people are so much more accepted now
> than the transgendered are so it seems like a gay child—I still see that parents
> would struggle with it—but nowhere near as difficult as it was for me because
> it's so much less understood and still so much stigma attached and the feeling
> of it being a freak.

Ann references name, pronoun, and physical changes that might occur during
transition as differences between transgender identity and sexual orientation,
the former entailing greater stigma, more difficult adjustment, and less privacy for the family. Perhaps the biggest difference in family members' adjustment to the disclosure lies in the distinction between revealing a non-normative *identity* and revealing a non-normative *aspect of identity*. In other words,
while sexual orientation is one facet of identity, gender identity may occupy
a more central role.

Olivia (interview #22), daughter of an MTF parent, touches on this distinction. When her parent first started growing her hair long and shaving her
facial hair, Olivia suspected her (then) father might be gay. Asked if she
would have felt differently if her father had come out as gay she said:

> I actually don't think it would have bothered me as much. I don't think it
> would have bothered me at all, quite frankly. Not having that as the situation I
> can't say for certain, but I had a lot of friends who were gay. I had no problem
> being around them, loving them, being affectionate with them—it's not dras-
> tic, it's not radical and transgender existence is a very radical existence! . . .
> It's a persona change . . . There's a shock to the eye when you first meet
> somebody who's finally come out as transsexual or transgender because the

physical presence is so changed, where your sexual practices are your sexual practices and that's not really something that's so noticeable.

Olivia implies that with transgender identity there is no avoiding coming out if the person chooses to transition. Again, the adjustment to transgender identity is characterized as greater due to the nature of transition changes and the inability to conceal them. As such, the family member's transition presents a challenge to family privacy management.

Finally, Carter discussed the difference in having his child come out as bisexual and then later as transgender, indicating that his concern for his child was greater upon the second disclosure. When asked how he felt when his child came out as bisexual, he said:

> Well, not surprised because we thought that sexual orientation could be part of what she was struggling with. We were glad to have her help us understand what was going on. You know, but we were also worried about all of the things parents who have a child whose sexual orientation is somewhat different worry about. How society will accept them and treat them. We felt relieved and worried at the same time.

Clearly, some of the same concerns parents expressed regarding transgender disclosure occur when a child comes out as LGB as well. But, when asked if he would describe the latter experience as easier, he said:

> Yes, I would. Because there are so many other issues besides discrimination on the basis of sexual orientation that come along with society's ideas about transgenderism. The problems are much more complicated and much more expensive. I mean, the therapies for those that want to transition. So, it was a second blow, I guess you could say, in terms of having issues to deal with.

While there seem to be some similarities in disclosures of LGB and transgender identities, without fail, participants who discussed the differences concluded that a disclosure or discovery of transgender identity entails a more difficult and more complicated adjustment. As Norwood (2013a) found, much of the complexity in adjustment seems to surround the conceptualization of the transitioned person as present or absent. However, stigma, challenges of transition, and privacy also are salient to the perception that transgender identity presents a greater stressor to families.

Clearly, transition elicits family stress as it necessarily involves change. Norwood (2013a) indicated that the meanings constructed for transition with regard to change or constancy of identity serve to relieve or complicate family members' struggles with transition. In this analysis we uncovered three additional factors in participants' narratives that either helped or hindered their adjustment to transition.

Factors that Ease or Exacerbate Stress Related to Transition

Factors that affected family stress related to transition centered on the participant's conceptualization and reconceptualization of the transgender person's identity. Family members' adjustment to the post-transition identity was connected to seamlessness vs. disconnection between the pre- and post-transition self as well as the speed of the transition.

Foreseen-Unforeseen

When participants described learning about their family members' transgender identities, there were numerous references to whether there had been signs of gender variance before that. Several participants indicated they had no inkling that their relative or partner had struggled with gender identity, which was often attributed to the perception that the person seemed quite traditionally gendered earlier in life. Olivia, for example, saw no signs of gender variance in her parent and described the father she knew as quite traditionally masculine, which increased her sense of shock related to the disclosure and transition. She said:

> My dad was always this tall, bearded gentleman. Suit and tie. Very much presented as a gentleman and then it was this shock when I finally saw my dad fully transformed for the first time . . . I saw her dressed in a dress, she was in a skirt, she had heels on, her hair was done, she had make up on, her nails were done, she had earrings in, and it was this, I—it was shocking to me just to see my father without a beard! . . . I had never seen her clean shaven before and that was this huge shock for me. And then these other little accouterments that went along with it. Seeing her trying very hard to present as female or present as woman . . . [it] was quite shocking because she hadn't quite settled into it yet either. So, it looked performative, it looked like an act. It was very strange.

For Olivia, her parent's gender expression was formerly so traditionally masculine that transition felt like a huge leap; for others, though, the transition was not much of a change at all. Isabella (interview #4), for example, described her sibling's transgender identity as all but expected or, at least, not a huge departure, given her sibling's pre-transition gender expression. Of her genderqueer sibling, Isabella said:

> I don't feel in any way that Jess is a different person. I don't feel like our relationship has changed significantly and I don't you know, probably because this felt like such a natural transition to me, like it wasn't out of left field.

Isabella explains that her sibling's transition away from the female sex category did not stretch her conceptualization of her sibling's identity.

Isabella was not the only participant to say or imply that the transition felt "natural" or "unnatural." Several commented on having seen "signs" or, conversely, having perceived the disclosure to come out of "left field." Participants found adjustment to transgender identity somewhat easier if they had long seen signs of gender variance. Whether the transgender identity was foreseen or unforeseen is connected to the next theme.

Sudden-Gradual

Many participants described their transgender family members' transitions as either sudden or gradual. When this was mentioned, participants indicated that changes were easier if they were perceived as gradual. Aaron (interview #17) talked about his sibling's transition from female to male and described his sibling as having an androgynous appearance for some time before he came out and officially transitioned. When asked if he believed that might have helped his adjustment, he said:

> Yeah, I definitely do. Even with my openness to homosexuality and theoretical openness to trans or anything else—I think that I would have been pretty shocked and probably felt—I certainly would have had a much harder time with it if it had been sudden.

Similarly, Liz, the spouse of an MTF transgender person, was asked if any of her spouse's transition changes were difficult for her. She said:

> No, not really . . . Beth took hormones and has now grown breasts . . . but it's not been an issue for us. So, no, because it was always so gradual. I always had time to adjust in stages, so it's not been a shock.

Liz's use of the word *stages* indicates that family members' adjustment to transition may be facilitated by a more gradual process where they can perceive more continuous change rather than an abrupt shift in identity. Asked to say more about significant moments that stand out in her experience of her spouse's transition, Liz contrasted the experience with other stressors. She said:

> We've had some other traumas in our life, so maybe those stick out more than this does. We've lost two children. And my mother passed away and Beth's parents passed away. Those things tend to be more important probably because they were more sudden. This gradual change and this constant communication, if there's been anything significant it has not been as significant as other things.

Liz describes sudden changes as more traumatic than gradual ones. Both Liz's and Aaron's descriptions connect the dimension of time to the conceptualization of the transitioned self, implying that it might be easier to adjust to an identity change if it occurs incrementally rather than in a concentrated manner. Time might dilute the sense of discontinuity and therefore ease feelings of shock and even loss connected to transition.

Erasure-Integration

The final theme related to family members' adjustment to transition was *erasure-integration*. Several participants said or implied that their adjustment was affected by whether they experienced continuity or discontinuity regarding the transgender person's identity. More specifically, some participants lamented the sense that there was an *erasure* of the past or the pre-transition identity while others were grateful for a sense of *integration* of the pre- and post-transition identities. The erasure-integration theme surfaced in talk about feelings of loss. Many times, feelings of erasure were connected to the fact that transgender family members asked others not to reference the past (e.g., former name), or to put away pictures from before the transition, or both. Other participants did these things out of respect for or to ease the transition of their loved one without being asked.

Chloe (interview #25), for example, expressed a desire for integration of the past and present when talking about how she reconceptualized her FTM child's identity. When asked how she makes sense of it, she said:

> I think I probably see that I had a daughter—I mean, you've got all these pictures and she hates to see them and doesn't want to know anything about them and doesn't want them displayed, but it really is part—and I hope she can find a way to accept that, you know, that that was her, but different and her parents didn't understand. Because I hate—it's almost like there is no birth to 3 or 4 [years old]—we wiped that out. You know, there's bows and there's pink, so it's hard to find a picture that she doesn't look like a girl in.

And, when probed about whether it is difficult to be asked to put away pictures from the past, Chloe responded:

> A little bit. Back then I was scrap-booking and I had all these girly pages. We don't ever get those out, and it's fine, it's fine, I just think it's something that we're all gonna have to find a way to incorporate and just deal with it and accept it and move on.

Chloe expressed hope that her child will find a way to be comfortable seeing pictures from his past so that those artifacts and memories do not have to be "wiped out" of their lives. Presumably, this erasure adds to the difficulty of coping with the stressor of transition.

John (interview #3), on the other hand, felt his adjustment to his MTF child's transitioned identity was eased by his daughter's ability to recognize and reconcile with her past. John explained that his child had not created an erasure of her past. He said:

> The past experiences are still there and this doesn't really alter them. She doesn't say, "You have to put away all the pictures." She's quite accepting of "this is a change that's happened" . . . she is so accepting of us and how we've responded and she hasn't said—she hasn't been demanding or difficult or unforgiving about mistakes we made. So, maybe it's because she's not demanded she's no longer that person, like she's gonna be somebody new and we better by God recognize it.

John cited his daughter's recognition of who she used to be as helpful to his adjustment. He implied that if she had insisted that he forget the son he had the experience would have been emotionally more difficult. He also indicated that his daughter's patience with the family as they adjusted to the transition, specifically with pronoun and name changes (he later said), was helpful to the process.

CONCLUSION

Our findings provide a glimpse into how transgender identity functions as a family stressor. However, the sample was small, drawn largely from support groups, and likely not representative of the wide range of family members' experiences. Still, the analysis has practical implications for family communication scholars, families with transgender members, and those who support transgender people and their families.

First, family members had complex emotional responses to the revelation of transgender identity and to transition. In addition to grief, they experienced shock, confusion, sadness, concern, and relief. Often, experiences of uncertainty motivated the communicative behaviors of information-seeking and support-seeking. While some discovered a lack of support for their needs, for the most part information and support-seeking behaviors aided their coping with the stress. Uncertainty has been found to induce stress (Lazarus & Folkman, 1984), and the type of uncertainty caused by insufficient information can be resolved by seeking information (Babrow, 2001). Thus, family members should be encouraged to seek more information, as well as support, as they cope with their experiences. Scholars and therapists should work to ensure that information is readily available. However, uncertainty might not always be present or easily alleviated in families with a transgender member. For some participants, discovery or disclosure was actually a relief because the transgender person's behavioral and/or emotional patterns finally made sense to them. Therefore, disclosure or discovery might relieve uncertainty rather than create uncertainty for the family, which might reduce rather than induce negative family stress. Moreover, other types of uncertainty may not be easily resolved by seeking information. Problematic integration theory (Babrow, 2001) posits that uncertainty arises from a number of experiences that make it difficult to resolve, including when uncertainty is rooted in contradiction. This seems particularly relevant for families with a transgender member, as Norwood (2012, 2013a) has shown contradiction to be at the heart of many family members' experiences of transition. Future research should look more closely at uncertainty related to this family stressor.

Second, transgender identity revelation is a qualitatively different experience than LGB identity revelation in families. Many family members did or would have found adapting to an LGB identity less difficult than adapting to a transgender identity. Transgender identity was perceived as more stigmatized and as a more drastic shift in identity than LGB sexual orientations. Further, transgender identities were perceived to be less concealable due to readily observable transition changes. Communication privacy management theory explains that people create rules for the ownership, revealing and concealing of private information in their relationships; when these rules are unclear or not followed, turbulence erupts (Petronio, 2002). The perceptible nature of transition changes seems to be associated with increased turbulence. A transgender person's family members may experience a negative emotional reaction to losing the ability to choose to reveal information about their family. This was found to be the case in families with a married same-sex couple. Some family members experienced negative emotions when the couples married because they lost the ability to conceal, perhaps through the use of euphemisms, the LGB identity of their family member (Lannutti, 2013). Despite this similarity, our results suggest that transgender individuals and their families may need means of social support that are distinct from what currently exist for LGB people and their families. Therapists and counselors should be aware of the uniqueness of experiences related to transgender identity in the family.

Finally, transitions that were foreseen, gradual, and that involved the integration of pre- and post-transition identities were less stressful for family members than those that were not or did not. The relational turbulence model, "a theory that focuses on transitions within close relationships as moments that make interpersonal communication relevant to relationship outcomes" (Solomon, Weber, & Steuber, 2010, p. 117), is helpful in making sense of this finding. Solomon et al. described *turbulence* as the disturbance that can occur in relationships in response to transition. They likened this turbulence to that experienced by airplanes; depending on the severe or sudden nature of the conditions outside the plane, the pilot will have to make more or less extreme adjustments to keep the plane moving smoothly. Applying this to relationships, it makes sense that the less abrupt and drastic the transition changes are, the less jolting the process of adjustment will be for family members. Therefore, transition changes that family members are relatively more prepared for, involved with, and have more time to adapt to will create less relational turbulence and a smoother emotional adjustment. Like our participant Liz explained, this could be achieved through constant communication and negotiation among family members.

Family acceptance and support are imperative for the transgender member's well-being during coming out and transition processes (Bockting, Benner, & Coleman, 2009). The transgender person faces the stress of coming out, deciding whether to transition, the transition process itself, and living with a stigmatized identity. Family members can engage in strategies to help ease these stresses. For example, they should seek information and support to gain a better understanding of transgender identity and to sort through their emotions. And, they should strive to be understanding toward the transgender family member. Presumably, allowing transgender persons the time and space to come into transgender or transitioned identities, or both, while offering support and respecting their wishes (e.g., pronoun use) would alleviate stress for them. In the case of young transgender persons, the family could also play an integral role in helping to facilitate transition by communicating with doctors, school officials, family members, and friends on behalf of the transgender member. In these ways, the family can be a source of positive rather than negative stress for the transgender person. Specific means of communication that can relieve stress for transgender persons should be one focus of future research in family communication.

Conversely, our study provides insights into how stress can be eased for the non-transgender family members. Given that so much of family members' struggles seem to center on reconceptualizing the transgender person's identity, there are some strategies that might aid this process, though some might be difficult to accomplish. If possible, transgender persons might ease stress for themselves and their families by demonstrating gender non-conformity some time before coming out. Of course, this is not something we imagine transgender children consciously doing, but older teens, young adults, and adults who are reticent to come out might consider this as a way to ease their families into the reconceptualization process.

If a transgender person decides to disclose, and if they are old enough to do so, they might ease the stress of this conversation by being ready with information about transgender identity. Having books, articles, or a Web site on hand for the family might speed along their information and support-seeking processes and help to take the onus to explain transgender identity off the transgender person. Furthermore, if the transgender person makes the choice to transition, doing so somewhat slowly, if possible, and with involvement of family members (e.g., choosing a new name together) could help the family in their process of reconstructing meaning for the transgender person's identity, lessen feelings of loss, and make adjustment to transition smoother. Additionally, families' reconceptualization processes are easier if they perceive there to be integration between the pre- and post-transition identity of the transgender person. For example, if a transgender person can be comfortable with pre-transition family pictures remaining on display or with conversational references to their pre-transition identity, this can lessen family members' feelings of loss. However, we are aware that these might prove to be difficult or impossible tasks for some transgender persons. At the least, transgender persons can ease stress in the family by showing patience as family members make their own transitions (e.g., allowing for sincere mistakes in pronoun use).

These applications mostly concern what the transgender family member can do to ease stress for others. Certainly, the reverse is just as, if not more, important. Studying the experiences of multiple members of a family system, ideally longitudinally, could further illuminate the dynamics of stress for everyone involved. Future research should strive to identify the "difference makers" for families who do not fare well under this stress compared to those who do. For example, it would be helpful to know whether resilient families have different family communication patterns than others (Ritchie & Fitzpatrick, 1990) and how much impact family members' global meaning systems have on acceptance and adjustment. Answers to these questions can help us to develop specific communication strategies for easing the negative and increasing the positive effects of this family stressor.

Chapter Five

Intercultural Communication

Pushing Boundaries: Toward the Development
of a Model for Transing Communication
in (Inter)cultural Contexts

Gust A. Yep, Sage E. Russo, and Jace Allen

Transgender has, in the twenty-first century, become a global assemblage.[1] Reminding us of the complex, evolving, productive, and contested nature of such an assemblage, Stryker (2006) wrote,

> "Transgender" is, without a doubt, a category of First World origin that is currently being exported for Third World consumption. Recently, however, engagements between . . . "transgender" . . . that [circulate] globally with Eurocentric privilege, and various non-European, colonized, and diasporic communities whose members configure gender in ways that are marginalized within Eurocentric contexts, have begun to produce entirely new genres of analysis. Such encounters mark the geo-spatial, discursive, and cultural boundaries of transgender . . . but also point toward [its] untapped potential. (p. 14)

As transgender embodiments, practices, subjectivities, communities, and politics traverse a wide range of geographical spaces and cultural systems, such boundaries are maintained and challenged, drawn and redrawn, perpetuated and transformed.[2] Indeed, social meanings of transgender have evolved within and between cultural spaces and geopolitical systems over time (e.g., Aiello, Bakshi, Bilge, Hall, Johnston, & Pérez, 2013; Bhanji, 2013; Horswell, 2005; Najmabadi, 2013; Stryker & Currah, 2014; Valentine, 2007; Williams, 2014). How do individuals and groups create and maintain identities, enhance and sustain cultural intelligibility, cultivate and increase a sense of belonging, and negotiate and contest social meanings—indeed communicate—within and across these complex boundaries? To begin to answer this question and to tap into the potential of the negotiation, crossing, and (re)definition of such boundaries, our chapter provides sketches of a model for transing communication in (inter)cultural contexts. To do so, our chapter consists of three sections. First, we discuss the process of transing communication and provide a brief description of our model. Next, using the four domains outlined in our model, we identify and review past research on transgender communication. We conclude by exploring the potential implications and new directions for transing communication research in (inter)cultural contexts.

TRANSING COMMUNICATION

Transing, introduced by Stryker, Currah, and Moore (2008), is a deconstructive tool that can be used within, across, and between gendered spaces and configurations.[3] More specifically, it is a practice that examines how gender is contingently assembled and reassembled with other structures and attributes of bodily being such as race and nation. Similar to processes of queering advanced by contemporary queer studies, transing is a critical practice that unpacks underlying relations of power within specific cultural, geopolitical, and historical contexts from a universalizing perspective which maintains that gender is a critical concern for *all* individuals inhabiting various positions in a gender system (e.g., gender normative and gender non-normative people in a given culture). In this sense, transing focuses on all gender embodiments and subjectivities across a broad cultural spectrum.

Transing communication is based on four fundamental premises. First, gender is understood and rendered meaningful in relation to other vectors of social and bodily difference (e.g., race, sexuality) within a specific cultural system. For example, one cannot fully and accurately understand the category of "woman" without examining how gender intersects with race, class, sexuality, ability, nation, and culture, among other social categories (Mohanty, 2003; Yep, 2013, in press). Second, gender is simultaneously a performative iteration and an administrative structure. In other words, it is both a set of repetitive acts that gives gender the illusion of substance (Butler, 1990) and a form of governance for individual and collective action that becomes institutionalized as "natural" (e.g., gender classification systems) in a social structure (Spade, 2011). Third, gender is characterized by multiplicity rather than duality (i.e., we prefer to think in terms of a gender galaxy rather than a gender binary). There are multiple genders that transcend the simplistic cultural classification of "woman" and "man" in various societies and historical periods (e.g., Bornstein, 2013; Horswell, 2005). Finally, transing communication highlights the centrality of the subjectivity of individuals inhabiting different genders rather than the social and cultural imposition of gender meanings and categories on such individuals. To put it differently, it prioritizes the experiences of people in their own gendered bodies as they engage with the social world—for example, how a trans person navigates a gender-oppressive cultural system (Spade, 2011). Taken together, transing communication provides a powerful tool for the examination of the relationship between gender and power, both microscopically (e.g., how gender influences identity and interpersonal relationships) and macroscopically (e.g., how gender is administered in social institutions such as media, education, and law, among many others).

Adhering to the above premises, we sketch a model for transing communication (see Fig. 5.1) that consists of two interdependent and orthogonal axes—degree of difference and degree of mediatedness. Degree of difference focuses on how cultural, social, and geopolitical systems inform and constitute conceptions of gender and sexuality between individuals and groups. As such, it outlines a continuum based on cultural distinctiveness ranging from low (e.g., individuals from the same cultural system interacting with each other) to high (e.g., individuals from very different cultural systems interacting with one another).[4] Degree of mediatedness focuses on the extent through which various technologies mediate communication. This axis outlines another continuum based on the qualities of communication influenced by technology ranging from low (e.g., two individuals engaged in face-to-face interaction without technological devices) to high (e.g., an individual or group communicating exclusively through multiple communication technologies with a potentially large audience). Together, the two axes intersect to form four domains of communication (see Fig. 5.1): (1) Low degree of difference and low degree of mediatedness (e.g., face-to-face interactions between gender normative and non-normative people from similar cultural systems); (2) Low degree of difference and high degree of mediatedness (e.g., mediated representations of gender non-normative people within a cultural system); (3) High degree of difference and low degree of mediatedness (e.g., face-to-face interactions between gender normative and non-normative people from different cultural systems); and (4) High degree of difference and high degree of mediatedness (e.g., popular discourses of gender non-normativity from two distinctive cultural systems). Characterized by broken boundary lines and potentially separate and sometimes overlapping areas, these domains are fluid and dynamic as communication shifts and changes along the continua of difference and mediatedness.

Our model provides both a structure for mapping research on transgender communication and a mode of analysis of such research. Given the recent surge of research on transgender communication and its increasing theoretical and methodological diversity, our model offers a structure and process for understanding these complexities. More specifically, by identifying past re-

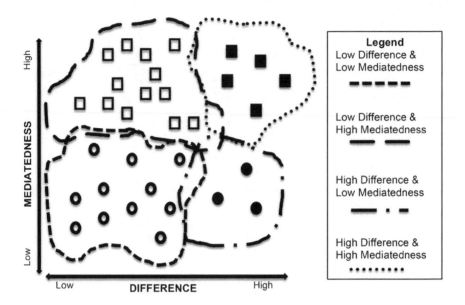

Figure 5.1.

search using our four research domains, we can more closely examine the construction of difference and cultural viewpoint in the study (degree of difference) as well as the nature and texture of the communication under investigation (degree of mediatedness). Such examination can provide a clearer perspective of cultural communication across the intracultural-intercultural continuum, as defined by degrees of difference, in a variety of settings featuring various degrees of mediatedness. In addition, our model provides a mode of analysis of the conceptualization and construction of gender in transgender communication research. Indeed, transing highlights the process of gender construction itself in research—for example, a study may conceptualize gender unidimensionally (i.e., gender by itself) or intersectionally (i.e., gender in relation to other vectors of difference), microscopically (i.e., gender as a set of individual traits or performances) and/or structurally (i.e., gender as an administrative structure and a form of collective governance), dualistically (i.e., gender as a binary) or multiplicatively (i.e., gender as a galaxy). Through the process of highlighting the construction of gender in research, our model provides ways to deconstruct gender and its underlying assumptions. For example, if a study constructs gender as an inherent, stable, and universal set of characteristics (i.e., gender as essential traits), the model, using the process of transing, calls attention to the ideologies and politics of the project. As such, it deconstructs the intricate relationship between gender and power within specific geopolitical and historical contexts (e.g., an essential and universal gender binary that transcends culture and history erases trans existence and subjectivity).

By offering ways to deconstruct gender and its underlying ideological and political assumptions, our model highlights the symbolic and material consequences of transgender communication research within and across various cultural contexts. The model, for example, calls attention to how the concept of "passing" in transgender communication research projects can further reinforce and maintain the gender binary, delegitimize trans expressions and subjectivities, and create social unintelligibility for this group in a cultural environment of symbolic erasure and annihilation. In addition to symbolic consequences, our model also provides ways to understand and examine the materiality of gender in and across cultural contexts (e.g., how the concept of "passing" harms—indeed limits and decreases the life chances—of individuals who cannot or will not pass in their own cultural communities and in the global stage, which can lead to local and, possibly, international efforts to change legal codes of gender administration). Finally, the deconstruction of gender in transgender communication research exposes, in Rubin's (1999) words, "the metaphysics of (trans) presence and absence" (p. 178). While trans presence signals the centrality of trans subjectivity and experience, trans absence focuses more on trans as a representation of gender enactment and achievement. More specifically, analysis of research using our model reveals whether trans people are objects of study (i.e., they are essentially voiceless, the researcher is speaking for them) or subjects of their own experiences (i.e., they have their own voice in the study, the researcher is speaking with them).

By providing a structure for mapping and a mode of analysis through the process of transing, our model can be a potentially useful tool to understand and examine gender, culture, power, and communication in transgender communication research. To illustrate, we use it to review and analyze past research before we explore new directions for transing communication in (inter)cultural contexts. Through the process of mapping past research, our review and analysis reveal that the first and second domains have been more heavily investigated than the third or fourth. In other words, work on transgender communication has focused more on intracultural than intercultural contexts, regardless of degree of mediatedness, which becomes evident in the next section.

REVIEWING RESEARCH ON
TRANSGENDER COMMUNICATION

Transgender communication research is becoming increasingly visible. After providing a more detailed conceptualization of our model, we provide, in this section, a review of representative research associated with each domain.[5]

The First Domain: Low Difference, Low Mediatedness

This domain explores interpersonal interactions within similar cultural systems. Talk show interviews (while highly mediated to a larger audience) are interpersonal interactions with varying degrees of low cultural difference. For example, an interview with Laverne Cox (star of the popular Netflix series *Orange Is the New Black*) and Carmen Carrera (TV personality and model) by Katie Couric has perhaps a slightly lower degree of cultural difference (similar avowed gender identity) than an interview between Janet Mock (author and former *People* magazine editor) and Piers Morgan (different avowed gender identity). To understand these interactions, we highlight three themes within the research in this area: (1) *issues surrounding language* (e.g., Blackburn, 2005; Hines, 2010; Iantaffi & Bockting, 2011; Irving, 2008; Levitt & Ippolito, 2013; Riley, Sitharthan, Clemson, & Diamond, 2011; Saltzburg & Davis, 2010; Sanger, 2008; Spade, 2011; Wiseman & Davidson, 2011), (2) *construction of identity* (e.g., Butler, 1990; Hancock & Helenius, 2012; Hansbury, 2011; Hines, 2010; Iantaffi & Bockting, 2011; Kuper, Wright, & Mustanski, 2014; Levitt & Ippolito, 2013; Pritchard, 2009; Riley et al., 2011; Saltzburg & Davis, 2010; Sanger, 2008; Wiseman & Davidson, 2011), and (3) *exploration of relationships* (e.g., Alegría, 2010; Bettcher, 2014a; Hansbury, 2011; Hines, 2010; Iantaffi & Bockting, 2011; Levitt & Ippolito, 2013; Riley et al., 2011; Tompkins, 2014; Wong, 2012).

Language

In this domain, researchers investigated how language refers to the creation, construction, and production of meanings in and through various linguistic systems within similar cultural contexts. Language constructs, affirms, and invalidates identities. When a language, such as English (both U.S. American and British), only has two socially accepted pronouns (i.e., him/he, her/she) to describe two legible genders (i.e., man, woman), those who do not fit the dichotomy become unintelligible. Unintelligibility produces invisible, invalid, and impossible identities and lives (Spade, 2011). For trans individuals, the issues surrounding language are threefold: the conflation of the terms *sex* and *gender*, the lack of a consistent definition of trans, and language as a source of regulation of trans identities.

Of the numerous issues surrounding language and the trans community, the conflation of the terms *sex* and *gender* is vital to examine. Much of the research in this domain addresses the fact that in Western cultures, colloquially using *sex* and *gender* as interchangeable terms invalidates trans identities by the inherent naturalization that occurs from the notion that biological sex (i.e., a specific phenotypic presentation of genitalia) should and must be concurrent with gender expression and identity (Hines, 2010; Iantaffi & Bockting, 2011; Levitt & Ippolito, 2013; Sanger, 2008; Wiseman & Davidson, 2011). Acknowledging gender as separate from biological features would create a space where trans identities could be as valid as genders that are already biologically celebrated by the hegemonic binary. Even with the acknowledgment that sex and gender should be separate terms, the consequences of their conflation remain. Most of the research conducted in Western cultures for this domain continues to address issues among "transmen" and "transwomen" or describe multiple trans identities as "transmasculine" and "transfeminine." Due to the lack of readily available, socially digestible language that acknowledges gender as a galaxy, research ultimately ends up perpetuating and reinforcing the dominant social systems.

As with sex and gender, there is some disagreement among researchers as to the definition of *transgender*, which is culturally specific. Some research does not acknowledge any differentiation of the multiple identities within the transgender "umbrella" (Levitt & Ippolito, 2013). Others specifically conflate *transgender* and *transsexual* to produce their own terms (e.g., "transpeople" [Sanger, 2008] or "gender variance" and "gender nonconformity" [Riley et al., 2011]). Still others simply condemn the use of *transgender* as an oversimplified umbrella term and call for a linguistic modification to the concept altogether (Hines, 2010; Iantaffi & Bockting, 2011). This lack of consensus and understanding preserves the confusing climate engulfing a perpetually muted and grossly misunderstood community.

The language we utilize in our everyday lives functions to validate and exclude certain people and identities in a culture. As such, it affects everyone (usually beginning at a young age), including those who are consciously working to deconstruct existing gender systems. Social scripts do this work without our conscious knowledge. Typical examples of Western social scripts include, "boy or girl?" as well as the prevalent focus on transitioning and genitalia in conversations with trans people (Iantaffi & Bockting, 2011). The reinforcement of the Western gender binary system, particularly through the English language, serves to maintain the gender hierarchy, which labels trans identities (or anything other than boy/man or girl/woman) as "unnatural" (Wiseman & Davidson, 2011). The notion of unnaturalness easily leads to the pathologization of trans bodies, namely, that trans people in U.S. American and English cultures (among others) must be diagnosed with Gender Identity Disorder (GID) to be able to receive hormone therapy, surgery, or other forms of medical intervention (Hines, 2010; Iantaffi & Bockting, 2011; Levitt & Ippolito, 2013; Riley et al., 2011; Wiseman & Davidson, 2011).

Identity

In this domain, identity refers to the creation, construction, and production of self and others in and through interactions within cultural contexts. Based on the research in this domain, identity is examined in terms of the construction and maintenance of self through language, discourse, and narrative; interaction with power; and, interaction with borders, specifically the gender binary.

Language, discourse, and narratives of trans voices that circulate in a culture influence how trans people construct their own identities. Because language and discourse in U.S. culture, for example, (re)create the gender binary, trans people are forced to conceive of their identities in terms of these two gender boxes. Much of the literature pointedly describes the ideas that trans people want or feel pressured to "pass" as either a stereotypically presenting man or woman. The "success" and "authenticity" of a trans person can be measured by the ability to pass as a particular gender for social legibility, perceived productivity, or safety (Hines, 2010; Iantaffi & Bockting, 2011; Levitt & Ippolito, 2013; Riley et al., 2011; Sanger, 2008; Wiseman & Davidson, 2011).

Constructions of self are intricately connected to power, including those of labeling and discourses of cultural intelligibility—that is, to be named, recognized, seen, and registered in the cultural imaginary. Although passing can be favorable in terms of access to privileges afforded to normative cisgender identities in a culture (Levitt & Ippolito, 2013), pressure to pass pertains to power relations. This pressure is inherently problematic because it reinforces the oppressive gender binary, invalidates trans identities (particularly for those who cannot or will not pass), and serves to protect the hegemonic cultural hierarchy of sex and gender through which heterosexuality is founded. In other words, the Western hegemonic sexual system based on gender object choice that produces the homosexual-heterosexual binary depends on the rigid separation of genders into "proper" (i.e., socially intelligible) women and men (Butler, 1990).

Trans identities work with and against the gender borders of a culture (i.e., the gender binary). This is manifested in a number of ways, including the health care establishment and sexual minority communities, among others. For a trans person to receive medical intervention in the U.S. or UK, for example, they are forced to gain social, cultural, and medical approval from their provider, giving the doctor the power to control and define the trans person's identity (Levitt & Ippolito, 2013; Riley et al., 2011). If a trans person does receive medical intervention (i.e., sex reassignment surgery or hormonal therapy), their shift in identity can be staggering.

Shifts in identity are inevitably coupled with shifts in power dynamics in intracultural contexts. Circulating within a cultural system, some trans people report gaining access to privileges that were not afforded to their previous gender (generally those who have specifically transitioned to "passing" masculine identities), while others were surprised by the apparent loss of privilege that was coupled with their transitions (generally those who transitioned to feminine identities or are unable/unwilling to pass as cisgender) (Levitt & Ippolito, 2013; Schilt, 2006).

Relationships

In this domain, relationships refer to the creation, maintenance, and negotiation of relational meanings in and through interpersonal interactions. Relationships with trans identities, based on published research, are explored through two lenses—interpersonal relationships and relationships to and within communities.

Interpersonal relationships with trans people can be complicated simply because of the gender systems trans people are forced to occupy. As previously stated, sexuality in most Western cultures is based on a strict gender structure that forces participants in a relationship to identify themselves and the relationship in particular ways (Levitt & Ippolito, 2013). For instance, if a person identifies as a man and is in a heterosexual relationship with a woman, but decides to transition to become a woman, do they become a lesbian couple? Their individual and collective sexual identities have inevitably shifted, regardless of the couple's willingness or desire to re-confirm the sexual and gender binary of the culture (Iantaffi & Bockting, 2011; Levitt & Ippolito, 2013). Due to the constraints and pressures of the current sex and gender systems, the couple will likely shift their sexual identities to be congruent with that of their gender identities.

The communal ties of trans people can be unfortunately complicated for a multitude of reasons. Experiences within these relationships can range from a sense of belonging and understanding to discomfort and violence (Iantaffi & Bockting, 2011; Levitt & Ippolito, 2013; Riley et al., 2011). Transphobia and genderism from the outside and within the LGBTQ[6] community are unfortunate realities for trans individuals (Bettcher, 2014b; Hines, 2010; Iantaffi & Bockting, 2011; Levitt & Ippolito, 2013; Riley et al., 2011). Internalized transphobia and genderism are likely the result of the Western social ideologies that are cultivated from (before) birth (Iantaffi & Bockting, 2011). Take, for example, a self-identified lesbian couple, in a Western culture, with a female-to-male (FTM) transitioning partner who has been shunned from lesbian communities for no longer fitting communal identity expectations of lesbianism. Trans narratives deem these instances of discrimination and violence as the most hurtful due to the fact that in these cases "the oppressed become oppressors" (Levitt & Ippolito, 2013, p. 57). In another trusted and seemingly safe relationship, parents grappling with their child's "gender nonconformity," unwilling to acknowledge their children as agents of their own identities, can end up harming the child's self-image by steering them toward cisgender identities that may not be the healthiest option for the child (Riley et al., 2011).

The Second Domain: Low Difference, High Mediatedness

This domain explores communication based on cultural homogeneity (i.e., low difference) in the context of mass communication technologies (i.e., high mediatedness). This often comes in the form of media portrayals of transgender people within the context of their own culture. *Self Evident Truths*, a U.S.-based photojournalism project depicting headshots of people who identify as anything outside of the culture's gender and sexual binaries, is an example of highly mediated communication with a relatively low degree of difference because of the U.S. American participants and audience. Grounded in the research within this area, we highlight three emerging themes: (1) *construction of identity* (e.g., Cavalcante, 2013; Mocarski, Butler, Emmens, & Smallwood, 2013; Sinnott, 2000; Steinbock, 2014; Tompkins, 2014; Wickman, 2003), (2) *sexual rights*[7] (e.g., Goodmark, 2013; Gressgård, 2010; Spade, 2011; Vitulli, 2010), and (3) *sexual activism*[8] (e.g., Hill, 2005; Thoreson, 2013).

Identity

In this domain's research, identity refers to the construction of self and others in and through public discourses within cultural contexts. Subthemes that arise surrounding identity include the conflation of the terms *gender* and *sexuality*, othering of trans identities, and visibility of trans identities.

While we have acknowledged that the conflation of *sex* and *gender* is inherently problematic and harmful, it is important to note that the conflation of *gender* and *sexuality* is also dangerous, but regrettably common. For example, U.S. and Thai media representations of trans people tend to conflate non-normative gender expression with an assumed "homosexual" identity. This assumption not only perpetuates the gender binary by presuming that all trans people will fall into conventional gender expressions that reify heteronormative understandings of sexuality, but also reduces the transgender person's gender and sexual identity to that of their gender expression (Sinnott, 2000). Though Brandon Teena identifies as a man in the 1999 film *Boys Don't Cry*, he is declared a lesbian by the intolerant townspeople, forcing him into inaccurate gender and sexual identities based solely on his genitalia

(Cavalcante, 2013). Similarly, media representations of trans people generally depict trans identities as a threat and betrayal to the cisgender and heterosexual populations. For example, representations of the *tom-dee* population (women who do not adhere to the socially acceptable feminine dress and performance codes) in Thai media have implied that not only is gender expression indicative of sexual identity, but that diverse representations of gender (and therefore sexuality) are a threat to Thai culture as a whole (Sinnot, 2000). In the U.S. reality television show *Dancing with the Stars*, Chaz Bono's gender identity is so confusing for the mainstream public that his sexuality is stripped from him altogether. While the spouses and partners of his fellow competitors are featured during the show, Bono's fiancé is rarely mentioned and never in a sexual context (Mocarski et al., 2013).

In order to preserve the prevalent heteronormative structures through media representation, both Thai and U.S. media consciously portray trans identities as inherently separate from the cultural mainstream—that is, normative cisgender. The creation of the "other" creates a space of uncertainty and anxiety about trans identities that further reinforces and solidifies the cultural gender hierarchy. For example, Thai media also portray the *tom-dees* as "brash" and "consumer-oriented," insinuating that masculine gender expression in women is intrinsically tied to unrelated personality characteristics that are viewed as divergent from ideal Thai culture (Sinnott, 2000, p. 43). Within these media contexts, trans identities are marked in obvious and debilitating ways. As a self-identified trans man in the beginning of the show, Bono, in *Dancing with the Stars,* is constantly separated from the other contestants. Though Bono attempts to perform heteronormative masculinity through song choice, the show undercuts his attempts with choreography that is generally aligned with the women on the show. While most dances on the show tend to be romantic or sexual, culminating in a close embrace, in six of eight dances that Bono performed, he and his partner were separated in the final pose (Mocarski et al., 2013).

In recent years, there has been some trans visibility in U.S. media. As people cultivate understandings of self through social comparison and self-reflection, it is vital that they see depictions of their identities within media contexts in order to validate their existence, legitimacy, and societal value. Keeping certain identities and their voices out of mainstream media insinuates that they are wrong, invalid, and inferior in the culture. This exclusion can be detrimental to the development of a healthy self-image for trans individuals and only serves to maintain the hierarchy of sex and gender systems that work to oppress non-normative identities. With such limited media representations of trans identities, it is crucial that trans individuals are presented consciously as multidimensional and humanistic. Unfortunately, U.S. popular media continue to present trans identities with simultaneously positive and negative valences. A promotional poster for *Transamerica*, a

2005 film starring Felicity Huffman, depicts a trans individual's struggle with everyday activities, such as bathroom use, providing visibility for trans identities and shedding light on the cisgender privilege afforded in those seemingly mundane acts. However, by depicting the main character, Bree, wearing all blue standing in front of an entirely pink background, the poster works to reify the established gender binary and highlight Bree's gender non-normativity in her culture (Cavalcante, 2013).

Sexual Rights

In this domain, sexual rights refer to the construction, regulation, and contestation of various sex and gender systems in and through public discourses within a singular cultural context. Perhaps not surprisingly, the research mostly focuses on laws.

Laws not only govern the ways we interact with the social world, but they also serve as a primary mechanism of the construction of cultural ideologies, including gender (Spade, 2011). According to Vitulli (2010), sexual laws in the U.S. serve to govern people's bodies, partially through the validation of gender and sexual identities. If people's genders are not aligned with their sex (and therefore do not adhere to the established Western cultural gender binary), they can be deemed inhuman and unworthy of the rights that are afforded to cisgender individuals (Gressgård, 2010). Within Western constructions of normative bodies, cisgender people are implicitly constructed as human and worthy of protection by law and further validated by social law (i.e., interpersonal and self-regulation of societal norms). On the other hand, non-normative bodies are pathologized as unhealthy and unstable, which might serve as justification for regulation and discrimination by both law and social law (Gressgård, 2010; Vitulli, 2010).

Sexual Activism

In this domain, sexual activism refers to the contestation, deconstruction, and reconstruction of various sex and gender systems in and through discourses within cultural contexts. The identified research on sexual activism focuses mostly on advocacy for trans communities and increasing the visibility of trans identities in mediated contexts.

As sexual activism becomes a more pressing issue throughout the world—including, for example, the "decline to state" option on birth certificates in Germany and the legal recognition of *hijra* identity in India—advocacy for sexual rights attempt to increase awareness to produce social change. South African trans activists, for example, have created a sundry approach to advocacy by encouraging solidarity among trans communities, addressing social law and the way that discrimination functions in everyday life, and deconstructing public discourses to break down the hegemonic forces plaguing sexual rights (Thoreson, 2013). Politics and legislation are a pressing concern for the trans community, as trans people are routinely denied access to basic human rights and subjected to discrimination within public services including medical care, among many others. However, many trans people engage in a form of advocacy by simply speaking publicly about their lived experiences and being represented through various media sources in a world that refuses to recognize and validate their existence (Hill, 2005).

The Third Domain: High Difference, Low Mediatedness

This domain is conceptualized through interpersonal interactions where there is a high degree of cultural difference. Dana International, an Israeli male-to-female (MTF) transsexual, and Guildo Horn, a German cisgender male, competed in the highly popular Eurovision Song Contest in 1998. Interpersonal interactions between Dana and Guildo during the event would exemplify this domain—face-to-face communication between two different individuals attempting to understand and relate to each other through their own linguistic and cultural filters. Research in this area is limited and generally takes the form of ethnographic accounts of cultural contexts with which the researcher does not identify. Three themes emerged from these cross-cultural interactions: (1) *use of language* (e.g., Blackwood, 2008; Roen, 2001), (2) *construction of identity* (e.g., Blackwood, 2008; Davidmann, 2014; Roen, 2001), and (3) *construction and maintenance of relationships* (e.g., Blackwood, 2008; Davidmann, 2014; Roen, 2001).

Language

In this domain, language refers to the creation, construction, and production of meanings in and through various linguistic systems across cultural contexts. When different languages are involved, such meanings become much more complex. As we have established, language holds an immense power in the construction and regulation of identity and relationships. When people attempt to understand the same concept (such as gender) across cultural contexts (such as Andean, Indonesian, Norwegian, South African, and U.S. American), meanings can be confounding (Blackwood, 2008; Roen, 2001).

Identity

In this domain, identity is referred to as the creation, construction, and production of self and others in and through interactions across cultural contexts. It would be highly ethnocentric and inaccurate to assume that non-Western cultures would (and could) readily adopt Western versions of sex and gender systems. However, these portrayals are available to anyone with access to the Internet and have a potential influence on other cultures throughout the world. Samoan culture, for example, has been negatively affected by Western trans ideologies. As reported by Roen (2001), a Samoan *fa'afafine* (i.e., a highly respected male who takes on feminine presentations of dress and familial duties) who visited the United States was referred to as a "cock in a frock" (p. 258), demonstrating an ethnocentric projection of U.S. culture (i.e., that cross-dressing is a joke or source of entertainment as opposed to a respected gender identity). On the other hand, Blackwood (2008) noted that some Indonesian identities derive their meanings from Western understandings of gender and sexuality, which gives them recognition and validation on a global scale.

Relationships

In this domain, we refer to relationships as the creation, maintenance, and negotiation of relational meanings in and through interactions across cultural contexts. Blackwood's (2008) experience with the *lesbis* and *tombois* of Indonesia serves as an example of Western influence on another culture's language systems that works to define and construct relationships through a Western lens. More specifically, Blackwood (2008) proposed that the word *lesbi* (used colloquially and in Indonesian media) is derived from the term *lesbian* and describes two females (note the reference to biology) in a relationship with each other. A *lesbi* relationship is comprised of a *tomboi* and a *girlfriend,* that is, a masculine-presenting female and a feminine-presenting female. *Tombois* do not consider themselves women, but rather feel that their performance of everyday life (e.g., sleeping wherever they choose, engaging in physical labor for work) falls more in line with Indonesian men, which is preferable considering the privileges afforded to men in Indonesian society. *Girlfriends* are feminine women. While the description of *tomboi* refers to gender expression and identity, in this case, sexuality is also implied. Due to the fact that *tombois* consider themselves to be closer to men than to women, they refer to themselves as heterosexual. Similarly, *girlfriends* do not consider themselves homosexual, though it is acknowledged that a *lesbi* relationship is a relationship between two females. Similarly, in the case of the Samoan *fa'afafine*, Roen (2001) observes that gender generally implies a homosexual identity and the terms *gender* and *sexuality* are practically interchangeable.

According to Blackwood (2008), the *lesbi* community will only acknowledge relationships where there is one masculine identified partner and one feminine identified partner, actively upholding a similar structure to the Western idea of heteronormativity. Adhering to the gender binary and acknowledging that there is one partner on either side is a crucial aspect of belonging to the *lesbi* community. However, these very particular understandings of gender and sexuality create a community where *lesbis* and *tom-*

bois can feel safe, free, and proud to express themselves and their love for one another.

The Fourth Domain: High Difference, High Mediatedness

This domain explores communication based on cultural heterogeneity (high difference) in mass mediated contexts (high mediatedness). To put it differently, it focuses on media representations of trans bodies from different cultural systems. An example of a highly mediated artifact that has spread across the globe is Thai pop singer Vid Hiper R Siam's music video "Lady-boy Never Cheats" (title loosely translated). Although problematic in various ways, the video has, as of 2014, reached well over 13 million viewers across the globe, including non-Thai speaking audiences, cisgender audiences, and audiences that know very little about Thai culture or transgender subjectivities (exemplifying this domain) as well as Thai audiences (exemplifying the second domain). Research in this domain is limited and highlights three central themes: (1) *identity* (e.g., Maurey, 2009; McLelland, 2000; Patel, 2010; Steinbock, 2014; Tompkins, 2014), (2) *sexual rights*[9] (e.g., McLelland & Suganuma, 2009; Patel, 2010), and (3) *sexual activism*[10] (e.g., McLelland & Suganuma, 2009; Patel, 2010).

Identity

In this domain, identity refers to the construction of self and others in and through public discourses, such as media representations, across cultural contexts. Research in this domain focuses on various conceptions of identity and conflation between gay and trans identities leading to a range of intelligibility of transgenderism.

Trans identity has been conceptualized in different ways ranging from stable to fluid. Patel (2010) describes *hijras*, individuals in Indian culture who are neither male nor female, as people who were born male but identify as female by performing femininity through bodily deportment, appearance, and dress. Often referred to as "third gender," which Patel (2010) translates into the Western conception of "transgender," the identity of a *hijra* is fairly fixed and stable (p. 836). On the other hand, identity has been characterized as the interplay between stability and closure as well as fluidity and ambiguity. Focusing on Dana International, the first Israeli MTF singer to represent her country and to win the Eurovision Song Contest, Maurey (2009) examined Dana's performance, choice of songs, and lyrics. The analysis suggested that Dana engages in a constant play with her identity ranging from reification of stable womanhood as passive and consumer-oriented to evolving performances of female agency as transgressive and highly sexual.

As stated previously, the literature we examined suggests that there is a pervasive conflation between *gender* and *sexuality*. In discourses across different contexts, we continue to see trans identity associated with homosexuality. In Japan, for example, McLelland (2000) noted that transgenderism, in the form of cross-dressing, is often conflated with homosexual desire and attraction. This error often results in elevating homosexual identity, with its accompanying markers of cross-dressing, entertainment, sex work, and effeminacy, at the expense of the intelligibility of trans subjectivity and identity. On the other hand, *hijras* have a trans identity that is distinctively different from homosexuality. Patel (2010) noted that there are two types of men who have sex with men—what the Western sexual system would call "homosexual"—in Indian culture: *panthis* (those who are masculine in gender performance and penetrators in sexual practice) and *kothis* (those who are feminine in gender performance and are sexually passive in practice). Although both *kothis* and *hijras* perform traditional femininity in their culture, *kothis* refers to a sexual identity while *hijras* adopt a culturally and religiously structured feminine way of living, which Patel (2010) equated to a transgender identity. In this cultural context, *hijra* identity is highly intelligible.

Sexual Rights

In this domain, sexual rights refer to the construction, regulation, and recognition of various sex and gender systems in and through public discourses across cultural contexts. Previous research continues to observe the conflation of sex and gender and different conceptualizations of trans identity, as reported above, and focuses on transgender rights as human rights. In India, for example, Patel (2010) noted that in spite of social acceptance, *hijras* struggle with their basic human rights, such as the lack of basic access to health care, sexual health information, and general political rights; employment and police discrimination; and ongoing gender-based violence and police brutality, among others. Such struggles have been placed in an international context and covered by various cultural media outlets as a battle for transgender rights.

Sexual Activism

In this domain, sexual activism refers to the contestation, deconstruction, and reconstruction of various sex and gender systems across cultural contexts. As such, it is both a symbolic and material extension of what researchers call "sexual rights." Not surprisingly, work in this area focuses on political and legislative change. Returning to the case of the *hijras* in India, a lot of focus was placed on Indian Penal Code (IPC) Section 377—imposed in 1860 by the UK, India's former colonizers, to criminalize sodomy. IPC 377, in many ways, serves as a classic example of how distinct cultural systems of sex, gender, and sexuality come into conflict through the process of colonialism and demonstrate how the colonizers—in this case, the British—used their power to impose, formalize, and enforce their cultural values on the native community. Legal discrimination against homosexuality and *hijras* in India is one of the results. Given the rampant employment discrimination and other forms of social regulation surrounding the workplace, most *hijras* turn to sex work to survive, and IPC 377 is used to intimidate, harass, target, and punish them (Patel, 2010). Using the language of transgender rights to fight legal discrimination against *hijras*, a legislative victory was achieved in April 2014, giving Indian *hijras* the right to be recognized as a "third gender."

TRANSING COMMUNICATION IN (INTER)CULTURAL CONTEXTS: EXPLORING NEW DIRECTIONS FOR RESEARCH

Without a doubt, our research indicates that there is a need to acknowledge the vast invisibility and invalidation of trans lives across cultural contexts. Utilizing the deconstructive method of transing to recognize and redefine the dominant sex, gender, and sexual systems within and between cultural spaces is the first step to dismantling the pervasive oppression of trans identities. By prioritizing the experiences of trans individuals, we can begin to construct communication that serves to challenge current social and ideological systems, validate diverse identities regardless of normativity, and produce research that reflects the rich complexities of trans lives within and across cultural systems. Recognizing that communication is always already cultural, our model offers a way to think about cultures in terms of difference, such as meanings and frameworks of intelligibility, views of self and others, embodiments and practices, as well as structures and social institutions, among others. Further, acknowledging the unprecedented changes and uses of technology in the last few decades, our model provides a way to consider its impact on communication and discourse, such as individual and collective identity, representation within and between cultures, construction of rights, and collective mobilization for social change, among others. Taken together, the model provides ways to map and examine current research and suggests new directions for transgender communication scholarship within and across cultures.

Using the model we developed and focusing on the studies we identified for each domain, we now discuss some implications for transing communication in (inter)cultural contexts and suggest new directions for research in these arenas. Our discussion focuses on two broad areas: (1) issues that emerged from the research *within* the four domains, which might be viewed as a "deep look from within," and (2) patterns that emerged from the research *between* the four domains, which might be characterized as a "panoramic view from above."

Transing communication, as stated earlier, demands that we examine how gender is assembled and reassembled with other qualities (e.g., race, sexuality) and structures (e.g., culture, systems of representation) of bodily being within geopolitical and historical contexts. A "deep look from within" the four domains—individually and collectively—suggests a number of potential implications and new directions for research.

First, researchers must be mindful of the ways they construct gender in their projects. More specifically, a number of the studies we examined, perhaps inadvertently, reified the gender binary by forcing trans people to conform to a system of gender duality rather than affirming multiple, even infinite, gender expressions, embodiments, configurations, and practices. In the process, trans people are othered and, in doing so, they will continue to be, as Suess, Espineira, and Walters (2014) forcefully reminded us, "defined as pathological" (p. 73). In addition to being symbolically and materially violent to trans people, such pathologization serves to reify gender norms (manifestations of societal gender standards), normativity (the culturally accepted belief that gender norms are "natural"), and ideals of normality (the creation of "natural" as distinct and separate from "unnatural" gendered bodies) in a culture. When researchers conceptualize normality as a dynamic relation rather than a static set of qualities (i.e., gender normality, such as the binary, is defined in relation to gender abnormalities, such as those who do not fit the binary, rather than defining gender normality as a "natural" or "given" group of traits), they expose the constructed, unstable, contingent, and improvisational nature of gender (Stephens, 2014). This is a critical move in future transgender communication research. Another critical move in this research is to examine gender inclusively through the trope of gender galaxy by having individuals and groups self-define—in other words, gender self-determination (Stanley, 2014)—rather than forcing them into existing categories.

Second, researchers must be attentive to how sex, gender, and sexuality systems are configured within a cultural context. Several studies point to the conflation of sex and gender; gender and sexuality; and sex, gender, and sexuality. In many Western cultures, for example, sex is always already gendered and normative gendered performances are intricately connected to the institutions of heterosexuality and patriarchy (Butler, 1990). In such a system, what is the potential of a trans body to reify or disrupt heteropatriarchy? Attention to this question as well as the relationship between microscopic interactions—for example, everyday conversations—and macroscopic structures and forces—for example, cultural ideology of cisgenderism that denigrates trans identities, bodies, genders, and sexualities (Lennon & Mistler, 2014)—are important in future work in transgender communication.

Third, researchers must examine how gender is defined and constituted through other salient cultural categories, such as race, class, sexuality, body, among others (Johnson, 2013; Yep, 2013, in press). In other words, gender must be examined intersectionally, which to us, means attending to both marked (i.e., non-normative identities within a culture such as non-White, non-middle class, non-heterosexual, etc.) and unmarked (i.e., normative identities within a culture such as White, middle-class, heterosexual, etc.) intersections (Yep, in press). Unfortunately, much of the research we identified focused mostly on gender and sexuality with little attention to race, class, or the body.

Fourth, studies that examined trans bodies and identities in the U.S. did not generally focus on culture while research on bodies and identities outside the U.S.—particularly non-Western societies—had a much greater emphasis on culture. As a result, Western cultures become an invisible and normative center through which "other" cultures are described, measured, and declared to deviate. A potentially productive direction in future transgender communication research is to examine how culture—visibly or invisibly—constructs gender, enforces gender normativity, and produces trans bodies and identities at particular moments in time and in various geopolitical contexts (Valentine, 2007; Yep, 2013).

Moving away from a focus on research *within* the domains and turning to the examination of research *between* the four domains of our model, a "panoramic view from above" emerges. It is clear that transgender communication research on various degrees of mediatedness is more common in intracultural settings (first and second domains) than in intercultural ones (third and fourth domains). Given the additional complexities and demands of intercultural research, this is, of course, hardly surprising. Intercultural communication research requires exploration into different ways of seeing, knowing, and living; constructing, reconstructing, and narrating bodies and subjectivities; and their subsequent translation into other systems of meaning, legibility, and cultural representation (Yep, 2013). This process of knowledge production exists in a complex field of power relations as Enke (2014) reminded us, "gay, queer, and transgender all comingle with imperialist institutions" (p. 242); in this sense, intercultural researchers, who act like translators, carry "the burden of destruction and creation" (p. 242). With sensitivity, care, and hope, the burden of creating new knowledge systems can be met in future transgender (inter)cultural communication research partly through "intersectional reflexivity" (Jones & Calafell, 2012, p. 963), which refers to the researchers' acknowledgment of and reflection on their own intersectional identity and their own self-implication in systems of privilege and marginalization in relation to their own culture as well as the culture of the group they are studying.

One obvious direction for future transgender communication research is to examine the production of gender—and its accompanying intersections—in cultural contexts beyond the U.S. and the global West (i.e., third and fourth domains). A perhaps less obvious future research direction is the examination of gendering processes in the West that focuses on whiteness, body normativity, and cisgender privileges (Johnson, 2013; Vidal-Ortiz, 2014). Such work is, in many ways, about unpacking invisible and unmarked systems of power and privilege, an important area of future transgender communication research. A final implication for researchers is to be mindful that in intercultural settings, identity, relationships, gender and sexual rights, and gender and sexual activism may have very different meanings for the individuals and cultural communities involved. Gender and sexual rights, for example, may look different from one cultural context to another depending on geopolitics, history, and the interplay between the local and the global (e.g., Balzer & LaGata, 2014; McLelland & Suganuma, 2009; Spade, 2011).

CONCLUSION

"Transgender" is itself an imperfect translation across cultural contexts, one that, as Enke (2014, p. 243) pointed out, "carries institutional and imperial discipline: to be named and to name oneself transgender is to enter into disciplinary regimes that distribute recognition and resources according to imperial logics," that is, systems of cultural intelligibility, value, and protection. As an imperfect translation, Enke (2014, p. 243) further noted, "transgender demands above all the need for more context, more story, and thus the translation into transgender never arrives and rests." Transing communication in (inter)cultural contexts is, in many ways, an invitation to engage with the boundaries and untapped potential of transgender and to participate in the necessary, risky, and hopeful act of unending, creative, and imperfect translation. We hope our model serves as a tool and a beginning of a journey to start thinking about communication and gender, within and across cultures, more critically, politically, expansively, and inclusively.

NOTES

1. Gust thanks Wenshu Lee and Philip Wander, John Elia and Gina Bloom, and Amy Taira, my "soul friends," for their ongoing inspiration and support; and Yogi Enzo and Pierre Lucas, my affectionate Pomeranian companions, for their sweet presence and unconditional love. Finally, Gust acknowledges his co-authors, Sage and Jace, for a collaborative project full of positive energy and mutual support; we make a great team.

2. For purposes of clarity and continuity, we use "trans people" and "trans identities" to describe the galaxy of gender expressions and identities that challenges the gender binary system (i.e., woman/man). See Stryker and Currah (2014) and Williams (2014) for a brief historical overview of the evolving meanings of the term.

3. We are using the gerund in our headings to highlight that these processes—transing, reviewing the literature, and exploring implications and future directions for research—are active, ongoing, and evolving. For example, our model is in a process of evolution and change

as new modes of communication emerge and transform and (inter)cultural encounters increase and magnify in our current era of neoliberal globalization.

4. Consistent with a critical approach to intercultural communication, our definition of culture is not restricted to the nation-state. As Yep stated elsewhere, "culture is a contested conceptual, discursive, and material terrain of meanings, practices, and human activities within a particular social, political, and historical context" (Collier, Hegde, Lee, Nakayama, & Yep, 2002, p. 231), which recognizes power in the construction and maintenance of differences. For further discussion of the definitions of culture in intercultural communication, see Moon (2008, 2013).

5. To illustrate the potential contours and content of each domain, we review the literature and provide examples of interdisciplinary research. Such review focuses more on qualities and patterns of representative research and should not be read as a comprehensive assessment of the literature.

6. LGBTQ (lesbian, gay, bisexual, transgender, queer) is an umbrella term used to describe non-heteronormative sexual and gender identities. LGBTQ has become the trademark of a community that mostly serves lesbian and gay identities.

7. Although it might be more accurately labeled as "gender/sexual rights," we are keeping the terms used by the researchers in this area.

8. Although it might be more accurate to label this theme as "gender/sexual activism," we are, once again, remaining close to the original terms used in the research we identified.

9. See note 7.

10. See note 8.

II

Media

Chapter Six

News

What's in a Name? Transgender Identity,
Metareporting, and the Misgendering of Chelsea
Manning

Jamie C. Capuzza

"As I transition into this next phase of my life, I want everyone to know the real me. I am Chelsea Manning. I am a female" (Manning, 2013, para. 1). These words began a media frenzy when Private Manning, convicted for violations of the Espionage Act and other offenses related to the release of classified information to WikiLeaks, announced to the world on August 22, 2013, that she was a transgender woman. The news industry's response to this announcement, her request to be called Chelsea instead of Bradley and to be referenced using feminine pronouns, ran the gamut from honoring her request immediately, to honoring her request eventually, to ridiculing her for making the request at all. Subsequently, certain news media were admonished for transphobic coverage by transgender advocacy organizations, transgender citizens, media watchdog groups, and media outlets themselves. By year's end, Manning was nominated for the Nobel Peace Prize and the *Huffington Post* ranked Manning's coming out as the "biggest transgender moment of 2013" (Nichols, 2013).

The following spring, Manning reappeared in the headlines when she petitioned for a legal name change, applied for clemency, and when the Army considered transferring her to a civilian prison to receive hormone therapy (civilian prisons are obligated legally to meet transgender healthcare needs whereas military prisons are not because Pentagon policy forbids transgender soldiers from serving openly). The extensive news coverage of Manning's announcement, her transition, and the heated response to that coverage prompted a much larger public debate about how journalists should best cover stories about transgender lives. This debate invites scholarly attention on the part of media critics interested in transgender communication.

The Manning case is well chosen because it illustrates many of the claims made by researchers and trans advocates regarding the role media play in regulating transgender identity. Specifically this chapter examines how this narrative functioned in three ways: to support an assimilationist definition of transgender, to contest Manning's transgender identity, and to divert public attention from other important matters.

In addition to illustrating the mediation of transgender identity and providing additional support for existing research, this chapter will extend this body of work by identifying and exploring another technique used to regulate transgender identity and expression, metareporting. How we talk about gender matters, and metareporting about how journalists write about transgender people such as Manning provides a prime opportunity to examine how public discourses construct, reconstruct, and potentially deconstruct gender. Because metareporting scholarship explores the symbiotic relationship between both press and publicity sources, this chapter also will add to transgender communication research by exploring messages produced directly by transgender advocates.

SCHOLARSHIP ABOUT NEWS COVERAGE
OF TRANSGENDER LIVES

Early media scholarship primarily examined representations of transgender people in entertainment media, and to a lesser extent news, with a focus on identity politics. Current research focuses on the politics of difference, specifically the roles media, including social and alternative media, play in producing and reproducing sex and gender normativity. Most research has taken the form of qualitative studies, both those that address questions of materiality and critical studies, informed by theories used in trans studies such as social constructivism, feminism, intersectionality, performativity, and queer theory.

The majority of this scholarship is message-centered rather than audience-centered. Little research in the form of traditional social scientific media effects studies or critical and audience reception studies exists. Ringo (2002) found that media facilitated the transgender self-identification process, and this form of internalization often led to negative self-perception among transgender people in terms of both identity and agency. *Trans Media Watch* (n.d.) measured British transgender people's attitudes toward media depictions of their community. Questionnaires revealed that the majority of respondents perceived these images to be inaccurate, negative, and at times, precipitating negative reactions and abuse.

When studying messages, researchers documented how media underrepresent this population and construct and reconstruct a standard definition of "transgender." According to this body of work, transgender lives historically were underrepresented by media much the same as other minority groups. However, more recently, an era of increased visibility has begun (Arune, 2006; Gamson, 1998b; GLAAD, 2013; Roen, Blakar & Nafstad, 2011). Transgender people such as Chaz Bono on *Dancing with the Stars*, Isis King on *America's Next Top Model*, and Laverne Cox in *Orange Is the New Black* or characters such as Bree in *Transamerica*, Zoe in *All My Children*, or Unique in *Glee* are taking their place in U.S. entertainment media.

In studies of news media, communication researchers have tracked and critiqued increased media attention producing primarily case studies about celebrities and sports figures such as Christine Jorgensen (Meyerowitz, 1998; Skidmore, 2011), Renee Richards (Birrell & Cole, 1990), Jenna Talackova (Tady, 2012), Steve Stanton (Kenney, 2008), and Christine Daniels (Pieper, 2013) or case studies about hate crime victims such as Brandon Teena (Sloop, 2000; Squires & Brouwer, 2002; Wilcox, 2003), Gwen Araujo (Barker-Plummer, 2013), Victoria Arellano (Chàvez, 2010), F.C. Martinez, Channelle Picket, and Rita Hester (Marcel, 2008).

While this research supported the claim that transgender lives are now more visible in the news, this quantitative increase in media attention did not equate with challenges to cisnormativity. Once media depicted transgender lives with more regularity, researchers found this coverage to be narrow and stereotypical on several levels. First, transgender people often were depicted as deceivers. Such coverage functioned as a means of disciplining marginalized populations. For example, crime news often sanctioned violence against transgender people by blaming them for hate crimes committed against them, a phenomenon known as "transpanic" defenses (Eckhardt, 2010; Marcel, 2008; Schilt & Westbrook, 2009; Sloop, 2000; Wilcox, 2003). Another example is Cloud's (2014) study which argued that Manning was disciplined both for her crimes related to espionage and because of her gender identity. Such news coverage also functioned to disparage trans identity by limiting depictions to either the "deceptive" or "pathetic" transsexual (Serano, 2007).

Second, increased news coverage medicalized the transgender body. For example, news media often focused on sex reassignment surgery (Buscar & Enke, 2011; Meyerowitz, 1998; Oberacker, 2007; Siebler, 2010). The fixation with genitals and reliance on "wrong body discourse" reduced gender identity and expression to reproductive systems, often in an exploitive manner (Barker-Plummer, 2013; Hollar, 2007; Kalter, 2008; Squires & Brouwer, 2002). As Woods summarized, transgender people in the media are "frozen in a permanent pathology" (Chuang, 2010).

Third, researchers found news coverage often conflated sex and gender, potentially undermining news consumers' understanding of the two. Furthermore, journalists typically over-emphasized transgender people's sexuality thus sensationalizing the news narrative (Birrell & Cole, 1990; Kenney, 2008; Meyerowitz, 1998; Schilt &Westbrook, 2009).

Fourth, researchers investigated problematic language use by journalists including the failure to use chosen names and pronouns as well as phrases such as "he wants to be called" or "she calls herself." This phrasing undermines a transgender person's ability to self-identify (Barker-Plummer, 2013; Pieper, 2013; Williams, 2010). Capuzza (forthcoming) found that while stylebooks journalists use to guide their writing accommodate certain aspects of transgender identity, they more often contribute to problematic language use and, potentially, to news consumers' misunderstandings.

Researchers also found that once transgender people do gain media attention, these representations typically were assimilative. For example, several studies investigated "passing" and determined that media seldom depict genderqueer identities (Mackie, 2008; Seibler, 2010; Skidmore, 2011; Squires & Brouwer, 2002; Wilcox, 2003). Hladky (2012) argued that the documentary miniseries *TransGeneration* constructed a standardized narrative around transgender identity "characterized by a progression from gender identity struggles, to therapy, to hormones, and finally to potential surgery, all in a specific time frame" (p. 107).

News narratives seldom challenge gender norms. Westbrook and Schilt (2014) found that even when news stories validated self-determinism for transgender people, they still maintained the gender binary. Journalists' sourcing patterns often limit transgender voices to personal narratives rather than interrogations of social assumptions related to gender, typically in soft rather than hard news, and silence genderqueer voices (Capuzza, 2014). Rarely did journalists use these stories as an opportunity to explain or to question the power of gender norms.

In sum, researchers have documented increased representations of transgender lives, but news stories often contributed to narrow views of transgender identity. Because gaining media visibility is an important first step to obtaining political power for minority populations, transgender people may feel compelled to court media attention, but in order to do so, often the price paid is assimilation, whether that is a desired outcome or not (Butler, 1990; Fejes & Petrich, 1993; Gross, 2001). In this regard, the media contribute to a narrow definition of transgender; this practice puts transgender people in the position of "proving" their identities using a standard that many find problematic.

METAREPORTING

Newer forms of media criticism focus not only on how media cover events, but also the mediation of those events. Journalists are becoming increasingly self-reflective about their own role in political processes (deVresse & Elenbaas, 2008; Esser, 2009; Haas, 2006). This self-reflection is a type of meta-communication sometimes called "metareporting." Specifically, metareporting is a trend in journalism that features both the news outlets themselves and publicity sources as important elements of the news narrative. Media scholars have used various terms to refer to this phenomenon such as "self-referential," "process news," "press self-coverage," "media self-criticism," "metacoverage," "media stories," and "media process frames" (D'Angelo, 1999; de Vreese & Elenbaas, 2008; Esser, 2009; Esser & D'Angelo, 2003; Esser, Reinemann & Fan, 2001; Gitlin, 1991; Haas, 2006; Kerbel, 1998, 1999; Wise, 2010).

The goals of this body of research are to document the frequency and tone of metareporting as well as the possible ways it shapes public opinion. Most often this research is quantitative and social scientific. Scholarship about metareporting typically focuses upon three features. First, there are two dimensions of metareporting including "press" and "publicity." Press metareporting spotlights the roles of the media in political affairs whereas publicity metareporting draws attention to the efforts of political actors courting the media's attention (de Vreese & Elenbaas, 2008). This research recognizes the fact that the media are not monolithic nor are they alone in creating public discourses. To this end, to be considered an example of metareporting, a story must make references to the press using terms such as "media" or "journalists" or proper nouns referring to specific news outlets as well as references to publicity sources (Esser, 2009; Esser & D'Angelo, 2003; Esser, Reinemann & Fan, 2001). Publicity sources include actors from across the political spectrum vying for media attention. This chapter focuses specifically on publicity sources that sought media attention in support of transgender citizenship.

Second, press and publicity dimensions always appear within specific frames. When journalists include the publicity dimension in their stories, the choice about how to frame this coverage is influenced by self-perceptions, industry standards, professional ideologies, and in this case, knowledge and attitudes about gender diversity. Similarly, when publicity sources frame their relationship to the press, they are influenced by similar factors and forward their own strategic communicative goals. Framing of metareporting is constructed in one of four ways: 1) as conduit; 2) as strategy; 3) as accountability; or 4) as personalization. According to Esser (2009), conduit frames present news organizations and advocates as pure brokers of information; strategy frames portray the news media and advocates as autonomous protagonists whose activities are consequential for the political process; accountability frames present the media and advocates as capable of self-criticism and concerned about journalistic standards and social responsibility; and personalization frames encompass stories about media personalities who make their subjective experiences the center of attention.

Third, metareporting appears within specific topic contexts. As news events are mediated, certain topics are revealed and others concealed. For example, in news coverage of political campaigns, candidate personality may appear more often than substantial discussions of policy issues. Previous scholarship focused initially on topic contexts related to election campaigns, war correspondence, and more recently, political policy initiatives. In this study, research on metareporting will be extended to news stories published about transgender-biased coverage.

DESIGNING A CASE STUDY OF MANNING'S NEWS COVERAGE

It is important to understand Manning's identity within a sociohistorical context. Manning leaked the largest number of classified documents in U.S. history at a time the country was involved in two controversial wars. Her identity was complicated first by the fact she was condemned by some as a traitor and honored by others as a whistleblower. Conservatives used her narrative as support for arguments about keeping gay and transgender people from serving in the military at the same time as liberals used her narrative as support for human rights, ending the wars, and prison reform.

Her identity was yet further complicated by the fact that the public was first introduced to Manning by the media as a gay man during her trial. As the trial progressed, however, the media reported that the Army knew Manning had a gender identity disorder and that she had created a female alter ego named Breanna Manning (Radia & Martinez, 2011). The Army knew about Manning's transgender identity because she gave her supervising officer a picture of herself dressed in a wig and lipstick attached to an email that stated, "This is my problem . . . I thought a career in the military would get rid of it" (Lewis, 2013, para. 2). Manning testified that she joined the Army hoping that living in a hyper-masculine environment would help her overcome her gender identity confusion. Although all of this information was readily available to the press during the trial, her August 22, 2013, statement regarding her transgender identity curiously surprised reporters and created confusion regarding how to write about her.

This textual analysis relied on three data sets. The first set of news articles, the announcement sample, dated from August 22, 2013, the day of Manning's coming out via her lawyer's televised statement, through the subsequent week. The second set of articles, the name change sample, was published March 19–21, 2014. The third set of articles, the clemency request and prison transfer sample, was published April 14–24, 2014. This method of sampling provided an opportunity to identify trends in news coverage over time.

After defining the time frame, the population to be studied was limited to print news stories, editorials, and blogs. Press articles included those written by professional journalists working for traditional outlets such as newspapers and news magazines as well as Internet-based news providers (such as the *Huffington Post*, *Salon,* and *Slate*), and Web sites and Weblogs produced by corporate news organizations based in the U.S. and aimed at a national audience. The resulting press sample represented a wide variety of outlets.

Press outlets do not work alone in the construction of transgender identity. Publicity outlets also participate in these regulatory discourses and, therefore, they should be included in the samples. Articles provided by national LBGTQ media watchdog groups, trans advocacy organizations, online support groups set up specifically for Manning and Weblogs maintained by transgender individuals were included in the data collection process. The publicity sample included online articles from organizations such as the Chelsea Manning Support Network, the National Center for Transgender Equality, GLAAD, and the American Civil Liberties Union, as well as from individuals such as Janet Mock and Lauren McNamara, and articles posted to Web sites such as *LBGTQ Nation*. Articles were obtained from Lexis/Nexis and by searching each outlet's own online archives for additional articles. The coding unit was the written text including headlines and articles, but not captions.

Stories then were coded using content categories based on the three features identified in scholarship about metareporting. The first content category identified patterns in press and publicity dimensions and revealed whose voices are centered in the public debate about news coverage of transgender lives. The second content category classified news frames as conduit, strategy, accountability or personalization for both press and publicity sources and revealed patterns in the framing of news coverage of transgender lives. The third content category identified topic contexts and revealed important information about what aspects of transgender identity and expression are most deeply embedded in press coverage and publicity efforts. The present study examined the following topic contexts: chosen names/pronouns, the role of transgender people in the military, incarceration of transgender inmates, and violence directed toward transgender victims. These topic contexts arose inductively from the samples.

THE AMOUNT OF NEWS COVERAGE ABOUT MANNING

A total of 136 stories were identified and coded (See table 6.1). The press provided 79% of the articles about Manning, and publicity sources provided 21% of the articles. A total of 39 different news outlets contributed to the samples, 25 press outlets and 14 publicity outlets. Newspapers, including the *Washington Post*, the *New York Times*, and *USA Today*, provided the most press articles about Manning and GLAAD and the ACLU provided the most publicity articles.

News coverage of Manning decreased over time by both press and publicity outlets. Sixty-one percent of the articles focused on Manning's coming out. This finding is consistent with previous claims that media forward a standardized coming out narrative. Once press and publicity outlets capitalized on the sensationalism of Manning's announcement, coverage of her name change, clemency application, and possible prison transfer dissipated.

The limited number of articles available from publicity outlets may reflect the controversial status Manning had at the time. News outlets already established the fact that Manning was convicted for espionage before her coming out, so her identity as a deceiver already was in place. What is interesting in this case study, however, is how a transgender person's damaged reputation resulted in the distancing of trans advocates. As transgender author Jennifer Finney Boylan published in the *Washington Post*, "any trans woman in the public eye has to behave in a manner above reproach. Lots of people wouldn't call Manning 'above reproach,' though; as a spokesperson she sets a very complicated example" (2013, para. 3). Additionally, Manning did not use the term "transgender" or a similar term in her coming out announcement to identify directly with this community; some people felt this omission was disrespectful. While publicity sources came to the public defense of Manning, their stated motivation came from a sense of mutual obligation to the transgender community rather than respect for her as an individual. Moreover, some transgender military personnel felt dishonored by Manning. As Gosztola (2014) summarized, "Numerous military veterans whether they were part of the LGBT community or not, reacted to the news of what Manning had done with profound disgust" (p. 40).

Table 6.1.

	# Outlets	# Announcement articles	# Name change articles	# Prison transfer/ clemency articles	Total # of articles
Press	25	61	30	16	107
Publicity	14	22	4	3	29

METAREPORTING: PRESS AND PUBLICITY DIMENSIONS
IN NEWS COVERAGE OF MANNING

Across all three samples, 30% were coded as examples of metareporting (see table 6.2). Specifically, 23% of press articles and 38% of publicity articles were coded as metareporting. Sixty-four percent of the press outlets and 43% of the publicity outlets participated in metareporting. These data illustrated the substantial level of metacommunication that occurred during the Manning narratives and how the mediation of Manning became newsworthy in and of itself.

References to the press far outnumbered references to publicity sources in both press and publicity metareporting articles (for the purposes of this case study, a term counted as a reference only the first time it was used in each article). Of the references to media in press metareporting articles, *The Today Show*, the Associated Press, NPR, CNN, and the *New York Times* were referenced most often, even more than generic terms such as "reporters" or "the media." Of the references to publicity sources in press metareporting articles, GLAAD was referenced most often. Journalists referenced national non-profit organizations that do not focus solely on transgender issues seldom mentioning grassroots organizations devoted specifically to transgender rights or individuals. Publicity metareporting articles similarly referenced CNN, the *New York Times*, the Associated Press, and GLAAD most often. The majority of publicity articles self-referenced rather than identify other organizations or transgender individuals.

Finally, the rate of metareporting in these samples decreased over time in both press and publicity articles. All but one metareporting article came from the announcement sample, indicating the debate over how transgender lives are discussed in news discourse was short-lived during the Manning narrative. Once the issue of how to refer to Manning was settled, the motivation to self-reflect about how the story of transgender lives is told in the news waned. In keeping with previous scholarship, again, the focus primarily was coming out narratives.

Table 6.2.

	Press	*Publicity*	*Total*
# Metareporting articles	24	15	39
# References to press source	106	57	163
# References to publicity source	24	13	37

In this case study, metareporting took on a variety of forms. Press meta-reporting articles largely included those that simply inventoried which media organizations used which name and pronoun and far fewer articles critical of media coverage. Press articles with headlines such as *USA Today's* "Media Torn in Manning 'he' or 'she' Pronoun Debate" (DiBlasio, 2013) illustrated the former category while *Salon's* "Media Willfully Misgender Chelsea Manning" (McDonough, 2013) illustrated the latter.

Publicity metareporting articles also ranged from a simple inventory of media organizations' use of name and pronoun and articles that merely en-couraged the press to follow stylebook guidelines to articles that were critical of media coverage. An example of the former included GLAAD's "Private Manning Will Be Called Chelsea, at Least by Some Media Outlets" (Murray, 2013). An example of the latter was Maza's (2013) editorial posted on *LBGTQ Nation* entitled, "CNN Guest Jokes Chelsea Manning Will Get 'Good Practice' Being a Woman in Prison."

METAREPORTING: FRAMING IN
NEWS COVERAGE OF MANNING

In metareporting, journalists highlight news and publicity outlets in their stories using specific frames (see table 6.3). In this case study, 49% of meta-reporting articles exemplified the strategy frame. The strategy frame illus-trates the tension between press and publicity outlets for control over the message. An example of a press article that contained a strategy frame, posted on *Politico*, was entitled, "Bradley Manning Explains Gender Change." This article detailed how Manning had hoped to come out after the publicity of the trial dissipated. The plan changed the day before her sentenc-ing when she found out Courthouse News Service was going to publish an article that stated she would not be provided hormone therapy while in prison (2013, para. 6). Manning and her lawyer strategized that it would be better for her to get ahead of the story and to take control of her coming out narrative.

Naturally publicity outlets also provided their own interpretation of events and sought to control messaging about Manning. The Transgender Law Center described the problematic relationship between the press and the transgender community they represent as follows, "The media has a long and poor track record of reporting on transgender people, and the coverage sur-rounding Private Chelsea Manning has brought that lack of fair and accurate coverage into sharp focus. The coverage that we have seen thus far has relied on stereotypical images, contrived confusion over names and pronouns, and an obsession with surgery" (2012, para. 3). In this regard, the Transgender Law Center clearly established an oppositional stance to the news media.

Typically strategy frames depict an antagonistic relationship between the press and publicity outlets. However, in this case study, the strategy frame transmuted into a new form in which the tension also arose among press outlets themselves. In the Manning narrative, metareporting primarily took the form of cross-media finger pointing depicting an antagonistic relationship between some media outlets on the one hand, and trans advocates *and* other media outlets on the other hand. Some press outlets were put on the defensive, publishing various rationalizations for their coverage while publicity sources and other media outlets pushed these press outlets to change that coverage. In their efforts to control the message, publicity outlets benefited from a highly competitive media landscape. While the media seldom self-critique, they occasionally criticize their rivals when it is to their strategic benefit. As Esser (2009) explained, media do not criticize each other "unless they are motivated by ideological animosity or business rivalry" (p. 713). This form of metareporting allowed press and publicity sources to capitalize on the sensationalism of the Manning narrative.

Twenty-eight percent of the metareporting articles typified the conduit frame. The conduit frame depicts media organizations in the neutral role of information brokers emphasizing a dissemination function. A press article that contained a conduit frame was the *New York Times*'s "He? She? News Media are Encouraged to Change" (Haughney, 2013) which described language used to refer to Manning by the Associated Press, National Public Radio, the *Huffington Post*, and the *New York Times* itself. The journalist quoted editors and stylebook guidelines throughout the article as well as GLAAD's style guidelines. In this manner, the newspaper became a simple conduit of information sharing with its readers a recap of style guidelines. The underlying message, a defensive one, is that the news industry has rules for discussing transgender lives already in place and many outlets are following them; the possibility that these guidelines have significant shortcomings is never broached. A publicity article that exemplified the conduit frame was

Table 6.3.

	Press	*Publicity*	*Total*
# Strategy frame articles	9	10	19
# Conduit frame articles	9	2	11
# Accountability frame articles	6	3	9
# Personalization frame articles	0	0	0

the Transgender Law Center's "Journalists: Commit to Fair and Accurate Coverage of Transgender People, Including Pvt. Chelsea Manning" (2013), which explained that the media have a poor track record of reporting on transgender people and provided a short list of problematic examples. The Web page's tone is neutral, documenting the simple fact the news media do not always get it right when reporting about transgender people.

The marked difference in the number of press conduit frames and publicity conduit frames illustrated the function each plays in society. Professional standards of journalism include objectivity which coincides with the definition of the conduit frame as a neutral dissemination of information. Publicity outlets, on the other hand, actively make a persuasive case for their cause rather than simply distribute information. In this regard, news consumers would expect to see more conduit frames in press articles than in publicity articles.

Twenty-three percent of metareporting articles contained accountability frames. Accountability frames present the press and publicity outlets as self-reflective and adaptive public advocates working to meet their responsibilities to create an informed citizenry. The article "NPR Issues New Guidance on Manning's Gender Identity" illustrated the press accountability frame as follows, "a healthy newsroom is open to debate and reflection. In the past day, we have been challenged by listeners and readers and by colleagues . . . raising a chorus of views, including requests to rethink, backed up by arguments that make good sense. We have been persuaded" (Perlata, 2013, para. 9). NPR held itself accountable for its news coverage and shared with news consumers a detailed explanation of how their thinking evolved and of the decision to change its coverage of Manning. An article indicative of the publicity accountability frame was National Lesbian and Gay Journalists Association's "NLGJA Encourages Journalists to Be Fair and Accurate about Manning's Plans to Live as a Woman" (2013). The author of this Web page used the Manning case as an opportunity to educate readers about important research about LBGTQ youth regarding high rates of depression and drug use.

Considering the fact that most news consumers are painfully uninformed about transgender lives, the limited number of accountability articles on the part of both the press and publicity outlets is problematic. Of all the metareporting frames, accountability is the most empowering because it illustrates growth on the part of media and those who court them and provides opportunities for public education. Most media organizations are prone to focus their stories about conflicts that naturally suits the strategy frame more than the accountability frame. Yet, because many citizens do not have regular opportunities to interact with transgender people directly due to the size of this population, people rely on mediated images to learn about transgender lives. Thus, it is all the more imperative that media fulfill an education function.

Additionally, while working to improve media representations of transgender people is critical, advocacy organizations need to use their time in the media spotlight to educate the public about key issues facing this community as much as to criticize media coverage if public understanding, acceptance, and respect is to increase.

METAREPORTING: TOPIC CONTEXTS IN NEWS COVERAGE OF CHELSEA MANNING

The next step in metareporting research is to examine the most frequent or typical connections between frames and topic contexts. The majority of press frames occurred in conjunction with stories about the use of Manning's preferred name and pronouns. Nineteen of the 24 press metareporting articles discussed this topic and did so across all three frames equally.

The majority of publicity frames also occurred in conjunction with articles about the Manning's preferred name and pronoun. Ten of the 15 publicity metareporting articles discussed this topic and did so mostly within the strategy frame.

Taking into consideration all of the press articles and thus putting the metareporting articles into a larger context, the majority used the name "Chelsea" and feminine pronouns to refer to Manning in all three samples. Of the 107 press articles, 70% used Manning's preferred name and pronoun. This number increased over time indicating that the press learned its lesson from the "pronoun debate" that defined the announcement sample. Every publicity article used Manning's preferred name and pronoun across all three samples.

All in all, one outcome of the Manning narrative is proof that the media can improve their coverage of transgender lives if there is a sufficient level of internal and external pressure to do so. However, it is important to recognize that metareporting also functioned as a means of regulating transgender identity. As Barker-Plummer (2013) argued, public debates are "both accommodating and containing gender challenges by allowing for, even capitalizing on the (empirically obvious and in some cases dramatic) gender nonconformity we see emerging around us, but then quickly moving to contain that nonconformity" (p. 720). While the increased use of preferred names and pronouns illustrated an accommodation of transgenderism and Manning's request, metareporting articles focused on language use, seldom mentioning other shortcomings of Manning's new coverage. For example, Manning's diagnosis of gender dysphoria and denial of hormone therapy by the military appeared regularly throughout all the articles, even those focusing on unrelated topics such as her applications for clemency and a name change.

Putting the metareporting articles in a larger context, across the sample of 136 articles, a variety of topics of concern to the transgender community were discussed including military service, violence, access to trans health care, and treatment of transgender inmates. However, in the 39 metareporting articles, these issues seldom were addressed and did not emerge as topic contexts. When the mediation of Manning was discussed in news articles, *how* journalists wrote about her was prioritized over *what* journalists wrote or, perhaps more importantly, failed to write about her and the very serious challenges she and other transgender people face. To be sure, this examination of metareporting revealed that the press's attention span for self-reflection is short.

DYNAMICS OF MANNING'S NEWS COVERAGE

Much the same as previous research on news coverage of transgender lives illustrated, the Manning case revealed how news narratives function in three ways: constructing an assimilationist definition of transgender, contesting transgender identity, and diverting public attention from other key concerns. First, the military's denial of Manning's hormone therapy certainly was newsworthy because it violated the World Professional Association for Transgender Health guidelines. But it also disrupted the existing assimilationist definition of transgender, and taking this position fueled the media frenzy. Hormone therapy became a major issue in the story line not only because denying therapy constituted cruel and unusual punishment, but also because it violated public expectations of what constituted a transgender life.

This case also illustrated that the press struggles with how to tell anything other than a standardized narrative about transgender people. Much the same as was found in previous research, journalists tried to fit Manning into a prescribed narrative. Stories of transgender people such as Manning who have not begun the transition process or who cannot transition push the established boundaries of news reporting conventions, and those who do not desire body modification or who are genderqueer are quite outside those boundaries.

Second, assimilationist definitions have consequences in that transgender people are put in the position of "proving" they meet a standard of transgender acceptability. The Manning narrative illustrated this form of gender policing. Because news consumers were accustomed to seeing Manning presenting as a man, her identity was contested even more vigorously. For example, in the first sample, almost every press article began with Manning's coming out statement, but press outlets never considered her word sufficient enough to establish her transgender identity. The press consistently followed the statement with discussions of her psychiatric diagnosis and her medical need for hormone therapy. As the author of the *Huffington Post*'s "Mainstream Media's Issue with Chelsea Manning's Gender Identity" explained, "news sources were unwilling to accept the veracity of Manning's claim to her gender identity" (DiLalla, 2013, para. 5). Additionally, the press regularly included "before and after" photographs of Manning, one photograph of Manning in uniform presenting as a man and one photograph of her presenting as a woman (a photograph that was submitted as evidence during her trial and used by media outlets repeatedly over many months of news coverage). In this regard, the media reconstructed a narrow definition of what constitutes an acceptable transgender body and debated whether Manning met this standard of acceptability.

While media reconstructed a standard definition of transgender and determined who is "trans enough" to meet that standard, they failed news consumers by not providing a deeper understanding of gender that would enable them to comprehend, and potentially accept and respect, transgender identities. Neither press nor publicity outlets explored gender assumptions meaningfully through an accountability frame. Across the three samples, only ten press articles indirectly explained or challenged gender assumptions: one article referenced the gender binary, five articles referenced sex and gender congruency, and four articles referenced gender stability. Remarkably not a single publicity outlet questioned gender assumptions in articles about Manning, thus indirectly reaffirming, rather than challenging, gender stereotypes. Consistent with other studies, the Manning case illustrated a discourse of rights and representations, not a challenge to the gender order or how journalists play a role in regulating transgender identity (Barker-Plummer, 2013; Sloop, 2004).

Third, in addition to concealing deeply embedded cultural assumptions about gender diversity, news articles about Manning's gender identity distracted public attention from the political truths she sought to expose. Both the leak itself and its contents undermined the public image of the U.S. military as in control of the wars and its own secrets. The military wanted the news consumers to view Manning as a threat to the state and then to the social gender order. This message dominated headlines rather than the controversies she revealed. In this regard, Manning's public identity constructed firstly as a traitor to her country and reconstructed secondly as a traitor to her gender certainly benefitted the military. As Cloud (2014) concluded, "Manning's coming out was allowed to negate the impact of her revelations of the atrocity of war" (p. 97).

DYNAMICS OF METAREPORTING

This chapter demonstrated that metareporting is another technique for regulating gender identities and explored the role publicity sources play in this dynamic. In this case, metareporting as a journalistic practice created the appearance of accommodating transgender identity and expression when, in actuality, it did not challenge assimilationist definitions of transgenderism. Metareporting constituted a significant portion of the first sample but decreased over time in both press and publicity sources, indicating that a consistent commitment to reflecting about news coverage of Manning was not sustained. Press and publicity sources both capitalized on the Manning narratives to forward their agendas during the coming out narrative and did so primarily using the strategy frame rather than the accountability frame which would have indicated a deeper commitment to public education about gender justice. Some press outlets used the narrative to appeal to their conservative base of readers while others positioned themselves as ideological rivals who were progressively trans friendly. Both press and publicity metareporting articles focused primarily on the topic context of language use with far fewer and less developed discussions of other shortcomings typically found in news coverage of transgender lives.

Additionally, this chapter demonstrated the limited and moderate role of publicity sources in news coverage about Manning. When the press did reference publicity sources, typically they were not advocacy groups focused solely on transgender justice nor were most grassroots organizations. Radical transgender activists who question the role of organizations with million dollar budgets such as the HRC and the National Lesbian and Gay Taskforce largely were silent during the Manning narrative. Bassichis, Lee, and Spade (2011) recognized this dynamic in their research about trans and queer social movements, "the most visible and well-funded arms of the 'LBGT movement' look much more like a corporate strategizing session than a grassroots social justice movement" (p. 654). The Manning narratives were ones of reform, not resistance. For example, publicity sources called for more humane treatment of transgender prisoners rather than calling into question the role of incarceration in the U.S. itself. Moreover, even though publicity sources openly supported Manning's right to be called by her chosen name and her access to hormone therapy, they still distanced themselves from the political truths she shared. Publicity outlets walked a fine line between supporting Manning and creating a positive image of the transgender movement. These organizations also found themselves in the difficult position of striking a balance between courting media visibility and criticizing media coverage.

CONCLUSION

While the body of research about news coverage is more developed than that of many other topics related to transgender communication, scholars in media and journalism studies have the potential to advance the field further. Textual analyses have identified and critiqued a variety of mechanisms used by news industries to ridicule and regulate transgender identities, such as metareporting, but other mechanisms remain unidentified and unexplored. For example, textual analysis of photojournalism, bridging visual communication research and journalism scholarship, would provide additional insight into how gender expression is framed in news coverage. Furthermore, most textual analyses have concluded that standard definitions of transgender render genderqueer identities almost invisible in news coverage. If and when this invisibility ebbs, scholars should critically analyze the role news industries play in the production of genderqueer identities.

This study focused on trans advocates as publicity sources. Media scholars and rhetorical critics alike could contribute significantly to a more in-depth exploration of the role communication plays in transgender rights activism. Additionally, anti-trans voices also vying for media attention as publicity sources warrant careful scrutiny, and this work would result in a more complete picture of trans mediation and metareporting.

Thus far, the majority of textual analyses have investigated messages produced by Western media industries. Cross-cultural analysis of news coverage would reflect current interests in trans studies related to the nation-state's role in gender expression, trans-feminisms, and post-colonialism. Similarly, textual analysis of news coverage generated by independent news producers, including transgender individuals and trans advocacy organizations, would be another fruitful research agenda. Alternative and social media play an increasingly important role in transgender communities; researchers would do well to investigate their use as modes of resistance. Such work also would provide deeper insight into the tension between press and publicity news sources in metareporting research. Moreover, researchers should not overlook nuanced though important differences among transgender advocates. Transgender veterans' organizations, Wiki communities, anti-incarceration groups, among others, may employ alternative and social media differently.

To date, the focus on textual analysis has been at the expense of audience and industry studies. Studies of transgender populations as news consumers are sorely lacking. The impact of news media, both corporate and those produced by the transgender community, on gender identity and politics would be an important complement to text-based research. Similarly, an investigation of the roles transgender professionals play in the news industry or the role of media watchdog groups also would generate meaningful data.

Undoubtedly, media scholarship will continue to make a significant contribution to the future of transgender communication research.

Chapter Seven

Television

The Provisional Acknowledgment of
Identity Claims in Televised Documentary

E. Tristan Booth

An episode of a television documentary series profiles the life of a young adult male-bodied individual. While the program makes clear that this individual identifies as a woman, it consistently refers to her with male pronouns. Finally, we see this individual in a hospital bed following a facial feminization surgery. The voice-over narration tells us, "Clint, now Jennifer, is joined in the recovery room by her mother and brother" (Keister & Butts, 2004). The narration suggests that this individual was a man named Clint until the moment that facial feminization surgery was completed; in this moment, she is "now Jennifer," and the narrator acknowledges this by using a female pronoun for the first time. But is facial feminization surgery typically perceived as the transwoman's rite of passage into womanhood? Another episode of the same series uses male pronouns for a transwoman until the completion of genital surgery. This depiction invites the question, at what point is a transwoman a woman? At what point has she "earned" the right to be described with female pronouns? Similar inconsistencies occur when transmen are depicted in television documentaries and documentary series.

As DeLuca and Peeples (2002) reminded us, "TV places a premium on images over words" (p. 133). They explained that U.S. culture has experienced a "pictorial turn" (p. 132) in that images dominate, not only on television, but in all other forms of mass media. As a result, they said, "most, and the most important, public discussions take place via 'screens'" such as television (p. 131), and that media are "the primal scene upon which culture is produced and enacted" (p. 132). The U.S. public learns about its culture, in no small part, from television, and its understanding of transsexualism is clearly rooted in those depictions presented on television and, to a lesser extent, in theatrical film.

This reliance upon the visual presents a problem for identity claims that cannot be verified by one's outward appearance. For transgender individuals whose public appearance does not correspond with their internal sense of identity, the communication of identity often begins with personal narrative, as delivered to friends, loved ones, and—in the case of transsexuals—a variety of medical professionals. Many transsexuals tell their stories verbally before they are able to display their identities visually. Unfortunately for television, however, a lengthy discussion of thoughts and feelings provides no visual content outside of the ubiquitous "talking head." While it is true that the body is "separable" from identity (Kerry, 2009, p. 706), the average viewer needs to *see* the identity on the body in order to believe it; in response, television dutifully assures that there is something to see by offering images related to various surgical procedures. While these images may not completely satisfy the viewer's need for visual confirmation of identity (e.g., a transwoman may be taller than the average woman with a visible Adam's apple, and a transman may be short in stature with hips more rounded than the average man's), hospital scenes do provide evidence of body alteration and, at the same time, satisfy television's need to present a constant stream of visual images.

The dependence upon images is not the only problem, however. On the subject of transsexualism, many members of the U.S. television audience will not be satisfied with an outward gendered appearance, even if it does meet the viewers' standards for an acceptable man or woman. This dissatisfaction is due to the fact that audiences may be unwilling to accept a gendered identity if they are aware that it does not correspond to the anatomical sex. These viewers do not expect unclothed genitals to be televised, but they do expect reassurance that the "correct" genitals exist before they will acknowledge an individual's claim to a gendered identity.

The presentation of transsexuals on television, then, faces three distinct challenges—namely, television's inherent dependence on images, the viewer's need for visual confirmation of gendered identity on the public body, and the viewer's insistence that physical sex must correspond to gendered presentation. From a production standpoint, these issues might be addressed in a variety of ways, depending on the genre of the program. This chapter engages in a close rhetorical-critical reading of the content of televised documentaries and episodes of documentary television series featuring transsexuals who are undergoing the transition process, and finds that, in some cases, the subjects' gendered identity claims are not fully acknowledged until *after* medical intervention has taken place, at which point the authoritative voice-over narration reflects a change in pronoun use for these individuals. The transsexual's self-identification as a man or woman is framed as a desire, but not acknowledged as a reality until the body has been transformed in some way. In other examples from the same programs, this self-identification appears to be respected consistently throughout the program, regardless of surgical status. In analyzing these production decisions, I argue that the documentary genre has reached a compromise in response to the three challenges it faces.

Because television is dependent upon visual images, and because many viewers insist upon genital surgery as a validation of gendered identity, a variety of transition-related surgeries are depicted visually and framed as rites of passage from one gender identity to another. These surgeries may include chest reconstruction for transmen, or facial feminization for transwomen, in addition to actual genital surgeries. In this way, television is able to provide a multitude of visual images, even for those transsexuals who are not undergoing genital surgeries at the time of filming. Because the non-genital surgeries are generally performed for the purpose of altering the public appearance (e.g., a flat chest for a man, a feminine face for a woman), the viewers' needs are partially satisfied. Either the public appearance or the genital configuration is being brought into correspondence with the self-identified gender, and the program's voice-over narration is constructed in such a way that viewers are encouraged to perceive these surgeries as sufficient to confirm the self-identified gender. Even when the patient's genitals have not been altered, an authoritative and omniscient voice tells us, with no hint of ambiguity, that Clint is "now Jennifer."

Following a summary of pertinent theoretical concepts, I review previous scholarly publications on the subject of transgender representation on television. I then proceed to analyze five televised documentaries and episodes of documentary series.

THEORETICAL CONCEPTS

Because the focus of this essay is restricted to televised depictions of transsexuals during the transition process, it is necessary to understand how the term *transsexual* has been defined. In this section I also address the somewhat antiquated term *sex change*, as well as concepts such as personal narrative, rhetoric, and synecdoche, which relate to the communication of identity on television.

The term *transsexual* is not always defined consistently. Some argue that an individual does not qualify as a transsexual until *after* he or she has undergone transition-related surgery. In this framing of the term, transition-related surgery, and genital surgery in particular, is presented as an inherent component of the definition. For example, sociologists Howard and Hollander (1997) stated that transsexuals are "people who have literally changed their sex—they have been surgically and hormonally altered" (p. 10). Others—including many transsexuals themselves—insist that surgery marks the *end* of transsexual status. This latter position suggests that the physical processes associated with transition define *transsexual* as a temporary state that is no longer occupied once these processes have been completed to the individual's satisfaction. For example, a transwoman might say, "I'm no longer trans-anything. I'm simply a woman." Still others, myself included, define transsexualism as identification with, and a desire to live as, the binary gender category that does not correspond with one's designated sex at birth, regardless of one's current or future surgical status. This definition is particularly significant for those who, for medical or financial reasons, are unable to pursue surgical treatment, though they may desire it. By this definition, the inability to undergo surgical reassignment, or even the lack of desire for actual surgery, does not disqualify the individual from categorization as a transsexual. In fact, many transsexuals live socially as men or women, having undertaken varying degrees of hormonal or surgical alteration, or sometimes none at all. Using this definition, it is the desire to live as one's self-identified binary gender that marks the transsexual status.

Stryker (2008) defined transsexuals as "people who feel a strong desire to change their sexual morphology in order to live entirely as permanent, full-time members of the gender other than the one they were assigned to at birth" (p. 18), without implying that this surgery must actually take place. An example of a definition that does not implicate the topic of surgery at all is suggested by Devor (1997) who stated, "When I use the terms *transsexual men* and *transsexual women*, I refer to persons who identify themselves as transsexual and who have begun to live full-time in their preferred gender statuses" (p. xxv). Devor actually expressed a preference for the term *transsexed*, rather than *transsexual*, in order to avoid the connotation that "sexuality is central to gender and sex dysphorias" (p. xxv). This is a key distinction, since transsexualism is not about sexual desire, nor does one's transsexual status automatically correspond to any particular sexual orientation.

Another contested term, the phrase *sex change*, has become a master narrative for transsexualism in U.S. culture. Corey (1998) defined master narrative as "the ongoing ideology passed from generation through generation by way of the stories we tell" (p. 250). Thorne (2004) referred to these stories as "culturally available scripts which speakers might use to create their own identities and those of others" (p. 362). For example, the parental expectation that one's male child will identify as a heterosexual man, marry a woman, produce children, and enter a particular type of profession is one common script or master narrative. In U.S. culture, the most common public scripts for stories relating to transsexualism have predominantly emphasized the surgical alteration of the genitals, thus, a "change of sex."

According to Gamson (1998a), the average television viewer believes that "the body tells the truth" (p. 163). Therefore, transgender people "are typically programmed [on television] in ways that emphasize anatomy as the only *true* gender marker" (p. 97). While the transsexual's personal narrative is present in televised depictions of transsexuals, often in the form of interview footage, the prospect of genital surgery is never left unaddressed, even for those who do not desire it. As a consequence, the subject of transsexualism tends to be defined, not as identification with the binary gender that does not correspond with one's designated sex at birth, but as the surgical solution to this problem, suggesting that one must be at least in the planning stages of genital surgery in order to call oneself a transsexual.

While Corey (1998) suggested that one's personal narrative has the capacity to undercut the master narrative's credibility, the transsexual's personal narrative is seldom given this opportunity in televised documentary. Because a conventional sex-gender alignment is hegemonic—considered normal and unquestioned—in U.S. culture, the television viewer not only expects it, but insists upon it. Therefore, "mass media coverage works, in a seemingly natural way, to reinforce dominant understandings of gender/sexuality" (Sloop, 2006, p. 325). Further, because television is a commercial medium, the need to attract a large number of viewers, preferably those with sufficient wealth to purchase advertised products, favors relatable programming that will not drive these viewers to change the channel. In a critical analysis, Condit (1989) speculated that "television, or any mass medium, can do oppressive work solely by addressing the dominant audience that also constitutes the public" (p. 112). She explained that television uses "a vocabulary that prefers the dominant audience's interests" (p. 112) rather than those of various marginalized audiences (including, in the present essay, transgender viewers). In other words, producers are somewhat obligated to consider the comfort level of the dominant public above that of the transgender public, even though transgender lives are being represented.

This obligation to favor the ideology of the dominant public should also be considered a rhetorical choice, in that rhetors must take into account the expectations of their audiences and tailor their messages accordingly. In other words, if they wish to persuade their audiences to think a certain way, rhetors must speak in a manner that audience members will find familiar and relatable. As Kenneth Burke (1950/1969) pointed out, "It is so clearly a matter of rhetoric to persuade a man by identifying your cause with his interests" (p. 24). If the filmed material allows for sufficient identification, such that viewers can take it seriously, they can then "validate the information and interpretations provided in a documentary against their own experiences and other sources of information" (Beattie, 2004, p. 12). In short, relatable material allows for the possibility of public education on a subject that is largely misunderstood.

All documentary contains this rhetorical or persuasive element because, even though "production discourses" are inclined to privilege "observation, verifiable evidence, and dispassionate reportage" (Macdonald, 2009, p. 658), a documentary that remains completely neutral about its subject matter cannot exist. Nevertheless, according to Nichols (1983), "many documentarists would appear to believe . . . that film-making creates an objective representation of the way things really are" (p. 18). Documentarists may believe this idea because they are filming their subjects' actual life experiences and allowing them to speak for themselves in interviews. However, various types of production decisions (choices as to which experiences are filmed and which are not, the angles at which scenes are filmed, the phrasing of the text used for narration, the type of voice chosen to read that narration, etc.) clearly construct an overall attitude toward the subject matter. As Nichols explained, "for a film to fail to acknowledge this and pretend to omniscience—whether by voice-of-God commentary or by claims of 'objective knowledge'—is to deny its own complicity with a production of knowledge" (p. 20). The viewers, themselves, also tend to see documentary as "a window on an unscripted, undirected, unrehearsed, and unperformed reality" when, in fact, those being filmed are "aware, actively or passively, of the camera and, by extension, of the spectator" (Waugh, 1997, p. 110).

With this knowledge that viewers will witness their words and actions, documentary subjects perform "self-expressive behavior carried out in awareness of the camera, with either explicit or tacit consent and/or in collaboration with the director" (p. 124). However, this awareness should not lead us to conclude that the transsexuals who appear in documentaries have full control over their public image. Macdonald (2009) insisted that "a dominant discourse is established, with interviewees' stories subordinated to this" (p. 661). While those interviewed are free to say what they will, the interview footage is edited, and the subjects' voices "are continually interrupted by the authoritative discourse of others (whether commentator, narrator, or experts)" (p. 661). This fact is particularly true in medical documentaries, where "human case studies tend to be co-opted for expository purposes, reinforcing a familiar hierarchy of professional knowledge over lay experience" (p. 662). In a variety of ways, directors, producers, and editors maintain ultimate control over the final product.

Bignell (2013) asserted that the specific subjects profiled in documentaries "have metonymic relationships with the reality of which they are a part." Strictly speaking, he is referring, here, to a specific type of metonymy known as synecdoche, in which the part stands in for the whole. For instance, if a documentary profiles one particular transwoman, she is being used to exemplify transwomen in general. Bignell argued that "this device . . . enables television [programs] to claim implicitly that they represent society to itself, and connect the specific subjects of [programs] to larger social contexts" (p.

222). Members of the dominant audience (i.e., the general public, as opposed to transgender viewers) might be led to assume that all transwomen exhibit attitudes, behaviors, desires, or even physical appearances similar to those they have seen depicted on screen, particularly if these viewers believe that they have never before encountered transwomen.

The implications of this phenomenon are especially concerning when the population being represented is culturally marginalized and largely unfamiliar to the dominant audience. This depiction creates an ironic tension, in that many such documentaries may be attempting to educate the general public about a misunderstood social group, yet in the attempt they may also create or perpetuate certain stereotypes about their subjects, since they clearly cannot depict the wide variety of attitudes, behaviors, desires, or physical appearances present throughout that group. It would not be surprising, then, to find some transsexual viewers complaining that the individuals profiled in documentaries do not accurately represent them. Indeed, it would be impossible to find one transman or one transwoman who could accurately represent all members of these particular social identities. Therefore, given that a total lack of representation is clearly not a viable alternative, transgender viewers as well as trans-positive scholars will likely continue in their efforts to influence production decisions and critique the subsequent programs.

SCHOLARLY ATTENTION

Television has offered depictions of fictional transgender characters, as well as nonfictional representations of transgender individuals in various genres beyond the documentary, and some of these programs have received scholarly analysis. However, while there have been an increasing number of articles on transgenderism in general, there are still relatively few that specifically address this topic in the context of television.

Since the inclusion of fictional transgender characters on television is a relatively recent phenomenon, the few scholarly articles on this subject are also limited in number. I was able to locate only four, published in the brief period between 2009 and 2011. In the first of these, linking the *Star Trek* franchise to queer and trans theories, Kerry (2009) examined an episode of *Star Trek: Enterprise* in which the character Trip, a human male, was used by an alien race to act as a "womb" for an alien fetus (p. 708). While Trip did not identify as transgender, Kerry described this male pregnancy as "an exemplar of the genderqueer who disturbs boundaries that hitherto had gone uncontested in science fiction and *Star Trek*" (p. 711). In another article from the same year, Reed (2009) made a similar point, arguing that when a female character on *The L Word* transitions from Moira to Max, this transformation "destabilizes the coherent subject that we most often see on television" (p. 170).

While Kerry (2009) and Reed (2009) saw this boundary disturbance as a step forward, Escudero-Alías (2011) had a more cynical reaction to the portrayal of drag kings on two series, *The L Word* and *Sex & the City*. Examining these portrayals, Escudero-Alías wrote that "drag king culture" did not "constitute any threat to the established gender identity categories. Rather, the series use drag kings ... to boost a commercial impulse to increase their audience ratings and incorporate the latest queer 'kicks' available in the market" (p. 270). Arguing that the "ultimate goal" of these series was to "showcase" gender disruptions for profit, Escudero-Alías described "a greedy capitalist consumer market" focused on "the depolitization and/or assimilation of any minority culture or style . . . which attempts to unsettle the *status quo*" (p. 271).

Finally, Morrison (2010) focused on audience reception rather than representation, examining how lesbian, gay, and bisexual (LGB) viewers reacted to a transitioning transsexual character on the series *All My Children*. Morrison found that members of the LGB community perceived transgender individuals as a "secondary ingroup," with greater concern for gay and lesbian individuals as the "primary ingroup" (p. 662). This concern was largely due to a "perceived threat" that transgender inclusion would result in some type of loss for gay men and lesbians. Morrison suggested that these findings indicated "a need to minimize any sense of competition between LGB and T populations" (p. 662).

Among the first scholars to address the representation of actual transgender people on television was sociologist Joshua Gamson (1998a; 1998b; 2001) whose book and related essays examined the presence of "non-conforming genders and sexualities" on television talk shows (Gamson, 1998b, p. 11). Gamson traced the regressive arc of these representations, explaining that the *Donahue* talk show model—in which "primarily white, middle-class, highly educated, organizationally affiliated guests came on to talk 'rationally' about issues"—was largely replaced by a new ratings-hungry model of shows with a "selection of nasty, rowdy, exhibitionist, not-great-to-look-at poor and working-class guests" (Gamson, 1998b, p. 14). Gamson argued that, in this model, "tolerance of visible gayness, put simply, is bought largely through the further stigmatization of bisexuality and gender nonconformity," leading "those interested in social acceptability to disown the visibility of some of their own" (p. 14). In other words, when bisexual and transgender individuals are framed as bizarre, "ordinary" gay men and lesbians appear acceptable in comparison.

Over ten years later, Riggs (2014) analyzed one particular episode of Oprah Winfrey's talk show featuring Thomas Beatie, a transman who was pregnant at the time. Riggs argued that Beatie was "constructed in the interview not simply as a 'wannabe' man, but moreover as a *failed* wannabe man" (p. 166) due to Winfrey's "use of a range of gender-normative (and indeed offensive) arguments that position Beatie as 'not quite'—not quite a father, not quite a man and thus not quite intelligible" (p. 160). Unlike many other talk shows, *Oprah* did not feature rowdiness or exhibitionism, yet it did tend to uphold gender-normative assumptions.

While the television talk show is one genre in which actual transgender people appear as themselves, another ubiquitous genre that allows for this is the broad category of reality television. In my own article on an episode of *Queer Eye for the Straight Guy*, I examined the one episode of the series to feature the makeover of a transman, arguing that the liminal nature of this man's body and social status caused the series to diverge from its established norms with respect to its content as well as the behavior of its five hosts. I also argued that transsexuals exist socially in a state of perpetual liminality, not in terms of personal identification, but in their "ability to negotiate that identity in a social context" should their trans status become known (Booth, 2011, p. 187).

Previous scholarly publications addressing the representation of transgenderism on television have focused their attention on the disruption or maintenance of gender boundaries, the LGB community's support for transgender identities, and the impact of liminal identities on television production norms. The following analysis finds that the representation of transitioning transsexuals on televised documentary places particular emphasis on audience comfort, sometimes to the detriment of transgender subjectivity.

TELEVISED DOCUMENTARY ANALYSIS

In this section, I turn to a rhetorical-critical reading of four televised documentaries about transsexual transitions: *Sex Change Soldier*, *My Secret Female Body*, *Sex Change: Her to Him*, and *Changing Sexes: Female to Male*, as well as a transsexualism-themed episode of the documentary health series *Super Surgery*. I selected these artifacts because they featured extended focus on transsexuals' lives and aired on mainstream cable channels.

The young transwoman named Jennifer, referenced at the beginning of this essay, was profiled on the television series *Super Surgery*—which ran on the now defunct cable channel, Discovery Health—in an episode titled "Gender Swap" (Keister & Butts, 2004). This episode contrasted the experiences of Jennifer with those of another transwoman named Brandi. In the first half of the episode, while neither woman had undergone surgery, the voice-over consistently referred to Brandi with female pronouns, but described Jennifer as "Clint," using male pronouns. For example, the narrator stated, "Brandi is still good friends with her spouse, but for the past two and a half years, she has been working to start a new life as a single woman." Meanwhile, "Clint" is profiled as a young man, and at one point the narrator explains, "He has been in a committed homosexual relationship with James." Here, the narration not only frames Jennifer as a man, but also frames this relationship as one between two gay men. This narration may be partially accounted for by the fact that Jennifer was presenting as a woman only part-time during high school, and it is possible that her partner, James, identifies as a gay man in a gay relationship. However, this construction completely negates Jennifer's self-identification as a woman, particularly since the "homosexual relationship" reference is made in the present tense. As stated earlier, she is only described with female pronouns once she has undergone facial feminization surgery toward the end of the episode, and this is the first time that the name Jennifer is even mentioned.

This depiction exemplifies the compromise that documentaries about transsexuals often make with their non-transgender viewers. While the general public might have been more comfortable if Jennifer had undergone genital surgery, thus creating a sex-gender alignment, they are partially satisfied with the fact that Jennifer had a surgery that would give her a facial appearance that is considered more conventional for a woman. In addition, by emphasizing this surgery, the documentary was able to fill the television screen with images, also exploiting the popularity of before-and-after comparisons.

Based on my research, examining televised documentaries and documentary series episodes, the inconsistent use of pronouns appears to be quite common, with narrators sometimes switching pronouns following a surgery, sometimes using the subject's preferred pronouns consistently, and sometimes switching pronouns for no apparent reason. While the voice-over for the documentary *Sex Change Soldier* (Preston, 2008) uses female pronouns for a transwoman even before surgery, it later switches to male pronouns in stating that "he now lives with a new girlfriend," even though this individual is clearly living full-time as a woman. Later still, the narrator switches back to using female pronouns. On the other hand, another documentary, *My Secret Female Body* (Patterson & Hackett, 2007), is notable for using pronouns more consistently. A young transman named Danny, prior to his chest surgery, is described with male pronouns throughout the film, except when profiling his early childhood. This example is laudable in that it acknowledges Danny's self-identification as a man, regardless of his surgical status, and without apparent concern for potential viewer disapproval. One reason for this may be the fact that Danny appears outwardly male.

The producers of the documentary *Sex Change: Her to Him* (Ulm & Grassie, 2004) faced an interesting challenge. While two transmen are profiled, one only very briefly, a large portion of the program is devoted to a transwoman (in contrast with the film's title) who is not undergoing any major surgeries that might provide an opportunity for a change of pronoun use. Rather, this woman, Michelle, has electrolysis to remove facial hair and spends a majority of the segment shopping for women's clothing with a style counselor. Early on, she is described as "a man who is about to step out for the first time as a woman." Here, Michelle seems to be framed as a man and a woman at the same time; however, all pronoun use is male: "Michael is waiting for his new life to begin. . . . A year ago, Michael made the decision to become Michelle." We learn that Michelle has been taking estrogen for over a year, and that the electrolysis and style counseling constitute the next steps in her transition. Finally, when she and the counselor are about to eat at a restaurant, we are told that "this is the moment when Michelle's life begins. She is about to step out in public for the first time." This sentence implies that Michelle did not even exist until she was able to appear in public as a woman, despite the fact that she had made the decision a year ago and clearly identifies as a woman. Rather than changing pronoun use following a surgery, the narrator begins to call her "she" upon her first public appearance. However, she is called "Michael" again at the end of the program when she is dressed more casually.

By contrast, the narrator refers to both transmen with male pronouns prior to their chest and genital surgeries. In this documentary, the men are considered men even before surgery, while the woman only becomes a woman when she appears in public. Again, it may be that the pronoun use is somewhat contingent upon physical appearance, since both men appear male prior to surgery, while the woman's appearance might be perceived as more ambiguous. Since Michelle has had no actual surgeries, many viewers might be reluctant to categorize her as a woman, and the documentary appears to recognize this reluctance in the way it describes her.

In a final documentary, *Changing Sexes: Female to Male* (Funk, Miller, & Soiseth, 2002), the narrator describes its subjects as "four transsexual women and their quest to live as men." This is a problematic sentence in two respects. First, the term *transsexual woman* refers to a transwoman. These individuals were born with sexed bodies that had been designated female, but *woman* is a term that signifies gender. It may be true that other people currently perceive these four men as women, based on physical appearance, but this is not the same thing as *being* a woman. Second, the sentence states clearly that these individuals *are* women, but they wish to live *as* men—a construction that implies deception. From a trans-positive standpoint, one would say that they are men who wish to live socially as men, clarifying that they are not yet perceived as men by others. The narration exemplifies Condit's (1989) assertion that "television . . . can do oppressive work solely by addressing the dominant audience" (p. 112), since the dominant audience would consider these men to be women so long as they appear to be women and inhabit bodies that are female sexed.

There is a difference in the way two of these men are described, and this difference seems to be at least partially explained within the narration. For Dirk, female pronouns are used only when his childhood is described. Once he is shown with his girlfriend, following his name change but prior to his chest surgery, the narrator makes the switch to male pronouns. However, Ryan receives female pronouns—as well as his female name, Rachel— throughout the majority of the program; his male name and male pronouns are not used until close to the end of the film, following his chest surgery. The primary difference between these men, noted in the narration, is the order of their transition processes. Dirk was already taking male hormones prior to his surgery, whereas "Unlike Dirk, Rachel has decided to have her breasts removed first." Because of this, Dirk's face is more male-appearing than Ryan's, and one could reasonably conclude that using male pronouns for Ryan would be confusing to the average viewer. On the day of Ryan's chest surgery, the narrator states that "she will today begin the process of acquiring a male body by having her breasts removed." This use of female pronouns continues throughout the hospital scenes, even after the surgery is complete. Near the end of the program, once Ryan has begun hormone treatments, the narrator informs us that "she has changed her name to Ryan and is living full time as a man." This is the first time we hear the name Ryan. As we see him hugging a woman, the voice-over finally uses a male pronoun in stating that "Ryan returns to Colorado to visit his identical twin sister."

Ironically, when Dirk is having his chest surgery, the narrator reverts to female pronouns, despite having used male pronouns up until this point: "Both breasts have been removed. Her original areolae and nipples will now be grafted onto her new chest." This narration seems particularly odd, given that Dirk has appeared male throughout the program.

One of the remaining two men in this documentary, Scott, is interviewed about having had a phalloplasty, a complex and physically invasive surgery which constructs a penis of average male size using tissue from the forearm. Most transmen do not pursue this particular surgery, partly due to the cost, and also because it leaves tremendous scarring. Speaking about this surgery in past tense, Scott is clearly pleased with the results. However, in describing Scott's reaction just after the surgery had been completed, the narrator commits an act of misrepresentation in stating that, "upon awakening, he was horrified at what he had done." We then hear Scott explain that he had experienced a great deal of pain, and considered it unfortunate that his body had to go through so much trauma, but he never expresses any regret about the surgery. This voice-over statement, unlike the majority of the narration used for this or any other documentary I have analyzed, strikes a sensational-istic tone. Perhaps a feeling of horror in reaction to this genital surgery was thought to be in keeping with the attitudes of some viewers, but the voice-over does not reflect the feelings implied by Scott's actual statements.

Taken together, these televised documentaries and series episodes do provide some basic education for the general public, yet they do so in tension with the actual self-identification of the transsexual men and women they are attempting to represent. The most obvious evidence of this tension shows up in the erratic use of gendered pronouns and preferred names. Ultimately, all of this confusion leads to an important question: At what point are transmen and transwoman considered men and women? Among the general public, there are some who would insist that these individuals will never be the men and women they claim to be because gender must correspond to birth sex. Others will acknowledge these self-identifications once genital surgery has been completed. Still others, more sympathetic and likely more educated on the subject, will understand that the individual's self-identified gender is authentic regardless of physical sex. Filmmakers, then, face the rhetorical challenge of educating and persuading a partially hostile audience while simultaneously attempting to avoid offending their transgender viewers.

CONCLUSION

Different viewers have different expectations and goals when they choose to watch documentaries that deal with transgenderism. Some may possess a genuine desire to learn, while others might simply wish to be entertained by the spectacle of "sex changes" and "men in dresses." Transgender people themselves might be seeking information, or they may be watching out of concern that the information presented is accurate.

While the inconsistent use of pronouns may appear to be an insignificant matter of etiquette, it indicates a foundational lack of understanding about transgender people that can lead not only to poor treatment interpersonally, but also to the passage of laws affecting how transgender people are able to live in the world. For example, the assumption that a transman is not a man and a transwoman not a woman until after the completion of surgery has prevented many transpeople from changing their legal sex designations because the U.S. government had, until recently, required proof of genital surgery before this change could be made. In many cases, surgery is desired, but too expensive, and most insurance plans will not pay for it. As a result of this conundrum, many transmen appear male but have identification cards listing them as female, and many transwomen appear female but have identification listing them as male. This "outs" their transgender status to authorities such as police, airport security, and customs agents. Fortunately, the Social Security Administration (2013) has lifted the genital surgery requirement for changing one's sex designation with the U.S. government, and a letter from a physician is now considered sufficient.

In this study, I found that narrators' pronoun use for transmen was often more consistent than that for transwomen, and this seemed to be related to outward appearance. One difference in the transition process between transmen and transwomen is the relative effectiveness of hormones. Because testosterone produces facial hair, transmen are usually perceived as male without facial surgery, whereas for transwomen, estrogen does not produce an equivalent marker of female-bodiedness, nor does it reduce one's height. If filmmakers continue to base their pronoun use on such factors, transmen will often be addressed more respectfully than transwomen. This greater respect for transmen may also be related to the fact that, socially, transmen are perceived to be transitioning "up" from a lower status as women to a higher status as men, while transwomen appear to be relinquishing their higher status for a lower one.

Documentaries about transsexuals must make a greater effort to explain transsexualism from the perspectives of those who experience it. For example, it should be made clear that genital surgery is less urgent than the alteration of outward appearance because one's day-to-day social interactions do not involve visible genitalia. Many transsexuals undergo genital surgery to fulfill private needs, but outward appearance is almost always considered a higher priority. Therefore, the most significant fact to convey is that the internal identification precedes transition. A transwoman does not "become a woman" when she transitions; rather, she is a woman who is making her identity visible to others.

Cisgender people often have difficulty grasping this concept because the gendered appearance of the pre-transition individual is assumed to represent internal identity. One innovative method of depicting internal identity on film would be to present the desired image of the person first, using an actor, prior to presenting the individual's actual appearance. For example, a female actor could speak to the camera, stating that she is happy and content as a woman with a female body, and that she feels comfortable interacting with others as a woman. The footage of this actor could then fade to footage of the actual transwoman, who continues speaking to the camera. She might say, "unfortunately, I was born into a body that looks like this, and I want to alter my appearance to look more like the actor you just saw so that people can more easily relate to me as a woman." In this way, viewers see the image of a woman first as a frame for their perception of the actual transwoman.

I have noted that some transsexuals do not desire surgery, yet they are transsexuals because they identify as the binary gender category that does not correspond to the sex designated at birth. Conversely, there are some gender variant individuals who desire various types of surgery, although they do not identify as transsexuals. In explaining that transsexualism has historically involved "surgical modification of the reproductive organs and chest" as well as hormone use and hair removal, Stryker (2008) added that "people who don't consider themselves to be transsexual have increasingly started using these same body modification practices, and they may do so without trying to change their legal gender" (p. 18). This move has led, she argued, to a "breakdown in familiar distinctions between who is a transsexual and who is not." Therefore, who is "considered an acceptable recipient of medicalized body modification procedures" is a "hotly debated topic" (p. 19).

I am not aware of any documentaries specifically focused on the non-transsexual modification of secondary sex characteristics (such as a female who desires a flat chest while not identifying as a man); however, an increasing number of documentary productions on the subject of gender variant identities may involve this phenomenon, and the topic of access to medical procedures is certainly worthy of analysis. For instance, a comparison is sometimes made between transsexuals and those suffering from body integrity identity disorder, described by Jordan (2004) as "amputee 'wannabes,' who desire amputation of one of their healthy limbs" (p. 329). Philosophically, some people support transsexual surgeries, arguing that "bodies are naturally inclined to be either male or female," but are opposed to amputations on the grounds that "bodies are also naturally inclined to be fully-abled, which in this context means having all of one's limbs" (p. 347). Scholars such as Nikki Sullivan (2005) have begun to explore these types of surgical access comparisons.

Those well versed in transgender theory will recognize that this essay is limited in scope, restricted to the topic of transsexuals who transition from one binary gender category to the other. There are few documentaries devoted to gender variant individuals, sometimes known as genderqueer, who do not identify with the conventional labels of *man* or *woman*. It is not surprising that we see fewer documentaries of this type on television because these identities are less relatable to the dominant audience. The average viewer might more readily accept the transsexual who identifies as a man or woman, while those who identify as a third gender, or multiple genders, will more likely be seen as confused or mentally ill. A filmmaker who wishes to educate the public about the full spectrum of transgender identities might be wise to produce a documentary series of episodes, to be shown in order, beginning with the least confusing information and progressing to that which is more complex and unfamiliar.

A comparison can be made, here, to the way in which television talk shows began to frame gay men and lesbians as socially acceptable in contrast to the less familiar categories of bisexuality and transgenderism (Gamson, 1998b). In keeping with this phenomenon, one might think that Winfrey's interview with a pregnant transman might make non-pregnant transmen (especially those who are masculine in appearance and behavior) seem relatively ordinary. However, because the general public has less familiarity with transsexuals than with gay men and lesbians, this is not likely the case. If

Beatie's choice to become pregnant is perceived as a sign of mental instability, this one representation may function, synecdochically, to paint all transsexuals with the same brush.

The fields of transgender studies and television studies present one another with a number of challenges. The field of television studies can influence transgender studies scholars to recognize that the use of television presents a rhetorical challenge, partly because it requires images and, therefore, a strategic use of those images, and partly because its audience is so broad; it is difficult to tailor one's message to an audience if that audience is, potentially, everyone. The field of transgender studies challenges television producers to acknowledge the non-visual through the use of language (such as gendered pronouns) as well as through the focus of program content, which tends to foreground physical appearance and the visual modification of the body over the voice of the televised human subject. Greater emphasis on transgender subjectivity would also allow for more nuanced discussions of surgical access, insurance coverage, and economic discrimination, both on television and within television studies.

With respect to fictional depictions of transgender identities on television, a related topic of some controversy concerns casting decisions for transgender roles. While some transgender activists insist that these roles should be given to transgender actors, others argue that playing a character unlike oneself is the very nature of acting; therefore, the best actor should be given the role, regardless of personal experience. This debate challenges television production practices and, as such, should also be considered within television studies.

The televised representation of a social group is always a matter of synecdoche—the one standing in for the many—and as such, television sets itself an impossible task that can never be met flawlessly. Well-meaning filmmakers can increase visibility for a marginalized social group but, as I noted elsewhere,

> Visibility is a risky prospect, particularly with respect to groups that are easily exploited for commercial purposes. Since transsexualism is not clearly understood by the U.S. public, an increase in media representation may be just as likely to further confuse the issue as to clarify it. (Booth, 2011, p. 191)

While this would seem to place a significant burden on those who create and control television content, not all of these individuals are willing to assume this burden. Some only wish to attract audience attention in order to make a profit, and this is when the burden gets shifted to those who belong to marginalized groups, particularly those activists who attempt to influence the media.

Chapter Eight

Film

*Becoming One of the Girls/Guys: Distancing
Transgender Representations in Popular Film Comedies*

Lucy J. Miller

In an iconic scene from the film *Tootsie* (1982), Dustin Hoffman as Michael Dorsey walks down a crowded New York City street dressed for the first time as his transgender alter ego Dorothy Michaels. The audience has not seen Michael as Dorothy until this very moment; the last shot before the cut to this scene is of Michael sitting in his agent's office. How do we know how to react to this scene? How do we know to laugh rather than to cry, get angry, be afraid, feel sympathetic, or any other of a number of emotions? What can this scene tell us about Western cultural attitudes toward transgender people?

Comedy is the most popular and well-known form of representation of transgender individuals in film. While these films have been successful, transgender comedies use that successful humor to distance the transgender characters as objects of ridicule. Cross-dressing in film represents the needs of comedy and society to have a subject to ridicule (Phillips, 2006). According to Phillips, "[c]omedy thus helps to ridicule and hence domesticate a transvestism that might otherwise prove threatening" (p. 81). The domestication of transgender identity is accomplished not only through the ridiculing of the transgender identities of the characters but also through the privileging of their cisnormative identities. Cisnormativity refers to the systemic expectation that there are only two mutually exclusive genders and the gender of all members of a society will match the sex assigned to them at birth, with attendant benefits given to those who adhere and the labeling of those who do not, transgender and queer individuals, as deviant. The films construct the cisnormative identities as the ones the audience should identify with while the transgender identities of these same characters should be laughed at.

I use cisnormative purposefully in this chapter, not just as a substitute for cisgender. Cisnormative is generally used in this chapter as a modifier of identity to illustrate the ways the characters are constructed to support the system of cisnormativity. The transgender identities of the characters are not presented as equal in these films, so to refer to their transgender and cisgender identities would imply that the characters could have chosen between either of their identities when this clearly is not the case. The purpose of a cisnormative identity is to assuage any fears by audience members that a character might find happiness, fulfillment, or purpose in her or his transgender identity. While film in general reflects the dominance of cisgender identities in Western society, cisnormative identities go a step farther in arguing that a cisgender identity is the only viable option for an individual. Pairing the cisnormative and transgender identities within the same characters only serves to make the argument in favor of cisnormativity more explicit, thus serving to distance the transgender identities of the characters from the audience.

I approach the filmic representations of transgender individuals through a cultural studies approach that views representation as both constitutive (Hall, 1997; Webb, 2009) and constraining (Heath, 1981), helping to shape our understanding of events and individuals while limiting the information available to us about those events and individuals. Transgender representations in film work generally to distance the transgender characters from the audience by evoking feelings of ridicule, fear, and sympathy. This chapter focuses specifically on the use of humor to position the transgender characters as objects of ridicule.

In this chapter, I classify transgender characters as characters who engage in extended dressing or living as a member of the sex they were not assigned at birth, regardless of whether the characters would self-identify as transgender. This focus deviates from that of other chapters in this collection that discuss individuals who identify as transgender or with a gender that differs from the one assigned to them at birth. While the characters in transgender comedies do not identify as transgender, the success of these films (box office receipts in excess of $100 million, numerous sequels spawned, and multiple Academy Award nominations and wins) ensures that they serve as some of the dominant cultural images of transgender people. Even though the characters themselves do not identify as transgender, their portrayals in these films place constraints on the lives of transgender people, assigning certain motives and meanings to their lived experiences. The fact that comedy is the most popular genre of transgender films is particularly limiting, with the humor in the films reinforcing the idea that transgender identities are not to be taken seriously and distancing transgender people further from an already unsympathetic public.

Humor has clear rhetorical functions in making arguments about how the audience should respond to the characters, and the humor in these comedies is farcical. "In farce, humor often results from mistaken identity, disguise, and other improbable situations" (Graves & Engel, 2006, p. 30). The implied wackiness of farce hides a specific constraining representation: the actions of the characters are never taken seriously because of the lighthearted tone of farce. The separation created through the lack of seriousness attributed to the actions of the characters positions the transgender characters as the objects of the humor rather than as active participants in the humor. In farce, according to Bermel (1990), "we laugh *at* the characters, never with them" (p. 54).

Laughing at someone implies a relationship between the audience and the character. Meyer (2000) identified four potential effects of humor based on that relationship: identification, clarification, enforcement, and differentiation. The humor in transgender farces is usually the result of the enforcement and differentiation effects; audience members laugh because they are happy to see a character facing difficulty while cross-dressed or because the experiences of the characters while cross-dressed are so distant from audience members' own lives that mocking the characters is acceptable. Humor based in difference is often used to assuage audience fears; what is feared "must be made fun of to exorcise the fear," with laughter providing a way of "asserting power over terrible threats" (Douglas, 2010, p. 65).

In this chapter, I analyze the ways transgender farces use narrative conventions and visual codes to communicate specific messages about transgender individuals. This chapter builds on analyses of transgender representation found in communication and film studies (Abbott, 2013; Bell-Metereau, 1993; Calvacante, 2013; Garber, 1992; Phillips, 2006). I begin with a review of scholarly literature on representations in transgender farces. I then analyze the following films: *The All-American Co-Ed* (1941), *Some Like It Hot* (1959), *Tootsie* (1982), *Victor/Victoria* (1982), *Just One of the Guys* (1985), *Mrs. Doubtfire* (1993), *Big Momma's House* (2000), *100 Girls* (2000), and *Sorority Boys* (2002). The films' narrative conventions (a crisis requiring cross-dressing, challenges to and reassertion of cisnormativity, and lessons learned) and visual codes (a successful transformation, the object and possessor of the gaze, and the big reveal) distance the transgender characters from the audience by privileging the cisnormative identities of the characters, thus opening up their transgender identities to ridicule. The scholarly literature on transgender comedies also focuses on the different ways the films support and create spaces for cisnormativity.

LITERATURE REVIEW

Feminist critiques of transgender comedies focus on the way the films rein-force cisnormativity and heteronormativity, the systemic privileging of heterosexuality. Butler (1993) singled out *Victor/Victoria, Tootsie*, and *Some Like It Hot* as examples of "forms of drag that heterosexual culture produces for itself" (p. 126). Transgender comedies "are functional in providing a ritualistic release for a heterosexual economy that must constantly police its own boundaries against the invasion of queerness" (p. 126). These films assist in the work of maintaining a cisnormative gender identity by providing clear examples of individuals who privilege their own cisnormative gender identities over any alternatives.

Scholars rightfully point out the privileging of cisnormativity in these films is often constructed at the expense of women (Collins, 2004; Douglas, 2010). Transgender comedies also privilege cisnormativity by reinforcing the gender binary through the assertion that the characters have one "natural" gender (Lieberfeld & Sanders, 1998, p. 130). A man returning to living as a man at the end of a film after spending time dressing as a woman is usually presented as a return to the character's true gender. While the endings of the films hint at a possible progressive identity for the characters through the lessons learned during their times spent cross-dressing, these lessons are applied to the characters' cisnormative identities while their transgender identities are discarded.

Other scholars (Garber, 1992; Tomasulo, 1996) argued that this gender tension is unnecessary because the characters never fully abandon their mas-culine or feminine identities and the cisnormative privilege accrued to them. A moment of this privilege is seen in Dorothy's speeches in *Tootsie* against her perceived harassment, which are "less a response to the oppression of women than an instinctive situational male reaction to being treated like a woman" (Garber, 1992, p. 6). While the characters may make clear assertions of their cisnormative identities at the end of the films, the characters never fully cede their claims to a cisnormative identity or the privileges that go with it even while cross-dressed.

Visually, the films are constructed around trans-misogyny. Trans-misogy-ny involves a transgender individual not only being objectified for her or his appearance but also for failing to perform femininity or masculinity accord-ing to cisnormative standards (Serano, 2007). Visual humor is derived mere-ly from the appearance of the characters' transgender alter egos in an attempt to deflect any ridicule the characters might receive for adopting transgender identities. Seeing the characters in their transgender alter egos stumble in their heels or rip their wigs off allows the audience to have a good laugh at the expense of transgender people without ever questioning cisnormativity.

In order to support the project of privileging cisnormative identities over transgender identities, transgender farces must create spaces in which the deviations from cisnormativity can be contained. The cross-dressing in *Some Like It Hot* serves the creation of a liminal, dream world (Cardullo, 1995). The dreams and desires of the characters are revealed within this liminal space. Through cross-dressing, the characters are able to address issues they are unable to deal with in their normal lives. The settings of many transgender farces support viewing the cross-dressing of the characters as a liminal escape from reality, whether it be sunny Florida (Phillips, 2006), Paris in the 1930s (Wood, 1986), or any other number of unusual locations, from a sorority house to an older Southern woman's home, that take the characters outside of their everyday existence. While in these dream worlds of luxury and frivolity, the characters are free to experiment with new identities. The liminality of the transgender identities in these films is further bolstered by the external nature of the crisis that leads the characters to the dream world and their new identities, absolving the characters of any blame that might accrue as a result of their experimentation. This "necessity for disguise is the genre's most fundamental narrative element" (Straayer, 1996, p. 44). All dreams must come to an end, though, and cisnormativity must be restored. The characters may be free to experiment with more fluid gender identities while in this liminal space, but they emerge to return fully to their cisnormative identities and once reestablished, all interest in their transgender identities disappears. By leaving their transgender identities in this liminal space, the films miss an opportunity to send a message about the inclusion of transgender individuals in society.

In my analysis, I build on the attention given in the scholarly literature on transgender farces to the ways the films reinforce cisnormativity. I extend this focus on cisnormativity by arguing that it is privileged in the films through the use of specific narrative conventions and visual codes. Transgender comedies construct the characters in particular ways that privilege their cisnormative identities at the expense of their transgender identities. To analyze this privileging of cisnormativity, I employ a qualitative textual analysis of the films.

METHODOLOGY

In this qualitative textual analysis, I conduct readings of the narrative conventions and visual codes of nine films featuring representations of transgender characters. The films selected for analysis serve as a representative sample of transgender representations in transgender farces. Moretti (2007) calls the analysis of groups of texts "distant reading," which he argues constitutes "*a specific form of knowledge*: fewer elements, hence a sharper sense of their overall interconnection" (p. 1). While I do not engage in the analysis of hundreds, if not thousands, of texts as Moretti does, I agree with his argument that taking a wider view of a group of texts can reveal information about the texts not available through the detailed analysis of individual works. The detailed reading of individual texts is still a highly valuable form of analysis, but it is not the goal of this chapter.

In this analysis, narrative conventions consist of the unfolding of story elements relative to similar film texts, including everything from significant plot events to the dialogue and interactions between characters. Visual codes are grounded in the concept of the male gaze (Mulvey, 1975) and consist primarily of mise-en-scène. I am concerned with what the audience sees on screen—how the characters are presented—including costuming, facial expressions, and body movements. Reference to camera movements (a slow tilt up a character's body from feet to head), transitions (cuts between scenes), and camera positioning (an overhead shot of a couple in bed together) are used when necessary to understand how the characters are visually presented to the audience. The focus of my analysis of visual codes is on the information presented on screen rather than on the ways the camera is manipulated to capture that information.

ANALYSIS

Through the use of narrative conventions and visual codes, the representations in transgender farces support the overall work of transgender representations to distance the transgender characters from the audience by positioning them as the objects of laughter and ridicule. Narrative conventions include a crisis requiring cross-dressing, challenges to and reassertion of cisnormativity, and lessons learned from the experience. Visual codes include a successful transformation, the object and possessor of the gaze, and the big reveal. The conventions and codes of these films work together to privilege cisnormative identities over transgender identities.

Narrative Conventions

The narratives of these films may seem to be aiming only for laughs but through the use of specific conventions, messages sent to the audience clearly privilege the cisnormative identities of the characters over their transgender identities. At various moments throughout the films, the cisnormative identities of the characters are given greater weight and importance than their temporarily adopted transgender identities. These moments range from the characters leaving their normal lives in face of a crisis by adopting transgender identities to regularly discarding those identities in order to pursue a heterosexual romance. At the end of these narratives, the characters are portrayed as having learned important lessons and grown as individuals through their experiences, but their transgender identities are cast aside as inconsequential, just part of their personal growth.

Crisis Requiring Cross-dressing

The characters in transgender farces never choose to cross-dress unless prompted by an external crisis. The crisis that leads a character to cross-dress is never an internal identity crisis but is always external, including everything from a desperate search for employment to trying to find an unknown one-night stand. Each character in the nine films under analysis must face her or his unique crisis. These characters would not otherwise choose to cross-dress and protest mightily when questioned about it, a feature that distinguishes them from genuinely transgender characters in other films.

The crises faced by the characters in transgender farces are structured around economic privilege: those with low economic privilege are desperate enough to cross-dress while those with high levels of economic privilege have the freedom to cross-dress. The economic privilege of the characters is rooted in heteronormativity. Part and parcel with heteronormativity's privileging of heterosexual romance and the nuclear family is the conception of the family as middle class, with the steady job and suburban home that accompanies traditional family values. The assumption being made by these films in constructing their narratives is that the majority of the audience is middle class and has neither experienced the economic desperation that might lead to cross-dressing as remedy nor the extravagant wealth and leisure that might lead to cross-dressing as a solution to simple problems. In an example of the differentiation function, the narratives are constructed to allow the audience to laugh at the characters' actions and decisions while never feeling that their own values are threatened since their experiences, particularly economically, are so different from those of the characters on screen.

Joe and Jerry in *Some Like It Hot*, Victoria in *Victor/Victoria*, Michael Dorsey in *Tootsie*, and Daniel in *Mrs. Doubtfire* all choose to cross-dress when faced with unemployment. Unemployment, another form of marginalization, creates a liminal space that allows for the subversion of gender norms. The employment status of all five characters is tenuous at best at the beginning of each film. Joe and Jerry, for example, are performing in a speakeasy that is raided by the police. While they manage to escape the raid, demonstrating their ingenuity when faced with danger, they do not get paid for the speakeasy gig and are desperate to obtain other work. Victoria is auditioning for a job singing in a nightclub, but she is told that her operatically trained voice is not right for the venue. Adopting a transgender identity in these films is presented as a last recourse for the economically desperate.

Because their transgender identities are adopted in moments of desperation, they can be discarded in favor of cisnormative identities when their situations improve. The lack of doubt the characters have that their situations will improve is further evidence of their cisnormative privilege.

Cross-dressing by those with low economic privilege is presented as a final act of desperation in order to improve their situations. For those characters with higher economic privilege, cross-dressing is presented as an almost fantastical solution to mundane problems. Wealth and steady jobs give these characters the freedom to explore nontraditional solutions to the crises they face. Terri in *Just One of the Guys*, Bob Sheppard in *All-American Co-Ed*, and the characters in *Sorority Boys*, particularly Dave, all come from wealthy families. A specific example of this privilege can be seen in the enormous size of the house Terri lives in and the fact that her parents go away for a two-week vacation, leaving her and her brother home alone and giving Terri the freedom to cross-dress. When she fails to win a newspaper competition at her high school, her journalism teacher says that while her article was well written, it was not outstanding. Infuriated, Terri asks, "Why? Because a pretty girl can't possibly have a brain?" She later complains to her brother Buddy about not being taken seriously because she's cute, "Sometimes I just wish I were a guy." Terri decides to attend the other school offering an internship disguised as a boy, and Buddy says that this "[m]akes perfect sense. You got a problem, you get in drag." Buddy's sarcastic comment reveals the ludicrousness of Terri's plan; she feels so entitled to the newspaper internship that she goes to the extreme measure of cross-dressing to ensure that it is hers.

The crisis requiring cross-dressing found in each of these films communicates the idea that transgender identity is the product of external factors. The search for an external reason is a common experience for many transgender individuals. A young transgender woman may search desperately for an external cause to explain her often confusing feelings or a transgender man may be asked what caused him to become transgender after coming out to family or friends. The distancing of transgender characters produced by transgender representations is supported by the external nature of the crisis that leads to cross-dressing; audience members can reassure themselves that they would respond differently when faced with similar situations. Instead of helping audience members identify with the characters by attributing the actions of the characters to the desperation in their situations, the external nature of the crisis can be interpreted by audience members as justification for the ridiculous choices the characters make in response to their situations. While cross-dressing may offer a temporary solution to the crises faced by the characters, it also calls into question their cisnormative identities so they must find ways to reassert those identities.

Challenges to and Reassertion of Cisnormativity

The distance created in transgender comedies between the transgender characters and the audience is a product of humor encoded into the transgender identities of the characters. This distance creates problems of identification for audience members in these films because the transgender characters are also the protagonists. The transgender positions of the characters seem to challenge cisnormativity, but the characters find other ways of reasserting their cisnormativity. Feeling distanced from a character's transgender alter ego, the audience may be motivated to identify with the masculine or feminine cisnormative identity of a character. An audience member may laugh at Michael in *Tootsie* while he is dressed as Dorothy while also rooting for him to end up with Julie in his cisnormative identity. The challenges to cisnormativity are overcome through the privileging of the cisnormative identities of the characters.

One way the films privilege the cisnormative identities of the characters is by demonstrating the difficulty the male characters have mastering feminine attire, particularly footwear. Michael stumbles as he walks down the street for his audition as Dorothy, and Jerry stumbles as he and Joe walk along the train platform. Daniel complains bitterly upon returning home after his interview as Mrs. Doubtfire, "If I find the misogynistic bastard who invented heels, I'll kill him." Jerry also raises questions about how easily women walk in heels. "How do they walk in these things, huh? How do they keep their balance?" Joe responds, "Must be the way the weight is distributed." Jerry ultimately comes to an essentialist conclusion about the difference between men and women after watching Sugar sashay down the platform, "I tell you it's a whole different sex!" Though they may not recognize the ways their cisnormative identities are being challenged, the poor gender performances of the characters demonstrate their lack of interest in fully adopting their transgender identities.

A second way transgender comedies privilege the cisnormative identities of the characters is the quickness with which they discard their transgender disguises. Joe abandons his feminine disguise on the beach and creates the identity of millionaire Junior to seduce Sugar, Matt only spends brief periods of time dressed as a woman while searching for his mystery girl, Malcolm repeatedly switches between himself and Big Momma in order to get closer to Sherry, and Bob readopts his masculine identity mere moments after arriving at Mar Brynn. Allowing the characters to spend extended periods of time not in their transgender disguises helps the audience identify with these cisnormative identities rather than their transgender identities. The relative ease with which the characters discard their transgender identities also reinforces the cultural perception of transgender people, especially women, as deceitful for not disclosing their transgender identities to everyone they meet and as complicit in their own victimization should someone respond violently upon learning of their transgender identities (Serano, 2007; Sloop, 2000, 2004).

Having shown the characters to be uncommitted to their transgender identities through poor gender performances and the frequent discarding of those identities, the final way the narratives privilege cisnormativity and heteronormativity is through the heterosexual romances featured in the films. Though the characters may adopt their transgender identities to escape a crisis, what they usually get out of the experience is a relationship. Nearly all of the characters are involved in some sort of romance in these films; Joe falls for Sugar, Bob for Virginia, Victoria for King, Michael for Julie, Terri for Rick, Malcolm for Sherri, Dave for Leah, and Matt for Patty. The clearly heterosexual romances the characters are engaged in function to assuage any fears the audience might have about the characters because of their adoption of transgender identities; audience members are not distanced further from the characters through same-sex romances on top of cross-dressing. Where cross-dressing creates distance, heteronormativity closes the gap.

The transgender identities of the characters may briefly and ostensibly challenge cisnormativity, but transgender comedies do nothing to entertain this challenge, working instead to solidify the cisnormative identities of the characters as sites of identification for the audience. Though the characters have discarded their transgender identities numerous times throughout the films, they reach a point where they must leave the liminal space of transgender identity and return with lessons learned about being better members of cisnormative society.

Lessons Learned

At the end of each film, the characters have made positive changes in their lives. Many have entered into relationships with the people they love. Almost all have learned something about the struggles of the so-called opposite sex. While self-improvement is all well and good, the lessons are applied to the characters' cisnormative identities while their transgender identities are discarded for good. Few attempts are made to incorporate their transgender identities as they return to their cisnormative lives.

The endings of the films are marked by returns. The characters clearly leave the liminal space of transgender identity and return to the cisnormative lives they left behind. Joe and Jerry ride across the waves in Osgood's boat with the Florida resort clearly in the background. Malcolm returns to his duties as an FBI agent by arresting Lester. Adam, Dave, Doofer, and Bob all return to their fraternity houses. Miranda tells her kids that they have a new nanny and opens the door to reveal Daniel standing on the steps. The endings of the films function as closure for the transgender identities of the characters. The happy endings are meant only for their cisnormative identities, so their transgender identities must be left behind.

Love is the most common happy ending in transgender comedies, though not without complications. An example of these complications is when Sherry tells Malcolm at the end of *Big Momma's House*, "You went through all this trouble trying to catch me in a lie but you were the one being dishonest." Malcolm responds, "That was fake but what I feel for you is real," and they seal their new relationship with a kiss. The message is that if there is a true connection, all is forgiven, even if one partner spent time cross-dressing. The transgender identities of the characters remain in the past and do not come back to haunt the characters in their cisnormative lives.

Most transgender farces show the improvement in the lives of the characters without direct reference to their transgender identities. *Tootsie* and *Mrs. Doubtfire* are the only films to feature explicit statements about how living as a woman made the male character better. Michael tells Julie, "I was a better man with you as a woman than I ever was with a woman as a man . . . I just gotta learn to do it without the dress." Miranda tells Daniel that Mrs. Doubtfire "brought out the best in you." Even though the adoption of transgender identities has clearly helped the characters improve their lives (everything positive, from their new relationships to their new jobs, comes as the result of their transgender identities), the positive influences are generally swept under the rug along with the discarded identities. Having constructed the narratives to privilege cisnormativity, suddenly acknowledging the positive benefits of their transgender identities would call the other events of the films into question.

Through the use of these narrative conventions, the transgender identities of the characters are distanced from the audience because the characters take these identities less than seriously. The visual codes of transgender farces continue the pattern of depicting the transgender identities of the characters as farcical.

Visual Codes

The visual codes of transgender farces distance the transgender characters from the audience through the use of trans-misogyny. Much of the visual humor in these films comes from framing shots and scenes as if the male gaze is in operation as it objectifies a woman. Once it has been made clear that the object of the gaze is transgender, the character is mocked for failing to live up to cisnormative standards of beauty. The visual codes distance the transgender characters from the audience through this combination of objectification and ridicule. As with the narrative conventions, the visual codes privilege the cisnormative identities of the characters through the lack of attention to their transformations, the situating of the object and possessor of the gaze, and the big reveal of the characters' transgender identities.

Successful Transformation

The successful transformation of the characters into their transgender alter egos is key to the narratives of the films but is presented visually. The successful transformation generally works only within the diegesis of the films; the audience is given too much information, whether it is hearing the characters devise their plans or seeing them don their disguises, to believe that a character has transformed into a man or woman. The transformations in these films work to distance the audience from the characters by reminding audience members that what they are seeing on screen are disguises rather than allowing them to identify with the characters as the men or women they appear to be as the other characters in the films are able to do.

The privileging of the characters' cisnormative identities is evident in the frequent use of quick cuts between scenes before and after the transformations. The cut uses the technique of montage to help the audience make the connection between the man or woman they were watching in the previous scene and the woman or man who appears on the screen now. The cisnormative identities of the characters are presented first before the transgender alter egos are ever seen. *Some Like It Hot, Tootsie, The All-American Co-Ed, Just One of the Guys*, and *Sorority Boys* all use this technique to signal a transformation. After Joe gets off the phone accepting the job in the girl's band, there is a quick cut to him and Jerry walking down a train platform dressed as women. Likewise, in probably the most famous example of this technique, after Michael's agent tells him no one in New York will hire him, there is a quick cut to Michael dressed as a woman walking down a crowded street. The use of the quick cut represents a general lack of interest in the process of transgender transformation and a desire to surprise the audience into laughter upon seeing either the man they just saw on screen now wearing a dress and heels or the woman they just saw now with slicked back hair and wearing a suit.

This lack of attention sends the message that the characters' transgender identities should be treated with a similar lack of attention; the cisnormative identities of the characters are what matter while their transgender identities are more insubstantial. Their transgender identities appear as if by magic and will disappear just as quickly. Once they have donned their transgender disguises, the characters now become objects and possessors of the gaze.

Objects and Possessors of the Gaze

Cross-dressed characters in transgender comedies problematize the standard workings of the cisnormative and heteronormative male gaze. While they maintain their cisnormative identities, their transgender identities make it difficult for audience members to adopt their point of view. This dual identity allows these characters to be both objects and possessors of the gaze.

Trans-misogyny is most evident in the scenes where the characters are the object of the gaze as their transformations are revealed. As is often the case with women in film, the characters are revealed via a tilt or other camera movement that begins at the characters' feet and moves slowly up their bodies before reaching their faces. *Some Like It Hot, Mrs. Doubtfire, Victor/ Victoria, Just One of the Guys, Sorority Boys, The All-American Co-Ed*, and *100 Girls* all contain variations on this visual representation of the characters, positioning them as objects to be looked at. A primary example is found in *Some Like it Hot*. As Joe and Jerry walk along the train platform dressed as women for the first time, the audience is invited to stare at their legs in the same way that numerous women have been stared at for centuries.

The cisnormative identities of the characters are also privileged through the manner in which they possess the gaze. As cisnormative individuals, they may be uncomfortable with and unaccustomed to being the object of the gaze, but this does not prevent them from possessing the gaze and objectifying other women. Malcolm as Big Momma cannot help but gawk at Sherry in her lingerie when she takes off her sweater after spilling jam on it. He also stares at her butt as she reaches for something on a high shelf in the cupboard that he asks her to get for him. During his audition for a soap opera, Michael as Dorothy lowers his glasses to stare at the butt of Julie, a fellow actress, as she walks away after helping him pick up some papers he dropped. The lowering of the glasses makes it clear that he is staring at her; Michael has no trouble seeing through the glasses so the action is meant to highlight the direction of his gaze. All of these moments happen while the characters are disguised as their transgender alter egos and so would be unusual actions for the heterosexual women they are positioned as. Yet again, a visual code is used to privilege the characters' cisnormative identities, which cannot be contained in the presence of an attractive woman.

In order to privilege the cisnormative identities of the characters, their transgender identities are belittled and mocked as objects of the gaze while their cisnormative identities are positioned as sites of power and control as possessors of the gaze. The final discarding of their transgender identities is accomplished visually through a big reveal.

The Big Reveal

Once ready to exit the liminal space of their transgender identities, the characters must discard these identities for a final time. The final abandoning of these identities is not done in private but in a big public reveal meant to confirm the cisnormative identities of the characters for any who might have questioned them. While images of the characters in the process of transformation are generally avoided in these films, images of the characters in a transitional identity that blurs their transgender and cisnormative identities function to privilege their cisnormative identities by framing the scenes as an inability to contain their identities any longer. By removing their wigs, the characters definitively assert their cisnormativity.

The removal of a wig or mask is the most common form of big reveal for male-to-female cross-dressers in transgender farces, making the argument that the hair and face are stronger signifiers of femininity than other aspects of a transgender woman's body. An example of this dramatic wig removal can be found at the end of *Sorority Boys*. Dave's big reveal is in service to the woman he has fallen in love with. During the KOKtail Cruise, a group of KOK alumni, led by Dave's father, decide Leah should be removed from the party using the fraternity's dogcatcher routine. Since the party takes place on a boat, this means throwing Leah overboard, but Dave steps forward dressed in a lavender party dress and heels to stop them. The other men pay no attention to him until he tells them to stop in his masculine voice and, very dramatically, removes his wig. His father is suddenly able to recognize Dave, as if his transgender alter ego is some kind of superhero disguise, and the other alumni cease attempting to throw Leah overboard. Having been ignored as his transgender alter ego, Dave removes his wig and reasserts his cisnormativity. Even wearing a dress is not enough to undermine the privilege associated with his cisnormative identity. Though his actions may be for Leah's benefit, they are also a clear assertion of his cisnormative identity; unaccustomed to being ignored when making demands, Dave discovers that what is hindering him is the trappings of his transgender disguise. Removing his wig restores the cisnormative privilege he feels entitled to.

Along with the narrative presentation of the characters as frequently discarding their transgender disguises, the big reveal most clearly demonstrates the privileging of the cisnormative identities of the characters. The characters are forced in these moments to make a choice, and they choose their cisnormative identities in the most dramatic fashion possible. The big reveal also puts to rest any readings of these films as gender fluid. The characters' identities are mutually exclusive; while they may learn lessons from their experiences, the purpose of these lessons is to help them function more effectively within the cisnormative system, not to help them recognize the wider range of gender performances and expressions available to them. A gender fluid reading of these films based on the fact that the characters temporarily occupy a liminal space that allows them to have gender experiences outside of the limited range of expression available within a cisnormative system ignores the clear ways these films reinforce the gender binary by privileging those identities that hew closest to it.

The big reveal is the final visual confirmation of the cisnormative identities of the characters. The fact that these reveals often involve very dramatic actions, such as wig removals or exposing breasts, sends the message that the cisnormative identities of the characters were very much at risk of being subsumed by their transgender identities. Bold and decisive action is needed to make their cisnormative identities crystal clear to any who might have doubts.

CONCLUSION

The narrative conventions and visual codes of transgender comedies work to distance the audience from the transgender identities of the characters while privileging the characters' cisnormative identities as potential sites of identification, and the distance produced by these representations reflects larger societal discomfort with transgender identities in Western cultures. At this time, Western cultures are still slowly coming to grips with identities outside of cisnormative expectations. Transgender acceptance even lags behind the progress made in the acceptance of gays and lesbians, as evidenced by the lack of attention to important transgender issues at the same time as same-sex marriage rights continue to advance and Don't Ask, Don't Tell is repealed. Transgender people, even children, are policed when they use the restroom, as in the case of Coy Mathis (Frosch, 2013). Transgender people can be arrested for walking down the street, as in the case of Arizona resident Monica Jones (Nichols, 2014), and have their murders go unsolved after charges are dropped against the initial suspect, as in the case of Islan Nettles (Molloy, 2013). These cases are not isolated incidents, with transgender people reporting high levels of abuse, harassment, homelessness, workplace discrimination, and suicide (Grant, Mottet, Tanis, Harrison, Herman, & Keisling, 2011).

In light of such injustices, the humor found in transgender farces may seem inconsequential, but both are a symptom of cisnormativity in Western culture. Transgender farces distance the audience from the transgender identities of the characters because the lived experiences of transgender people are so far removed from the experiences of the audience members or are seen as deserving of disdain that laughter is deemed an appropriate response. This attitude also manifests in the daily lives of transgender people. A common reaction for many people upon encountering a transgender person for the first time is laughter, either behind a barely concealing hand or directly to the individual's face. Can we really expect anything different from people, regardless of how harmful it is to transgender people themselves, when this is the reaction prompted by the dominant transgender filmic representation? Films reflect cultural attitudes and values, and the continued success of trans-

gender farces that feature narrative conventions and visual codes that distance the transgender characters as objects of ridicule are reflective of current
Western cultural attitudes toward transgender people.

This chapter also responds to Spencer's (2014) call to analyze popular
media texts, even those not featuring representations of transgender people,
through a transgender lens. While also analyzing films often considered to
not be representations of transgender people, the main contribution of this
chapter to the analysis of media texts through a transgender lens is the concept of a cisnormative identity. Cisnormative identity reflects a transgender
lens on analysis by highlighting the ways films are constructed to privilege
cisnormativity at the detriment to transgender and other gender non-conforming identities. While future research could apply the concept in an analysis of
a particular film, a more interesting project would be to analyze genres (action, romantic comedy) or the work of individual actors (Johnny Depp, Julia
Roberts, Denzel Washington) to further determine the characteristics of a
cisnormative identity. Analysis of transgender representation in film and
other media continues to be important, and future research must continue to
bring attention to the myriad ways transgender people are distanced by these
representations, but the privileging of cisnormativity in all films also works
to maintain separation between transgender and cisgender people. If transgender people are ever going to be fully and accurately represented in film
and other media, the construction of cisnormative identities that present being cisgender as the only valid option must be addressed at all levels of the
film experience, from those who make the films to those who view them.

Chapter Nine

Visual Communication

From Abomination to Indifference: A Visual Analysis
of Transgender Stereotypes in the Media

Paul Martin Lester

In Deuteronomy, the fifth book of the Hebrew Bible, the Jewish Pentateuch, and the Old Testament, Moses revealed a long list of laws. More famous for his Ten Commandments, these rules, although not cut in stone, were also part of his constant concern to keep the Israelites in line. Not making it on his top ten list were essentials he thought were needed for a pious life, such as: If you come across an ox on the ground, you must try to pick it up; if you find a bird's nest, the eggs may be taken, but leave the mother alone. However, another important law for Moses was not related to walking along a road: "A woman shall not wear a man's garment, nor shall a man put on a woman's cloak, for whoever does these things is an abomination to the Lord your God" (22:3–6). Although Moses reportedly lived to the age of 120, it is probably good he did not exist in more recent times to watch the infamous cloak wearer Bela Lugosi in *Dracula* (1931) or the adorable tie and vest sporter Diane Keaton in the eponymous *Annie Hall* (1977). As a religious fundamentalist, Moses was so disgusted by cross-dressers that he labeled such persons abominations.

This work is not so concerned with actual or fictionalized cross-dressers played with hammy gusto by John Travolta in *Hairspray* (2007) or with reserved aplomb by Julie Andrews in *Victor Victoria* (1982). This chapter concentrates on visual messages of persons who were swaddled as babies with a blanket that should have been a different color. Focused on visual communication and through analyses of selected popular culture examples presented in film, on television, and for the Web, this chapter argues that transgender stereotypes that rely on visual messages get their power from the concept of disgust, a basic response to a particular stimulus that, for most persons, has emotional as well as physical reactions. With such powerful responses, it is no wonder that creators of pornographic materials often use disgust as a lure to attract viewers who find the visual messages entertaining. When transpersons are part of storylines that purposely evoke disgust in viewers, whether for dramatic or comedic purposes, the use of disgust becomes another form of pornography while the visual stereotypes shown are difficult for many to erase from their minds.

IMAGES MUST BE ANALYZED

Mass media function as one primary source of visual stereotypes. Because images—whether in print or on screens—affect a viewer emotionally more than words alone, repeated visual stereotypes often contribute to misinformed perceptions that have the weight of established facts. As Hill and Helmers (2004) explained, "like verbal texts, [images] can be used to prompt an immediate, visceral response, to develop cognitive (though largely unconscious) connection over a sustained period of time, or to prompt conscious analytical thought." Consequently, visual messages are the best media to "instantiate values and stir up strong emotions" (pp. 5, 11).

The mass media are about the only place where persons regularly and over a long time see members from other cultural groups. Views of the "other" fill the pages of newspapers and magazines, are shown on television, projected within darkened movie theaters, and glow on computer screens. However, when most of those media images are stereotypical, viewers are not challenged to examine the bases for their personal prejudices. For example, media often portray transpersons as needing to "pass" as their chosen gender using outlandish makeup and costumes and dramatizing bizarre behaviors that support preconceived stereotypes. Passing as a concept became necessary when persons considered as "others" wanted to participate in the benefits afforded those of the dominant culture without detection. Passing may be required because of perceived differences in race, class, religion, gender, or another identity among dominant and non-dominant individuals. In dark-skin cultures, it is called "colorism." For example, those with African and Indian backgrounds have learned that if they have lighter skin they will have a perceived advantage over those darker in hue. Some resort to skin bleaches and other techniques. Think of Michael Jackson's quest to fool everyone into believing he was Anglo or *Elle* magazine executives accused of lightening the skin of Aishwarya Rai Bachchan and Gabby Sidibe (Hilton, n. d.). Other cultural groups have their own forms of passing. In F. Scott Fitzgerald's novel *The Great Gatsby*, those without economic means try to blend with the wealthy classes. Religious passing has a more sinister history. For example, the motion picture *Europa Europa* (1990) tells the story of Jewish men who attempted surgery to restore their foreskins to pass as Gentiles in order to escape the horrors of the Holocaust. Passing then, is a thoroughly visual phenomenon, not only for transpeople, but for other groups as well.

Because images are so powerful, we must take them seriously. Theorists John Berger and Roland Barthes offer field-defining perspectives for thinking carefully about images. Berger is most known for his works *About Looking* (1980) and *Ways of Seeing* (1972). In *Looking*, he wrote that image analysis must be "seen in terms which are simultaneously personal, political, economic, dramatic, everyday and historic" (1980, p. 51). In studying any image—whether still or moving—adequate time and seriousness must be afforded to the analytical process because of the multiple meanings and contexts any image exhibits. Barthes's *Camera Lucida: Reflections on Photography* (1981) is considered a classic in the field. For Barthes, certain images that have strong emotional content, from news photographs of disasters to personal snapshots of loved ones, can affect and be remembered by a person until death.

All communication, whether verbal or visual, is composed of two major types of messages: the literal and the symbolic, otherwise known in semiotic terms as denotative and connotative. For Barthes (1981), images that are denotative are similar to the literal concept because they describe actual experience. Literal or denotative messages can cross cultural boundaries for a more global, universally intended meaning. Almost anyone, regardless of group membership, will recognize and understand literal meanings in words and pictures. A traditional toothy smile of a person posing for a snapshot, for example, usually translates well across cultures and is quickly understood. Conversely, symbolic signs often require in-depth analysis in order to discern their meaning or function. Almost all members of the same cultural group will understand connotative communications. That shared meaning is what helps form and bond a group because they have the same history, experiences, language, and so on. Many times, however, symbolic images are a mystery for outsiders because they form their meaning from specific cultures and historical contexts. A close-lipped ironic smile of a death row prisoner may be considered more symbolic than literal.

Barthes (1981) attempted to combine the literal elements of an image into the term he named *studium*. He then combined the symbolic and connotative terms into another, the *punctum*. *Studium*, Latin for "hobby," stands for an image analysis role that is a long-term, culturally informed, and carefully considered interpretation of the meaning of a picture. The term referred to "a kind of general, enthusiastic commitment" (p. 26).

From the Latin for *puncture* or *wound*, the *punctum*, however, is a raw "hit in the gut" reaction that one sometimes feels when an image is so powerful it resists immediate interpretation because of, perhaps, its disgusting content. For Barthes (1981), the *punctum* "is that accident which pricks me (but also bruises me, is poignant to me)" and can be an entire image or a detail within a frame. These often shocking pictures can make a person audibly gasp at a first viewing because of their content. They are retained in a person's long-term memory without a filter or a need of verbal interpretation (pp. 27, 43). For Barthes, portrayals that are meant to shock audience members are examples of *punctum*; visual messages meant to educate others form his *studium* concept.

Julia Serano's *Whipping Girl* (2007), a seminal work concerned with transpersons and femininity, illustrates the concept of *punctum*. For Serano, the media usually portray two stereotypical archetypes of transpersons—the deceptive and the pathetic. Deceivers as shown in media productions are usually considered a threat as they successfully pass as women in order to retaliate against men in "an unconscious acknowledgment that both male and heterosexual privilege is threatened by transsexuals" (p. 38). Both of Serano's archetypes fall into Barthes's *punctum* concept—audience members are surprised at the reveal. In the deceivers camp, Serano named the characters Dil (played by Jaye Davidson) in *The Crying Game* (1992), police lieutenant Lois Einhorn (played by Sean Young) in *Ace Ventura: Pet Detective*, the title character in *Myra Breckinridge* (1970) (played by Rachel Welch), as well as transwomen coming out in television episodes of *Jerry Springer* and the British reality show, *There's Something About Miriam*. Because pathetic characters are almost always included as a kind of humorous diversion, they are not considered a threat and include Mark Shubb (played by Harry Shearer) in *The Mighty Wind* (2003) and John Cabell "Bunny" Breckinridge (played by Bill Murray) in *Ed Wood* (1994) (Serano, 2007, pp. 36–40). Such pathetic depictions rely on an audience member aware of the feeble attempt at passing.

The underlying and enduring message inherent in the *studium* and the emotive power of the *punctum* combine through the use of metaphors. It is through the human convention known as the metaphor that meaning and a viewer's experiences are combined. Aristotle wrote in *Rhetoric*, "It is a great thing, indeed, to make proper use of poetic forms. But the greatest thing by far is to be a master of metaphor" (Lakoff & Johnson, 2003, p. 190). The importance of metaphors for human understanding is that they bring the outside in. What is experienced and what is known are shaped and altered by the ways persons describe connections between the outside world and its interpretation in the mind. "Metaphors serve," wrote Kaplan (1990), "as interpretive frameworks for organizing information about the world and making sense of experiences" (p. 38). Lakoff and Johnson (2003) go further.

For them, images are powerful because "no metaphor can ever be compre-hended or even adequately represented independently of its experiential ba-sis" (p. 19). Experience matters.

Rozin, Haidt, and McCauley (2008) wrote that North American psycholo-gists, social workers, and others identify nine experiences related to disgust including "food, body products, animals, sexual behaviors, contact with death or corpses, violations of the exterior envelope of the body (including gore and deformity), poor hygiene, interpersonal contamination (contact with unsavory human beings), and certain moral offenses" (p. 757). As the term literally means *bad taste*, most of the history of research related to disgust involves the contact or consumption of revolting foods. However, there is growing interest in the moral foundations of disgust associated with three of the nine—sexual behaviors, violations of the exterior envelope of the body, and certain moral offenses—as they can be linked to many criticisms of storylines that involve transpersons.

Disgust as an emotional response from a member of the dominant culture can also be exhibited by care professionals who should know better and by some transpersons who should be helped to overcome their repulsion toward their own bodies. As Landau noted (2012), for many older members working in the health fields, "transsexuality was a 'pathological' term used to describe people who cross-dressed and/or modified their bodies through sex reassign-ment surgery" (p. 184). Consequently, medical doctors, psychotherapists, and other professionals often did not receive adequate training to counsel transgender individuals and were "unaware of the therapeutic needs of trans-gendered [*sic*] people." As a result, such clinicians hid their biases and exhib-ited "a tone of cynicism and disgust" (Lev, 2004, p. 19). Peers, of course, also have a tremendous influence. In a survey of 129 students from an afflu-ent suburban New York high school, Fortuna (2007) discovered that "stu-dents were more likely to believe that transgender people are disgusting compared to gay, lesbian, and bisexual people" (p. 37). When therapists and acquaintances feel disgust, it is not surprising that clients and schoolmates can feel the same way about themselves. Califia (1994) attributed self-hatred to such actions as not practicing safe sex and in statements from survey respondents such as "We can't get rid of all that programming that says we are inferior, filthy, disgusting, godless, and pathological" (p. xxv). In her book, *How Sex Changed*, Meyerowitz (2004) wrote that doctors reported that their transmen patients had "a sense of humiliation or 'disgust' as their breasts developed and menstruation began, and some [transwomen] ex-pressed a feeling of hatred or revulsion toward their genitals" (p. 136).

Disgust has also found its way into the legal system. Cram (2012) de-scribed attacks on transpersons by individuals experiencing a "transpanic," an extreme reaction that often leads to a physical confrontation when passing is not an option. Defense attorneys have used disgust as a legal argument to justify violent outbursts that sometimes lead to death. Cram wrote, "Although there may be a cluster of negative emotions such as animus, rage, or anger that motivate an individual to commit a bias crime, defense pleas that rely upon 'deception' or 'panic' attempt to legitimize feelings of disgust toward the person(s) attacked" (p. 418). In such crimes of passion, juries can be manipulated. "The logic of the defense," wrote Cram "rests on mobilizing the collective disgust of potentially sympathetic jurors and public witnesses as a way of exonerating the perpetrator" (p. 420). Of course, disgust as a defense is only as successful as an attorney's talent at choosing sympathetic jurors who are easily disgusted. Nevertheless, disgust may also help explain why flamboyant transgender stereotypes persist in the media—disgust as entertainment—or perhaps more succinctly—disgust as pornography.

The technical term, *qualia*, or revulsion, is thought to be the most critical component of disgust. When subjects are asked to reveal when they ever felt disgusted by moral violations, most of the respondents admitted disgust was connected with "betrayal, hypocrisy, and racism" (Rozin et al., 2008, p. 762). Although repulsed, disgust makes one feel superior to those who for example, "have sexual preferences at odds with the majority" (Rozin et al., 2008, p. 766). One of the reasons producers of television and motion picture programs create stereotypes of transpersons is because viewers who feel disgust for a so-called outlandish character can also be amused by such presentations. "The delicate boundary between disgust and pleasure" is often considered socially acceptable when the experience is not personally threatening. However, on the streets, violent behavior can be the result when disgust toward a transperson is linked with hypocrisy, alienation, contempt, and anger (Rozin et al., 2008, pp. 769).

DISGUST, PORNOGRAPHY, AND VISUAL IMAGES

Even people who have no known acquaintance with a transperson likely hold stereotyped views about transpeople. Where does that knowledge come from? Family, friends, personal experiences, and educational and religious institutions all contribute to what a person believes. However, this chapter is not concerned with those influences. As the most powerful contributors to the formulation of cultural values—negative and positive—the mass media hold a special place in the inculcation of transgender (and almost all other cultural) stereotypes. As McAvan (2011) wrote, "Transsexual and transgendered people have long been a figure of fascination and disgust in our culture, typically being analyzed as pathological in . . . sensationalist fashion in the media" (p. 24). Meyerowitz (2004) agreed with McAvan when she wrote, "In the popular culture, various media frequently cast transsexuals as 'freaks' or 'perverts'" (p. 11).

In an honest article on the Web that described his stereotypical past as a 12-year-old, Jefferson (2011) told of his amusement at seeing the disgust fellow actors exhibited toward transpersons by gagging, vomiting, and telling bad jokes in such films as *Ace Ventura: Pet Detective* (1994), *Naked Gun 33 1/3: The Final Insult* (1994), *Soapdish* (1991), and *The Hangover Part II* (2011). The Internet Movie Database lists about 125 feature films that have a transgender character since the earliest flicker of a celluloid strip moving through a motion picture projector. *Boys Don't Cry* (1999), *Hedwig and the Angry Inch* (2001), and *Dallas Buyers Club* (2013) are notable examples with critics mostly raving about their plots and performances. However, as Nicola Evans's (1998) analysis of *The Crying Game*, with its cultural sleight-of-hand in which the female love interest is revealed at the end as a man provoking disgust, made clear, "Drag in contemporary Hollywood cinema gives us a touch of innovation (cross-dressing) in order to sell us some very bland forms of sexism and racism" (p. 214). Critical viewers must always consider the meaning of the symbolism of iconic images presented on the screen as well as, particularly for this discussion, the level of disgust evoked by the ways transpersons are portrayed. As Lacan famously wrote, "Whatever is refused in the symbolic order, reappears in the real" (Miller, 1993, p. 71). That is, an unperceived perception eventually becomes an uninvited mental irritant.

Disgust is certainly in play as a motivating factor compounded by alienation, contempt, and anger in the murder of Brandon Teena in *Boys Don't Cry*. It is nevertheless difficult for most to understand why anyone would be so disgusted and so enraged as to commit such a crime after it was discovered that a friend hid such a personal secret. While the reason for the behavior of the killers is answered, the tragic consequence of passing unsuccessfully was not the point of the work. As Cooper (2002) noted, the motion picture "has far broader liberatory and societal implications than just contradicting media's traditionally negative stereotypes of sexual minorities [because it depicts] heteronormativity's bigotry toward gender transgression and [condemns] the lack of social or political change that could help eradicate such prejudice" (pp. 57–58). The film therefore transcended the storyline of a specific act of brutality when passing was unsuccessful and made a general statement on violence. It was a noble and honest depiction without resorting to stereotypes that elevated the work to Barthe's *studium* level of impact. Despite all the good intentions expressed by the director and others, it was a plus that Hilary Swank, a ciswoman who was awarded an Oscar for her performance, was shown in the movie as a handsome young man with dark, close-cropped hair, side-angled, diffused lighting that brought out the bone structure on his face that often brightened with an endearing, infectious smile, and a thin physique casually hidden inside an open-collar shirt and blue jeans. His appearance was designed to be a metaphor for innocence and adventure. Part of the success of the movie was that an audience member, whether lesbian, gay, bisexual, transgender, queer, or cisgender could therefore feel sympathetic and be allowed to feel a socially acceptable attraction to a transman character rather than disgust.

Directed, written, and acted by John Cameron Mitchell, *Hedwig and the Angry Inch* is a tale of an East German transwoman singer who falls in love with an American soldier and elects to have surgery to complete her transformation and please the man she loves. However, the operation goes terribly wrong and leaves a one-inch penis lump. Gay actor Neil Patrick Harris, fresh off his performance as a misogynistic cisman in *How I Met Your Mother*, played the title role on Broadway for which he won the best actor in a musical Tony in 2014. The film featured ample examples of show-stopping over-the-top theatrical stereotypes that included rooms full of wigs. There was also lively double entendre salad bar banter from the star such as, "When you think of huge openings, many of you will think of me," an ironic reference given the condition of the maligned inch. With all of Hedwig's challenges, in the end the story was simply about looking for love and living with choices. Since its first performance as a stage musical in 1997, it has inspired and aided many trans-curious persons and has attracted a cult following (Jones, 2006, p. 465) similar to the success of *The Rocky Horror Picture Show* (1975) with Dr. Frank-N-Furter played by Tim Curry. Nevertheless, transgender critics of *Hedwig* have described the musical as disgusting primarily because of its stereotypical storyline. As described by one blogger, the musical features

> a transgender woman with botched SRS [sex reassignment surgery] who appears to be completely insane and who in the end of the production is portrayed as a streetwalker, calls herself a misfit and loser, and appears to be incredibly gender-confused [and] portrayed by a gay man with a questionable history regarding transgender sensitivity. It is disgusting, revolting, and disheartening. (Transas City, 2014)

Although not a transgender movie, one of the main characters in *Dallas Buyers Club* was Rayon, a transwoman played by cisactor Jared Leto who was awarded an Academy Award for his performance. *Time* magazine writer Steve Friess (2014) expressed the outrage many felt at the shrill stereotype that was Rayon:

> What did the writers of *Dallas Buyers Club* and Leto as her portrayer decide to make Rayon? Why, she's a sad-sack, clothes-obsessed, constantly flirting transgender drug addict prostitute, of course. There are no stereotypes about transgender women that Leto's concoction does not tap. She's an exaggerated, trivialized version of how men who pretend to be women—as opposed to those who feel at their core they are women—behave.

About the popular stereotype of Rayon, one scholar wrote, "Representation is important. And when a flawed version of a community of people wins a prestigious award, it serves as a gateway for flawed understanding and perceptions of that community to arise and persist" (Reddy, 2014, p. 4). Compared with Brandon in *Boys Don't Cry*, Rayon became more obviously an object of pornographic entertainment and an unfortunate model for future characterizations. As Reddy noted, *Boys*:

> treats Brandon as not only a character, but a human in his own right, someone that despite his inherent "otherness" is equal to the surrounding characters. *Boys Don't Cry* trusts Brandon and tries to understand him, an integral component of representation and one that is completely absent Rayon. (p. 41)

In addition to movies, television relies upon visual depictions of transgender people that evoke disgust. Talk and reality shows on television are easy targets as their overt purpose is almost always to sensationalize, trivialize, and consumerize. Maury Povich, the discredited journalist turned DNA-obsessed father-finder on many of his confrontational daytime programs, is a master of Barthe's *punctum*. He is especially infamous in the lesbian, gay, bisexual, transgender, and queer (LGBTQ) community for his "Man or Woman?" episodes in which he surprised his audience members by revealing the sex assigned at birth of his studio guests who were dressed in bathing suits or lingerie. The airings were exploitive and mean-spirited (Fagerberg, 2013).

Special condemnation, however, is reserved for the television personality RuPaul Andre Charles of Atlanta. On his reality show modestly named *Ru-Paul's Drag Race*, he sponsored a competition named "Female or Shemale" in which contestants were asked whether someone pictured was "a biological woman or a psychological woman." Rooted in transgender pornography and drag queen culture, "shemale" is, according to GLAAD, defamatory and "serves to dehumanize transgender people and should not be used" (Molloy, 2014).

In contrast, programs available to watch through Web sites on computer monitors, tablets, and smart phones seem to show fewer visual stereotypes than their traditional media partners because they are produced by entities run by executives who can afford to take chances. The pressures are not as high to bring in large numbers of viewers. United Kingdom's Sky Atlantic with show runner Paul Abbott produced only six episodes of *Hit or Miss*, available on the movie rental company Netflix (n.d.). The show featured the ciswoman Chloë Sevigny as an Irish transwoman assassin-for-hire, Mia. The plot became more interesting after she learned of a son she never knew existed and met her extended family with a multitude of challenges. The production was noteworthy for its high quality acting, cinematic visual elements, and a full-frontal nude shower scene in the first episode revealing that Mia had a penis. The shot is acted so casually that Barthes's *punctum* is never evoked. The sensitive portrayal of a hardened killer coping with passing as a woman and softened by an inherited family was a credit to the genre.

THE IMPACT OF DISGUST, PORNOGRAPHY, AND VISUAL STEREOTYPES

Transgender stereotypes portrayed visually invite negative interpretations by those who have no independent personal experiences for a contrary viewpoint. Consequently, these portrayals invite the inference that all transpersons behave in the same way. The *punctum* hits the viewer in the gut before the *studium* can soften the emotion in the mind. Media images of transgender people often rely on prurient, pornographic objectification—a *punctum* approach—or guide a viewer toward a more reasoned reaction—a *studium* perspective—mainly through the relative success or failure of an individual's efforts at visually passing. Positive examples are more *studium* than *punctum*—they make viewers think more than they shock. The difference between visual messages that stereotype and are thus vilified by scholars and programs that are admired for the stories they tell has to do with the ways images are analyzed by the audience. They evoke a higher level of consideration by their reliance on symbolism rather than literal portrayals. Finally, they stimulate long-term memories by providing metaphors that help link a spectator with the character's story. The impersonal becomes personal as objective and casual viewing becomes subjective and engaged learning.

Disgust as an emotional construct that includes hatred is important to consider as it can be linked to the commodification of violence against transpersons as entertainment, a form of visual pornography. Pornography can be understood as any extreme expression of speech, anger, or physical conflict. Any producer of visual messages who shows persons as objects in scenarios of degradation, injury, torture, fifth, or inferiority in a context that makes these conditions voyeuristic is a pornographer. When aggression toward transpersons is shown in mass media presentations for entertainment purposes, the result can be considered a form of pornography. In *Regarding the Pain of Others*, Sontag (2003) wrote, "All images that display the violation of an attractive body are, to a certain degree, pornographic" (p. 85). Visual portrayals that sensationalize transpersons to a level of disgust for audience members would qualify under Sontag's rubric.

FUTURE RESEARCH TOPICS FOR VISUAL COMMUNICATION

Looking forward, I contend that future research at the intersection of transgender studies and visual communication would benefit from the implementation of six perspectives for analysis—personal, historical, technical, ethical, cultural, and critical. These lenses for analysis will enable future researchers to analyze past and contemporary transgender representations as well as audience reactions pertaining to disgust and indifference (Lester, 2014, pp. 128–146).

As an initial, subjective opinion, the personal perspective should be employed for studies that determine the before-and-after views of subjects from diverse demographic backgrounds after viewing programs that feature transgender storylines—exploitive, stereotypical, and illustrative. The research should attempt to discover the personal reasons disgust is often tied to dramatic and comical transgender productions.

The historical perspective approach should include in-depth biographies written by researchers that delve deeply into the psyche of producers and actors responsible for transgender presentations. Such work may uncover whether any historical trends have common bonds that need to be broken or strengthen by contemporary creators. Researchers should also conduct content analyses, framing, and gatekeeping studies that reveal the trends in transgender visual stereotypes particularly related to the practice of passing and the concept of disgust as displayed in newspapers, magazines, and advertisements for print and screen media.

As the technical perspective concentrates on the decisions made to create works, future researchers should study production values associated with transgender motion pictures and television shows and discern how technical factors such as hairstyles, makeup, clothing, mannerisms, dialog, lighting, settings, camera angles, and so on affect viewer perceptions of passing while contributing or ameliorating disgust reactions.

Evaluating the choices made by producers is part of the ethical perspective. The role-related responsibility of a maker of visual materials related to the topic of transgender culture should be to educate, rather than to simply entertain, viewers. If such a goal is attempted, then that creator is acting ethically as long as any harm sensed by viewers can be justified. Academics should be invited to oversee the production of programs to make sure fascination with a storyline is not contingent on disgust and revulsion.

The cultural perspective concentrates on the symbolic messages used to tell stories. The popular concept of pornography, with disgust as its chief component, should be expanded to include a critique of non-traditional forms of objectification and abuse as featured by many transgender storylines.

Finally, the critical perspective is employed to take a long-term, thoughtful, and objective viewpoint of the transgender genre as shown by visual presentations. For example, British actor and comedian Eddie Izzard was interviewed on NPR ostensibly for his ability to perform his stand-up act in English, French, Spanish, or Arabic, depending on the preference of his audience. Inevitably the conversation turned to his more famous proclivity of dressing as a woman with (usually) a conservative dress, makeup, and heels. Sounding a bit exhausted and perhaps disappointed by the question of why he dons this visual motif, Izzard replied with an answer that sums up the future of LGBTQ stereotypes:

> If you think about it, gays and lesbians have now got more boring than it was in the '50s, and ever in history before that. So if you come in and say, I am a plumber, I happen to be gay, you go, OK, well, you any good at plumbing? Yeah, I'm pretty good at plumbing. Fine, I don't really care if you're gay or straight or whatever, the plumbing thing is the main thing I hired you for. And that's what it's got to get to, you know? That's where transgender has to get to. (NPR Staff, 2014)

CONCLUSION

Rubin (2006) lamented the often stated and unnecessary divisions that are invariably created when language is used to divide rather than to unite persons. She wrote,

> The fact that categories invariably leak and can never contain all relevant "existing things" does not render them useless, only limited. . . . Instead of fighting for immaculate classifications and impenetrable boundaries, let us strive to maintain a community that understands diversity as a gift, sees anomalies as precious, and treats all basic principles with a hefty dose of skepticism. (p. 479)

When critical evaluations of transgender productions are accomplished by thoughtful writers and researchers whether from academia or popular culture, presentations should be created of transpersons with little regard to birth physicality, with words and images that do not stereotype, and with storylines, actors, and production decisions that promote positive values. It is then possible for the goal of indifference to be realized. In a world where no one questions the gender of any other person is a world where a plumber is judged by the quality of the work rather than the size of her hands.

Chapter Ten

Social Media

Fleshy Metamorphosis: Temporal Pedagogies of Transsexual Counterpublics

Joshua Trey Barnett

On April 2, 2008, Joshua Riverdale took his first shot of testosterone.[1] Excited to have access to the chemicals that would help him transform his body, Riverdale chronicled the experience on his blog, *Gender Outlaw*: "I didn't really feel anything with the injection," he wrote, "just a very small pin prick. Immediately, however, I felt something different coursing through my system, like an adrenaline rush after I get stung by a wasp. I also noticed a different taste in my mouth within a few minutes" (Riverdale, 2008b). Though the immediate side effects may seem anticlimactic, the first dose of hormones is generally a momentous occasion for transsexuals. As one popular online transitioning guide put it, "Testosterone HRT [hormone replacement therapy] is perhaps the largest physical step between passing as male versus appearing female" ("Testosterone," n.d.). Marking the occasion, Riverdale blogged more details on how he spent the rest of his day, which included a hike with his pets and the planting of a commemorative tree, which, he noted, his girlfriend dubbed the "T-Tree." Regular readers of *Gender Outlaw* would know that Riverdale had been working up to this moment since previous posts had tracked his first talk with his family physician about top surgery (Riverdale, 2007a) and even detailed accounts of meetings with his therapist (Riverdale, 2007b). For Riverdale, the blog is a scene for sharing information about his own experiences of transitioning so that others might benefit.

The day before he took his first shot of testosterone, Riverdale posted five photographs of his body prior to beginning the HRT regimen. Each photograph shows Riverdale differently posed, showing off certain parts of his body: one from the shoulders up, front and back shots of Riverdale flexing his arm muscles, a headless photo of his torso (with a black line concealing his breasts), and a final image of his lower half, covered in part by underwear. Though it is unclear whether Riverdale intended to take more photos at the time, over the next six years he amassed a large collection of images of his body in various states of transition. In fact, between April 1, 2008, and April 29, 2013, Riverdale uploaded 115 photographs of himself to *Gender Outlaw*, effectively creating a continuous visual archive of a body in-the-making (Riverdale, n.d.). In the beginning, Riverdale posted a photo set every month, but as time went on the postings became less and less frequent, likely because noticeable visible changes to his body also became less frequent. Each of the subsequent photographs, however, follows the pattern marked out in the first set, showing a similarly posed Riverdale in five different positions. The visual archive, which Riverdale titled "My Physical Evolution on Testosterone," documents the visible effects of both testosterone injections and surgeries on a body born with female sexual characteristics.

As the photographic sequence progresses through time, noticeable changes in Riverdale's body morphology take shape and become visible to viewers. From the minute to the magnificent, visible changes can be traced from photo set to photo set as viewers scroll down the Web page and magnify individual photographs. For instance, from month six to month seven Riverdale's facial hair begins to fill in and a light moustache covers his upper lip. Over the course of that same month, Riverdale's acne flares up into dozens of red spots dotting his upper back and shoulders, a tell-tell sign of testosterone HRT in female-to-male (FTM) transsexuals. Unappealing as it may be to some, acne is one way that the body signals changes—likely a welcome sign for those on testosterone HRT. In a lengthy blog post dated June 18, 2008, for instance, Riverdale offered readers an account of his experiences with testosterone-related acne along with a litany of treatment suggestions (2008c). In month seven, even the hair on Riverdale's upper legs and thighs seems to have filled in significantly. The documentary style of Riverdale's photographic sequence, which attempts to present the body in precisely the same way over time, not only enables but also invites viewers to watch his bodily transformation take shape.

Although these are only the most obvious visible changes to Riverdale's appearance, my brief reading of them above demonstrates the kind of visual spectatorship that I explore in the following pages. The photographic sequence, I contend, invites viewers to trace bodily changes, enacting what I call a *temporal pedagogy*, or modeling a way of seeing and thinking about the human body as a site of change and transformation across time. Unlike "emergence" narratives, exemplified by sensational before-and-after photographs of remarkably different transsexual bodies, Riverdale fittingly likens his transition to an "evolution" in which the body develops and is cultivated over long periods of time. Thus, alongside other ways of conceptualizing the body, Riverdale's photographic sequence encourages viewers to understand the body not as a stable, immutable entity but rather as a site of what Donna Haraway (2008) has called "becoming with," a complex process of constituting the body in relation with others (human, non-human, chemicals, etc.). By generating a space for understanding the body differently, Riverdale's photographic sequence also makes room for a transsexual counterpublic in which a version of what Judith Halberstam (2005) has called "queer time" can flourish. Queer time, for Halberstam, is in part "about the potentiality of a life unscripted by the conventions of family, inheritance, and child rearing," and, as I argue throughout this chapter, the conventions of sexed and gendered bodies (2005, p. 2).

Within the field of rhetorical studies, scholars have begun to trace the role of the visual in, for instance, discourses of transgender pregnancy (Landau, 2012) and transgender citizenships (Cram, 2012). In this essay, I extend these efforts by tracing the visual rhetorical history of Riverdale's photographic sequence along three lines: production, reproduction, and circulation. Following Cara Finnegan's model of performing rhetorical histories of the visual, this chapter tracks "the ways in which images become inventional resources in the public sphere" (2008, p. 198). For Finnegan, rhetorical histories of the visual enable us as critics to understand how certain photographs become useful, persuasive even, within a given social, political, and historical context. Moreover, the visual becomes a way of understanding those various contexts and of making sense of why and how particular ideas and concepts take hold. Rather than offering a rhetorical history of an individual or iconic image of the transsexual body, I locate the rhetorical significance of Riverdale's project in its cumulative presentation over several years. Accordingly, I begin with questions of production by exploring the conditions under which Riverdale's photographic sequence emerged. Then I turn to issues of reproduction as they relate to digital photography, blogging aesthetics, and the online transsexual community. Finally, I attend to concerns about circulation, or how the photographs reach audiences. In this section I most fully develop my notion of temporal pedagogies by analyzing how viewers encounter Riverdale's photographic sequence.

VISUALIZING TRANS BODIES IN THE BLOGOSPHERE

Why did Riverdale's photographic sequence emerge in this way and at that time? What cultural conditions, technological apparatuses, and political motivations would lead a young FTM transsexual to photograph himself transforming over time? In other words, what were the conditions under which Riverdale produced this set of self-portraits? As Finnegan noted, "Production must be accounted for if we are to know where images come from (literally) and why they appear in the spaces where we find them" (2008, p. 200). The goal of asking such questions is to trace the amalgamation of social, political, and technological conditions that converge to make a moment "ripe" for production of a particular kind. In the case of Riverdale's photographic sequence, self-portraiture must be understood within a long line of medicalized and documentary photography aimed at providing evidence of particular bodily morphologies.

Portraiture, and specifically photographic portraiture, has played an important role in visualizing medicalized bodies. This is, at least in part, because "Reference … is the founding order of Photography" (Barthes, 1981, p. 77). In other words, photography has provided to medical and scientific discourses a degree of evidence needed to substantiate claims about the body. As Ludmilla Jordanova noted in an introduction to *Medical Humanities*, "Portraits are ubiquitous in medicine" (2013, p. 2). For instance, the early heliotherapist Auguste Rollier used multiple photographs of his patients to demonstrate the healing powers of the sun. As Tania Woloshyn noted of Rollier's images, "these photographs were imperative as records of the patients' physical transformation, from diseased and pallid to dark, healed bodies" (2013, p. 39). Photographs of patients' bodies, which began sickly and gradually improved in health, gave credence not only to Rollier's practices of solar therapy but also to the institution of medical practice more generally. At other times, as both Finnegan (2005) and Rachel Hall (2009) noted, portraits were used to extend racist and xenophobic attitudes in practices like phrenology. Similar photographic practices would be employed throughout the history of medicine, but perhaps in recent years the most documented morphological changes have been produced by plastic surgeons hoping to offer evidence of their work (Spear & Hagan, 2008). Though the connections between photography and medicine are much more complex than this brief review can account for, suffice it to say that the two practices are routinely intertwined in ways both banal and extraordinary.

While artists have produced images of trans or gender-ambiguous bodies for centuries (for one early case study, see Taylor, 2004), photographs of the transsexual body have only recently proliferated within certain circles, the most obvious of which are online trans communities. For the Halberstam of *In a Queer Time and Place*, "when it comes time to picture the transgender body in the flesh, it nearly always emerges as a transsexual body" (2005, p. 97). This is problematic in her view since, as she put it, "the transgender body is not reducible to the transsexual body, and it retains the marks of its own ambiguity and ambivalence" (Halberstam, 2005, p. 97). Halberstam's claims referred to work by transsexual artists like Loren Cameron (1996) and

Del LaGrace Volcano (2000), both of whom routinely invoked something of an "emergence" narrative in which the transsexual body is figured in striking before-and-after comparisons or posed in ways that heighten masculine or feminine aesthetics. Cameron's (1996) *Body Alchemy: Transsexual Portraits*, for example, was among the very first sets of transsexual portraits to circulate publicly,[2] predating Riverdale's photographic sequence by more than 10 years. In it, Cameron reproduced several portraits of himself and other FTM transsexuals. Before starting testosterone HRT, Riverdale (2008a) wrote a review of *Body Alchemy*, calling the images "beautiful" and "evocative."

While Riverdale's photographic sequence certainly builds on the burgeoning visual archive detailed above, perhaps even taking some inspiration from Cameron's work, it also diverges in important ways from the emergence narrative by harkening back and extending the more medicalized, documentary style of presentation engaged by physicians and scientists. At the end of Riverdale's photographic sequence, he noted that his documentary project was inspired by a similar Web site on which an FTM transsexual posted photographs of himself while transitioning (see Ethan, n.d.). The Web site to which he referred includes dozens of close-up photographs of Ethan's body as it changed over the course of several years on testosterone HRT. Ethan's photographic sequence, which began in 2004, is divided into six categories (head, arms, legs, stomach, facial hair, and acne) and includes several photos in each category at various integrals over the span of five-and-a-half years. At the time, Ethan's page was one of only a very few publicly circulating digital archives of transsexual photographs, so it is not surprising that Riverdale would take inspiration from the presentational style developed there. Alongside the before-and-after shots so prevalent in both Cameron and LaGrace Volcano's work, both Ethan and Riverdale offer an evolutionary aesthetic that imagines the body in processual terms.

Notably, the production of this evolutionary aesthetic was in some significant sense related to the proliferation of digital cameras and blogging technologies. By the time Riverdale began his photographic sequence, not only had digital cameras become pervasive but some 40 percent of users also shared their photographs online (Schurman, 2009). Whereas before the advent and proliferation of digital cameras personal photographs were just that—mostly personal and private—afterwards these images were increasingly likely to be shared far and wide.

At about the same time, the blogosphere was taking off as an important scene of cultural and countercultural practice, growing from a single venue to include an entire community of independent writers (Siles, 2012). Online spaces such as blogs and social media sites have played a particularly important role for transsexuals and others who experience any number of oppressions, providing scenes of community making and information sharing that often are not otherwise available (Shapiro, 2003; see also Spencer & Barnett, 2013). A Transgender Law Center guide even called the Internet a "vibrant virtual community for transgender people" (Transgender Law Center, 2012, p. 28), and recent social science research demonstrates that many transgender people find blogging an empowering practice (Lin, 2006; Mitra & Gajjala, 2008).

CONJURING TRANSSEXUAL COUNTERPUBLICS

Once they have been produced, to what ends are digital photographic sequences like Riverdale's put? How are they mobilized within complex rhetorical situations? What positions, literally and figuratively, do these photographs occupy, and what do those positions tell us about the process being visualized? How does this position change how we relate to the images? To put these questions in Finnegan's terms, what are the stakes and rhetorical effects of reproducing Riverdale's photographic sequence online? "We need to understand," she urged, "not only where images 'come from,' but also what they are made to do in the contexts in which we discover them" (Finnegan, 2008, p. 204). The question of reproduction thus goads the rhetorical scholar to consider things like the medium on or in which images are published, the way one image relates to another, and the correspondence between text and images. Focusing on these issues, Finnegan noted, means acknowledging "that images are hybrid entities, that we do not encounter them in isolation, and that their arrangement (at least in the spaces of print culture) is always the result of particular editorial choices and framing of ideas" (2008, p. 200). What I argue here, through an analysis of how Riverdale reproduced his digital images, is that the online photographic sequence itself constitutes a *transsexual counterpublic* in which certain ideas about the body are able to emerge and flourish.

Riverdale's photographic sequence invites viewers to trace bodily changes across time by presenting the photographs in chronological order, with the oldest photos at the top of the page and the most recent ones toward the bottom. On an individual page of *Gender Outlaw*, titled "My Physical Evolution on Testosterone," Riverdale routinely uploads five photographs of his body, each one posed so that the viewer can take stock of the bodily changes that have occurred, say, on his legs and back. The photographs, in thumbnail form, are arranged according to a grid in which the five images taken on a certain day run across the page parallel to one another (see Figure 10.1). Each set of photographs, taken on a different day, is then positioned below the prior set such that viewers can trace changes to the individual body parts. When viewers scroll down the photographic sequence, they also advance through time. But, of course, viewers are not limited to scrolling forward through time; they can also return to the top of the page, go back as it were, and click on any of the photos to magnify them. At several intervals in the timeline, Riverdale has posted videos and time-lapse image sequences to supplement the photo sequence. These videos offer additional archival footage of Riverdale from before he began testosterone, including images culled from childhood photo albums and candid shots of Riverdale while on HRT. Though the videos are not my primary concern here, they do supplement viewers' experiences with the photographic sequence by opening up the archive to account for other parts of Riverdale's life.

More specifically, the sizing and arrangement of the individual photographs in the sequence draws on and exemplifies a certain documentary or scientific approach to the human body as a site of transformation. The small thumbnails are arranged side-by-side and one-above-the-other, a type of display that calls attention to the temporal relationship between each photograph by suggesting that one leads to another. That every subsequent shot builds on the compositional style of the one before it also helps to substantiate the photographic sequence's claim that it represents a chronological string of events.[3] As opposed to showing larger versions of each photograph, which would have enabled viewers to see more detail without magnifying an image, Riverdale placed the photos on the Web page in a way that allows viewers to see multiple sets at a time. In fact, viewers cannot encounter any one of the sets on their own; they must always first see them as relational. The smallness thus invites viewers to look at the photographs across time, as a cumulative archive of how the body-in-transition transforms with the continuous use of testosterone. As viewers scroll down through the sequence, then, they understand that they are tracing one particular body as it transforms. Thus,

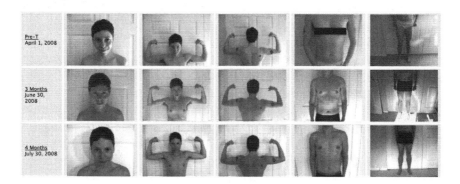

Figure 10.1. Screenshot of Joshua Riverdale's photographic sequence, "My Physical Evolution on Testosterone." Reproduced here with the permission of Riverdale. Access the interactive version at http://genderoutlaw.wordpress .com/evolution/.

the most recent photographs, which show a burly, muscular Riverdale, seem to be a sensible extension of those earlier images of a small-framed, beardless, boyish-looking figure. Rather than heightening the stark differences involved in transsexual transitions, as so many before-and-after shots do, the processual style of Riverdale's sequence actually makes sense of how a body becomes otherwise.

In addition to the relationship between individual photographs, text also plays an important role in how viewers experience Riverdale's photographic sequence. Scholars of visual rhetoric have long acknowledged that text and image cannot be divorced from one another, and that we need to study both in order to better understand each one (Mitchell, 1994; Olson, Finnegan, & Hope, 2008). Riverdale's photographic sequence is supplemented by three different textual elements. First, there is the title that frames and thematizes the photographs: "My Physical Evolution on Testosterone." Second, there are the time markers that are positioned to the left of each chronological set of photographs. Each one includes both a general marker of time (e.g., "3 Months") as well as the particular date on which the set was taken (e.g., "June 30, 2008"). Both the title and the time markers foreground the temporal dimensions of Riverdale's photographs by calling attention to the fact that this archive is a cumulative, longitudinal project. The chronological markers also invite viewers to do comparative interpretation across dates, to look for ways Riverdale's body has transformed. Third, there are the comments that both Riverdale and his followers post at the bottom of the page. Some 47 comments had been posted at the time this chapter was written, and that number continues to grow as more viewers post their own comments. Though a few of the comments border on patronizing (one poster, a self-described "predominately straight female," longwindedly calls Riverdale "brave" and "inspiring"), the majority of comments either expressed gratitude for the photographic sequence or raised specific questions that Riverdale might be able to answer. For instance, one commenter said, simply, "I appreciate the work you've put into documenting your story. Sharing it with us is a gift" (see Riverdale, n.d.). Another asked about Riverdale's exercise regimen, to which Riverdale responded with a detailed list of physical activities he engaged in after he began testosterone HRT. Taken together, the textual components that accompany the photographic sequence both guide the viewer's interpretation and open up a space for engagement with the images themselves.

Once reproduced in this way, Riverdale's photographic sequence conjures an audience made up of strangers, what Michael Warner (2002) called a *public*. For Warner, all texts have publics; indeed, even this chapter (and this book) has a public. According to Warner, publics are self-organized relations among strangers who come together around some personal or impersonal text, which has itself been reflexively circulated in a particular temporal context. All it takes for a text to conjure a public is attention, that is, for someone to pay attention to the text. Importantly, publics are scenes of rhetorical invention, or what Warner called "poetic world making" (pp. 114–116).

Most publics are organized in ways that speak to dominant, white, masculine, patriarchal, heteronormative, and cisgender understandings of the world. However, some publics, like Riverdale's photographic sequence, are organized in ways that run counter to those dominant logics. Warner called these *counterpublics*. Counterpublics, he argued, "mark themselves off from any general or dominant public" and are composed of strangers who "are understood not merely to be a subset of the public but constituted through a conflictual relation to the dominant public" (2002, pp. 117–118). Like other forms of gay and queer literature, *Gender Outlaw* can presume that its readers will make up a subordinated class and that certain idioms and styles need not be explained or tempered for palatability. Put another way, Riverdale's photographic sequence addresses already subordinated social actors and invites them to resist the pull of dominant bodily logics, which value stability over change, legibility over confusion.

The fact that Riverdale's photographic sequence runs counter to such dominant logics can be discerned in the mode of reproduction outlined above. Extending the temporal horizon of transsexuality beyond mere categories like "before" and "after," a point discussed at length in the following section, Riverdale's photographic sequence challenges dominant logics of time and embodiment (Halberstam, 2005) by refusing to make transsexuality legible as a corporeal product that can once and for all be stabilized, disciplined, and read. Indeed, counterpublics are "defined by their tension with a larger public" in which "exchanges remain distinct from authority and can have a critical relation to power" (Warner, 2002, p. 56). In dominant publics, stability and legibility are routinely demanded of bodies, such that individuals can be "read" as either male or female, but within a transsexual counterpublic ideas of mutability and transformation, along with practices of bodily poesis and representation, are able to surface as legitimate areas of conversation, spectatorship, and imagination. Ideas like mutability and transformation are culled from otherwise stagnant discourses of the body through particular kinds of reproduction. In the case of Riverdale's photographic sequence, the documentary style and arrangement of images invites viewers to imagine the body outside of dominant temporal logics, to see the body as a site of change, and to engage with strangers in meaningful dialogue about what it means to inhabit such a body.

Although it is true that most anyone with a computer and an Internet connection could view Riverdale's photographic sequence, it should be clear that his visual archive does not then constitute another dominant public. Not only are Riverdale's photos reproduced on a Web site that appeals to a subordinated group of people whose view of the human body often runs counter to dominant logics, but the very mode of reproduction itself challenges those logics and understandings of the body. For sex and gender to maintain their hegemonic role in society, they must remain stable and legible. Riverdale's photographic sequence unhinges both sex and gender by presenting a series of photos that chronologically undoes dominant understandings of the body. As photo set gives way to photo set, viewers are invited to imagine the body as a scene of becoming in relation to chemicals and surgeries, neither of which are necessary for the basic vitality of the human body. The rhetorical force of such an undoing is not that it makes transsexuality palatable or amenable to dominant, cisgender publics, but that it confronts them, resists them, and refuses to be usurped by them.

TEMPORAL PEDAGOGIES

What happens when photographic sequences of the transsexual body-in-transition circulate online? What are the social, political, ontological, and epistemological consequences of showing the body-in-transition within transsexual counterpublics? Who and what benefit, and who and what lose, when such images become accessible, searchable, downloadable, and sharable? What new ways of seeing, and thus acting, are reflected and deflected by photographic sequences like Riverdale's? To answer these questions, a rhetorical analysis of circulation is helpful. For Finnegan, an analysis of circulation is integral if one is to understand how photographs function rhetorically: "Circulation must be accounted for" because "it is the fundamental property of photography" (Finnegan, 2008, p. 200). Moreover, to analyze circulation means that "we attend to the feature [photograph] in terms of the way it fits into broader social, political, and institutional discourses" about the body in general and the transsexual body in particular (Finnegan, 2008, p. 208). In the case of Riverdale, I suggest that his photographic sequence intervenes in and provides material support for discourses of the mutable, trans body. Within these discourses, the photographic sequence puts forth what I am calling a *temporal pedagogy* of the body.

I employ the term *temporal pedagogy* to signal the way in which Riverdale's photographic sequence instructs viewers to see and understand the (transsexual) body as a site of fleshy metamorphosis, of what Haraway (2008) called "becoming with." To suggest that Riverdale's photographs are pedagogic is merely to repeat an oft-stated axiom of rhetorical theory and criticism: namely, that communication offers us ways of approaching the world around us. Or, as Kenneth Burke put it, that communication and language offer us "equipment for living" (1973, p. 304). Similar theses have taken on particular significance within the narrower field of visual rhetorical studies, which has attended broadly to how visual artifacts help us make sense of and act within the world (see e.g., Cram, 2012; DeLuca, 1999; Finnegan, 2003, 2005; Hariman & Lucaites, 2001, 2003, 2007a, 2007b; Harold & DeLuca, 2005; Johnson, 2007; Landau, 2009, 2012; Peeples, 2013; Thornton, 2013). Publicly circulating photographs are constitutive, or at least suggestive, of certain worldviews and behaviors. Since Riverdale's photographic sequence circulates within a transsexual counterpublic, it makes particular attitudes toward the body available while curtailing others.

To suggest that Riverdale's photographic sequence offers viewers a way of seeing and understanding the transsexual body as a fleshy site of "becoming with" is to argue that it works against dominant logics of the body as an immutable, bounded entity. Namely, Riverdale's photographic sequence challenges hegemonic notions of embodiment, stability, and time as they relate specifically to questions of medicalized and chemical interventions. Essentialist attitudes toward gender, for instance, maintain that "man" and "woman" are natural, inevitable social categories directly linked to an individual's sexual characteristics (i.e., whether they have a penis or vagina). Susan Stryker critiqued this attitude in her play, *Rage Across the Disciplines*, in 1993: "The transsexual body is an unnatural body. It is the product of medical science. It is a technological construction. It is flesh torn apart and sewn together again in a shape other than that in which it was born" (1994, p. 238). Whereas Stryker spoke somewhat ironically, the perspective she characterized is nonetheless pervasive. Such a perspective, perhaps rooted in an understanding of the body as sacred, condemns the "unnatural" intervention of medicine, the "technological construction" as opposed to the natural growth and change of the body, and the degree to which morphological transformations are at the forefront of transsexual embodiment.

Embracing the instability and mutability of the transsexual body-in-transition, Riverdale's photographic sequence invites viewers to imagine this body as a scene of fleshy metamorphosis on and in which transformation occurs. For Haraway, "the body is always in-the-making; it is always a vital entanglement of heterogeneous scales, times, and kinds of being webbed into fleshy presence, always a becoming, always constituted in relating" (2008, p. 163). This "entanglement" is one of multiple bodies together, "relating," and becoming differently. In his photographic sequence, Riverdale visualizes the transsexual body as a scene of evolution, that is, as a scene of bodily change and transformation that is "webbed into fleshy presence" through a complex array of chemical relations, surgical interventions, and physiological developments. As viewers scroll through the sequence, what they encounter is a processual body slowly transforming, slowly manifesting differently. This metamorphosis is not merely representational, but also fleshy, a point that the photographic sequence evinces through its referentiality. The changes are sometimes easily recognizable in the photos, such as when a tuft of hair on

Riverdale's upper lip appears between months six and seven, or when his back begins to broaden and his muscles swell up in the first two years of testosterone HRT. Other transformations are less perceptible in any one set of images and instead become recognizable only when viewers comparatively work their way through the photographic sequence. Unlike its counterpart, the emergence narrative, Riverdale's evolutionary sequence encourages viewers to look at the body not for drastic developments but rather for minute, slow changes that occur on and in the body. For transsexual viewers, this temporal pedagogy not only resists dominant body logics but also provides a way of imagining their own bodies transforming. Whereas before-and-after photographs foreground the dramatic, Riverdale's photographic sequence emphasizes slow change over time.

The temporal pedagogy of Riverdale's photographic sequence thus also refuses the legibility of before-and-after images, which tend to suggest that a transition *happened* (in the past tense) and that a new identity, a new body, has *emerged*. In its place, the photographic sequence proposes an understanding of the body in which process is foregrounded, in which flesh continually gives way to something new. Indeed, Riverdale's "Evolution" depicts transformation as it unfolds, as it manifests on a particular body. With each new photo set, viewers encounter another iteration of Riverdale's morphological journey. But this cumulative archive builds over time not in order to settle or finalize Riverdale's aesthetic appearance, as so many visualizations of the transsexual body seek to do, but rather to call attention to its continual transformation. In *Cruising Utopia*, the late queer theorist José Esteban Muñoz generated a similar attitude toward queerness, arguing that queerness is always on the horizon, just out of reach, "not yet here" (2009, p. 1). For Muñoz, queerness is a destination, a different time and place. In a similar fashion, Riverdale's photographic sequence figures gender as a horizontal phenomenon, always constituted in a kind of reaching forward and looking back. Viewers can only understand the present, however it happens to be presented in the most up-to-date set of photographs, by looking back. And yet, what lies ahead is precisely unclear. There is always the potential that Riverdale will upload another set of photographs that reaffirm or complicate the last. Thus figured, the body is always indeterminate, always becoming.

Against the backdrop of supposedly stable, immutable bodies, whose sex and gender presentation remain constant throughout life, Riverdale's photographic sequence offers another way of seeing and thinking about the body. As Warner noted, a public is always the scene of poetic world making. For counterpublics, this world making project seeks to subvert or undermine dominant logics, to be "transformative, not replicative merely" (Warner, 2002, p. 122). Riverdale's temporal pedagogy is a certain kind of training, to be sure, but it might be one in which "failure" to reproduce legibility (or, at the very least, a failure to settle things once and for all) is a central and defining practice (see Halberstam, 2011). Visualized and imagined otherwise, the transsexual body can be instructive more generally insofar as all bodies, regardless of one's choice to seek hormonal or surgical interventions, are scenes of becoming. This lesson was important when Riverdale began his photographic sequence, and it remains important today.

The political import of Riverdale's temporal pedagogy is in some significant sense also maintained by his unwillingness to let the photographic sequence circulate broadly. Indeed, this is another reason his photographic sequence constitutes a counterpublic despite its availability online. Although he routinely receives requests for reproducing some or all of the photographs, during a personal conversation he revealed that he rarely allows others to circulate his images: "I turn down most requests, but not all," he said. "It just depends on context." Within the context of his blog, the photographic sequence is able to offer its temporal pedagogy precisely because the images are presented together. Outside this context, the photographic sequence is less likely to provoke the kind of imagination I have outlined above. In other words, in order to retain its rhetorical force the photographic sequence needs *not* to circulate widely within dominant publics but to remain within the context of the transsexual counterpublic it produced in the first place. It is within this space, already constituted as counter to dominant logics, that the photographic sequence can offer up its radical understanding of the body as a scene of fleshy metamorphosis.

CONCLUSION

Drawing on Riverdale's photographic sequence, in this chapter I have traced out a rhetorical history of one way of visualizing the transsexual body as a site of fleshy metamorphosis. In doing so, I have mapped, as Finnegan put it, "the ways in which images become inventional resources in the public sphere" (2008, p. 198). By generating a *transsexual counterpublic*, Riverdale's photographic sequence posits a *temporal pedagogy* that invites viewers to see and understand the human body as a scene of becoming. Working against dominant logics of cisgender embodiment and temporality, Riverdale's temporal pedagogy refuses the immutable, stable body in favor of a richly transformative, processual body. This pedagogy is predicated, at least in part, on the social, political, historical, and technological contexts within which it emerged. Indeed, the proliferation of digital cameras, the blogosphere, and trans visibility has generated a space in which Riverdale's temporal pedagogy can flourish online—and perhaps be lived most fully by other bodies.

But, like Riverdale's photographs, this essay is only one in a series of ongoing, cumulative postulations and provocations toward further inquiry. A

number of areas warrant additional intellectual labor. For starters, communication scholars should investigate the broad array of visual documentaries of
transitions now prevalent online. Dozens of self-made YouTube videos, for
example, visually chart hormonal transitions (Riverdale's [2009] alone has
garnered more than one million views). The nuances of that genre, which
produce a different kind of visual encounter, merit further study. Moreover,
as trans visibility continues to increase within the public sphere, modes of
self-representation should be compared to, and judged against, popular forms
of representation. As I have suggested in this essay, it is precisely because
Riverdale's photographic sequence appears within a transsexual counterpublic that it maintains its ability to posit a radical understanding of the body as a
scene of fleshy metamorphosis. It is unclear whether such a rhetorical effect
could be accomplished within dominant publics, but this possibility ought to
be explored since it could transform how we all think of the human body.

In addition to probing this topical area, scholars of visual rhetoric should
also continue to develop methodologies that productively account for the
accumulation of photographs in addition to those that become iconic. Processes that occur over relatively long periods of time, such as transitioning
and toxic exposure, often provoke substantial archival projects. If we are to
understand these processes we must embrace the accumulation, even if that
complicates some of the more traditional means of approaching visual artifacts, such as the close analysis of singular photographs. Jennifer Peeples
(2013) has offered one way of approaching archives of accumulated photographs in which visual narratives are traced over time, but a robust rhetorical
approach to such accumulations must also confront those visual archives that
resist being placed within narratives or that intentionally escape the gaze of
dominant publics.

Finally, as this chapter has suggested, communication scholars should
further interrogate the productive possibilities and limitations of what I have
called temporal pedagogies, or ways of seeing and imagining the body in
relation to time. To develop this idea, I have drawn on Haraway's (2008)
notion of "becoming" and Halberstam's (2005) theory of "queer time,"
though other theories might usefully elucidate additional features of temporal
pedagogies not addressed here. While Riverdale's photographic sequence
posits an important temporal pedagogy, it is only one of many ways that
viewers can be instructed to see and imagine the body. The emergence narrative, captured best in before-and-after photographs, is a pervasive temporal
pedagogy within transsexual discourses. We need to attend more fully to how
that form of visualization affects its viewers, as well as how it works alongside and against the evolution narrative I have discussed here. Within and
beyond the transsexual counterpublic where I have located one such temporal
pedagogy, the ways that we choose to see and understand bodies as temporal-
ly diverse matter. We might, following Halberstam, set out to trace other

"forms of representation dedicated to capturing these willfully eccentric modes of being" (2005, p. 1). In doing so, we will also open ourselves up to being transformed by time.

NOTES

1. As with everything I write, this chapter is the result of much community engagement. I would like to thank the editors of this volume, along with Jane Goodman and Daniel Grinberg, for their generous engagement with the ideas presented in this essay. Moreover, I am grateful to Joshua Riverdale for answering numerous questions as this essay was developed. Finally, audiences at the International Conference on the Image in Chicago and at the Indiana University (Corpo)Realities Symposium, both held in 2013, provided meaningful commentary on early versions of this paper for which I am thankful.

2. Photographs of trans people have, of course, been a part of private collections for much longer. The Kinsey Institute for Research in Sex, Gender, and Reproduction's archives, for instance, include hundreds of private photographs taken and preserved by individuals.

3. Other forms of bodily transformation are presented using a similar visual presentation. For instance, there are few among us who have not witnessed photographs of extreme weight loss or of the pregnant body as it develops through gestation. The familiarity of this visual style may contribute to viewers' capacity to make sense of the transsexual body not as a scene of emergence but of evolution across time.

III

Public and Rhetorical Communication

Chapter Eleven

Language

*Traversing the Transcape: A Brief Historical
Etymology of Trans* Terminology*

Mary Alice Adams

The intersection of transgender studies and issues related to language interests scholars from a variety of disciplines and perspectives. This chapter
begins with a historical discussion of the development of transgender terminology. I next discuss frame shifting as a strategy of rhetorical definition that
facilitates some understandings and forecloses others. I then offer a critique
of GLAAD's *Media Reference Guide-Transgender Issues*, highlighting the
opportunities and liabilities of the guide's framing choices. This chapter
concludes with an invitation to communication students and scholars to consider language as an important object of analysis and tool for potential social
change.

IN THE BEGINNING

The earliest language for describing gender nonconformity tended to conflate
gender identity and sexual orientation. The categorization of transgender
individuals according to their sexual orientations was probably due to the
popularization of the terms *bisexual* (Beemyn, 2004), *lesbian*, and *homosexual* in the mid- to late-19th century (O'Connor & Kellerman, 2009). In the
mid-19th century, Karl Heinrich Ulrichs wrote about "a female soul in a male
body," which referred to an individual who was bisexual or sexually attracted
to members of both sexes (Beemyn, 2004). An 1868 letter from the writer
and "sex-law reformer" Karl Maria Kertbeny to Ulrichs featured the first
recordings of the terms *heterosexual*, "erotic acts" performed by men with

women, and *homosexual*, "erotic acts performed by men with men and women with women" (Katz, 1995, p. 52).

The heterosexual and homosexual labels were first used in the United States in a Chicago medical journal article by Dr. James G. Kiernan in 1892 (Katz, 1995). For Kiernan, both heterosexual and homosexual were perverted terms signifying non-procreative sex regardless of one's sexual partner (Katz, 1995). According to Kiernan, heterosexuals' depravity was due to their "psychal hermaphroditism" which caused them to have "inclinations to both sexes," while homosexuals were those whose "general mental state is that of the opposite sex" (Katz, 1995, p. 20). Kiernan erroneously attributed the notion of the depravity of heterosexuals to Dr. Richard von Krafft-Ebing (Katz, 1995). The English translation of Krafft-Ebing's *Psychopathia Sexualis* in 1893 helped to familiarize Americans with the term *heterosexual* (Katz, 1995). Unlike Kiernan, Krafft-Ebing did not view non-procreative heterosexual sex as deviant; rather, for Krafft-Ebing, heterosexuality "implicitly signifies erotic normality," while homosexual sex was pathological because it was non-procreative (Katz, 1995, p. 22).

Heterosexual and homosexual were not the only sexually oriented terms to enter public consciousness at the turn of the twentieth century. According to the *Oxford English Dictionary*, *lesbian*, an adjective pertaining to female homosexuality, appeared in 1890, while the word *gay* began to be used to denote male homosexuality, although not exclusively, starting in the mid-20th century (O'Connor & Kellerman, 2009).

The shift away from conceptualizing transgender persons as homosexuals, bisexuals, or heterosexuals with the fetish to dress as members of a different sex began in 1910 with the publication of *The Transvestite* by Dr. Magnus Hirschfeld (2006), a sexologist and early advocate for transgender patients. Hirschfeld coined the term *transvestite* to describe people who wore the clothing of members of a different sex. He argued that transvestitism was not reducible to "homosexuality, fetishism, or some form of psychopathology" (Hirschfeld, 2006, p. 28). Instead, *transvestites* were one kind of "sexual intermediaries" who existed on a hypothetical spectrum from "pure male to pure female" (Hirschfeld, 2006, p. 28).

Hirschfeld's use of the term *transvestite* referred not only to people who dressed as members of a different sex, but also to those who sought sexual reassignment surgery (Hirschfeld, 2006). After the term transsexual entered the lexicon in the mid-1950s, *transvestite* came to represent only those who wore the clothes of members of a different sex (Stryker, 2008). Eventually, the transvestite label fell out of favor because it was deemed to be derogatory; *cross-dresser* has emerged as a more suitable replacement (GLAAD, 2014b).

In 1954, Dr. Harry Benjamin, another early advocate for transgender health, published an article noting that there was a significant difference between *transvestites*, who performed the role of a member of a different sex, and *transsexuals* who "want to be [a member of a different sex] and function as one, wishing to assume as many characteristics as possible, physical, mental, sexual" (Benjamin, 2006, p. 46). Moreover, *transsexuals* were those with a gender identity different from their biological sex. For Benjamin, transsexuals may undergo medical treatments to change their biological sex, often times to align it with their gender identity, or they may live their lives as the so-called opposite sex (Killermann, 2013). Despite not coining the word *transsexual*—that distinction belonged to David O. Caldwell who used it in the title of his 1949 article "Psychopathia Transsexualis" (Stryker, 2008)—Benjamin did much to popularize it.

Benjamin's article, "Transsexualism and Transvestism as Psycho-somatic and Somato-psychic Syndromes," was the first to mention the transsexual variant *transsexualist*, to refer to a transsexual individual, and *transsexualism*, to refer to the transsexual experience (Benjamin, 2006). Benjamin also wrote the seminal 1966 transsexual treatise, *The Transsexual Phenomenon* (Benjamin, 2006). *The Transsexual Phenomenon* was called the bible of transsexuality (Williams, n.d.). In addition to arguing that gender identity was immutable, *The Transsexual Phenomenon* created a methodical approach for addressing the interconnected and varied relationships between the "sexed body, gender identity, and sexual desire" (Benjamin, 2006, p. 45).

For Benjamin, the word *transsexual* was an umbrella term covering those who lived part-time as members of a different sex and did not want sex reassignment surgery (SRS); those who lived full-time as members of a different sex and may or may not require SRS; as well as those who lived full-time as members of a different sex and required SRS. SRS was essential for those who wanted to change their biological sex, by way of a medical process, so that they would be in alignment with their gender identity (Killermann, 2013; Williams, n.d.). Individuals who underwent a medical process to change their biological sex from male to female were designated as *MTF*, while those who underwent the medical process to change their biological sex from female to male were designated as *FTM* (Killermann, 2013).

Benjamin was also a proponent of SRS for transsexuals who were suffering from substantial *gender dysphoria* when individuals feel significantly disconnected from their biological sex and gender role (Williams, n.d.). The American Psychiatric Association (APA) acknowledged gender dysphoria as a psychiatric condition when it released the third edition of the *Diagnostic and Statistical Manual of Mental Disorders* in 1980 (Valentine, 2007). The APA called the condition *gender identity disorder* (GID) and stated that it entailed identification with another gender; disturbance with one's sex; persistent feelings of the unsuitability of the "the gender role of that sex"; and "clinically significant distress or impairment in social, occupational or other important areas of functioning" (American Psychiatric Association, 2000, p. 581).

The APA's acknowledgment of GID was a double-edged sword, however. On one hand, the inclusion of GID in the *Diagnostic and Statistical Manual of Mental Disorders* legitimized it in the eyes of the medical community and subsequently the general public through the establishment of diagnostic criteria and treatment standards. On the other hand, this designation served to stigmatize the condition by labeling it a disorder (Transgender Equality Network Ireland, 2014).

After decades of debate, the APA revised its diagnostic criteria for GID in 2013 and renamed it *gender dysphoria* (American Psychiatric Association, 2013). In the fifth edition of the *Diagnostic and Statistical Manual of Mental Disorders*, the APA added a "post-transition specifier for people who are living full-time as the desired gender (with or without legal sanction of the gender change)" to enable transgender individuals to receive medical treatment and/or counseling to assist in their gender transitioning process (American Psychiatric Association, 2013, p. 452).

THE ARRIVAL OF TRANSGENDER

Renaming GID not only updated the clinical nomenclature, it also broadened the scope of the criteria for diagnosing gender dysphoria. Furthermore, the name change mirrored the etymological shift in terminology from *transsexual* to *transgender* decades before. As had been the case with the transvestite label during the first half of the twentieth century, the transsexual label was found to be lacking by the late 1970s. *Transgender*'s predecessors: *transgenderism, transgenderal,* and *transgenderist,* were developed to describe those who felt uncomfortable with either the transvestite or the transsexual labels. The early proponents behind the drive to adopt the first transgender variants wanted to create specific terminology for people who found themselves somewhere between transvestites and transsexuals on the gender spectrum (Gressgård, 2010; Rawson & Williams, 2014). In particular, they were looking for labels for individuals who permanently changed their genders without permanently changing their sexual organs (Rawson & Williams, 2014; Stryker, 2008; Valentine, 2007).

Transgenderism, the earliest of the transgender variants, appeared in print in 1965. Psychiatrist John F. Oliven used the term in the second edition of *Sexual Hygiene and Pathology* to clarify the difference between transgenderism and transsexualism (Rawson & Williams, 2014). He stated that the desire to change one's gender was called transgenderism while the desire to change one's genitals was called *transsexualism* (Rawson & Williams, 2014). This clarification was very important because, prior to this, there was no distinction between gender and sex. Thus, those whose gender identity differed from their sex at birth and those who underwent SRS were thought to be one and the same (Killermann, 2013).

The next early transgender variant to appear in print was *transgenderal*, which was reportedly coined by pioneering transgender activist Virginia Prince in 1969 (Williams, n.d.). For Prince, the word transgenderal described people like her who lived as members of a different sex without surgically altering their sexual organs (Rawson & Williams, 2014; Williams, n.d.).

The last early transgender variant to appear in print was *transgenderist* in 1975. In a newspaper article written by Ariadne Kane and Phyllis Frye, transgenderists were said to have two healthy and diverse identities (Rawson & Williams, 2014; Williams, n.d.). The following year, Kane elaborated on this idea, adding that the male transgenderist goes "beyond cross dressing to convey an image and express feelings we usually associate with femininity" (Rawson & Williams, 2014).

Throughout the 1970s, *transsexual, transgenderism, transgenderal*, and *transgenderist* all jockeyed to become the preferred term to refer to transgender individuals. By the 1980s, the word *transgender* had eclipsed the others to become the label of choice (Williams, n.d.). Unlike *transsexual, transgenderism, transgenderal*, or *transgenderist*, the word *transgender* was conceived as an:

> umbrella term for people whose gender identity and/or gender expression differs from the sex they were assigned at birth. [This includes FTM, MTF], transsexuals, cross-dressers and other gender-variant people. Transgender people may or may not decide to alter their bodies hormonally and/or surgically. (GLAAD, 2014b)

The advantage that the transgender label had over its predecessors was that it was deliberately developed to function as a universal term. In contrast, the word *transvestite* was applied to cross-dressers while, despite Benjamin's intentions, *transsexual* was not perceived as an umbrella term by the public since it was used to describe Christine Jorgensen, who gained notoriety after undergoing SRS in the early 1950s (Williams, n.d.). *Transgenderal* never caught on because it was too awkward, while *transgenderist* like *transgenderism* eventually ended up being shortened to transgender (Rawson & Williams, 2014; Williams, n.d.). The key to the appeal of the transgender label was its applicability to more people by focusing more generally on gender variation or nonconformity.

Throughout the rest of the 20th century and continuing into the early 21st century, *transgender* remained the blanket term to describe people whose gender identity differed from the sex they were assigned at birth as well as "those who cross over, cut across, move between or otherwise queer socially constructed sex/gender boundaries" (Gressgård, 2010, p. 540). In the 1990s, *trans**, a shorthand version of the word transgender, rose to prominence (TransAdvocate, 2014). The word *trans** was envisioned to be a more inclusive iteration of transgender (Killermann, 2012b; TransAdvocate, 2014; Transgender Equality Network Ireland, 2014). Additionally, *trans* was used as a prefix to designate those whose gender identity differed from their sex at birth, thus *transman* was used for a person who was female-assigned at birth but identified as a man, while *transwoman* was used to describe a person who was male-assigned at birth but identified as a woman (Killermann, 2013).

In 1994, biologist Dana Leland Defosse coined the word *cisgender* to describe those whose sex at birth was in congruence with their gender identity (Enke, 2013). The label cisgender was developed to highlight the fact that everyone has a gender identity (Enke, 2013; Killermann, 2013; Transgender Equality Network Ireland, 2014). As was the case with transgender, the *cis* prefix was combined with both man and woman to create the terms *cisman* to denote those who were born male and identified as male and *ciswoman* to denote those who were born female and identified as female (Enke, 2013; Killermann, 2013; Transgender Equality Network Ireland, 2014).

The 1990s also saw the emergence of the field of queer linguistic studies. According to linguists Bucholtz and Hall, "queer linguistics puts at the forefront of linguistic analysis the regulation of sexuality by hegemonic heterosexuality and the ways in which non-normative sexualities are negotiated in relation to these regulatory structures" (2004, p. 471). Consequently, queer linguists are interested in understanding how language use replicates the power relations between marginalized and non-marginalized groups, especially groups who do not conform to society's hegemonic heteronormative ideal.

THE TRANS* UMBRELLA EXPANDS

As the trans* umbrella opens further, new terms continue to emerge, including an update of the acronym for the lesbian, gay, and bisexual community; transgender terms from other cultures; and other non-cis terms. The acronym LGB, an abbreviation of the collective lesbian, gay, and bisexual community, is now more often figured as LGBTQ to include T for transgender and Q for queer, which denotes those who exist outside gender and sex binaries (Killermann, 2013). Terms from other cultures that address issues of gender variance such as two spirit and third gender have also appeared more prominently in the early part of the 21st century. For some Native Americans, the label *two spirit* designates individuals who possess masculine and feminine traits

(Killermann, 2013). The term *third gender* is a label for people who do not identify with either the masculine or feminine gender (Killermann, 2013).

Bridging the gap between two spirit and third gender is the term *bi-gender* which describes those whose gender identity fluctuates between male and female thereby giving them the fluidity to identify with both genders and sometimes a third gender (Jakubowski, 2014; Killermann, 2013). *Agender* individuals are the opposite of those who identify as bi-gender (Jakubowski, 2014). Agender people lack attachment to any gender (Jakubowski, 2014). Agender, bi-gender, two spirit, and third gender are all examples of gender-queer orientations (Killermann, 2013).

On the whole, I celebrate the continued growth and emergence of an expansive cornucopia of transgender terminology. I agree with Kulick (2000) who argued that the development of terms that adequately represent the expression of gender identities is essential because the process of labeling gender "confers existence" (p. 244). While the absence of a label that fits may feel like symbolic annihilation, the ability to embrace a label is often an important step in accepting and recognizing one's own identity (see, e.g., Bucholtz & Hall, 2004; Coates, 2013; Iantaffi & Bockting, 2011; Motschen-bacher & Stegu, 2013).

A RHETORICAL FRAMING ANALYSIS
OF GLAAD'S MEDIA GUIDE

In addition to naming, which leads to the conferral of existence, language also works to frame mainstream narratives about transgender identity in a manner that privileges hegemonic cisnormativity. According to David Zaref-sky, definitions serve to frame a rhetorical situation by supporting a state-ment and presenting backing for it (2004). What is more:

> The definition of the situation affects what counts as data for or against a proposal, highlights certain elements of the situation for use in arguments and obscures others, influences whether people will notice the situation and how they will handle it, describes and identifies remedies, and invites moral judg-ments about circumstances or individuals. (Zarefsky, 2004, p. 612)

An example of framing is using SRS as the determining factor when discuss-ing whether someone is transgender. Framing the discussion in such a man-ner not only insults the dignity of the transgender individual, but it is also incredibly problematic because not all transgender people have or want SRS, and just because a transgender individual has not undergone SRS does not negate the individual's transitioning process (GLAAD, 2012; GLAAD, 2014b).

The framing process also acts as a conduit between cognition and culture, meaning that it helps people to make sense of the world around them. The transgender community's displeasure with the media's use of the phrase "bathroom bill" is a case in point. A number of media outlets have used the offhanded phrase "bathroom bill" in discussions about passing non-discrimination laws and ordinances establishing gender neutral restroom facilities for queer and transgender individuals. In addition to being flippant, "bathroom bill" is a derogatory phrase that was created to cause fear and havoc in the minds of members of the cisgender community (GLAAD, 2014b).

Communication students and scholars are uniquely positioned to promote transgender advocacy through the lens of rhetorical framing. The combination of queer linguistic analyses with rhetorical framing techniques offers communication scholars and students the opportunity to assess the language and the perspectival positions of mediated messages about transgender lives. To that end, I take as a case study in this chapter the eighth edition of GLAAD's transgender reference guide for media practitioners. While the eighth edition of the media reference guide admirably offers helpful suggestions for language use, tone, and media coverage more broadly, it falters in its framing of transgender subjects as Othered or always already criminalized/victimized.

I now turn my attention to my analysis of the eighth edition of the *GLAAD Media Reference Guide-Transgender Issues*, which can be downloaded from GLAAD's Web site, in order to investigate how the presentation and dissemination of information on transgender awareness created by a well-known LGBT organization has the potential to invite contradictory interpretations of transgender narratives and lives. I argue that the frame of so-called journalistic objectivity in the media reference guide constrains GLAAD's otherwise progressive potential. I discuss and analyze the content components of the Web site first. Next, I examine how the choice of certain linguistic conventions over others assists in the selection of information and the establishment of salience. Finally, I offer suggestions for future research at the nexus of transgender studies and language.

Since 1985, GLAAD has worked as a media advocacy organization for the LGBT community. GLAAD persuaded the *New York Times* to revamp its editorial policy regarding LGBT individuals as well as allowing same-sex couples to be featured in its Weddings & Celebrations pages (GLAAD, 2014a). Additionally, GLAAD convinced the Associated Press to update and revise the AP Stylebook to include terminology that inclusively describes LGBT persons (GLAAD, 2014a).

There is great potential in and much to celebrate about GLAAD's work over the last three decades and about the *GLAAD Media Reference Guide-Transgender Issues* more particularly. The guide features brief lexicons focusing on "general terminology" and "transgender specific terminology," including elucidations of terms pertaining to gender identity, sexual orientation, transitioning, and GID, among others. The glossary sets the stage for the next section, "transgender terms to avoid." There are three subheadings in the "transgender terms to avoid" section. The first two sub-sections, "problematic terms" and "defamatory terms," highlight words that should not be used when speaking to or about transgender individuals and encourages journalists not to refer to trans people as "pre-operative" or "post-operative." The last section "names, pronoun usage and descriptors" offers useful suggestions to media practitioners such as using the chosen names and preferred pronouns of transgender individuals and avoiding the use of phrases like "she calls herself" or other linguistic constructions tantamount to accusing transgender people of deception. The guide also warns journalists against grammatical errors such as using the word "transgendered" or "transgenders." The advice related to language echoes much of the advice this volume offers and represents the best and most up-to-date standards for journalistic professionalism and inclusiveness. On that point, I give the guide high marks.

The progressive potential of the eighth edition of the *GLAAD Media Reference Guide-Transgender Issues*, however, is regrettably offset by unfortunate framing from the very beginning. I first note the oddity of the document's title, *GLAAD Media Reference Guide-Transgender Issues*. The use of the word "issues" denotes objects or items, as opposed to people, lives, experiences, or communities. Referring to transgender *issues* instead of *individuals* emphasizes the importance of ideas and concepts at the expense of the dignity of transgender persons. In essence, referring to *Transgender Issues* instead of, for instance, *issues related to reporting about transgender people*, Others transgender individuals by objectifying them. In discourse about human identity, the word issue has a far from innocent past: consider, for instance, the reduction of entire worldviews and perspectives into that one word, a strategy often invoked by people with more power to further marginalize someone who dares to resist (e.g., "Let's not get distracted by the issue of race" or "Do you mean the gay issue?"). Furthermore, even if GLAAD means to address issues related to reporting rather than addressing transgender people (such as the issue of which pronoun or name to use in a news report, for instance), the title of the document relies on an awkward adjective-noun relationship. The "issue" (if we want to call it that) of which pronoun or name to use is not a transgender issue as much as a language issue. Therefore, even though GLAAD's intentions are good on this matter, the actual language they use invites confusion at best. We might expect such errors from the media outlets who constitute the rhetorical audience for the GLAAD media reference guide, but when the media reference guide itself makes such blunders, we who study language must begin to ask who exactly is watching the genderqueer henhouse.

The guide's mission is discussed in three brief and distinct explanatory paragraphs that are found under the title. The opening paragraph explains what the media resource guide is—a resource for media professionals and entertainers who seek to provide "fair" and "accurate" coverage of LGBT issues. The paragraph concludes with a disclaimer that states that the resource is not meant to be a "prescriptive" guide for media outlets reporting about LGBT people nor is it an extensive glossary. In the first paragraph, then, the guide frames its audience, justifies its purpose, and delineates what it is not.

To its credit, GLAAD here speaks in a language that journalists identify with, and to the degree that GLAAD's advice here leads journalists away from using slurs such as "tranny" or perpetuating stereotypes about transgender people in general, I affirm the guide's utility. However, the use of the terms *fair* and *accurate* works to flatten the perspective of the media guide and reifies a journalistic mythos of objectivity. Being fair and accurate means that everyone is treated the same, which is an admirable idea in theory but unlikely in practice due to the hegemonic hetero- and cisnormative power structure. Encouraging a fair and accurate perspective in all situations requires a position of privilege as only those who have a powerful social location can espouse such a notion. For example, a journalist reporting about an elementary school student who comes out at school as transgender might feel compelled by a sense of journalistic objectivity to present "both sides of the story"—that is, to interview a supportive school administrator and the parent in the school district who feels the most incensed about sending her kid to school with a transgender classmate. While the guide does not address this situation explicitly, contributing to the journalistic mythos of objectivity can clearly have beneficial and harmful consequences. More simply, we expect "That's the way it is" from Walter Cronkite, but GLAAD ought to know better. An advocacy organization that fancies itself a media watchdog does its transgender constituents and any other critical thinking auditor a serious disservice when it contributes to the grand narrative of journalistic objectivity as a reasonable goal. Furthermore, I wonder if journalistic objectivity were possible, should GLAAD advocate it. For journalists or anyone else to claim (feign?) objectivity in the face of news reports about transphobic hate crimes, discrimination, suicide rates, or other related topics borders on thoughtless absurdity at best and crass inhumanity at worst.

The second paragraph narrows the focus from LGBT concerns generally to those of the transgender community specifically, which is the topic of the rest of the guide. In sharp contrast to the previous two paragraphs, the third paragraph begins with a cautionary note. The word "important"—written in boldface and all capital letters—immediately increases the salience of this paragraph. The word "important" is the only word to be written in all capital letters in the introduction and the only boldface word in the introduction.

Both of these typographical flourishes visually call attention to the word and subsequently the sentences that follow. This is also the only paragraph to contain two hyperlinks. The first hyperlink deals with specific resources for covering transgender individuals who have been involved in crimes, while the second hyperlink focuses specifically on reporting about Private Chelsea Manning.

The third paragraph's focus on crime is noteworthy because it betrays the impossibility of the first paragraph's call for fair and balanced reporting. This paragraph serves to frame transgender individuals as criminals, victims, or both. Focusing on transgender criminology or victimage perpetuates the stereotype that transgender individuals are deviants who should be marginalized or targets-in-waiting. Transgender people, then, occupy a precarious position, always already implicated as aggressors or objects of violence—not only in the parlance of mainstream media stereotypes, but also in the framing of the very guidelines that purport to offer advice to those media. GLAAD's own media reference guide undermines its emphasis on fair and accurate coverage from just two paragraphs earlier.

Moreover, while mentioning Chelsea Manning makes some sense because of the salience of her case at the time, featuring only Manning is problematic. Singling out Manning individualizes and personifies the pernicious implications of the entire section on criminology and victimage. GLAAD itself sees transgender persons as especially newsworthy only or primarily when they are involved in a crime; as the touchstone for this section of the media guide, Manning concretizes the criminology/victimage framing. Again, the media reference guide replicates the errors in mainstream media GLAAD ostensibly rails against.

The importance of analyzing frames, then, cannot be overstated. Frames serve as lenses through which we view and subsequently interact with society (Zarefsky, 2004). By emphasizing certain elements over others, frames shape the transgender narrative in a manner consistent with hegemonic culture. More specifically, the frame of journalistic objectivity undercuts the guide's otherwise laudatory elements by objectifying transgender people and reinscribing stereotypes of transgender people as criminals or victims. Because society is cisnormative, discourses about transgender individuals and issues are framed in cisnormative terminology which privileges the cisnormative experience at the expense of transgender individuals. Even organizations like GLAAD that set out to offer advice to the rest of the media function from within the hegemonic power structure that produces stereotypes, misunderstanding, and harm.

During the summer of 2014, when this book chapter was under revision, GLAAD released the ninth edition of the *GLAAD Media Reference Guide-Transgender Issues*. I am delighted to report that in the ninth edition the highly contentious paragraph focusing on crime has been deleted. However, the guide continues to use the phrases "transgender issues" and "fair" and "accurate."

CONCLUSION

As the abovementioned analysis indicates, critical language studies with a focus on rhetorical framing can benefit communication students and scholars. Paying careful attention to linguistic conventions will assist in the creation of messages that respect the human dignity of all transgender individuals. Additionally, the importance of analyzing how messages are rhetorically framed cannot be overstated because frames act as lenses through which we come to understand and interpret phenomena.

For communication students and scholars interested in the intersection of critical language studies and rhetorical framing, at least two potentially promising areas for future research deserve our attention. The first relates to the contradistinction between Western and non-Western transgender perspectives, while the second deals with the political, ideological, and axiological differences between types of media guides. Being mindful of the variance between Western and non-Western cultural perspectives will allow for more globally inclusive analyses of transgender narratives, whereas an awareness of the differences between the political, ideological, and axiological variations between media guides has the potential to foster insightful discussions pertaining to the ethical use of language by media practitioners.

The first potentially promising area of future research for communication students and scholars interested in the intersection of critical language studies and rhetorical framing relates to the difference between Western and non-Western perspectives. As the trans* umbrella continues to expand, more research is being conducted about the transgender experience. Encouraging as this is, it is also problematic because global trans* narratives are almost exclusively written from a Western cultural frame of reference that restricts non-Western cultural perspectives (Towle & Morgan, 2002). Consequently, Eurocentric transgender research turns a blind eye to transgender cultural experiences that complicate Western notions of a gender binary. Language choices, of course, reveal assumptions and often entire ontologies. The aforementioned example of two spirit identities in the Native American tradition illustrates the problem: For tribes that revered two spirit persons, European imperialists brought not only genocide and disease, but also a metaphysics of gender binarism and hierarchy. To research language for describing the vastness of gender identity diversity in humankind, we must continually question Western reliance on binaries.

A second potentially promising area of future research is to continue the project of critically analyzing media guides' advice about language standards for reporting about transgender individuals. Media guides attempt to contribute to the journalistic mythos of objectivity, however the politics, ethics, and values of the media outlets that created them subtly influence not only the material covered in the guide but the manner in which it is discussed. Media guides highlight items that particular media outlets deem most important. The *GLAAD Media Reference Guide-Transgender Issues* is but one resource media practitioners can consult when reporting on the transgender community. Both Trans Pride Canada and the United Kingdom's Trans Media Watch have produced media guides to assist in the coverage of transgender individuals. It would be interesting to note any differences between the guides' terminology and mission statements based on the nation of origin. Additionally, what roles do national politics and ideology play in the creation of media guides? Analyzing the role that ideology plays in the creation of media guides enables students and scholars to study the ethical politics of language. A cross-cultural comparison of advocacy group media guides might highlight common themes to address when promoting transgender awareness worldwide.

Additionally, the juxtaposition of advocacy group media guides with those created by media organizations might yield a wealth of information about how media institutions report on the transgender community. Studying the editorial policies of a major mainstream media promises to highlight how institutional politics shape so-called journalistic objectivity. Further, researchers might compare corporate policies with advocacy guides.

Whether these or other future directions, communication scholars must begin to contribute to the multi-disciplinary project of thinking critically and carefully about language use, especially with sensitivity to culture and with particular attention on those who fancy themselves arbiters of others' language choices. I hope this chapter is a step in that direction.

Chapter Twelve

Religious Discourse

Coming Out, Bringing Out: God's Love,
Transgender Identity, and Difference

Leland G. Spencer IV

On August 30, 2009, the Reverend David Weekley stepped into the pulpit at Epworth United Methodist Church in Portland, Oregon, and revealed that he had undergone sex reassignment surgery in the 1970s before he entered ordained ministry (Goldman, 2009; Weekley, 2009). The announcement garnered national media attention. Weekley's congregation embraced the announcement, but Weekley knew his revelation put him on dangerous terrain. The Institute for Religion and Democracy, a conservative para-church organization led by Mark Tooley, launched a campaign against the Reverend Drew Phoenix, a Baltimore pastor who had come out as transgender in 2007 (Burke, 2007). Despite Tooley's anger about transgender clergy, no church law prohibits transgender clergy. Conservatives in the denomination tried but failed to enact proscriptive legislation at the 2008 General Conference, the denomination's law-making body that meets quadrennially. The Reverend Karen Booth, for example, submitted a petition "that would spell out church policy by stating that neither transgenderism nor transsexuality 'reflects God's best intentions for humankind'" (United Methodist News Service, 2008). Though the General Conference did not adopt Booth's petition, the denomination's stance against lesbian and gay clergy, including the defrocking of the Reverend Beth Stroud in 2004 after she came out as a lesbian to her Pennsylvania congregation, gave Weekley reason to fear for his own credentials ("Methodist Court," 2005).

Despite the risk, Weekley delivered a coming out sermon that not only told his own story, but also included his congregation in the story; he made

his coming out *their* coming out. In this chapter, focused on the intersection
of transgender studies and religious communication, I offer a close reading of
Weekley's sermon, originally published on the congregation's Web site
(Weekley, 2009) and later reprinted in Weekley's (2011) book *In From the
Wilderness.*[1] I argue that Weekley's coming out also functioned as a *bringing
out.* Weekley first positioned his transgender identity as a God-given difference. Then, through a definitional move of rhetorical association, Weekley
established difference as a God-given gift to all persons. As such, Weekley
came out as transgender and brought the whole congregation out with him.
The call to embrace difference as evidence of God's love stands as an invitation for the entire denomination to join Weekley in coming out of closets of
narrow cisgender-only theologies like that of Tooley and other conservative
United Methodists. Likewise, I conclude, communication scholars who study
questions of gender identity and human sexuality might come out of their
own closets: closets that define religion too narrowly as always heteronormative and cisnormative. Explaining communicative strategies for navigating
the intersections of gender identity and religious identity requires recognition
of the deep complexity of many such intersections.

WEEKLEY'S TWO TRUTHS

In the months leading up to his sermon, Weekley told his congregation he
had been working on a book manuscript, but they did not know the topic.
Weekley titled the sermon "My Book Report," and in revealing the topic of
his book, disclosed his identity as a post-operative transman. Throughout the
sermon, Weekley sustained a focus on two central beliefs he had held since
his childhood. Throughout this chapter, I refer to these as Weekley's truths
because he holds them as axiomatic: "From earliest memory, I saw myself as
a boy. The boy who would grow in to the man you see here today" (para.16).
Just as Weekley identified as a boy, he also identified as a child of God:
"Another early, formative memory and experience that forms and informs
who I am today is my love of God, and sense of being loved, and connected"
(para. 24). Weekley calls these two truths his "two earliest memories and
formative experiences" (para. 29).

Weekley's early sense of identification as a boy resonates with the generic elements of transgender coming out stories. As a genre, transgender coming out stories, while not monolithic, often include themes of mind-body
dissonance (Fraser, 2009; Morgan & Stevens, 2008), an affinity for clothing
and artifacts consistent with one's gender identity rather than the societally
assumed gender (Bilodeau, 2005; Gagne, Tewksbury, & McGaughey, 1997),
and the felt need to monitor or censor one's behavior based on context
(Morgan & Stevens, 2008).

Weekley's story departs from the generic norm at the intersection with religion. Many coming out narratives ignore religion or figure religion as a hindrance or an obstacle to overcome. For example, Levy and Lo's (2013) interviews with transgender Christians revealed that "It was often because of their gender identity that many [participants] initially questioned church doctrine" (p. 79). Justin Tanis (2003) found that transgender people of many faiths struggle with whether their religious traditions consider transgender identity sinful and whether their traditions support the transitioning process. By contrast, Weekley elevates his religious identity as a child of God to the level of certainty, the same level where he puts his gender identity. Religious identity for Weekley serves as the counterpart to his gender identity. For Weekley, religious identity operates not a problem to overcome, a villain to vanquish, a cross to bear, or a yoke to abandon. Instead, religious identity works with gender identity in mutually forming him into the *man* he becomes.

Weekley continued to refer to this pair of truths throughout the sermon, always connecting his gender and spiritual identities. Weekley noted that during his teenage years, he overheard someone talking about Christine Jorgensen, the transwoman whose series of sex reassignment surgeries in the 1950s made national and international news. Weekley said, "As I listened, I learned that she had not always been seen as a woman, but had been born a male. She had undergone what was then called sex-reassignment surgery in Sweden" (para. 34). For Weekley, overhearing that conversation gave him "new hope," and thereafter, "grace seemed to intervene at the right moments" (para. 39). Weekley went on to say that he eventually learned of a team of medical specialists for transgender persons in his hometown of Cleveland, Ohio. He met with medical experts there for three years, and finally "underwent a series of surgeries to help make [his] external gender match [his] internal one as a man" (para. 48). Weekley recounted that "the night before my first surgery, I prayed a prayer of both thankfulness and intercession to God from my hospital bed, and I fell asleep at peace" (para. 49).

Again, this segment of Weekley's story reads as a typical transgender coming out narrative. Christine Jorgensen's well publicized sex reassignment surgery features as a notable touchstone in many such stories (Gagne et al., 1997; Hill, 2013; Spencer, 2014; Stone, 1991). Yet where we might expect in the story to find religious opposition in the form of a disapproving family member, faith community, or clergyperson, instead Weekley reports that "grace seemed to intervene." The grace of God—not luck, coincidence, or good fortune—explains Weekley's learning about Christine Jorgensen and then about his own medical options. Weekley's story revises the tired old script of religious opposition in coming out narratives. He understands his faith as an asset in the gender transition process. Bringing his body into alignment with his internal gender identity allowed Weekley to live out his first truth: his maleness. The means by which Weekley arrived on the surgeon's table represented the other truth: his identity as a child of God, and in this case, God whose grace intervened to facilitate Weekley's transition. Furthermore, God offers Weekley peace in the midst of that transition. Weekley's faith, then, supports him throughout his whole gender journey. His religious faith appears not as a minor character or antagonist in his narrative, but a source of succor for the duration.

Weekley then said that coming out represented a sort of culminating spiritual experience for him. Before his August 2009 sermon, Weekley had anonymously shared parts of his story in a 1992 sermon at a Reconciling United Methodist Church, a congregation that openly welcomes lesbian, gay, bisexual, and transgender people. Reflecting on the 1992 sermon, Weekley noted, "In that message I was able for the first time, to connect in public, my life journey as a transgender man with my faith journey as a disciple of Jesus" (para. 54). Although the link between his gender and spiritual identity made sense to Weekley, he had "learned how unsafe a transgender candidate for ordained ministry was" (para. 64). To resolve the tension between his call to ministry and his arguably valid perception of the denomination as unsafe for transgender ministerial candidates, Weekley concluded that he would "become the best pastor possible" and then "share my story when I was close to retirement" (para. 65). Weekley reasoned, "I thought that if I interacted with as many persons as I could, and they experienced me as a good person and pastor, it might be part of a witness" (para. 65). Described in this way, both Weekley's decision to remain closeted in the past and his locutionary act of coming out in the present cohere intelligibly with the two truths that comprise his identity: Maintaining the secret allowed Weekley to live out his call to ministry and express his love for God without being defrocked because of his gender identity, while coming out permitted him to make a public witness to both of the truths he affirms so passionately. Weekley's resolve to do the best work he could do in order to find acceptance when he eventually came out reflects a paradox not uncommon among marginalized groups: one much perform exceptionally well in order to be considered normal. If a good pastor just happens to be transgender, maybe people will accept transgender ministers. In Weekley's own construction, the potential acceptability of Weekley's story of transgender identity hinged on his skill as a minister.

For the first time in Weekley's narrative, his faith ostensibly presents a problem. The conflict, though, relates not to Weekley's faith as much as to his career. In other words, Weekley does not doubt his faith in God or his status as a beloved child of God. His anxiety centers on potential backlash from official channels within the United Methodist Church. Despite the apparent contradiction, Weekley's faith remains helpful to his coming out. Even if denominational hierarchies prosecute or persecute him, Weekley's coming out will have been a witness to the centrality of God's love in his life. Having told the story of his childhood truths, those truths' abiding sustenance of his journey through surgery, and the practical culmination of those truths in his coming out sermon, Weekley then made two turns in the sermon that shifted its focus from him to his congregation.

ONE MORE TRUTH

After transitioning and serving in ordained ministry for twenty-seven years, Weekley added "one more truth to the two" that he had embraced since his childhood:

1. I am a little boy, who in some ways is different from other boys, and from other people,
2. I am loved by God, and I love God, and
3. Most people are different from most other people in some way. (para. 69)

Weekley extended the core truths he holds in two important ways. First, he added the notion of difference to the truth about his gender identity. Earlier in the sermon, he identified as a boy (period). Now he acknowledges that identification as a difference that sets him apart from other boys. The move toward *difference* may seem regressive at first blush, as though the two truths Weekley previously affirmed confidently now needed hedging, amendment, or qualification. However, the shift toward difference in the first truth sets up for the move Weekley makes in the new truth he added to his list. Where Weekley's amended first truth sets him apart from other boys, his third truth insists that "most people are different from other people in some way." Engaging in a form of rhetorical definition David Zarefsky (2004, p. 612) called association, "expanding the meaning of a term to cover the new case at hand," Weekley widens the boundaries of normal, God-given difference to include gender identity. In other words, that which seems to divide Weekley from other boys actually makes him part of the majority, experiencing difference just as "most people" do.

Second, Weekley's new truth introduces a social dimension to a story hitherto focused on Weekley himself. By bringing "most people" into the sermon, Weekley invites his congregants to understand themselves in relationship to these three truths, a point he would underscore in the sermon's conclusion. Between the amended first truth (Weekley's difference) and the newly added third truth (most people's difference), Weekley repeated his love for God and his assurance of God's love for him. In this organizational structure, God's love connects Weekley's individual difference to the differences of "most people," cementing Weekley's association of his own gender identity with the theologically positive-inflected term *difference*. God's love brings Weekley's story from an individual and potentially shameful difference held in secret to a communally affirmed sign of the diversity of creation. Weekley's difference neither separates him from God nor from others. Instead, God's love puts Weekley's difference into a network of mutuality[2] with everyone else's difference.

Weekley accentuates the communal implications of the message in his conclusion. He asks the congregation to reflect on three truths:

> Today, I pray for this same healing and freedom for each one of us here, as we move to a new level of community together, and as we become comfortable with these basic truths:
>
> 1. We love God and God loves us.
> 2. We are all different from most other people in some way.
> 3. We still love God, and God still loves us. (para. 80)

Notably, Weekley altered the order and intensity of the truths in the sermon's denouement. Throughout the sermon, Weekley began with his gender identity (later made consubstantial with difference), then affirmed the love of God in his life. Here, when Weekley first explicitly asked the congregation to join him in accepting his basic truths, Weekley put God's love first and last. Where previously "*most people*" were different from others, now "*we* are all different from most other people in some way." This time, the truth about difference includes everyone. The creative and potentially revolutionary move, though, comes in one word repeated twice in the last truth: *still*. With the word *still,* Weekley underscored that difference, even his expanded definition of difference, does not separate anyone—himself or his congregation—from the love of God. In the mind of Tooley and many other conservative Christians, Weekley's difference—his gender identity—disconnects him from God. Having associated gender identity with difference and established the universality of difference, Weekley put the whole congregation on the same level with him: different, and different in a way some people would understand to be incommensurate with Christianity.

Weekley's unifying use of difference as an all-inclusive category also anticipates and answers some of the opposition he knew he would face. The congregation gave Weekley full support, most immediately by applauding him at the end of the sermon (Goldman, 2009). But the Institute for Religion and Democracy took Weekley's coming out as an opportunity to decry what it understands to be an increasingly dangerous liberalization of mainline Protestant Christianity in the United States. Tooley wrote an inflammatory blog post blasting Weekley:

> Did you know that United Methodism now has TWO publicly announced transsexual ministers? [. . .] Contrary to previous claims by sexual orientation

activists that everything is predetermined before birth, the latest fad is to claim that orientation AND gender are completely in flux and self-determined. Some call this "omnigender." Most of us would call it ridiculous. (Tooley, 2009, emphasis in the original)

Not surprisingly, Tooley's blog post ends with a hyperlink where concerned readers may make a pledge: "Your donation for church reform is urgently needed" (Tooley, 2009). Despite the blog post's purported exigence, Weekley's coming out sermon, Tooley must alter everything about Weekley's message in order to sustain his own ideology and the hysteria he hopes to inspire among readers (and potential donors). Tooley refuses to use the language Weekley uses to refer to himself. Weekley (2009) identifies as "a transgender man" (para. 54). Tooley calls him "transsexual." Without citing which "sexual orientation activists" he means (and with evidently little reflexivity about the awkwardness of such a sobriquet), Tooley mischaracterizes decades of research on gender and sexuality as concluding that "everything is predetermined before birth." Other research Tooley disagrees with Tooley dismisses as "the latest fad." He then uses the term "omnigender," again without citing exactly who the "some" are who use it. Finally, in an error even students in an introductory argumentation course could spot, Tooley resorts to an ad hominem fallacy, calling the hypothetical straw man (or straw genderqueer person?) he set up "ridiculous."

I dwell on Tooley's vitriolic and uninformed remarks to highlight the effectiveness of Weekley's rhetorical association. Weekley never claimed that "everything is predetermined before birth" nor that "orientation AND gender are completely in flux and self-determined." Instead, Weekley claimed that he always knew he identified as a boy and that he always knew God loved him. Weekley acknowledged the difference his identity imbued him with, but he defined difference as God-given, and eventually, difference as characteristic of everyone. Where Tooley seems insistent that activists should pick one "side" of the so-called debate between "predetermined" and "in flux" and stick to it, Weekley side-steps the nature/nurture binary entirely. Weekley states clearly that he has always seen himself as male, but he eschews making sweeping essentialist claims or resorting to biological determinism. He begins by coming out and offering his own reflexively perspectival truths, but he finishes by bringing the whole congregation out with him. By declaring everyone's difference as falling within the realm of God's love, Weekley disrupts the argumentative ground of his potential detractors. Tooley misses Weekley's point entirely because engaging with what Weekley actually said would presumably require Tooley to disagree either with the claim that difference is part of God's creation or that God loves everyone. These positions prove untenable, even for Tooley, so he fabricates claims that never appear in Weekley's sermon and then dismisses those claims as "ridiculous."

COMING OUT WITH WEEKLEY: AN INVITATION FOR STUDENTS AND SCHOLARS OF COMMUNICATION

Weekley's association of transgender identity with difference and in turn, of difference with the love of God, imagines a different relationship between transgender identity and faith than that often proffered by religious leaders and transforms his coming out sermon into a bringing out sermon. Anyone who identifies as different (i.e., everyone) can come out with Weekley. I suggest that students and scholars of religious communication and transgender communication ought to embrace that invitation and come out with Weekley as well. From what closet ought we to come out? Simply put, the closets of narrowness that prevent us from understanding fully one another's perspectives.

When I read queer and feminist scholarship, I often wish for more nuance in discussions of religion. For example, in laying out the prescriptive main tenets of "gaga feminism," J. Jack Halberstam writes sweepingly of religion:

> When it comes to gender norms and sexual mores, religion really is the root of all evil, and that cuts across many religions. [. . .] religion is a no-no and God has got to go-go. Christianity in particular has not been held accountable for all of the violence and misery that it has brought upon the world through its missions, morality, and miserable notions of salvation. As an anti-Christian doctrine, gaga feminism will not be your salvation, it will not save or redeem you, it will not forgive you for your sins, but instead it encourages you to be a nonbeliever, and to keep your spiritual beliefs to yourself. (2012, p. 28)

In the beginning of his "creative nonbelieving" rule, Halberstam seems to put all religion in the same handbasket and condemn the whole enterprise; however, he reserves special hostility for Christianity. Then, in a sentence I find more vexing every time I read it, he contends that gaga feminism simultaneously encourages nonbelief and the keeping of one's beliefs to oneself. The insistence for gaga feminists to practice creative nonbelief seems itself to violate the final clause of Halberstam's imperative. He has not kept his beliefs to himself.

Even so, I endeavor here no more to probe the internal coherence of Halberstam's gaga feminist principles than to refute Tooley's position about biblical gender identity (whatever his position may be). Instead, I want to suggest that communication scholars of religion, of transgender studies, and of both ought to seek out the space between the extremes of Tooley and Halberstam. Students and scholars of religious communication must acknowledge the existence of transgender people and further acknowledge that at least some transgender people also identify with a religious or spiritual tradition. In 2010, Helen Sterk argued that the *Journal of Communication and Religion* "would benefit in range and diversity through publishing more sophisticated gender and feminist-based articles" (2010, p. 207). I agree with Sterk, and I would extend her point to the sub-discipline of religious communication more broadly (i.e., regardless of publication outlet) and beyond gender-based articles to include analyses that center on gender identity as well. Religious communication scholars have much to offer to the study of transgender lives, particularly as transgender lives intersect with, transition among, or move within religious traditions. Messages like Weekley's—which affirm transgender and religious identity—deserve the attention of communication scholars from humanistic and social scientific traditions alike. Jewish and Christian theologies of transgender inclusion and transgender religious narratives have circulated for more than a decade (Cheng, 2011; Dzmura, 2010; Isherwood & Althaus-Reid, 2009; Ladin, 2012; Tigert & Tirabassi, 2004; Mollenkott, 2001; Tanis, 2003). Given that communication scholars have particular training on attending to context, explaining rhetorical strategies and methods of persuasion, and the importance of audience, surely some of these narratives and theologies offer fodder for our analysis. Additionally, students and scholars with a social scientific orientation may find intrigue in questions about whether attitudes about lesbian, gay, and bisexual inclusion within organized religious traditions change at the same or different rates as opinions about transgender inclusion. Applied communication scholars and others with a goal of reaching practitioners and service providers should especially consider contributing to scholarly conversations about transgender persons of faith. Articles on the topic in social work and counseling journals provide some helpful conclusions but commonly take too cavalier an approach to language choices. From insisting on reporting their research participants' "biological sex" (Levy & Lo, 2013) to using *transgender* as a noun (Joan of Arc "shared many characteristics with today's male-to-female transgenders," according to Bockting and Cesaretti [2001, p. 292]), to presumptuously correcting a participant's self-identification (Yarhouse & Carrs, 2012), social work and counseling psychology scholars interested in the experiences of transgender persons of faith misstep with language in potentially harmful ways. Scholars with more training in the nuances and importance of inclusive language may contribute richly to these discussions in ways that could lead to better care and treatment for people who seek social or mental health services.

While my own preference lies with people and messages that we might identify as affirming all of human dignity, I submit that oppositional messages also deserve scholarly attention. Surely some who share Tooley's view about the incompatibility of transgender identity with Christianity or any other religious tradition articulate that view more thoughtfully and carefully than Tooley. The field of communication can learn from analysis of these arguments and strategies as well. Regardless of what students and scholars of religious communication believe on these questions—and I recognize that many sincere, faithful people arrive at different conclusions than I—transgender people produce messages and find messages produced about them that have real, material effects in their lives. These messages and these lives deserve our attention.

To communication scholars whose primary interests lie in the study of gender identity, I offer a similar exhortation. When writing about sexual orientation, gender identity, or both, we must resist the temptation to use the words *religion* or *Christianity* as handy stand-ins for the primary source of conservatism and opposition on a host of issues related to gender, sexuality, and gender identity. Even when most people who hold a particular political position do so because of their religious convictions, painting entire religious traditions with the same brushstroke misses a great deal of diversity within each religious tradition. Sometimes, the judicious use of a carefully defined modifier goes a long way toward managing the problem: *conservative Christians* or *Orthodox Jews* at least offer implicit recognition that great multiplicity exists within the broader categories *Christian* and *Jew*. For instance, in *Toward a Civil Discourse: Rhetoric and Fundamentalism*, rhetorical scholar Sharon Crowley (2006) exemplifies both the problem I identify here and a way forward toward a solution. I admire that she uses modifiers like "Right wing," "fundamentalist," and "apocalyptic" to qualify which Christians she means in her analysis of evangelical Christian political activism, but after she carefully defines her terms, she ends up functionally collapsing all or most of Christendom into one end of a binary with American liberalism on the other end. The coherence of her argument depends on diametric opposition, so while she tacitly acknowledges that "the phrase 'liberal Christian' is not an oxymoron," liberal Christians remain invisible throughout her analysis (Crowley, 2006, p. 7).

Scholars committed to intersectionality ought to realize that like sex, gender, sexual orientation, gender identity, race, ethnicity, and social class, religious identity informs (at least some) people's social locations and subject positions. A scholar need not subscribe to a particular set of beliefs to recognize that the religious views of those they study matter and to consider the implications of their research subjects' spiritual lives when applicable. My objection to Halberstam (2012) stems not from his rejection of religion, or even from his conviction that everyone ought to reject it. Though I personally arrive at different conclusions on both points, the real tragedy of his perspective and those who embrace it wholesale lies in the propensity to overlook the importance of religiosity for understanding and explaining others' lives. Many transgender people (and for that matter, many cisgender people, many straight people, many gay and lesbian people, and others) reject religion, and for good reason. But many others do not. From where I stand, transgender folks (and, again, gay and lesbian people, women, people with disabilities, and others) who intentionally remain part of religious traditions that may or may not fully accept them invite a number of questions that communication scholars have the tools to answer: Why do people stay in less than hospitable religious traditions? What strategies of resistance do they employ in such contexts, and to what effect? Do the more welcoming parts of the religious tradition talk to (work within, cooperate alongside) the more traditional or conservative sects? Previous work in communication studies begins to explore some of these questions, particularly for women (Cetin, 2010; Foss, 1984; Jablonski, 1988; Kraidy, 2009; Lengel, 2004; Macdonald, 2006; Maddux, 2011; Spencer, 2013; Sterk, 1989, 1993) and lesbian, gay, and bisexual persons (Bennett, 2003; Chávez, 2004; Johnson, 2008; Lynch, 2005; Spencer & Barnett, 2013; Spencer, 2015; Zukic, 2008), but more work remains to answer these questions and pose new questions about transgender persons' encounters with religion.

My analysis in this essay and several of the articles I have cited consider the intersections of religion and gender or sexuality within Christianity. While a few articles address Judaism and Islam, the intersections of Eastern religious traditions with gender, sexuality, and gender identity offer promise for future communication scholarship. With the notable exception of Abhik Roy's work on Hindu masculinities (Roy & Hammers, 2014; Roy, 2006), religious communication scholarship about gender and sexuality tends to reflect a monotheistic, Western, and often Christian bias. As contrasted with the three major monotheistic religions, Eastern religious traditions and polytheistic traditions differ significantly in their ontological, epistemological, axiological, and metaphysical assumptions about unified human subjects and the importance of the self. We might then reasonably expect the communicatively constructed gender norms and life experience for transgender Buddhists or genderqueer Hindus to differ greatly from Jewish or Christian trans folks.

In sum, I call on transgender studies scholars in communication to engage more often, more seriously, and more fairly with religious communication. And I charge scholars of religious communication in particular to recognize the significance of transgender lives to religion and religion to at least some transgender people's lives. I urge all of us to resist conflating *religion* with *Christian(ity)* or with monotheism or major Western religious traditions writ large. In this way, transgender studies scholarship in religious communication holds great potential for explaining hitherto under-examined phenomena and, more important, making transgender lives more livable.

CONCLUSION

Sadly, the support Weekley received in the immediate aftermath of his coming out eventually abated. In 2013, Weekley left Epworth United Methodist Church and moved across the country to begin a doctoral program in ministry at Boston University School of Theology. Explaining his decision on his blog, Weekley wrote:

> After publicly disclosing my history as a transgender man I struggled for three years to continue local church ministry and provide leadership and education for my denomination concerning the authenticity and spiritual experiences of many transgender persons of faith. Despite verbal support promised by many people, actions by my bishop, district superintendents, several colleagues, and some members of the congregations I served proved otherwise. One of the most painful personal truths I learned through this process is exactly how deep, and often subconscious trans-phobia actually is in our culture. I still believe some of those who hurt and abused me and my family do not accept as true that they did so. (2013)

Taken as a whole, Weekley's experience reflects a wide range of the influence of religious communication on transgender lives. Weekley's faith in God and trust in God's love sustained him for many years, abiding through his transition and nearly three decades of ordained ministry. Religious faith not only made meaning for Weekley, but offered hope and promise in the midst of his bodily transition. After coming out, Weekley discovered how quickly the honeymoon could end (and I invoke a cisnormative and heteronormative metaphor here intentionally and reflexively). Religious communities, for Weekley, also functioned as a source of transphobia, of violence, of fear. People's real, material, embodied lives intersect and interact with religious communication. Sometimes, those encounters act violently on trans lives. Other times, those encounters offer tremendous hope for transformation—or perhaps even transfiguration.

NOTES

1. I originally accessed Weekley's sermon from the Epworth United Methodist Church Web site in February 2010, though the sermon has since been removed from the site. Weekley (2011) expanded on his story in his memoir, *In from the Wilderness*. A substantial excerpt of "My Book Report" appears in the book itself.

2. I borrow this phrase from Martin Luther King, Jr.'s "Letter from a Birmingham Jail." See King (1992).

Chapter Thirteen

Legal Discourse

The Trans-Exclusive Archives of U.S. Capital Punishment Rhetoric

Peter Odell Campbell and Cory Holding

The official language of U.S. law has a significant, and sometimes understated, degree of sovereign control not only over those individuals forcibly subject to its immediate jurisdictions (such as someone brought up on criminal charges), but also over all possibilities of present and future life within the borders of the United States (Campbell, 2012, 2013). U.S. legal language should be studied as something to be feared and strategized against. A specifically transgender approach to such a project, however, poses some difficulty. The vast body of U.S. institutional legal rhetoric contains within it what K. J. Rawson (2009) has called ambiguously transgender archival spaces. In this chapter, we turn in particular to U.S. judicial and administrative rhetorics of capital punishment and incarceration. The total set of these discourses forms legal rhetorical archives wherein the exploration of "trans people and trans lives" (West, 2013, p. 9) is a morally questionable undertaking. To name many people caught up in these archives' discursive fields "trans" would be unwelcome, a violent act. But, U.S. rhetorics of capital punishment and prison administration are core tools in the ongoing statist project of "gender policing" trans people (TransJustice, 2005, pp. 227–228).

Trans personhood can exist both variously and simultaneously as an identity form and a more or less "temporary" set of "contextualized experiences" and practices (West, 2013, p. 14). We argue that transgender studies in legal rhetoric must find ways to answer the question of how to approach fields of discourse (such as official capital punishment rhetoric) wherein trans personhood is "unrealizable" (Butler, 1999, p. viii), but to do so in ways that do not replicate the appropriation of "transgender" as a "mere tropological figure" in academic arguments about the various limits of linguistic categorization (Namaste, 2000, pp. 14–15; see also, West, 2013). In what follows, we offer a rhetorical distinction between certain *de jure* and *de facto* forms of U.S. capital punishment rhetoric. From this distinction, we argue for building a space conducive to critical analysis of state-institutional legal language within the field of transgender communication studies. We hold together: the absence and unrealizability of named trans life in the official language of capital punishment law and the unofficial deadly consequences of articulations of transgender life-in-prison by judicial and administrative rhetors. We view this critical combination as an opportunity to turn these archives of erasure, absence, and failure toward a productive and hopeful end. By mapping the discursive structure of cisnormative punishment institutions, trans rhetorical study can provide useful resources to the effort to abolish those very institutions.

TRANSGENDER STUDY IN THE RHETORIC OF LAW

In writing a chapter about transgender studies in legal rhetoric (which is largely, although not exclusively, a sub-field of communication studies), we face a productive challenge. Existing legal rhetorical work in transgender studies is rich, useful, provocative—and rare. Few transgender-inclusive studies of U.S. judicial or administrative punishment rhetoric have been published by communication scholars in communication studies outlets (for examples of the exceptions that prove the rule, see Chávez, 2011; Cloud, 2014). This may be because the turn in queer and trans communication, history, and legal studies away from the policy pronouncements of statist institutions and toward the language and procedures of the administrative entities responsible for implementing law in the daily lives of U.S. residents is relatively new (Canaday, 2009; McKinnon, 2011; Spade, 2011). But it could also be due to the procedural, ethical, and political difficulties inherent to any transgender study about a body of rhetoric that works to exclude and punish any form of trans identification within its boundaries. Our goal in this chapter is to help articulate a mode of explicitly transgender inquiry about the rhetoric of U.S. punishment and prison administration. While our focus in this chapter centers on civilian prisons, many of our conclusions could apply just as strongly to military prisons.

Any form of transgender study is necessarily rhetorical. "Transgender" is a recent addition to our lexicon. The word itself is a collocation, an assemblage of two words constellated on the basis of overlapping relationships of similarity, difference, and mutual reference (Threadgold, 1997, p. 102).[1] As Rawson and Williams (2014, p. 2) described it, transgender is simultaneously: a floating discursive signifier for an active "rhetorical landscape" of identity categories and subject positions and an ontology demarcated by a set of various "*trans*-gender" practices of being and relation (Rawson, 2009, p. 131, emphasis in original).

In the language of U.S. legal institutions (the language of courtrooms, legislatures, and governmental administration) *transgender* functions more as a device for violently defining trans people in terms of previously constructed categories of illness and deviance than as a progressive statist recognition of trans people's self-identification. Most often, however, *transgender* works as both at the same time (see, for example, Havlik, 2012). Isaac West (2008, 2010, 2013)—the critic responsible for much of the communication studies work in transgender legal rhetoric—works accordingly through an inversion of legal scholarship's typical focus on state-institutional authors. Following in part David Valentine (2007), West takes a subject-focused, ethnographic approach to transgender study. He writes about quotidian legal rhetoric as trans people both experience and produce it. For West (2013), the practice of writing about law via trans people's everyday legal articulations of law and citizenship works as a necessary corrective to scholars interested in *transgender* only as a hermeneutic device for their own self-referential, theoretical explorations of categorical failures in legal discursive forms. In this way, West's work runs parallel to other recent writing by queer, trans, and activist communication scholars who focus on the possibility of trans life per se as a form and strategy of performative resistance to oppressive cisnormative rhetorics produced by statist institutions (see, for example, McKinnon, 2014).

But conceiving of transgender study as rhetorical entails a recognition of *transgender*'s inherent polysemy. Transgender is a term both for self-identification and for the organizational and institutional interpellation of others. It is a device used for good and ill by activist, medical, and legal organizations and institutions seeking to make sense of evolving realities of sex and gender identity. As an umbrella term (Rawson & Williams, 2014, p. 2), transgender is a vital resource for many different people erased by subsumption into other umbrella terms like *queer* (or *female, male, person*). It is also a pernicious terminological force for the collapsing together of race, sexual, class, sex, and gender difference under the sign of a single new identity form (Valentine, 2007; Rawson, 2009; West, 2013; Rawson & Williams, 2014). Here at the intersection of transgender studies and trans-exclusive institutional legal rhetoric, we are mindful of Rawson's (2009, p. 131) eloquent description of transgender research in an archive of sources that pre-date the term—because in such an archive it would be difficult, in a certain terminological sense, to "explore trans people and trans lives" as the primary focus of an explicitly transgender scholarly inquiry.

Rawson (2009, p. 131) considers a hypothetical archivist's interaction with a set of papers written by a "female-born person of colour who often passed as male and used the identity label 'bulldagger.'" If the archivist names this person, or labels their papers, as transgender, the archivist "disrespectfully and oppressively" names "an identity . . . that already has a name." The name the scholar chooses interpellates a person of color into a rhetorical form that, for all of its necessity and potential, is also freighted with practices of white-normative racial erasure. Naming this person "trans" might erase who they are or were. But this possibility must be weighed always against the possible consequences of not naming. If the researcher, aware of the violence they might do, chooses *not* to name the archival subject, or label their papers, as transgender, they risk participating in the archival subject's erasure from the "long lineage of other people who *trans*-gender"—and in this way, also participate in the ongoing white-normative erasure of trans, gender nonconforming, and genderqueer people of color.

Rawson's scenario invites the question of whether transgender communication study should privilege a focus on the communicative outputs and experiences of self-identified trans people (as we believe West argues). In general, we believe transgender communication study should do so. But in this chapter, we depart from this standard on methodological and terminological grounds. From our outsider, public archival research perspective, no self-identified trans people live on death row. The rhetorical archives constituted in officially produced discourses of U.S. capital punishment and prison administration are so effective in their violent cisnormativity that they erase any possibility of meaningful trans life for many who are caught up in their jurisdiction. We take the tension in Rawson's hypothetical scenario between the choice to name or not name an archive as *transgender* as the basis for refusing either choice. Instead, we suggest a transgender rhetorical study of archives that *trans-gender*, but should not be named *trans**—this is, a study of those "archives of failure" wherein transgender articulation and identification carries the least possibility and the greatest risk.

The officially produced discourses of U.S. capital punishment and prison administration form a de facto—existing in reality, if not by right in law—system of cisnormative capital punishment that operates in two forms. First, it demands execution for people whose trans personhood is either non-existent or unspeakable, but nonetheless marks them for death. Second, it operates through laws and procedures whose de jure—in law—purpose of protecting vulnerable prison populations works as a cover for the laws' de facto function of acting as a transgender death penalty.

West's practice of legal inquiry in communication is generally consistent with the broadly anti-establishmentarian foci of queer legal studies. Transgender scholarship that focuses on what the queer legal theorist Leslie J. Moran (2009, p. 295) called "black letter" law—that is, research focused literally on the letter of the law—risks reproducing what West (2013, p. 21) called an "archive of failure." Research limited to this "black letter" archive, West argued, moves attention away from powerful and innovative forms of anti-cisnormative resistance found in everyday transgender legal articulations. Again, we tend to agree—except that an overbroad application of this anti-black letter method ignores the particular context of de jure U.S. punishment rhetoric and other U.S. legal rhetorics that work de facto to punish and even to kill (Campbell, 2012).

There is in fact a death penalty for being trans (and in particular, trans and poor, trans and black, trans and immigrant, trans and queer) in the United States. This rhetorical death penalty is rooted in prisons and death rows, but it reaches out from spaces of incarceration to affect transgender, gender nonconforming, and genderqueer life "on the outside." There are trans people who experience relative safety from the effects of this de facto death penalty—but this safety is in no small part a function of structurally inherent forms of race, citizenship, gender, class, familial, and other privileges. Analysis grounded in *transgender* that would avoid replicating racialized and other problematic blind spots often implicated in the use of the term must take up transgender as a varied and intersectional identity form (Spade, 2011; West, 2013). In particular, any study of U.S. transgender legal rhetorical identifications and articulations should be grounded in the fact that trans people of color specifically are more subject to official and unofficial forms of state violence than any other identity group in the United States (Davis, 2014; Wideman, 2014). This means that if the language procedures of U.S. punishment administration imply trans failures, these failures help to delineate those transgender subject positions (intersectionally implicated in race, ethnicity, gender, class, sexuality, nationality, family, and citizenship status) through which people are more capable of everyday articulations of trans resistance. Any such resistance, of course, is often met with violent repression and death. But these violent responses are most likely to be directed at trans people who are poor, black, and queer. Turning our rhetorical critical attention away from legal "archives of failure" will not help to change this fact.

As we argue elsewhere, rhetorical legal methods offer an opportunity for an anti-establishmentarian insistence on the value of understanding "how" certain state-institutional rhetors make their claims (Campbell, 2012; Constable, 2004, p. 78). An occasional focus on legal rhetorical archives of [trans] failure need not fall into the trap of trans-effacing scholarship that West (2013) and Viviane K. Namaste (2000) warned us of. Instead, we call for trans, legal, rhetorical study as one tool in the multi-pronged scholarly and activist effort to abolish the places of incarceration where these archives of failure are produced and maintained.

Peter Odell Campbell and Cory Holding

DE FACTO PUNISHMENT

Two concepts in legal scholarship represent potential resources for realizing a transgender archive of trans-exclusive death penalty rhetoric. The first is a collection of theories that examines sentencing procedures in trials of women convicted of death-eligible crimes to argue that capital punishment serves as the ultimate arbiter for policing and maintaining patriarchal gender norms in the United States. The second is a concept called the "accidental death penalty"—a legal rhetorical construction designed to frame administrative failures in the treatment of mentally ill inmates as violations of the U.S. Constitution's Eighth Amendment prohibition on cruel and unusual punishment. These theories seek to explain the de facto discriminatory reality of legal statutes and procedures that might seem like "facially neutral" attempts at distributing and ordering justice (Siegel, 1998, p. 31). Taken together, they suggest a hermeneutic for an explicitly transgender study of judicial and other discourses of legal administration that assumptively deny the legitimate existence of transgender people. But we do not want to take an add-trans-and-stir approach to existing theories—or to existing institutional archives (Butler, 1990; Morton, 1994). We aim instead to join existing projects that attempt to force a space for transgender inquiry within certain violently cis-normative legal rhetorical archives—archives that exclude but matter to trans lives.

The distinction between de jure and de facto law is common in U.S. judicial practice and scholarship. The terms are not necessarily mutually exclusive: de jure means "by right" or "according to law"; de facto, "in fact." The juxtaposition of the two terms is used by legal rhetors (both judicial and critical) to signal instances where judicial precedent or legal statute might not explicitly require a certain consequence, but nonetheless in actual fact make it so. Reva Siegel (1998, p. 31) used the distinction between de jure and de facto forms of racial segregation to argue that even after the end—indeed the constitutional outlawing—of legally mandated (de jure) racial segregation, "many facially [de jure] neutral state practices" are in actual fact (de facto) continued forms of mandated discrimination. In this example, the "demise of de jure segregation" did not bring an end to, or even a substantial diminishment of, racial caste in the United States because de jure segregation has been replaced with various statutes and judicial precedents that maintain a system of de facto white supremacy (Siegel, 1998, p. 56).

Comparisons among de jure and de facto forms of law can be useful for rhetorical legal analysis because they enable a consideration of the meaning and effect of legal language beyond the prima facie statements of policies, statutes, and judicial opinions (Constable, 1998, 2004).[2] We think this is particularly true in the context of jurisprudential rhetoric implicating trans people in capital punishment. An exclusive focus on the discourses of either de jure or de facto systems of execution would not be adequate for the project of mapping out the rhetorical system through which U.S. polities kill trans people, and people who trans—especially not for the purpose of helping to abolish that system. Our alternative, a rhetorically constituted de facto death penalty, exists as a collocation of deadly punishment discourses targeted simultaneously at all transgender people in the United States, and also toward non-trans identified people subject to U.S. capital sentencing procedures, who are executed because they somehow "*trans*-gender."

TRANS(-)GENDER CAPITAL PUNISHMENT

To read the official archives of U.S. law, one would think that trans people are not subject to capital punishment. Presently, there appear to be no persons who are imprisoned for capital crimes and awaiting execution in U.S. state or federal prisons who publicly identify or have been identified in popular media or public legal documents as trans people. It may or may not actually[3] be the case that there are no trans people on death row—but trans people are disproportionately represented in all forms and levels of jail and prison as a result of systematic legal, racial, and economic marginalization and active targeting by police and citizens (Spade, 2006; Tarzwell, 2006; West, 2013). Sydney Tarzwell (2006) and Dean Spade (2011) argued accordingly that there is a coherent, multi-level punishment system of targeted anti-trans administrative violence directed especially against immigrants, non-citizens, people of color, queer people, and poor people who are transgender (Spade, 2011). This system of administrative violence is not specifically mandated in any U.S. law—but its effects are real, and sometimes deadly (Bassichis, 2007; Spade, 2011). The question of whether any trans persons are presently subject to capital punishment is, therefore, mostly irrelevant to the fact that every day trans people face the threat of death at the hands of the state.

One possible reason for the absence of any explicitly transgender voices in the archives of U.S. capital punishment rhetoric is that any trans-identification "on the row" could have potentially deadly consequences. The late 1970s saw the enactment of a series of state and federal statutes written with the de jure purpose of eliminating arbitrary and capricious decision making from capital sentencing procedures (Baldus et al., 1998; Banner, 2002). These statutes require comparative evidence about the "aggravating and mitigating circumstances" of a capital convict's crimes to be presented in the post-conviction, sentencing phase of a capital trial as a guide for a jury's deliberations about whether to hand down a death sentence (§ 921.141, Fla. Stat., 2013). In the late 1990s, a group of feminist law students, including Jenny Carroll (1997) and Melinda O'Neil (1999), published a series of influential law notes arguing that aggravating and mitigating circumstances laws, as applied in particular to women convicted of death-eligible crimes, have had the de facto effect of establishing the U.S. system of death penalties as a mechanism by which the nation-state enforces normative expectations for femininity.

Prosecutors charged with making "aggravating circumstances" arguments in favor of executing women (persons whom the court defines as female) convicted of capital crimes frame their targets as "evil women"—"'crazed monsters' deserving of nothing more than extermination" (Carroll, 1997, p. 1416; O'Neil, 1999, p. 221). Prosecutors accuse these people of performing—in the commission of the crime they are convicted of, in their daily lives, or both—such grossly "'unladylike' behavior" that they can no longer be eligible for the paternalistic protective impulses of U.S. judicial actors (Shapiro, 1999, p. 459). They are found guilty of the de facto crime of murder *particularly inconsistent with a judge or jury's notions of feminine ideals*. For Carroll (1997, p. 1451), the apparent "scarcity" of women on death row is actually the best evidence for the gender-disciplinary "power" of U.S. capital punishment. Death row, according to these theories, is our national society's ultimate demarcation of a "limit-experience" of tolerable feminine behavior (Foucault, 1991, p. 18).

We find these theories persuasive. But one problem with them, as Barbara Cruikshank (1999, p. 1115) put it, is that "not all women" convicted and sentenced to death "are 'women,'" and, we add, not all men who must undergo U.S. capital sentencing are men. Both the prosecution of capital punishment in the United States and its contrarian study by feminist anti-death penalty scholars are simultaneously and mutually gendered and *cis*gendered. The dominant abolitionist archives of sex- and gender-implicated U.S. capital punishment discourses are places wherein trans people have been presumptively erased.

We argue that an appropriate corrective would not, in this case, lie in Rawson's "naming" option. It may be more productive—and perhaps more ethical—to recognize that *transgender*'s potential as a progressive mode of signification and self-identification might begin to break down within the most oppressive and circumscribed spaces of U.S. incarceration. As Ruthann Robson (1998, p. 35) observed, "while sexual identity is arguably always socially constructed, it is difficult to fathom more 'constructing' circumstances than the threat of being executed." In any de jure punishment context (as we will discuss in a following example), an accused or convicted person's identity is forcibly subordinated to legal rhetorical identification at the whim of judicial and bureaucratic state officials. A person's means for resisting the consequences of this oppressive identification is heavily determined by intersectional circumstances of racial, class, citizenship, gender, sexuality, and other forms of privilege that are beyond their control. The study of "trans people and trans lives" as they exist and resist under the sign of U.S. capital punishment rhetoric would often be a study that privileges the resistive potential of those certain people who are more able to *be who they are* in incarceral spaces.

Instead, we suggest that the unrealizability of trans life within the archival space of U.S. capital punishment rhetoric's discursive field signals the de facto operation of de jure capital punishment as a deadly warning directed not just at transgender people per se, but at people who dare to trans-gender within the long reach of U.S. law. Such a theory disaggregates the gender policing effects of capital punishment away from the supposed targeting of gender transgressive members of putatively fixed identities (women convicted of murder). Instead, the procedural rhetoric of capital sentencing can be approached and resisted for what it is: one of many statist tools in the violent administration of cisnormativity.

THE "ACCIDENTAL DEATH PENALTY"

In 1992, Michelle Lynne Kosilek was convicted in Massachusetts of first-degree murder for the death of Cheryl Kosilek. From the year of her conviction, Kosilek has been in litigation with the Massachusetts Department of Corrections (DOC) over the DOC's refusal to provide her access to sex reassignment surgery. On January 17, in *Kosilek v. Spencer* (No. 12-2194, 1st Cir. 2014), a panel for the United States Court of Appeals for the First Circuit upheld the District of Massachusetts's 2012 order that DOC Commissioner Luis S. Spencer must provide Kosilek this "medically necessary" surgery, as failure to do so without "penological justification" subjects her to "'unnecessary and wanton infliction of pain'" in violation of the U.S. Constitution's Eight Amendment prohibition on cruel and unusual punishment (*Kosilek v. Spencer*, 2012, p. 115; *Kosilek v. Spencer*, 2014, p. 3). The case is now awaiting an "en banc" decision from the entire First Circuit bench.

Throughout the process of her investigation, arrest, trial, appeal, and Eighth Amendment litigation, Kosilek has been subject to a variety of forms of "gender policing" by agents of the state. In the 1996 Massachusetts Supreme Judicial Court opinion upholding Kosilek's conviction, Justice Neil L. Lynch insisted on referring to Kosilek by her male birth certificate name and with masculine pronouns—despite the fact that Kosilek had *legally* taken the name Michelle, and that, in Lynch's words, a "single justice of this court [had permitted] the defendant . . . to refer to himself [*sic*] as Michelle Kosilek" throughout the high court's consideration of her appeal (*Commonwealth v. Kosilek*, 1996, p. 449n1). Lynch's diction is not some accident of procedure in judicial composition. We read it as a deliberate judicial rebuke to Kosilek for both being and living as trans. Writing for the District of Massachusetts in *Kosilek v. Spencer* (889 F. Supp. 2d 190, D. Mass., 2012) District Judge Mark L. Wolf used Kosilek's name, Michelle, but referred to her throughout the District Court's opinion with the masculine pronoun. Wolf's pronoun use is subsequently explicitly corrected in direct quotations of his opinion by First Circuit Judge Ojetta Rogeriee Thompson (2014, p. 55). Both name and pronoun use are, therefore, clearly a *choice* available to judges. Lynch seems to complain that Kosilek was "permitted" to call herself by her own name during her appeal proceedings; the evident contempt Lynch displays for this permission may have had some influence on the Massachusetts Supreme Judicial Court's negative view of Kosilek's claims in her own defense (McKinnon, 2009).

We dwell on Lynch and Wolf's cissexist naming decisions to emphasize how Kosilek has been treated by both prison administrative and judicial rhetors. As Kosilek (2011, p. 9) writes:

> I'm a prisoner, a transsexual currently transitioning to female while living in a men's prison. It is . . . the most humiliating and reactionary environment in which to transition from one identified gender to another, but I had no choice in the matter . . . the realities of prison life are too complex to properly explain . . . but some have results that are so far out of proportion to their intended purpose that they can fill one's days with grief.

This set of de facto results of seemingly mundane prison policies has material and even deadly consequences for any prisoners situated similarly to Kosilek. Federal courts have so far recognized the medical necessity of Kosilek's demand for access to sex reassignment surgery. In an amicus brief filed with the First Circuit on Kosilek's behalf, lawyers for Gay and Lesbian Advocates and Defenders (GLAD) and other organizations characterize the Massachusetts Department of Corrections as a cynical state institution that would rather risk the death of a prisoner than face the possibility of public opposition to providing Kosilek with necessary care (GLAD et al., 2013). Taken at face value, GLAD's framing of Kosilek's case is evocative of a legal theory developed by Elizabeth Alexander in support of her own Eighth Amendment litigation—what Alexander calls an "accidental death penalty" for mentally ill prisoners.

In 2008, Alexander (pp. 3–5)—the director of the National Prison Project of the American Civil Liberties Union Foundation—coined the term "accidental death penalty" in reference to certain policies common to U.S. prison administration treatment of mentally ill prisoners. One of Alexander's clients, Timothy Souders, was a physically and mentally ill person imprisoned in March 2006 at the Southern Michigan Correctional Facility. Souders died on August 6, 2006, in administrative segregation, or solitary confinement—where he was held in conditions so severe that his death became a predictable outcome. Broadly, "accidental death penalty" references the deadly consequences Souders and many other prisoners face as a direct consequence of a series of intersecting "public policy choices" in an era of mass incarceration. The "accidental death penalty" works as a legal rhetorical tool for positing that "systemically inadequate care" (including the use of solitary confinement as a form of treatment) in the treatment of mentally ill prisoners represents a violation of U.S. constitutional prohibitions on cruel and unusual punishment (Alexander, 2008, p. 7).

Kosilek's case, which depended on Kosilek's (2011, p. 9) self-identified and legally recognized gender identity disorder (GID), suggests that trans prisoners may also form a set of incarcerated people who are subject to this "accidental death penalty," constituted simultaneously in medicalized administrative policies toward trans prisoners, and the medical interpellation of certain prisoners as transgender or transsexual regardless of their self-identification. "Systemically inadequate care" is a reality for transgender, gender variant, gender non-conforming, and genderqueer prisoners. Trans people are almost always denied access to gender affirming medical treatment while they are incarcerated (Tarzwell, 2006, p. 170). Rare exceptions to this denial occur in situations involving trans, gender non-conforming, and genderqueer people who—with and without their consent—have been given a diagnosis of GID. A GID diagnosis represents one of the only chances for any incarcerated person to experience transgender affirmation from their supervising institution. But at the same time, the prison views the diagnosis as a label of mental illness. GID diagnoses thus render trans people (and/or people interpellated by prison medical staff as trans) doubly vulnerable to prison policies that use solitary confinement as a catch-all mechanism for both "treating" mentally ill inmates, and for addressing violence directed against trans prisoners by prison guards and by other prisoners at the direction and behest of prison guards (Tarzwell, 2006).

If the rhetorical archive of Alexander's accidental death penalty included the experiences of trans prisoners, then Kosilek's eventual victory in court could be celebrated as a repudiation of the accidental death penalty—an example of a prisoner rescuing herself from prison administration policies so incompetent as to be deadly. The District Court's language of no "penological justification" for the DOC's denial of Kosilek's requested care could set a powerful precedent for raising instances of administrative incompetence (not just toward trans people) to the level of willful constitutional violation.

We argue, however, that Kosilek's case represents something more insidious than an "accidental death penalty." Kosilek might win—even at the United States Supreme Court—and we do not diminish the significance of such a victory, one resulting from a person courageously taking up the only arms available to her in the fight to live her life. But the rhetorical study of judicial rhetoric must include an analysis of certain judicial argumentative choices in addition to the immediate consequential effects of judicial opinions. The success of Kosilek's Eighth Amendment claim depends on continued judicial recognition that her case meets various brightline criteria—specifically, that the DOC's refusal of sex reassignment surgery does not constitute a "good faith" effort to further a "legitimate penological objective" (*Kosilek v. Spencer*, 2012, p. 115). The Supreme Court's Eighth Amendment finding in *Furman v. Georgia* of capricious and arbitrary procedures in capital sentencing led directly to the creation of aggravating and mitigating circumstances statutes (Baldus et al., 1998). Kosilek's case will also inspire the creation of new de jure procedures for treating trans inmates that purport to meet whatever criteria for good faith "legitimate penological objectives" judicial rhetors choose to set. We should not assume that these criteria would have a net positive impact on the lives of trans people subject to the U.S. criminal justice system. In fact, based on precedent, we should probably assume the opposite. District Judge Wolf's casually violent discursive treatment of Kosilek occurs in the context of what is otherwise a relatively "favorable" instance of judicial treatment of a trans person. As such, Wolf's pronoun use underwrites a broader reality. The death penalty for trans prisoners is not the "accidental" result of cruelly incompetent prison policies for mental illnesses or GID. It is instead a de facto death penalty constituted in existing official and unofficial policies directed specifically against trans people.

A trans person's experience of life in prison and jail is likely to be characterized primarily through violence. This is a rhetorical reality, produced and maintained through the persuasive language of prison administration. Prisoners interviewed for the Sylvia Rivera Law Project's (SRLP) "Report on the Treatment of Transgender and Intersex People in New York State Men's Prisons" (Bassichis, 2007) reported not only that prison guards and other correctional employees are primarily responsible for violence against trans prisoners, but that this violence is accompanied, enabled, and *committed via* rhetorics of cisgendering discipline. Bianca, "an SRLP client . . . imprisoned in the general population," stated in the report that "the administration is against us. Something has to be done, and all they say is 'Act like a man!' . . . the Inspector General said officers have a right to [rape] me. That I'm just a man and shouldn't be dressing like this" (Bassichis 2007, p. 19).

Trans people are disproportionately subject to rape and sexual assault in U.S. prisons and jails (Bassichis, 2007). But as Spade (2011) argued, the primary legislative corrective to rape and sexual assault in prisons, the Prison Rape Elimination Act (PREA), is a highly effective mechanism for prison administrators inclined to inflict violence against "prisoners of color and queer and trans prisoners," because the PREA's implementation guidelines unsurprisingly emphasize "punishment tools" including both protective and punitive solitary confinement.[4] In sum: trans people are shunted into prison via other bureaucratic agencies; prison administration policies are written to punish any instance of gender variance or non-conformity; legal statutes written for the ostensible purpose of protecting prisoners from assault have the opposite effect; prison officials consistently perform sometimes deadly violence against trans inmates; and this violence is both immediately physical and conveyed performatively through official and everyday cissexist speech.

The concept of a de facto death penalty for trans prisoners facilitates the charge that when a trans person is injured or killed in the context of interaction with prison institutions, it is not merely an accident, or the result of an oversight stemming from an individual officer's criminal negligence, or even the by-product of unconstitutional and potentially criminal sets of prison administrative practices. Trans deaths in prison are the deliberate result of a rhetorically constructed system of cisgender discipline. Because prison policies purportedly designed to aid trans people work instead to hurt and kill them, the discursive procedures governing U.S. prison administration of trans people are in fact, if not in law, a rhetorical system of capital punishment for the de facto crime of being transgender. Officially, of course, such a thing is impossible. There could never be a de jure punishment for being trans—at least not in the present version of our constitutional state. A legal rhetorical perspective looks beyond the surface meaning of legal language, enabling an understanding of how the discursive operation of certain administrative policies nonetheless results in a set of de facto punishments for any person whose life stands in violation of cisgender legal normativities.

CONCLUSION

In this chapter, we attempt to follow some of K. J. Rawson's archival advice for the transgender study of sets of institutional legal discourses that both implicate transgender people and presumptively exclude them. The collocation of rhetorics of U.S. capital punishment sentencing procedures directed against people who trans-gender and rhetorics of U.S. prison administration directed at transgender people forms an overlapping set of institutional legal arguments about the relative value to the U.S. polity of normatively stable vs. gender-divergent bodies, lives, ways of being, and relations. These explicit (de jure) and implicit (de facto) arguments have equally sovereign effects (Butler, 1997; Campbell, 2013). They have potentially deadly consequences for all gendered life within the reach of U.S. law. Cruikshank (1999, p. 1115) defines gender specifically on death row not as a form of identity, but rather a "terrain of contestation open to the condemned" for the purposes of anti-juridical resistance. We take Cruikshank's definition as our first example of possible future study in trans legal rhetoric. Rather than ignore or erase "trans people and trans lives," the transgender study of capital punishment rhetoric as an archive of trans unrealizability could enable future rhetorical critical celebrations of a certain possibility; namely, the possibility that people who are not, cannot, or must not be transgender might still, in certain circumstances, rhetorically perform transgender resistance to cisnormative legal institutions.

Isaac West's pathbreaking work in queer and trans legal rhetoric warns of the danger in constantly reproducing "archive[s] of failure" related to trans life in the United States—something that our insistent focus on the interpellation of trans people into official punishment discourses certainly risks doing. But the critical positing of a rhetorically constituted, de facto death penalty for both transgender people in prison and people who trans-gender in U.S. legal jurisdictions can also be one contribution of communication studies scholarship to a growing anti-statist and anti-establishmentarian transgender archive of capital punishment and prison abolitionist resistance. That is, by promoting an understanding of its existence, rhetorical teaching and research about this de facto death penalty can be beneficial to those abolitionist scholar/activists in queer, feminist, and trans legal studies already working to resist the cisnormative state's disparate operations and effects (Meiners, 2011; Spade, 2011). We argue that this benefit places an obligation on scholars who carry out transgender rhetorical studies of U.S. legal language. In the context of U.S. punishment systems, a transgender rhetorical project intending to contribute to such an archive of resistance must be grounded in an uncompromising, antinormative *telos* of prison abolition.

Our field includes a rich tradition of explicit opposition to the death penalty, to incarceration, and to other forms of judicial and statist rhetorical violence (see, for example, Hartnett & Larson, 2006; Morris, 2005). This tradition includes recent work in both queer and trans-focused rhetorical study (Chávez, 2011; Cloud, 2014; McKinnon, 2014; Rand, 2013). Some of this work is explicitly abolitionist—that is, focused on strategies for resisting and eliminating those statist and cultural institutions most responsible for racist, cisnormative, and heteropatriarchal violence. Dana L. Cloud (2014) and Sara L. McKinnon (2014), for example, recently explored ways in which the study of de jure institutional punishment rhetorics can help to celebrate and forward the potential for trans-identification to act as a powerful form of "political resistance" to legal structures of statist domination (Cloud, 2014, p. 81).

At the same time, suspicion of overtly anti-establishmentarian political *teloi* has been, and remains, a persistent trend in rhetorical legal studies (Ono & Sloop, 1992). In their essay on the "Rhetorical Boundaries of 'The Law,'" Marouf Hasian, Jr., Celeste Michelle Condit, and John Louis Lucaites (1996) insisted on separating critical legal *rhetoric* from critical race theory, critical legal studies, and other traditions that they argue do not take a nuanced enough approach to the complex role that judicial rhetors play in the negotiated processes of culture formation within the U.S. state. Indeed, we agree that one of the great benefits of rhetorical inquiry into law is in U.S. rhetorical studies' methodological ability to recognize the simultaneously inherent and limited polysemy of any discourse, such that no given example of political/rhetorical enterprise can be entirely hegemonic, assimilationist, or revolutionary (Condit, 1989).

In this vein, West (2013, p. 168) has recently urged transgender *rhetorical* scholarship to stand as a corrective to the insistent antinormativity common to much of contemporary queer and trans theory, particularly in the context of antinormative calls to reject the ethical and political utility of "demands for equality" within a heteronormative state. Unlike Hasian, Condit, and Lucaites's analyses of judicial rhetoric-in-culture, West forwarded his anti-antinormative arguments in the context of a methodological shift away from institutional legal discourse in favor of critical celebrations of everyday forms of transgender resistance to cisnormative power structures. West's (2013, p. 173) response to anti-establishmentarian critics of "left legalism" is refreshingly not an apology for statist legal rhetors who speak superficially of rights even as they further laws and policies designed primarily to maintain cisnormative, racist, and heteropatriarchal "hierarchies of value" in U.S. culture (Singh, 2004, p. 24). Instead, West (2013, pp. 176–177) called attention to trans advocates who demonstrate the "radical potential of performative contradictions" in forms of trans advocacy that celebrate the mutual *compatibility* of legal-institutional and anti-establishmentarian movement efforts.

As such, we propose a chiasmatic, simultaneous departure from and alignment with West in our own vision of a possible future for trans legal rhetorical scholarship in communication studies. West's legal rhetorical work is characterized by what we would call an anti-legal institutional and establishmentarian *object-focus*, even as he articulates an opposition to certain kinds of normative anti-establishmentarianism in the political *teloi* of his scholarship. In this chapter, and in some of our previous work, we insist on the value of focusing on legal institutional and establishmentarian archives for rhetorical analysis, even as we tend to argue for the normative position that rhetorical criticism of institutional legal discourses *should be* carried out in the service of anti-statist and establishmentarian politics. In short, if West's scholarship involves extra-legal institutional object foci in the service of anti-antinormative political goals, our work offers a limited defense of normative anti-establishmentarianism via the critical analysis of establishmentarian rhetoric. Broadly, we would like to see trans legal rhetorical scholarship occurring at all points within the matrix of antinormative or anti-antinormative positions and institutional or extra-institutional contexts. We take McKinnon's (2009, 2011) ongoing foray into the study of quasi-judicial, bureaucratic legal speech as one major point of guidance for just such a future.

For West (2013, pp. 177–178), leftist critics of "left legalism" often make the fundamental error of assuming that "demands for equality" work unidirectionally against anti-establishmentarian projects that seek to craft "discursive systems of meaning free from already contaminated liberalism." West's analysis reminds us that law is rhetorical; it includes quotidian, ceremonial, and institutional languages. Calls like ours to reject certain "transgender articulations of law" that engage with institutions may then be at best dangerously naïve, and at worst an elite academic form of disciplinary violence that repudiates the legitimacy of choices made by folks who are risking their lives, as it were, on the ground. West's view of transgender rhetorical scholarship might caution us, for example, to temper our earlier description of Kosilek's left-legal resistance with a more explicit acknowledgment of the various, unpredictable, and possibly even abolitionist effects that might flow from the success of her Eighth Amendment claims.

Our caution, however, is that West's representation of antinormative theories is fair with respect to some antinormative critiques of left-liberalism, but more accurately a caricature of other examples of this critical activist tradition. Many queer and trans antinormative objections to left-legal equality projects do not work in the way that rhetoricians are often tempted to claim. Rather, as Livingston and Campbell (forthcoming, p. 306) argued, it is more productive to describe many queer and trans antinormative critiques as establishing certain uncrossable brightlines for the "acceptable use" of left-liberal "legal reform" tools including legislative efforts to achieve legal mandates for equality and anti-discrimination. We follow Spade (2011, p. 162) in urging a particularly stringent version of this brightline test in situations where "law reforms [cannot] be part of dismantling violent regimes of administering life and death." It is true that academic critics can be too quick, as West (2013) argued, to dismiss activists' rhetorically strategic and creative reasons for pursuing legal equality projects for a variety of ends. But we believe that the ability through rhetorical methods to describe the existence of a de facto trans death penalty in de jure U.S. punishment discourses sets one such clear (if simultaneously fuzzy and contestable) brightline for future trans legal work.

We advance the normative claim that future trans legal scholarship should not contribute any labor toward the further existence of incarceration institutions in the United States. As the disciplines of rhetoric and communication continue to exist as a component part of this incarceral nation-state, we as rhetorical and communication scholars should be wary of participating in any project that has the potential to facilitate the *improvement* of administrative discourse in U.S. prisons and other punishment systems. We should maintain this wariness even in situations where such improvement appears to foment greater protections or equality for the most oppressed members of U.S. prison populations. The present reality of rhetorical violence directed at trans people in U.S. prisons is an urgent crisis. It demands an unqualified, anti-state equality, angry, abolitionist response (Spade, 2012). Our chapter does not do enough to celebrate daily articulations of trans resistance to the rhetorical structures of U.S. punishment systems. But future legal rhetorical studies of "trans people and trans lives" must do more to privilege trans folks who have to this point in our nascent sub-discipline been marginalized or ignored: that is, queer, person of color, poor, migrant, homeless trans activists whose articulations of law are explicitly anti-establishmentarian, anti-statist, anti-legislative, anti-equality, and abolitionist.

West (2013, p. 177) argued that the law,

> As a performative enactment . . . is a diachronic resource invoked by individuals, and . . . synchronically interpreted, redeployed, and modified. Viewed in this light, legal cultures must not be understood as hegemonically solidified cultural formations that inhibit agentic practices upon one's entrance into these discursive regimes.

This demand for legal scholarship to embrace and so foment possibilities of agentic resistance even within what seem to be the most oppressive enactments of U.S. legal culture is the basis for West's (2013, p. 177) urge that legal scholars recognize "the need to approach legal cultures from the perspective of undoing rather than domination and subordination." Our perspective in this chapter is on domination and subordination, rather than undoing. West (2013, p. 177) called his "shift in perspective" from domination to undoing "an important supplement to institutionally based analyses of the law." We reverse this relationship, and offer our mode of trans investigation into trans-exclusive institutional legal rhetorical archives as an important supplement to West and other's quotidian rhetorical legal study.

Ultimately, we hope that an institutionally focused mode of transgender legal rhetoric can become a basis for an abolitionist practice of legal rhetorical criticism. We hope this rhetorical critical practice can help underwrite specifically trans understandings of judicial and administrative arguments about sex, gender, and identification, as a form of scholarly resistance to this country's de jure and de facto cisnormative regimes of capital punishment.

NOTES

1. We take this particular definition of collocation from Terry Threadgold's (1997, p. 102) *Feminist Poetics: Performance, Histories*. Threadgold's collocation references "patternings of lexical words recognized [and constituted by critics] on the basis of similarity, difference, and part/whole metonymic relations."

2. Angela P. Harris (2011), for example, has described the generalized operation of hetero-patriarchal violence (carried out as a device for establishing and maintaining hetero and andronormative power hierarchies) in the U.S. criminal punishment system. This violence tends to be state-produced, state-enabled, and/or state-approved. It "stretches across civil society and the state"; it is indiscriminate in its targets, and all too real in the lives of its victims (Harris, 2011, p. 17). But it is not reducible to or describable in terms of any one official form of state-punishment. It is the de facto result of a collocation of de jure punishment policies and discourses.

3. Prisons rarely keep records on trans inmates (Spade, 2006). When they do, the judicial and prison-administrative conferral of the terms "transgender" or "transsexual" on a subject of U.S. law is generally reserved for persons with an official, court-recognized diagnosis of "gender identity disorder" (GID) (p. 5, 46n1–2). Many trans people do not have a GID diagnosis, and persons with a diagnosis may also not identify as "transgender" (Bassichis, 2007). Finally, a condemned person seeking to still avoid execution would incur significant additional risk by publicly identifying or being identified as trans.

4. The recent case of Zahara Green is an instructive example. Green, a trans inmate held in a men's prison, filed suit against the facility alleging that when she was admitted into protective custody, prison officials deliberately placed her in the same cell as the potential assailant she had requested protection from (*Green v. Calhoun*, 2014).

Chapter Fourteen

Public Memory

Historical Trans-cription: Struggling with Memory in Paris Is Burning

Thomas R. Dunn

Over the last twenty-five years, director Jenny Livingston's documentary *Paris Is Burning* (hereafter, *PIB*) has emerged as a consequential artifact for remembering the recent transgender past. Depicting the lives of largely Black and Latino gay men and transgender people—often referring to themselves as "queens"—performing in the drag ball scene of 1980s New York City, the film continues to reach audiences in unexpected ways. While some members of the transgender community have thanked Livingston for preserving this era of the transgender past on film (Jones, 2013), *PIB*'s reach far exceeds this community alone. Since 1990, the film has become a staple at film festivals, college campuses, academic conferences, and annual LGBT history celebrations (Prosser, 1998). It is assigned watching in feminist, queer, LGBT, and transgender history courses worldwide. The film is even required viewing for all contestants on the hit television series *RuPaul's Drag Race*, which remediates the film's jokes, readings, and lingo for a new generation (Juzwiak, 2010). Meanwhile, the film's subjects, quotations, and performances have transfixed popular culture (Juzwiak, 2013; Jones, 2013). In short, while much of transgender history goes unrecognized (Feinberg, 1996), few rhetorical artifacts so broadly circulate the lives of transgender people in the past as *PIB*.

Given the film's iconic status in U.S. culture, *PIB* has received significant critical attention (hooks, 1992; Butler, 1993; Prosser, 1998). However, despite its growing symbolic clout, *PIB* has not been considered from the standpoint of memory, particularly public memory. Over the last two decades, public memory—the study of how the past is mobilized in specific ways for persuasive intent in the present—has become an important topic within rhetorical scholarship (Phillips, 2004; Dickinson et al., 2010). Unlike history, which Pierre Nora (1989) describes as representational, static, and "incomplete," memory emphasizes the sociability and versatility of the past. Rather than following history's efforts to pin down the past, memories are in "permanent evolution" (Nora, 1989, p. 8), willfully open to deformations, manipulations, and appropriations. Given their symbolic force and pliability, memories therefore become extremely useful in public communication, in general, and rhetoric, in particular. By displaying, debating, rethinking, and recasting the past in particular ways before others, communities and individuals can come to see memories as a valuable resource for understanding who we have been, who we are, and who we can be.

Viewing *PIB* through the lens of public memory prompts important questions: Why has *PIB* been afforded such a privileged place within conceptions of the transgender past? What does this prominence reveal about the state of transgender public memory? Moreover, how do representations, non-representations, and mis-representations of the transgender community in the film shape historical understandings of that community and direct contemporary attention to the transgender past? In the pages that follow, I consider these questions by taking *PIB* as a rhetorical artifact to chart out the past, present, and future of transgender public memory, particularly within the Communication Studies discipline.

Before undertaking this analysis, I must acknowledge I write this chapter as a gay, white, cisgender man, transgender ally, and communication scholar interested in public memory. As such, I bring specific expertise and privileges to critiquing the film that I hope will make this contribution worthwhile. However, I must also acknowledge my anxieties in speaking for the transgender community and its past, particularly because, as Julia Serano notes, transgender and intersex lives have been co-opted by cisgender academics in recent years (2007). This concern is more pressing in this chapter given persuasive charges that Livingston co-opted the film's transgender subjects for her own gain (hooks, 1992; Butler, 1993). Cognizant of these concerns, I have tried to observe two principles in this chapter's execution. First, following Audre Lorde's claim that "unused privilege is a weapon in the hands of our enemies" (as cited in Olson, 2014), I have chosen to use my privilege to bring to light concerns I hope can better be illuminated by members of the transgender community. Second, in this essay, I attempt as much as possible to use my privilege thoughtfully, only tentatively "speaking for others" and instead *pointing toward others* without some of my privileges (Alcoff, 1991, p. 5). I do so by citing scholarship by transgender intellectuals and activists inside and outside the discipline and taking seriously the voices of the people in the film. While I will not always agree with these voices, giving them serious consideration is the least that can be expected in promoting more inclusive future debates about these issues.

My argument in this chapter is that *PIB* represents a key rhetorical memory text from which broader lessons about the prospects for a transgender public memory project can be gleaned. Therefore, by assessing the productive qualities of and challenges facing the film, greater reflection can be brought to bear on what a transgender memory project must do in the future if it is to be fully realized. As such, this chapter proceeds as follows. First, I review current considerations of memory and transgender lives within extant literature. Next, I illustrate why *PIB* has become a prominent public memory text about the transgender community. I follow by examining how this film does and does not represent the transgender past on screen, highlighting particular stakes for a transgender public memory project. Finally, I offer a glimpse at two deeper issues that must be grappled with for theorizing transgender public memory moving forward.

PUBLIC MEMORY: TRANSGENDER POLITICS AND SCHOLARSHIP

Before assessing the film in relationship to the possibilities for a transgender public memory project, it seems prudent to ask two questions. First, who counts as transgender in transgender public memory? While the term transgender is by all accounts relatively new, its terrain is contested along temporal and definitional lines (Rawson & Williams, 2014). However, in considering transgender public memory, this chapter defers to Susan Stryker's definition of transgender to "refer to people who move away from the gender they were assigned at birth, people who cross over (*trans-*) the boundaries constructed by their culture to define and contain that gender" (2008, p. 1). I embrace this broadest definition of the term so nearly every person who appears in *PIB* could make some claim to transgender identity.

Second, does transgender public memory yet exist? The answer is both/ and in nature. On one hand, transgender public memory does not (yet) seem to exist as a proper entity of its own. Scholarly searches reveal no use of the term in published essays or books, either inside or outside the discipline, though I suspect it appears in unpublished work at this time. On the other hand, the discipline is increasingly concerned with transgender lives and recounts those lives within notable work. Simultaneously, transgender lives have been addressed through public memory scholarship, not as distinctive entities, but subsumed under interests in gay, lesbian, bisexual, *and* transgender memory or queer public memory scholarship (Morris, 2004, 2007; Dunn, 2010, 2011). This state of affairs should not be surprising at this time since transgender lives and theories are rarely found in a distinctive cultural home (Stryker, 2004).

While limited scholarship expressly links the issue of public memory to transgender lives in the discipline, there are prominent intersections between transgender studies and the past in other academic fields. Memoir and auto-biography, for instance, have long been a powerful resource for transgender persons like Kate Bornstein to bring their experiences before public audiences (1994). Historians and others doing historical work, like Leslie Fein-berg (1996) and Stryker (2004), have produced important volumes on the transgender past to disrupt contemporizing views of transgenderism and undercut narratives of uninterrupted social deviance. K. J. Rawson, a rhetori-cal scholar in English, has illuminated how different terminologies and ve-nues for the transgender experience do or do not make transgender lives visible and accessible for public audiences (2009, 2014). In addition, as recent proceedings at the Transgender Archives at the University of Victoria illustrate, oral history and public history have also begun to play an important part in (re)constructing transgender pasts (2014). Vital and significant work by individuals and communities to preserve, recover, correct, and marshal the transgender past also occurs outside academia (Rawson, 2014).

Therefore, while transgender public memory may not exist as a distinc-tive entity at the moment, much evidence suggests we are on the verge of this undertaking. Communication Studies seems like a strong place for such work to commence given its interest in public memory, gender, contingent forms of knowledge, identity and difference, and persuasion and audience. Howev-er, a cisgender man calling into existence something like transgender public memory seems untoward. Rather, in the remainder of this chapter, I consider *PIB* as a rhetorical artifact that might presage a broader interest in transgen-der public memory. My goals in the pages that follow are less to theorize what transgender memory is now than to ask what the film tells us about how a transgender public memory might come into existence. Furthermore, I wonder what *PIB* reveals about the prospects for a transgender public memo-ry separate and distinct from other forms of remembering the past.

AUTHORIZING *PARIS IS BURNING* AS A SITE OF MEMORY

Given ongoing struggles to secure transgender rights, freedoms, and well-being (Currah et. al, 2006), transgender public memories may offer signifi-cant resources for changing public perceptions of transgender people and gender generally. However, much like queer public memories, the transgen-der past is difficult to marshal when it has been actively suppressed, erased, silenced, and destroyed (Morris, 2007; Devor, 2014). Despite these obsta-cles, *PIB* has somewhat surprisingly emerged as the leading edge of what could become a widely recognized transgender memory project. But why has *PIB* entered the public consciousness rather than other artifacts of the transgender past? By answering this question, we can develop a better understanding of the prospects for similar types of transgender rhetorical acts.

In my view, at least four factors led to *PIB*'s significant public uptake. One of the most important factors is the film's *access* to and not unproblematic privileging of transgender voice. As opposed to turning transgender people into spectacular objects to be witnessed but not understood, the people in *PIB* are the focus of the text. Unlike popular, onscreen accounts of the transgender experience in which cisgender actors often portray transgender roles (e.g., *Boys Don't Cry, To Wong Fu, Thanks for Everything! Julie Newmar, Transamerica, Dallas Buyers Club*), the documentary genre provides transgender persons substantive screen time to describe their lives, to convey their personal experiences, and to document (to the best of their knowledge) the history of the ball scene from first person perspectives. In this way, the film operates as public memory to the extent that the transgender subjects of the film make their private memories publicly accessible to general audiences (Phillips, 2004). Certainly, documentary is not the direct form of public address it often seems. There are consequential filters through which the voices of *PIB*'s transgender subjects inevitably pass, most importantly a white, upper-middle class, lesbian cisgender director (hooks, 1992). Nonetheless, as a text in which real transgender persons (not cisgender actors) are able to convey their real lives (not fictional accounts) to large cisgender audiences, the film is a rare and valuable artifact demanding public attention.

Another factor making *PIB* consequential is it *timeliness* or the *kairotic* moment of film. Shot between 1987 and 1989, *PIB* recounts an instant in transgender memory that has become increasingly inaccessible in the wake of the HIV/AIDS crisis. As NPR recently described, the film "immortalized a very specific moment in both gay and trans culture and in New York City, before both were changed forever by the dual clouds of AIDS and gentrification" (Shepherd, 2012). Despite shooting during the worst days of the epidemic in the United States, *PIB* barely addresses HIV/AIDS onscreen, though the disease certainly haunts the film. HIV/AIDS took a horrific toll on the community, and the ball scene did not escape unscathed. Indeed, all of the major figures in the film are now deceased, and many of the film's primary subjects are known to have been touched by or died early deaths from AIDS-related illnesses. As a result, just as the personal, cultural, and institutional reminiscences of the gay community were decimated by the epidemic, the transgender past likewise suffers a devastating "memory void" (Morris, 2007, p. 95). In short, it would have been impossible to make the same film even five years later because so many of its central figures had died of the disease. Therefore, one of the film's greatest values is that it captured these memories prior to the subjects' eventual passing. Through

PIB, a moment that feels pre-AIDS (even if it is not) becomes available for contemporary audiences, filling, in some small way, the gaping transgender memory void.

The *intersections* of race, class, gender, and sexuality in *PIB* also influence its persistent appeal, giving the film a distinctiveness rarely matched by even more contemporary transgender texts. Critiques highlighting the whiteness of LGBT histories and memories are ubiquitous in current scholarship for good reason: As rarely as the transgender past is witnessed, a rich, intersectional image of that past is even more uncommon. In this regard, *PIB* is a notable exception. The film centers the experience of largely Black and Latino gay men and transgender persons, prioritizing their voices in an era in which minorities were rarely empowered in most popular media formats. However, the film's value goes beyond representation alone. *PIB* actively investigates intersections between race and class, celebrity, gender identity, and sexuality in ways few other media texts attempt. Indeed, the film's complex cultural critiques are still sought out in classrooms and public dialogues where the intricacy of identity is discussed, perpetuating *PIB*'s appeal more than two decades after its release. While the film's attention to race and class is laudable, critics have also highlighted the film's handling of race as problematic. For instance, bell hooks claims *PIB*'s emphasis on the gender bending of black men in particular functions to support ongoing white supremacy (hooks, 1992). Nonetheless, from the perspective of memory, the racial diversity and cultural criticisms brought to bear in *PIB* are fundamental to its appeal.

Finally, more than any other single factor, the film's *publicness* has been immensely influential in describing its persistence. Despite claims to the contrary, the transgender community is not a people without a past. It is, however, a community whose past has been less accessible to those outside of it. As the *New York Times* reports, "Drag balls, the product of a poor, gay and mostly nonwhite culture, had been held in Harlem since the 1920's. But it wasn't until Jennie Livingston's award-winning documentary, *Paris Is Burning*, was released in 1991 that anyone outside that world knew much about them" (Green, 1993). While the newspaper overstates public ignorance of the drag ball scene—and transgender people generally—the film did circulate transgender lives before wider audiences. Indeed, the film medium made *PIB* significantly more accessible to popular audiences who might be wary to visit actual drag balls themselves. In addition, the producer's decision to release *PIB* in film festivals *and* theatrically in urban centers further contributed to its persistence (Hernandez, 2005). The unusual circulation of a transgender film before public audiences continues to expand today. While *Paris Is Burning* was "difficult to see except at late-night art house showings and on vintage VHS" for years (Shepherd, 2012), today, the film is available on Netflix streaming, iTunes, and has been illegally uploaded to YouTube, dramatically increasing its accessibility. Unlike any other film of its kind, *PIB* has made past transgender lives more available than ever before.

As Del Marquis, a member of the band The Scissor Sisters, stated in remembering the film: "Most institutions exclude the study of LGBT history in education, but this documentary is one of the main chapters we will look back on" (Shepherd, 2012). Our ability to look back on that past—indeed to marshal it for present and future needs—is not coincidental. *PIB* is influential because of the right mix of access, timeliness, intersectionality, and publicity. Therefore, it seems likely these elements would be essential to any wider transgender public memory project. However, while these points help explain why *PIB* is so pervasive a transgender memory, they do not reveal the simultaneous threats that privileging this film over other texts presents to the transgender past. Investigating these threats is just as crucial to understanding the prospects for transgender public memory as its possibilities.

TROUBLES FOR TRANSGENDER PUBLIC MEMORY IN THE FILM

While the points described above help explain why *PIB* has come to equate a transgender public memory for popular audiences, the film itself also illuminates challenges that limit or undermine the prospects for transgender public memory. As such, identifying and grappling with these challenges is necessary if transgender public memory will succeed as an important political and rhetorical project. While other challenges also exist outside the film's purview, the three most prominent issues in *PIB* are the gay frame, scope, and who speaks for the transgender past.

The Gay Frame

The most immediate constraint to transgender public memory in the film is that *PIB* is largely shot through what we might call "the gay frame." By gay frame, I mean that all the queens featured in *PIB*—and the drag ball culture they participate in—are represented as gay, particularly gay *men*. While it is unquestionable that gay men feature prominently in *PIB*, the sweeping language and imperializing framing of the film also sublimate other identities we might read as transgender, leaving transgender pasts ignored or unrecognized in the public sphere. We might understand the film's flattening of distinctions between gay men and transgender people to be an artifact of the time. The contours of the term "gay" have long been malleable and represented people identifying as male, female, and otherwise for decades (Minter, 2006). In addition, despite the long history and diverse uptake of the term "transgender" (Rawson & Williams, 2014), it is likely that the queens in *PIB* preferred other terms for non-cisgender experiences that were popular at the time. Indeed, several of the film's subjects— including major players like

Angie Xtravaganza, Venus Xtravaganza, and Octavia St. Laurent—describe themselves as "transsexuals," "transvestites," "having a transsexualism operation," "being a woman," and being "no longer a man." However, while academics and scholars knowledgeable about such evolving terminologies may appreciate these idiosyncrasies, for less informed popular audiences, *PIB*'s gay frame confuses real distinctions between sex, gender, and sexuality, making the different experiences of transgender lives in the past unrecognizable.

There are two related means by which the gay frame becomes the central terministic screen in the film (Burke, 1966). First, *PIB* explicitly and regularly labels drag balls and their performances as acts of gay men. This framing becomes clear in the first minute of the film as a young queen, Kim Pendavis, recounts his father's warning about life as a gay man: "You have three strikes against you in this world. Every black man has two—that they're black and they're male. But you're black and you're male and you're gay. You're going to have a hard fucking time." With these simple phrases, before viewers see a queen or the ball scene in any way, a particular perspective is set: Audiences should read all the people on screen as *gay*, black men. Whether "gay" does or does not accurately describe Pendavis, the epigraphic placement of these sentences directs the audience's attention toward racial difference, same-sex desire, and the gender binary as central lenses for interpreting the film. Leaving Pendavis behind, the camera quickly refocuses on one of the film's primary subjects, Pepper LaBeija, as she enters the ball scene in full, other gendered splendor. LaBeija's appearance may prompt the audience to question the gay frame—is that a man? Is that a gay man? However, the film quickly dispatches doubts and reinforces the gay frame in voice over: "Gay people—men gather together under one roof and decide to have a competition amongst themselves—balls….this movie is about the ball circuit and the gay group that's involved with it." Again, the film authorizes the gay frame as *the* correct way to view the events to follow. This frame recurs repeatedly in *PIB*. For instance, LaBeija later explains "realness" as "not giv[ing] away the fact you're gay" when performing a different gender and describes her relationship with young queens as based in the fact that "I'm gay and they're gay." Similarly, another prominent queen interviewed in the film, Dorian Corey, affirms reading the various families of performers (called "houses") who battle at balls as "gay street gang[s]." The film even asserts the gay frame after the credits roll, summarizing in a final scene that "this is what gay life is about." As such, the audience is encouraged to interpret all participants in the ball scene as gay men. As a result, other queens on screen who might identify as transgender or transgender *and* gay often go unacknowledged.

Second, when the film does acknowledge transgender lives, it subordinates them under the rubric of gay life. As we have already discussed, despite the film's persistent gay filter, transgender identities are voiced on screen in *PIB*, even if the term "transgender" is not. However, when transgender identities are expressed in the film, they are instantly cast as sub-identities within a larger gay community. For instance, Angie, a "legendary" queen in the House of Xtravaganza, describes her "new tits" in one moment and her pleasure in teaching other queens about "the gay life" in the next. Earlier, a young queen in the House of Xtravaganza named Venus describes herself as "gay" but also "want[ing] my sex change to make myself complete." As such, even while parts of their testimonies seem to authorize reading the queens as transgender women, they seem to end up claiming gay male identities by the conclusions of their statements. By doing so, they highlight how many people were navigating coming to see themselves in multifaceted ways in relation to sex, gender, and sexuality in a pre-queer moment, and even today (Minter, 2006). Therefore, it would be untrue to say transgender identities are actively being disciplined in the film. Nonetheless, the effect of this framing remains: The film collapses intricate identities—including ostensibly transgender identities—under a single, unified gay moniker. As a result, the gay frame authorizes a reading that understands transgender lives as dominated by gay politics which (over?)emphasizes same-sex desires. In such a case, the prospect for a transgender public memory project separate and distinct from LGBT and queer concerns is put at risk.

Scope

The scope of the film is also disconcerting in forwarding a productive transgender public memory. For Burke, scope significantly affects the representativeness and success of any text (1969). In the case of *PIB*, the scope of the film is particularly narrow, allowing for an in-depth analysis of the people and culture of the ball scene. However, as a memory text with few contemporaneous artifacts for comparison, this constricted focus portends a troublesome assessment of the transgender past. Two important factors fall out of the transgender past in *PIB*: geography and history.

Geographically, the frame for *PIB* is the drag ball scene in Harlem, New York. Harlem has a long, historical affiliation with drag balls and the transgender community; as such, there is significant cultural value in highlighting this location on screen. Yet, this narrow scope simultaneously implies problematic historical understandings about transgender lives. For instance, the film largely locates transgender people exclusively within the ball scene. While the docks, participant's homes, the streets of Harlem, and stock footage all appear in *PIB*, the vast majority of the film occurs in one of several drag balls. In addition, many (but not all) queens pictured outside the ball scene do not appear in other gendered apparel. As a result, viewers can falsely assume that most queens do not violate gender conventions outside of the ballroom space. Such an assumption is valid for many ball participants; however, it is also true that other queens live their everyday lives performing a gender different from the one most people would associate with their biological sex. In other words, the limited geography of the film suggests transgender identities do not exist in contexts other than the ball scene. As a result, while *PIB* affirms historical transgender lives, it also suggests (often incorrectly) that those lives are part-time and space-specific. As a result, much of the transgender past is lost on screen.

Equally disconcerting, the film's limited geography reconfirms popular beliefs that transgender people reside exclusively in urban areas. While urban centers surely offer at least the appearance of security and anonymity that may be conducive to leading a transgender life safely, transgender people and performances certainly exceed city limits, in the present and past. Drag balls in the 1980s occurred in both urban and rural areas, on the coasts and in Middle America, though some were smaller and more secretive affairs. Transgender identities and practices, meanwhile, have existed through time anywhere people perform gender (Feinberg, 1996). Yet, by fixating the film in New York City, the outer limits of transgender geographies are further marginalized. To be fair, the film never says it represents the *only* instantiation of this community; however, the film's failure to acknowledge other spaces of transgender existence invites contemporary audiences to underestimate the reach of the transgender past.

Similarly, decades of contemporary transgender identity and performance are potentially ignored by affixing *PIB* as a starting point for transgender public memory. In several instances in the film, *PIB* suggests it is investigating a unique moment in time for the viewer. This is most evident as the film opens to a black screen reading "1987, New York." By so consciously marking the film's temporal instant, viewers are invited to consider the events in *PIB* as special and exceptional in history (and geography). Unfortunately, this rhetoric of temporal and geographic distinction unintentionally wipes away decades of the transgender past. For example, the "Hamilton Lodge Ball" in Harlem (later known as the "Faggots' Ball") featured female impersonators nearly continuously since its founding in 1869. By 1926, the ball was so infamous that city newspapers openly reported on it and the high number of "fairies" in attendance (Chauncey, 1994). Regrettably, this rich transgender past is absent from *PIB*.

Certainly, the queens in the film cannot be held accountable for all of this transgender history; indeed, by 1987, many of the most canonical LGBT histories had not yet been written. George Chauncey's *Gay New York*, which would help popularize the history of the Harlem drag balls, would not be published until 1994, and Feinberg's *Transgender Warriors* would not be written until 1996. But the film does have its own unofficial historian who, in presenting her private memories as public memories, also circumscribes the transgender past. Dorian Corey represents this historical voice in the film. According to Corey, her first ball experience was an "early type ball" which featured "all drag queens interested in looking like Las Vegas show girls." By estimating these date cues, the earliest Corey likely attended a ball was the 1950s. But by describing this time period as "early," a significant string of transgender memory sites intimately connected to *PIB* is cast aside. At some level, this failure is Livingston's; interviews with other queens at other balls and at other times would inevitably have told a different or at least more complex history of the community. But, by privileging Corey's account, the public's memory of the transgender past is severely limited by *PIB*. Unfortunately, that challenge persists today as venues like the *Huffington Post* continue to describe *PIB* inaccurately as the place "where the ballroom tradition began" (Anderson, 2012).

Who Speaks the Past?

A final dimension limiting *PIB* as a transgender public memory is whom the film authorizes to speak about and represent the transgender past. In bell hooks's (1992) assessment of the film, there are two primary voices authorized to speak for the past: Dorian Corey and Pepper LaBeija. While hooks lauds Corey as "both historian and cultural critic in the film" and denigrates LaBeija as someone who "constructs a mythic world to inhabit" (pp. 155–156), both are given credibility through the filmmaker's extended attention to describe the transgender past for a novice viewing public. In these roles, both subjects detail important facets of the past that other subjects do not, including what inspired ball culture, trends through time, and how a queen becomes "legendary." However, despite this value, each speaker's ability to represent transgender memory adequately is limited. Many of these limitations relate to the narrators' identities as men "who act or dress like a woman." This does not disqualify Corey or LaBeija as transgender persons by our contemporary definition; however, neither Corey nor LaBeija expresses a transgender identity as other people in the film do. Corey and LaBeija identify themselves in the film with the terms "gay," "man," or "drag queen," emphasizing their circumscribed performance of gender trouble rather than its everyday realities experienced by other queens. In the film, Corey even goes so far as to say drag is her "profession," not a part of her identity. Therefore, while both narrators are able to speak about the transgender past through their particular subject positions, their memories do not necessarily well represent the pasts of other transgender people in the film, particularly transsexuals and transvestites.

When only a particular segment of the transgender community is authorized to speak for the entire community, significant representational issues emerge. The stakes in empowering only Corey and LaBeija's voices in *PIB* become apparent where LaBeija reflects on her views about sex reassignment surgery. According to LaBeija:

> I can only say how a man who acts or dresses like a woman feels. I never wanted a sex change. That's taking it a little too far . . . A lot of kids I know, they got the sex change . . . [but] I've never recommended it. And I would have never got it. I'm so thankful that I was that smart.

The implication in LaBeija's statement is clear: While gender bending itself may not be problematic, even a drag queen can see the biological desires of some transgender persons are unwarranted. LaBeija claims her transgender peers are not smart but naïve in their pursuit of a body that better reflects their gender identities, confirming prejudicial viewers' concerns about the limits of acceptable gender trouble. In doing so, LaBeija betrays herself as an unreliable narrator of the transgender past, disparaging other transgender persons for whom the film authorizes her to speak. With only limited historical voices like LaBeija's in the film, the broad diversity of the transgender community is not merely minimized but maligned at great expense.

At the same time as LaBeija and Corey are given free rein to describe their view of the transgender past, people representing different kinds of transgender experience in the film—particularly transvestites, transsexuals, and others who have expressed a desire to change their sex physically—are never asked to share their memories in a public sense. Certainly, people like Venus and Angie Xtravaganza speak of their private and personal pasts on screen; however, neither is asked to speak about the transgender past in a broader, public sense like Corey and LaBeija. This absence is felt most clearly when a long-standing queen like Angie Xtravaganza, who explicitly identifies as transsexual—unlike Corey and LaBeija—is not asked about the shared transgender past. If she was ever asked to share such memories by Livingston, those memories must have ended up on the editing room floor. Instead of describing the past, transvestite and transsexual voices in the film are asked to speak exclusively about the present and future: their hopes, desires, and dreams. In doing so, *PIB* essentially divides the transgender community into two. Drag queens like LaBeija and Corey, who put on and take off their genders through performance alone, become authorities about the past while queens who have or desire to change their sex are authorized to discuss *transitioning* only. In short, drag queens are asked to linger on the past while transvestite and transsexual subjects are prompted to dwell on what will come next. As a result, transsexual and transvestite memories of the ball scene and its participants are enveloped by LaBeija and Corey's more normative and less threatening personal experiences, leaving the rich and diverse pasts of others underneath the transgender umbrella largely unrecognizable for the viewing public.

In summation, no matter how influential *PIB* has become for preserving and translating the transgender past into public memory, there are significant reasons to be wary in adopting the film's representations. While much is preserved in the film worth remembering, much is also at stake, both for the film's participants and for those of us who rely upon this rhetorical telling of the past to know our common history.

CONCLUSION

The ongoing emergence of *PIB* into the public consciousness reveals opportunities and obstacles facing a wider transgender public memory project. Through the film, *PIB*'s most rhetorically salient features are put on display, inviting contemporary transgender memory-makers to consider adopting similar strategies. At the same time, the challenges of the gay frame, scope, and representational authority that appear in *PIB* offer warnings for what may face a fully realized transgender public memory project. Indeed, I believe the challenges identified in *PIB* stem from deeper issues inherent in remembering the transgender past. Ultimately, these deeper issues must be detailed and addressed by the field before the benefits of this undertaking can fully materialize. These issues are twofold.

The first root issue impeding transgender public memory is affirming memory as a valuable resource for transgender people and politics. Despite the recent "*turn toward* memory" in queer communities (Morris, 2007, p. 95), many transgender people remain rightly suspicious of viewing memory as a site of power rather than a source of pain. On several counts, transgender misgivings about the past mirror anxieties about closets, discrimination, violence, and the trauma of the HIV/AIDS epidemic shared by gay, lesbian, and bisexual people. However, transgender pasts also maintain unique difficulties for taking memory seriously as a tool for rhetorical action. For instance, for transgender people who have been put painfully at odds with their bodies in the past, the transitioning process becomes an *opportunity to forget* by adopting new names, homes, and even memories to preserve their safety and new gender identities (Bornstein, 1994). Similarly, transgender persons who may not wish to be "denied the joy of our histories" (Bornstein, 1994, p. 127) are still pushed by persistent medical, psychological, and cultural forces to abandon memories of their earlier lives. Therefore, a successful transgender public memory project must begin, not only with recovering transgender memories, but by validating memory as a productive space of rhetorical action.

Second, the discipline must also answer whether transgender public memory can push beyond the boundaries of queer public memory to offer something genuinely new, radical, and productive. As we have seen, transgender memories to date have largely been addressed under the auspices of LGBT or queer memory. However, as Stryker (2004) has argued, lumping transgender experiences underneath a broader queer studies label can further marginalize transgender lives and concerns. Constituting a separate transgender memory project distinct from queer memory may solve this dilemma, but invites the question: What might a transgender public memory project offer that a queer public memory project cannot or will not? While this question remains to be fully answered, I believe there are some ways already evident in which a transgender public memory project may, at least potentially, make a real contribution.

For one, a transgender public memory project may (re)integrate gender more fully into analyses of the LGBT past. While queer memory scholarship references gender in important ways, it can also adopt highly limited gendered perspectives. For instance, in Christopher Castiglia and Christopher Reed's book *If Memory Serves* (2012), the authors actively choose to focus only on the memory culture of gay *men*. While there are meaningful reasons for their narrow scope, the book's framing nonetheless reifies a male/female binary that limits transgender lives from being recognized. By contrast, I am certain a transgender public memory project would demand no less than the full integration of sexuality, identity, desire, *and gender* in examining memory in public life. Likewise, a transgender public memory project may excel at bringing bodies more fully into discussions of the queer past. While bodies are not altogether absent in extant queer memory scholarship, one of the major aims of transgender studies is "enacting a new narrative of the wedding of self and flesh" (Stryker, 2004, p. 213). A transgender public memory project, then, may more forcefully articulate the (dis-)embodied and material dimensions of the LGBT past and proffer innovative opportunities to understand them. Lastly, a transgender memory project may better disrupt homonormativity than queer public memory. While public memories *writ large* need not necessarily be conservative, their users often adopt normative impulses to align the past with those in power in the present. With increasing frequency, these normative impulses have infiltrated queer public memory, privileging homonormative images of the LGBT past that, among other things, stabilize the gender binary to the disadvantage of others expressing "minoritized and marginalized manifestations of gender" (Stryker, 2004, p. 214). A transgender public memory project, itself not immune to similar normative impulses, may nonetheless be better situated to disrupt the domestication of radical queer subjectivities around gender and ensure the LGBT past not become the domain of only the "safest," most "respectable," and most "normative" protagonists.

Addressing the issues above is vital to establishing a successful transgender public memory project. Future scholars should not take these issues lightly, but they should also not be considered insurmountable. Indeed, as transgendering communication studies advances, I have great faith that prospects for addressing these issues will outstrip new obstacles. If that is the case, a vibrant and radical transgender memory project—one that goes beyond sexuality, prioritizes gender identity, and disrupts normativity deep into the past—may offer the world and the discipline a new, distinct, and compelling site in the struggle for liberation.

References

Abbott, T. B. (2013). The trans/romance dilemma in *Transamerica* and other films. *Journal of American Culture, 36*(1), 32–41. doi: 10.1111/jacc.12011

Aiello, G., Bakshi, S., Bilge, S., Hall, L. K., Johnstone, L., & Pérez, K. (2013). Here, and not yet here: A dialogue at the intersection of queer, trans, and culture. *Journal of International and Intercultural Communication, 6*(2), 96–117. doi:10.1080/17513057.2013.778155

Alcoff, L. (1991). The problem of speaking for others. *Cultural Critique, 20*, 5–32. doi: 10.2307/1354221

Alegria, C. A. (2010). Relationship challenges and relationship maintenance activities following disclosure of transsexualism. *Journal of Psychiatric and Mental Health Nursing,17*, 909–916. doi: 10.1111/j.1365-2850.2010.01624.x

Alegria, C. A. (2011). Transgender identity and health care: Implications for psychosocial and physical evaluation. *Journal of the American Academy of Nurse Practitioners, 23*(4), 175–182. doi: OI: 10.1111/j.1745-7599.2010.00595

Alegría, C. A., & Ballard-Reisch, D. (2012). And then he was a she: Communication following a gender-identity shift. In F. C. Dickson & L. M. Webb (Eds.), *Communication for families in crisis: Theories, research, strategies* (pp. 77–101). New York, NY: Peter Lang.

Alexander, E. (2008). Litigating under the Eighth Amendment: Prison health care, political choice, and the accidental death penalty. *University of Pennsylvania Journal of Constitutional Law, 11*, 1–22. Retrieved from http://scholarship.law.upenn.edu/cgi/viewcontent.cgi?article=1140&context=jcl

Allen, B. J. (2000). Learning the ropes: A black feminist standpoint analysis. In P. M. Buzzanell (Ed.), *Rethinking organizational & managerial communication from feminist perspectives* (pp. 177–208). Thousand Oaks, CA: Sage.

Alpert Reyes, E. (2014, January 28). Transgender study looks at 'exceptionally high' suicide-attempt rate. *Los Angeles Times.*

Altemeyer, B. (2001). Changes in attitudes toward homosexuals. *Journal of Homosexuality 42*, 3–76. doi: 10.1300/J082v42n02_04

American Psychiatric Association. (2000). *Diagnostic and statistical manual of mental disorders* (4th ed., text rev.). Washington, DC: Author.

American Psychiatric Association. (2013). *Diagnostic and statistical manual of mental disorders* (5th ed.). Arlington, VA: Author.

Anderson, J. C. (2012, June 20). "Paris Is Burning" ballroom community serves as case study in HIV prevention, coping in LA. *Huffington Post.* Retrieved from http://www.huffingtonpost.com/2012/06/20/paris-is-burning-ballroom-study-hiv-prevention-in-la_n_1598667.html

Arune, W. (2006). Transgender images in the media. In L. Castaneda & S. Campbell (Eds.), *News and sexuality: Media portraits of diversity* (pp. 110–133). Los Angeles: University of Southern California Press.

Babrow, A. S. (2001). Uncertainty, value, communication, and problematic integration. *Journal of Communication, 51*, 553–573. doi: 10.1111/j.1460-2466.2001.tb02896.x

Baldus, D., Woodworth, G., Zuckerman, D., Weiner, N. A., & Broffitt, B. (1998). Racial discrimination and the death penalty in the post-*Furman* era: An empirical and legal overview, with recent findings from Philadelphia. *Cornell Law Review, 83*, 1638–1770. Retrieved from http://www.lawschool.cornell.edu/research/cornell-law-review/upload/baldus.pdf

Ballinger, G. A., & Schoorman, F. D. (2007). Individual reaction to leadership succession in workgroups. *Academy of Management Review, 32*, 118–136. Retrieved from http://aomarticles.metapress.com/content/e31p124821410g74/

Balzer, C., & LaGata, C. (2014). Human rights. *TSQ: Transgender Studies Quarterly, 1*(1–2), 99–103. doi:10.1215/23289252-2399731

Banner, S. (2002). *The death penalty: An American history.* Cambridge, MA: Harvard University Press.

Barker-Plummer, B. (2013). Fixing Gwen. *Feminist Media Studies, 13*(4), 710–724. doi: 10.1080/14680777.2012.679289

Barnett, J. T., & Johnson, C. W. (2013). We are all royalty: Narrative comparison of a drag queen and king. *Journal of Leisure Research, 45*, 677–694.

Barthes, R. (1981). *Camera Lucida: Reflections on Photography.* (R. Howard, Trans.). New York, NY: Hill and Wang.

Bassichis, D. M. (2007). *It's war in here: A report on the treatment of transgender and intersex people in New York State men's prisons.* Retrieved from http://srlp.org/files/warinhere.pdf

Bassichis, M., Lee, A. & Spade, D. (2011). Building an abolitionist trans and queer movement with everything we've got. In E. Stanley & N. Smith (Eds.), *Captive genders: Trans embodiment and the prison industrial complex* (pp. 15–44). Oakland, CA: AK Press.

Bauer, G., Boyce, M., Coleman, T., Kaay, M., Scanlon, K., & Travers, R. (2010, July 26). Who are trans people in Ontario? *TransPULSE E-Bulletin, 1*(1).

Bauer, G., Hammond, R., Travers, R., Kaay, M., Hohenadel, K. M., & Boyce, M. (2009). 'I don't think this is theoretical: this is our lives': How erasure impacts health care for transgender people. *Journal of the Association of Nurses in AIDS Care, 20*(5), 348–361. doi: 10.1016/j.jana.2009.07.004

Beagan, B., Chiasson, A., Fiske, C., Forseth, S., Hosein, A., Myers, M., & Stang, J. (2013). Working with transgender clients: Learning from physicians and nurses to improve occupational therapy practice. *Canadian Journal of Occupational Therapy, 80*, 82–91. doi:10.1177/000841713484450

Bean, H. (2014). U.S. national security culture: From queer psychopathology to queer citizenship. *QED: A Journal in GLBTQ Worldmaking, 1*(1), 52–79. doi:10.14321/qed.1.1.0052

Beattie, K. (2004). *Documentary screens: Nonfiction film and television.* New York, NY: Palgrave Macmillan.

Beemyn, B. G. (2004). Bisexuality. [Web log message]. Retrieved from http://www.glbtq.com/social-sciences/bisex.html

Beemyn, G., & Rankin, S. (2011). *The lives of transgender people.* New York, NY: Columbia University Press.

Bell-Metereau, R. (1993). *Hollywood androgyny* (2nd ed.). New York, NY: Columbia University Press.

Benjamin, H. (2006). Transsexualism and transvestism as psycho-somatic and somato-psychic syndromes. In S. Stryker & S. Whittle (Eds.), *The transgender studies reader* (pp. 45–52). New York, NY: Routledge.

Bennett, J. A. (2003). Love me gender: Normative homosexuality and "ex-gay" performativity in reparative therapy narratives. *Text & Performance Quarterly, 23*(4), 331–352. doi:10.1080/1046293042000190603

Berger, J. (1972). *Ways of Seeing.* London: Penguin.

Berger, J. (1980). *About looking.* New York, NY: Pantheon Books.

Bermel, A. (1990). *Farce: A history from Aristophanes to Woody Allen*. Carbondale, IL: Southern Illinois University Press.

Besnier, N. (2005). Crossing genders, mixing languages: The linguistic construction of transgenderism in Tonga. In J. Holmes & M. Meyerhoff (Eds.) *The handbook of language and gender* (pp. 279–301). Malden, MA: Blackwell Publishing.

Bettcher, T. M. (2014a). When selves have sex: What the phenomenology of trans sexuality can teach about sexual orientation. *Journal of Homosexuality, 61*(5), 605–620. doi:10.1080/00918396.2014.865472

Bettcher, T. M. (2014b). Transphobia. *TSQ: Transgender Studies Quarterly, 1*(1–2), 249–251. doi:10.1215/23289252-2400181

Bhanji, N. (2013). Trans/scriptions: Homing desires, (trans)sexual citizenship, and racialized bodies. In S. Stryker & A. Z. Aizura (Eds.), *The transgender studies reader 2* (pp. 512–526). New York: Routledge.

Bignell, J. (2013). *An introduction to television studies* (3rd ed.). New York, NY: Routledge.

Bilodeau, B. (2005). Beyond the gender binary: A case study of two transgender students at a midwestern research university. *Journal of Gay & Lesbian Issues In Education, 3*(1), 29–44. doi:10.1300/J367v03n01_05

Birrell, S., & Cole, C. (1990). Double fault: Renee Richards and the construction and naturalization of difference. *Sociology of Sport Journal, 7*(1), 7–21.

Blackburn, M. V. (2005). Agency in borderland discourses: Examining language use in a community center with black queer youth. *Teachers College Record, 107*(1), 89–113. doi:10.1111/j.1467-9620.2005.00458.x

Blackwood, E. (2008). Transnational discourses and circuits of queer knowledge in Indonesia. *GLQ: A Journal of Lesbian and Gay Studies, 14*(4), 481–507. doi: 10.1215/10642684-2008–002

Blanch, D., Hall, J., Roter, D., & Frankel, R. (2009). Is it good to express uncertainty to a patient? Correlates and consequences for medical students in a standardized patient visit. *Patient Education & Counseling, 76*, 300–306. doi:10.1016/j.pec.2009.06.002

Bockting, W. O., Benner, A., & Coleman, E. (2009). Gay and bisexual identity development among female-to-male transsexuals in North America: Emergence of a transgender sexuality. *Archives of Sexual Behavior, 38*, 688–701. doi 10.1007/s10508-009-9489-3

Bockting, W. O., & Cesaretti, C. (2001). Spirituality, transgender identity, and coming out. *Journal of Sex Education & Therapy, 26*(4), 291.

Bockting, W. O., Robinson, B., Benner, A., & Scheltema, K. (2004). Patient satisfaction with transgender health services. *Journal of Sex and Marital Therapy, 30*, 277–294. doi:10.1080/00926230490422467

Bockting, W. O., Robinson, B., & Rosser, B. (1998). Transgender HIV prevention: A qualitative needs assessment. *AIDS Care, 10*, 505–526. doi:10.1080/09540129850124028

Bokser, J. A. (2010). Sor Juana's *Divine Narcissus*: A new world rhetoric of listening. *Rhetoric Society Quarterly, 40*(3), 224–246. doi:10.1080/02773941003617418

Bono, C. (2011). *Transition: The story of how I became a man.* New York, NY: Dutton Adult.

Booth, E. T. (2011). Queering *Queer Eye*: The stability of gay identity confronts the liminality of trans embodiment. *Western Journal of Communication, 75*(2), 185–204. doi: 10.1080/10570314.2011.553876

Bornstein, K. (1994). *Gender outlaw: On men, women, and the rest of us*. New York, NY: Routledge.

Bornstein, K. (2013). *My new gender workbook*. New York: Routledge.

Boss, P. (1988). *Family stress management*. Newbury Park, CA: Sage.

Boss, P. (1992). Primacy of perception in family stress theory and measurement. *Journal of Family Psychology, 6*, 113–119. doi:10.1037/0893-3200.6.2.113

Bradford, A., & Meston, C. M. (2011). Sex and gender disorders. In D. H. Barlow (Ed.), *The Oxford handbook of clinical psychology* (pp. 446–468). New York, NY: Oxford University Press.

Bradley Manning explains gender change. (2013, August 26). *Politico*. Retrieved from http://www.politico.com/story/2013/08/bradley-chelsea-manning-gender-change-95928.html

Brennan, J., Kuhns, L., Johnson, A., Belzer, M., Wilson, E., & Garofalo, R. (2012). Syndemic theory and HIV-related risk among transgender women: The role of multiple, co-occurring health problems and social marginalization. *American Journal of Public Health, 102*, 1751–1757. doi : 10.2105/AJPH.2011.300433

Brill, S. A., & Pepper, R. (2008). *The transgender child: A handbook for families and professionals*. Pittsburgh, PA: Cleis Press.

Brown, R., Bylund, C., Gueguen, J., Diamond, C., Eddington, J., & Kissane, D. (2010). Developing patient-centered communication skills training for oncologists: Describing the content and efficacy of training. *Communication Education, 59*, 235–248. doi:10.1080/03634521003606210

Bucholtz, M., & Hall, K. (2004). Theorizing identity in language and sexuality research. *Language in Society, 33*, 469–515. doi: 10.1017/S004740450044021

Budge, S., Katz-Wise, S. L., Tebbe, E. N., Howard, K. A. S., Schneider, C. L., & Rodriguez, A. (2013). Transgender emotional and coping processes: Use of facilitative and avoidant coping throughout the gender transition. *The Counseling Psychologist, 41*, 601–647.

Burdge, B. J. (2007). Bending gender, ending gender: Theoretical foundations for social work practice with the transgender community. *Social Work, 52*, 243–250. doi: 10.1093/sw/52.3.243

Burke, D. (2007, November 3). Transgender pastor allowed to keep post in Baltimore. *Washington Post*, p. B09.

Burke, K. (1966). *Language as symbolic action: Essays on life, literature, and method*. Berkeley, CA: University of California Press.

Burke, K. (1969). *A rhetoric of motives*. Berkeley and Los Angeles: University of California Press. (Original work published 1950)

Burke, K. (1969). *Grammar of motives*. Berkeley, CA: University of California Press.

Burke, K. (1973). *The philosophy of literary form: Studies in symbolic action* (3rd. ed.). Berkeley, CA: University of California Press.

Buscar, E., & Enke, A. (2011). Unlikely sex change capitals of the world: Trinidad, United States, and Tehran, Iran as twin yardsticks of homonormative liberalism. *Feminist Studies, 37*(2), 301–328.

Butler, J. (1990). *Gender trouble: Feminism and the subversion of identity*. New York, NY: Routledge.

Butler, J. (1993). *Bodies that matter: On the discursive limits of sex*. New York, NY: Routledge.

Butler, J. (1997). *Excitable speech*. New York, NY: Routledge.

Butler, J. (1999). Preface. In J. Butler, *Gender trouble: Feminism and the subversion of Identity* (pp. vii–xxviii). New York, NY: Routledge.

Bylund, C. L., Peterson, E. B., & Cameron, K. A. (2012). A practitioner's guide to interpersonal communication theory: An overview and exploration of selected theories. *Patient Education and Counseling, 87*, 261–267. doi:10.1016/j.pec.2011.10.006

Byne, W., Bradley, S., Coleman, E., Eyler, A., Green, R., Menvielle, E., & Tompkins, D. (2012). Report of the American Psychiatric Association task force on treatment of Gender Identity Disorder. *Archives of Sexual Behavior, 41*, 759–796. doi:10.1007/s10508-012-9975-x

Califia, P. (1994). *Public Sex: The culture of radical sex*. Pittsburgh, PA: Cleis Press.

Cameron, L. (1996). *Body Alchemy: Transsexual Portraits*. Berkeley, CA: Clevis Press.

Campbell, P. O. (2012). The procedural queer: Substantive due process, *Lawrence v. Texas*, and queer rhetorical futures. *Quarterly Journal of Speech, 98*, 203–209. doi: 10.1080/00335630.2012.663923

Campbell, P. O. (2013). *Judicial rhetoric and radical politics: Sexuality, race, and the Fourteenth Amendment* (Doctoral dissertation). Retrieved from Illinois Digital Environment for Access to Learning and Scholarship.

Canaday, M. (2009). *The straight state: Sexuality and citizenship in twentieth-century America*. Princeton, NJ: Princeton University Press.

Capuzza, J. (forthcoming). Who defines gender diversity? Sourcing routines and representation in mainstream U.S. news stories about transgenderism. *International Journal of Transgenderism, 15*(3). doi: 10.1080/15532739.2014.946195

Cardullo, B. (1995). The dream structure of *Some Like It Hot. Etudes Anglaises, 48*(2), 193–197. Retrieved from http://www.cairn.info/revue.php?ID_REVUE=ETAN

Carroll, J. (1997). Images of women and capital sentencing among female offenders: Exploring the outer limits of Eighth Amendment and articulated theories of justice. *Texas Law Review, 42*, 1413–1454.

Casey, M. K., Miller, V. D., & Johnson, J. R. (1997). Survivors' information seeking following a reduction in workforce. *Communication Research, 24*, 755–781. doi: 10.1177/0093650297024006007

Castiglia, C., & Reed, C. (2012). *If memory serves: Gay men, AIDS, and the promise of the queer past.* Minneapolis: University of Minnesota Press.

Cavalcante, A. (2013). Centering transgender identity via the textual periphery: *Transamerica* and the "double work" of paratexts. *Critical Studies in Media Communication, 30*(2), 85–101. doi:10.1080/15295036.2012.694077

Cavanagh, S. L. (2013). Affect, performance, and ethnographic methods in *Queer Bathroom Monologues. Text and Performance Quarterly, 33*(4), 286–307. doi:10.1080/10462937.2013.823513

Celega, D., & Broz, S. (2012). Physician communication skills training: A review of theoretical backgrounds, objectives, and skills. *Medical Education, 36*, 1004–1016. doi:10.1046/j.1365-2923.2002.01331.x

Cetin, I. (2010). Veiled representations. *Feminist Media Studies, 10*(4), 409–419. doi:10.1080/14680777.2010.514113

Chamberland, L., & Saewyc, E. (2011). Stigma, vulnerability, and resilience: The psychosocial health of sexual minority and gender diverse people in Canada. *Canadian Journal of Community Mental Health, 30*(2), 1–5.

Charmaz, K. (2006). *Constructing grounded theory: A practical guide through qualitative analysis.* Thousand Oaks, CA: Sage.

Chauncey, G. (1994). *Gay New York: Gender, urban culture, and the making of the gay world, 1890–1940.* New York, NY: Basic Books.

Chávez, K. R. (2004). Beyond complicity: Coherence, queer theory, and the rhetoric of the "gay Christian movement." *Text & Performance Quarterly, 24*(3/4), 255–275. doi:10.1080/1046293042000312760

Chávez, K. R. (2010). Spatializing gender performativity: Ecstasy and possibilities for livable life in the tragic case of Victoria Arellano. *Women's Studies in Communication, 33*, 1–15. doi:10.1080/07491401003669729

Chávez, K. R. (2011). Identifying the needs of LGBTQ immigrants and refugees in southern Arizona. *Journal of Homosexuality, 58*, 189–218. doi:10.1080/00918369.2011.540175

Chávez, K. R. (2013). Pushing boundaries: Queer intercultural communication. *Journal of International and Intercultural Communication, 6*(2), 83–95. doi:10.1080/17513057.2013.777506

Chávez, K. R., & Griffin, C. L. (Eds.). (2012). Introduction: Standing at the intersections of feminisms, intersectionality, and communication studies. In *Standing in the intersection: feminist voices, feminist practices in communication studies* (pp. 1–31). Albany: SUNY Press.

Cheng, P. S. (2011). *Radical love: An introduction to queer theology.* New York, NY: Seabury Books.

Chuang, A. (2010). Woods: We miss the normal part of people's lives when covering diversity. *Poynter.* Retrieved from http://www.poynter.org/how-tos/newsgathering-storytelling/diversity-at-work/100473/woods-we-miss-the-normal-part-of-peoples-lives-when-covering-diversity/

Clayton, M., Latimer, S., Dunn, T., & Haas, L. (2011). Assessing patient-centered communication in a family practice setting: How do we measure it and whose opinion matters? *Patient Education and Counseling, 84*, 294–302. doi:10.1016/j.pec.2011.05.027

Clements-Nolle, K., Marx, R., & Katz, M. (2006). Attempted suicide among transgender persons: The influence of gender-based discrimination and victimization. *Journal of Homosexuality, 51,* 53–69. doi:10.1300/J082v51n03_04

Cloud, D. L. (2014). Private Manning and the chamber of secrets. *QED: A Journal in GLBTQ Worldmaking, 1*(1), pp. 80–104. doi:10.1353/qed.2014.0012

Coates, J. (2013). The discursive production of everyday heterosexualities. *Discourse & Society, 24*(5), 536–552. doi: 10.1177/0957926513486070

Collier, M. J., Hedge, R. S., Lee, W., Nakayama, T. K., & Yep, G. A. (2002). Dialogue on the edges: Ferment in communication and culture. In M. J. Collier (Ed.). *International and Intercultural Communication Annual, 24,* (pp. 219–280). Thousand Oaks, CA: Sage.

Collins, P. H. (2004). *Black sexual politics: African Americans, gender, and the new racism.* New York, NY: Routledge.

Commonwealth v. Kosilek, 423 Mass. 449 (1996).

Condit, C. M. (1989). The rhetorical limits of polysemy. *Critical Studies in Mass Communication, 6*(2), 103–122. doi: 10.1080/15295038909366739

Condit, C. M., Lynch, J., & Winderman, E. (2012). Recent rhetorical studies in public understanding of science: Multiple purposes and strengths. *Public Understanding of Science, 21*(4), 386–400. doi:10.1177/0963662512437330

Constable, M. (1998). Reflections on law as a profession of words. In B. Garth and A. Sarat (Eds.), *Justice and power in sociolegal research* (pp. 19–35). Evanston, IL: Northwestern University Press.

Constable, M. (2004). On not leaving law to the lawyers. In A. Sarat (Ed.), *Law in the liberal arts* (pp. 69–83). Ithaca, NY: Cornell University Press.

Coolidge, S. (2014, August 25). City covering transgender surgery. Retrieved from http://www.cincinnati.com/story/news/politics/2014/08/25/cincinnati-transgender-lgbtq-insurance/14591839/

Cooper, B. (2002). *Boys Don't Cry* and female masculinity: Reclaiming a life & dismantling the politics of normative heterosexuality. *Critical Studies in Media Communication, 19* (1), 44–63. doi:10.1080/07393180216552

Corbin, J., & Strauss, A. (2008). *Basics of qualitative research.* Thousand Oaks, CA: Sage.

Corey, F. C. (1998). The personal: Against the master narrative. In S. J. Dailey (Ed.), *The future of performance studies: Visions and revisions* (pp. 249–253). Annandale, VA: National Communication Association.

Cram, E. D. (2012). "Angie was Our Sister:" Witnessing the trans-formation of disgust in the citizenry of photography. *Quarterly Journal of Speech, 98*(4), 411–438. doi: 10.1080/00335630.2012.714899

Crowley, S. (2006). *Toward a civil discourse: Rhetoric and fundamentalism.* Pittsburgh, PA: University of Pittsburgh Press.

Cruikshank, B. (1999). Feminism and punishment. *Signs: Journal of Women and Culture in Society, 24,* 1113–1117. doi:10.1086/495409

Currah, P. (2008). Expecting bodies: The pregnant man and the transgender exclusion from the employment non-discrimination act. *Women's Studies Quarterly, 36,* 330–336. doi: 10.1353/wsq.0.0101

Currah, P., Juang, R. M., & Minter, S. P. (Eds.). (2006). *Transgender rights.* Minneapolis: University of Minnesota Press.

D'Angelo, P. (1999). Framing the press: A new approach to assessing the cynical nature of press self-coverage and its implications for information processing. *Paper presented at the International Communication Association,* San Francisco, CA.

Davidmann, S. (2014). Imag(in)ing trans partnerships: Collaborative photography and intimacy. *Journal of Homosexuality, 61*(5), 535–653. doi:10.1080/00918369.2014.865481

Davis, A. (2014). *Keynote.* Address presented at the *Race & Pedagogy National Conference,* University of Puget Sound, Tacoma, WA.

Davy, Z. (2011). *Recognizing transsexuals personal, political and medicolegal embodiment.* Burlington, VT: Ashgate.

De Cuypere, G., Van Hemelrijck, M., Michel, A., Carael, B., Heylens, G., Rubens, R., et al. (2007). Prevalence and demography in Belgium. *European Psychiatry, 22*(3), 137–141. doi: 10.1016/j.eurpsy.2006.10.002

del Piccolo, L., Mazzi, M., Scardoni, S., Gobbi, M., & Zimmermann, C. (2008). A theory-based proposal to evaluate patient-centered communication in medical consultations: The Verona Patient-Centered Communication Evaluation scale (VR-COPE). *Health Education, 108*, 355–372. doi:10.1108/09654280810899984

DeLuca, K. M. (1999). *Image politics: The new rhetoric of environmental activism*. New York, NY: The Guilford Press.

DeLuca, K. M., & Peeples, J. (2002). From public sphere to public screen: Democracy, activism, and the "violence" of Seattle. *Critical Studies in Media Communication, 19*(2), 125–151. doi: 10.1080/07393180216559

Denker, K. J. (2009). *Co-constructing work-life concerns: An examination of couples' discourse* (Doctoral dissertation). Retrieved from http://hdl.handle.net/10355/9874

Devor, A. H. (2014). Preserving the footprints of transgender activism: The Transgender Archives at the University of Victoria. *QED: A Journal of GLBTQ Worldmaking, 1*, 200–204. doi: 10.1353/qed.2014.0043

Devor, H. (1997). *FTM: Female-to-male transsexuals in society*. Bloomington: Indiana University Press.

deVresse, C., & Elenbaas, M. (2008). Media in the game of politics: Effects of strategic metacoverage on political cynicism. *Press/Politics, 13*(3), 285–309. doi: 10.1177/1940161208319650

DiBlasio, N. (2013, August 23). Media split in Manning "he" or "she" pronoun debate. *USA Today*, 2A.

Dickinson, G., Blair, C., & Ott, B.L. (Eds.). (2010). *Places of public memory: The rhetoric of museums and memorials*. Tuscaloosa: University of Alabama Press.

DiLalla, A. H. (2013, August 23). Mainstream media's issue with Chelsea Manning's gender identity. *The Huffington Post*. Retrieved from http://www.huffingtonpost.com/alex-hayden-dilalla/mainstream-medias-issue-w_b_3798402.html

Distel, M. A., Rebollo-Mesa, I., Abdellaoui, A., Derom, C. A., Willemsen, G., Cacioppo, J. T., & Boomsma, D. (2010). Familial resemblance for loneliness. *Behavior Genetics, 40*(4), 480–494. doi: 10.1016/j.tics.2009.06.005

Dixon, J., & Dougherty, D. S. (2014). A language convergence/meaning divergence analysis exploring how LGBTQ and single employees manage traditional family expectations in the workplace. *Journal of Applied Communication Research, 42*, 1–19. doi: 10.1080/00909882.2013.847275

Doty, A. (1993). *Making things perfectly queer: Interpreting mass culture*. Minneapolis: University of Minnesota Press.

Douglas, S. J. (2010). *The rise of enlightened sexism: How pop culture took us from girl power to Girls Gone Wild*. New York, NY: St. Martin's Griffin.

Dow, B. J., & Condit, C. M. (2005). The state of the art in feminist scholarship in communication. *Journal of Communication, 55*, 448–478. doi:10.1111/j.1460-2466.2005.tb02681.x

Dunn, T. R. (2010). Remembering Matthew Shepard: Violence, identity, and queer counter-public memories. *Rhetoric & Public Affairs, 13*, 611–52.

Dunn, T. R. (2011). Remembering "a great fag": Visualizing public memory and the construction of queer space. *Quarterly Journal of Speech, 97*, 435–60. doi: 10.1080/00335630.2011.585168

Dzmura, N. (Ed.). (2010). *Balancing on the Mechitza: Transgender in Jewish community*. Berkeley, CA: North Atlantic Books.

Eckhardt, K. (2010). This is a test: The visual framing of transgender victims of bias-motivated homicide. *Paper presented at the American Society of Criminology Annual Meeting*, San Francisco, CA. Retrieved from http://citation.allacademic.com/meta/p431769_index.html

Ekins, R., & King, D. (2006). *The transgender phenomenon*. London: Sage.

Enke, A. F. (2013). The education of little cis: Cisgender and the discipline of opposing bodies. In S. Stryker & A. Z. Aizura (Eds.), *The transgender studies reader 2* (pp. 234–247). New York, NY: Routledge.

Enke, A. F. (2014). Translation. *TSQ: Transgender Studies Quarterly, 1*(1–2), 241–244. doi:10.1215/23289252-2400163

Epstein, R., Franks, P., Fiscella, K., Shields, C., Meldrum, S., Kravitz, R., & Duberstein, P. (2005). Measuring patient-centered communication in patient-physician consultations: Theoretical and practical issues. *Social Science & Medicine, 61*, 1516–1528. doi:10.1016/j.socscimed.2005.02.001

Epstein, R., & Street, R. (2007). *Patient-centered communication in cancer care: Promoting healing and reducing suffering.* Bethesda, MD: National Cancer Institute.

Escudero-Alías, M. (2011). Ethics, authorship, and the representation of drag kings in contemporary US popular culture. *Journal of Popular Culture, 44*(2), 256–273. doi: 10.1111/j.1540-5931.2011.00831.x

Esser, F. (2009). Metacoverage of mediated wars: How the press framed the role of the news media and of military news management in the Iraq wars of 1991 and 2003. *American Behavioral Scientist, 52*(5), 709–734. doi: 10.1177/0002764208326519

Esser, F. & D'Angelo, P. (2003). Framing the press and the publicity process: A content analysis of metacoverage of network news. *American Behavioral Scientist, 46*(5), 617–641. doi: 10.1177/0002764202238489

Esser, F., Reinemann, C., & Fan, D. (2001). Spin doctors in the United States, Great Britain, and Germany: Metacommunication about media manipulation. *Harvard International Journal of Press/Politics, 6*, 16 – 45. doi: 10.1177/0002764202238489

Ethan. (n.d.). *Transition > Testosterone > Photo Documentation. FTM Transition.* Retrieved from http://www.ftmtransition.com/transition/testosterone/tphotos.html

Evans, N. (1998). Games of hide and seek: Race, gender and drag in *The Crying Game* and *The Birdcage. Text and Performance Quarterly, 18*, 199–216.

Fagerberg, M. (2013, October 17). Maury Povich - Man? woman swimsuit segment. Retrieved from https://www.youtube.com/watch?v=TvqLzYFD2kQ

Feinberg, L. (1996). *Transgender warriors: Making history from Joan of Arc to Dennis Rodman.* Boston, MA: Beacon Press.

Fejes, F., & Petrich, K. (1993). Invisibility, homophobia and heterosexism: Lesbians, gays and the media. *Critical Studies in Mass Communication, 10*(4), 395–422.

Feldman, C. D. (1981). The multiple socialization of organization members. *Academy of Management Review, 6*, 309–318. Retrieved from http://www.jstor.org/stable/257888

Finnegan, C. A. (2003). *Picturing poverty: Print culture and FSA photographs.* Washington, DC: Smithsonian Books.

Finnegan, C. A. (2005). Recognizing Lincoln: Image vernaculars in nineteenth-century visual culture. *Rhetoric & Public Affairs, 8*(1), 31–57.

Finnegan, C. A. (2008). Doing rhetorical history of the visual: The photograph and the archive. In C. A. Hill & M. Helmers (Eds.), *Defining Visual Rhetorics* (pp. 195–214). Mahwah, NJ: Lawrence Erlbaum Associates.

Finney Boylan, J. (2013, August 22). Longing for the day that Chelsea Manning and I both seem boring. The *Washington Post.* Retrieved from http://www.washingtonpost.com/lifestyle/style/longing-for-the-day-when-chelsea-manning-and-i-both-seem-boring/2013/08/22/7bf52c42-0b5d-11e3-b87c-476db8ac34cd_story.html

Flores, G., Gee, D., & Kastner, B. (2000). The teaching of cultural issues in U.S. and Canadian medical schools. *Academic Medicine, 75*, 451–455. doi:10.1097/00001888-200005000-00015

Fortuna, D. B. (2007). *Alone among many: Faculty and student perceptions of harassment and violence toward gay, lesbian, bisexual, transgender and queer students* (Master's thesis). Retrieved from http://digitalcommons.brockport.edu/edc_theses/33/

Foss, S. K. (1984). Women priests in the Episcopal Church: A cluster analysis of establishment rhetoric. *Religious Communication Today, 7*, 1–11.

Foster, E. (2008). Commitment, communication, and contending with heteronormativity: An invitation to greater reflexivity in interpersonal research. *Southern Communication Journal, 73*(1), 84–101. doi: 10.1080/10417940701815683

Foucault, M. (1991). *Remarks on Marx: Conversations with Duccio Trombadori.* (R.J. Goldstein & J. Cascaito, Trans.). New York, NY: Semiotext(e) and Autonomedia.

Fox, R. (2010). Charting the *Yeast Radio* virus: Exploring the potential of critical virology. *Western Journal of Communication, 74*(4), 417–435. doi:10.1080/10570314.2010.492820

Fraser, L. (2009). Depth psychotherapy with transgender people. *Sexual & Relationship Therapy, 24*(2), 126–142. doi:10.1080/14681990903003878

Friess, S. (2014, April 22). Don't applaud Jared Leto's transgender "mammy." *Time.* Retrieved from http://time.com/10650/dont-applaud-jared-letos-transgender-mammy/

Frosch, D. (2013, March 17). Dispute on transgender rights unfolds at a Colorado school. The *New York Times.* Retrieved from http://www.nytimes.com/2013/03/18/us/in-colorado-a-legal-dispute-over-transgender-rights.html?pagewanted=all&_r=0

Funk, M. [Writer & Producer], & Miller, N. J., & Soiseth, T. V. [Executive producers]. (2002). *Changing sexes: Female to male* [Documentary]. Silver Spring, MD: Discovery Communications.

Gagne, P., Tewksbury, R., & McGaughey, D. (1997). Coming out and crossing over: Identity formation and proclamation in a transgender community. *Gender and Society,* (4), 478. doi:10.2307/190483

Galvin, K. M. (2006). Diversity's impact on defining the family: Discourse-dependence and identity. In L. H. Turner & R. West (Eds.), *The family communication sourcebook* (pp. 3–20). Thousand Oaks, CA: Sage.

Gamson, J. (1998a). *Freaks talk back: Tabloid talk shows and sexual nonconformity.* Chicago, IL: University of Chicago Press.

Gamson, J. (1998b). Publicity traps: Television talk shows and lesbian, gay, bisexual, and transgender visibility. *Sexualities, 1*(1), 11–41. doi: 10.1177/136346098001001002

Gamson, J. (2001). Talking freaks: Lesbian, gay, bisexual and transgendered families on daytime talk TV. In M. Bernstein & R. Reimann (Eds.), *Queer families, queer politics: Challenging culture and the state* (pp. 68–86). New York, NY: Columbia University Press.

Garber, M. (1992). *Vested interests: Cross-dressing & cultural anxiety.* New York, NY: Routledge.

Gates, J. G. (2011, April). How many people are lesbian, gay, bisexual, and transgender? The Williams Institute, UCLA School of Law, Los Angeles, CA. Retrieved from www.law.ucla.edu/williamsinstitute

Brief *Amicus Curiae* of Gay and Lesbian Advocates & Defenders, EqualityMaine, Human Rights Campaign, MassEquality, Massachusetts Transgender Political Coalition, National Center for Transgender Equality . . . & Transgender New Hampshire in Support of Plaintiff-Appellee and in Support of Affirmance; *Kosilek v. Spencer,* No. 12-2194 (2013, February 27).

Girshick, L. B. (2008). *Transgender voices: Beyond women and men.* Hanover: University Press of New England.

Gitlin, T. (1980). *The whole world is watching: Mass media in the making and unmaking of the new left.* Berkeley, CA: University of California Press.

Gitlin, T. (1991). Bites and blips: Chunky news, savvy talk and the bifurcation of American politics. In P. Dahlgren & C. Sparks (Eds.), *Communication and citizenship: Journalism and the public sphere in the new media age* (pp. 119–136). London: Routledge.

GLAAD (2012). *An ally's guide to terminology: Talking about LGBT people & equality.* Retrieved from http://www.lgbtmap.org/allys-guide-to-terminology

GLAAD (2014a). *GLAAD history and highlights: 1985–present.* Retrieved from http://www.glaad.org/about/history

GLAAD (2014b). *GLAAD media reference guide-transgender glossary of terms.* Retrieved from http://www.glaad.org/reference/transgender

Goldman, R. (2009, September 30). *Congregation embraces transgender minister. ABC News.* Retrieved from http://abcnews.go.com/Health/MindMoodNews/congregation-embraces-transgender-minister-larger-church-rift/story?id=8706416

Goodmark, L. (2013). Transgender people, intimate partner abuse, and the legal system. *Harvard Civil Rights-Civil Liberties Law Review, 48*(1), 51–104.

Gosztola, K. (2014). How the LBGT community helped create the caricature of Private Manning. *QED: A Journal in GLBTQ Worldmaking, 1*(1), 30 -46.

Grant, J., Mottet, L., & Tanis, J. (2010). *National transgender discrimination survey report on health and health care*. Washington, DC: The National Center for Transgender Equality and the National Gay and Lesbian Task Force.

Grant, J. M., Mottet, L. A., Tanis, J., Harrison, J., Herman, J. L., & Keisling, M. (2011). Injustice at every turn: A report of the *National Transgender Discrimination Survey*. Washington: National Center for Transgender Equality and the National Gay and Lesbian Task Force.

Graves, M. A., & Engle, F. B. (2006). *Blockbusters: A reference guide to film genres*. Westport, CT: Greenwood Press.

Greatheart, M. S. (2010). *The Fred study: Stories of life satisfaction and wellness from post-transition transgender men* (Unpublished master's thesis). University of British Columbia, Vancouver.

Green v. Calhoun, CV614–103 (Southern D. Statesboro Div. 2014).

Green, J. (1993, April 18). Paris has burned. The *New York Times*. Retrieved from http://www.nytimes.com/1993/04/18/style/paris-has-burned.html?src=pm&pagewanted=1

Gressgård, R. (2010). When trans translates into tolerance-or was it monstrous? Transsexual and transgender identity in liberal humanist discourse. *Sexualities, 13*(5), 539–561. doi:10.1177/1363460710375569

Gross, L. (1991). Out of the mainstream: Sexual minorities and the mass media. *Journal of Homosexuality, 2*, (1–2) 19–46.

Gross, L. (2001). *Up from invisibility: Lesbians, gay men, and the media in America*. New York, NY: Columbia University Press.

Grossman, A. H., D'Augelli, A. R., Howell, T. J., & Hubbard, S. (2005). Parents' reactions to transgender youths' gender nonconforming expression and identity. *Journal of Gay & Lesbian Social Services, 18*(1), 3–16. doi: 10.1300/J041v18n01_02

Haas, T. (2006). Mainstream news media self-criticism: A proposal for future research. *Critical Studies in Media Communication, 23*(4), 350–355. doi 10.1080/07393180600933196

Halberstam, J. (2005). *In a queer time and place: Transgender bodies, subcultural lives*. New York, NY: New York University Press.

Halberstam, J. (2011). *The queer art of failure*. Durham, NC: Duke University Press.

Halberstam, J. (2012). *Gaga feminism: Sex, gender, and the end of normal*. Boston, MA: Beacon Press.

Hall, S. (1997). The work of representation. In S. Hall (Ed.), *Representation: Cultural representations and signifying practices* (pp. 13–64). London: Sage.

Hall, R. (2009). *Wanted: The outlaw in American visual culture*. Charlottesville, VA: University of Virginia Press.

Hancock, A., & Helenius, L. (2012). Adolescent male-to-female transgender voice and communication therapy. *Journal of Communicative Disorders, 45*(5), 313–324. doi:10.1016/j.jcomdis.2012.06.008

Hansbury, G. (2011). King Kong & Goldilocks: Imagining transmasculinities through the trans-trans dyad. *Psychoanalytic Dialogues, 21*(2), 210–220. doi:10.1080/10481885.2011.562846

Haraway, D. (2008). *When species meet*. Minneapolis: University of Minnesota Press.

Hariman, R., & Lucaites, J. L. (2001). Dissent and emotional management in a liberal-democratic society: The Kent State iconic photograph. *Rhetoric Society Quarterly, 31*(3), 5–31.

Hariman, R., & Lucaites, J. L. (2003). Public identity and collective memory in U.S. iconic photography: The image of "Accidental Napalm." *Critical Studies in Media Communication, 20*(1), 35–66. doi:10.1080/0739318032000067074

Hariman, R., & Lucaites, J. L. (2007a). *No caption needed: Iconic photographs, public culture, and liberal democracy*. Chicago, IL: University of Chicago Press.

Hariman, R., & Lucaites, J. L. (2007b). The Times Square kiss: Iconic photography and civic renewal in U.S. public culture. *The Journal of American History, 94*(1), 122–131. doi:10.2307/25094781

Harold, C., & DeLuca, K. M. (2005). Behold the corpse: Violent images and the case of Emmett Till. *Rhetoric & Public Affairs, 8*(2), 263–286. doi:10.1353/rap.2005.0075

Harris, A. P. (2011). Heteropatriachy kills. *Washington University Journal of Law and Policy, 37*, 13–65. Retrieved from http://openscholarship.wustl.edu/law_journal_law_policy/vol37/iss1/3/

Hartnett, S. J., & Larson, D. M. (2006). "Tonight another man will die": Crime, violence, and the master tropes of contemporary arguments about the death penalty. *Communication and Critical/Cultural Studies, 3*(4), 263–287. doi:10.1080/14791420600984102

Hasian, M. Jr., Condit, C. M., & Lucaites, J. L. (1996). The rhetorical boundaries of "the law": A consideration of the rhetorical culture of legal practice and the case of the "separate but equal doctrine." *Quarterly Journal of Speech, 82*, 323–342. doi: 10.1080/00335639609384161

Haughney, C. (2013, August 22). He? She? News media are encouraged to change. The *New York Times*, p. A17.

Havlik, G. (2012). Equal protection for transgendered employees? Analyzing the Court's call for more than rational basis in the *Glenn v. Brumby* decision. *Georgia State University Law Review, 28*, 1315–1340.

Heath, S. (1981). *Questions of cinema*. Bloomington: Indiana University Press.

Heinrich, L. M., & Gullone, E. (2006). The clinical significance of loneliness: A literature review. *Clinical Psychology Review, 26*, 695–718. doi .10.1016/j.cpr.2066.04.002

Heinz, M. (2012). *Transmen on the web: Inscribing multiple discourses.* In Karen Ross (Ed.) *The Handbook of Gender, Sex, and Media* (pp. 326–343). Chichester, West Sussex: Wiley-Blackwell.

Heinz, M. (2014a). *Transgender health communication needs*. Paper presented at the Western States Communication Association Convention, Anaheim, CA.

Heinz, M. (2014b). *The common feeling of isolation: Vancouver Island transgender experiences*. Paper presented at the Central States Communication Association Convention, Minneapolis, MN.

Heinz, M., & McFarlane, D. (2013). Island lives: A trans community needs assessment for Vancouver Island. *Sage Open 3* (3). doi: 10.1177.2158244013503836

Hernandez, E. (2005, August 6). Five questions for Jennie Livingston, director of "Paris Is Burning" and "Who's the Top?" *Indiewire*. Retrieved from http://www.indiewire.com/article/5_questions_for_jennie_livingston_director_of_paris_is_burning_and_whos_the

Hill, C. A., & Helmers, M. (Eds.). (2004). *Defining visual rhetorics*. Mahwah, NJ: Lawrence Erlbaum.

Hill, D. B. (2005). Coming to terms: Using technology to know identity. *Sexuality and Culture, 9*(3), 24–52. doi:10.1007/s12119–005-1013-x

Hill, R. (2013). Before transgender: Transvestia's spectrum of gender variance, 1960–1980. In S. Stryker & A. Aizura (Eds.), *The transgender studies reader 2* (pp. 364–379). New York, NY: Routledge.

Hilton, P. (n.d.). A new skin lightening controversy for *Elle*! Retrieved from http://perezhilton.com/tag/skin_lightening/#.U3PAzscWIgY

Hines, S. (2006). Intimate transitions: Transgender practices of partnering and parenting. *Sociology, 40*, 353–371. doi: 10.1177/0038038506062037

Hines, S. (2010). Queerly situated? Exploring negotiations of trans queer subjectivities at work and within community spaces in the UK. *Gender, Place, and Culture, 17*(5), 597–613. doi:10.1080/0966369X.2010.503116

Hirschfeld, M. (2006). Selections from *The Transvestites*: The erotic drive to cross-dress. In S. Stryker & S. Whittle (Eds.), *The transgender studies reader* (pp. 28–44). New York, NY: Routledge.

Hit & Miss. (n.d.) IMDB.com. Retrieved from http://www.imdb.com/title/tt2232345/?ref_=fn_al_tt_1

Hladky, K. N. (2013). The construction of queer and the conferring of voice: Empowering and disempowering portrayals of transgenderism on *TransGeneration*. In T. Campbell & J. Carilli (Eds.), *Queer media images: LBGT perspectives* (pp. 101–110). Lanham, MD: Lexington Books.

Hollar, J. (2007). Transforming coverage: Transgender issues get greater respect – but anatomy remains destiny. *Fairness & Accuracy in Reporting*. Retrieved from http://www.fair.org/index.php?pages=3216

Holman, C. W., & Goldberg, J. M. (2006). Social and medical transgender case advocacy. *International Journal of Transgenderism, 9*(3–4), 197–217.

hooks, b. (1992). *Black looks: Race and representation*. Boston, MA: South End Press.

Horswell, M. J. (2005). *Decolonizing the sodomite: Queer tropes of sexuality in colonial Andean culture*. Austin: University of Texas Press.

Horvath, K., Iantaffi, A., Grey, J., & Bockting, W.O. (2012). The content and format of transgender-related webpages. *Health Communication, 27*, 457–466. doi:10.1080/10410236.2011.610256

How transgender people experience media. (n.d.). Trans Media Watch. Retrieved from http://www.transmediawatch.org

Howard, J. A., & Hollander, J. (1997). *Gendered situations, gendered selves*. Thousand Oaks, CA: Sage Publications, Inc.

HRC (2014a). Corporate Equality Index: Rating American workplaces on lesbian, gay, and transgender equality. *Human Resources Campaign*. Retrieved from: http://www.hrc.org/campaigns/corporate-equality-index

HRC (2014b). Sample equal opportunity policies. *Human Resources Campaign*. Retrieved from: http://www.hrc.org/resources/entry/sample-equal-employment-opportunity-policies

Hundley, H. L., & Rodriguez, J. S. (2009). Transactivism and postmodernity: An agonistic analysis of transliterature. *Communication Quarterly, 57*(1), 35–50. doi:10.1080/01463370802662473

Iantaffi, A., & Bockting, W. O. (2011). Views from both sides of the bridge? Gender, sexual legitimacy, and transgender people's experiences of relationships. *Culture, Health & Sexuality: An International Journal for Research, Intervention and Care, 13* (3), 355–370. doi: 10.1080/13691058.2010.537770

Ilyasova, K. A. (2009). The personal, the political, and the divisive: ENDA and other LGBT conversations. In B. Drushel & K. German (Eds.), *Queer identities / Political realities* (pp. 81–96). Newcastle upon Tyne, UK: Cambridge Scholars Publishing.

Irving, D. (2008). Normalized transgressions: Legitimizing the transsexual body as productive. *Radical History Review, 100* 38–56. doi:10.1215/01636545-2007-021

Isherwood, L., & Althaus-Reid, M. (Eds.). (2009). *Trans/formations*. London: SCM Press.

Israel, G. (2006). Translove: Transgender persons and their families. In J. J. Bigner (Ed.) *An Introduction to GLBT Family Studies*, (pp. 51–65). New York, NY: Haworth Press.

Jablin, F. M. (1982). Organizational communication: An assimilation approach. In M. E. Roloff & C. R. Berger (Eds.), *Social cognition and communication* (pp. 255–286). Beverly Hills, CA: Sage.

Jablin, F. M. (2001). Organizational entry, assimilation, and disengagement/exit. In F. M. Jablin & L. L. Putnam (Eds.), *The new handbook of organizational communication: Advances in theory, research, and methods* (pp. 732–818). Thousand Oaks, CA: Sage.

Jablonski, C. J. (1988). Rhetoric, paradox, and the movement for women's ordination in the Roman Catholic Church. *Quarterly Journal of Speech, 74*, 164–183. doi:10.1080/00335638809383835

Jack, J. (2012). Gender copia: Feminist rhetorical perspectives on an autistic concept of sex/gender. *Women's Studies in Communication, 35*(1), 1–17. doi:10.1080/07491409.2012.667519

Jackson, P. A. (2004). Gay adaptation, tom-dee resistance, and kathoey indifference: Thailand's gender/sex minorities and the episodic allure of queer English. In W. L. Leap & T. Boellstorff (Eds.), *Speaking in queer tongues: Globalization and gay language* (pp. 202–230). Chicago: University of Illinois Press.

Jakubowski, K. (2014, March 4). Too queer for your binary: Everything you need to know and more about non-binary identities [Web log message]. Retrieved from http://everydayfeminism.com/2014/03/too-queer-for-your-binary/

Jefferson, C. (June 30, 2011). How I learned to hate transgender people. Retrieved from http://magazine.good.is/articles/how-i-learned-to-hate-transgender-people

Jensen, I. W., & Gutek, B. A. (1982). Attributions and assignment of responsibility in sexual harassment. *Journal of Social Issues, 38,* 121–136. doi: 10.1111/j.1540-4560.1982.tb01914.x

Johnson, C., Levenkron, J., Suchman, A., & Manchester, R. (1988). Does physician uncertainty affect patient satisfaction? *Journal of General Internal Medicine, 3,* 144–149. doi:10.1007/BF02596120

Johnson, D. (2007). Martin Luther King Jr.'s 1963 Birmingham Campaign as image event. *Rhetoric & Public Affairs, 10*(1), 1–25. doi:10.1353/rap.2007.0023

Johnson, E. P. (2008). *Sweet tea: Black gay men of the south.* Chapel Hill: University of North Carolina Press.

Johnson, J. R. (2013). Cisgender privilege, intersectionality, and the criminalization of CeCe McDonald: Why intercultural communication needs transgender studies. *Journal of International and Intercultural Communication, 6*(2), 135–144. doi:10.1080/17513057.2013.776094

Jones, J. (2006). Gender without genitals: Hedwig's six inches. In S. Stryker and S. Whittle (Eds.), *The transgender studies reader* (pp. 449–467). New York, NY: Routledge.

Jones, R. G., & Calafell, B. M. (2012). Contesting neoliberalism through critical pedagogy, intersectional reflexivity, and personal narrative: Queer tales of academia. *Journal of Homosexuality, 59*(7), 957–981. doi:10.1080/00918369.2012.699835

Jones, S. (2013, March 22). Filmmaker Jennie Livingston on life and loss after *Paris Is Burning*. *Buzzfeed.* Retrieved from http://www.buzzfeed.com/saeedjones/youwannatalkaboutreading

Jordan, J. W. (2004). The rhetorical limits of the "plastic body." *Quarterly Journal of Speech, 90*(3), 327–358. doi: 10.1080/0033563042000255543

Jordanova, L. (2013). Portraits, patients and practitioners. *Medical Humanities, 39*(1), 2–3.

Juzwiak, R. (2010, April 28). My own private *Untucked*. *VH1.* Retrieved from http://blog.vh1.com/2010-04-28/my-own-private-untucked-behind-the-scenes-at-the-rupauls-drag-race-season-2-reunion/

Juzwiak, R. (2013, January 30). Go ahead and throw all the shade you want, straight people. *Gawker.* Retrieved from http://gawker.com/5980303/go-ahead-and-throw-all-the-shade-you-want-straight-people

Kalter, L. (2008, October). Catching up. *American Journalism Review, 30*(5), 10–11. Retrieved from http://search.ebscohost.com.ezproxy.mnsu.edu

Kanai, R., Bahrami, B., Duchaine, B., Janik, A., Banissy, M. J., & Rees, G. (2012). Brain structure links loneliness to social perception. *Current Biology, 22,* 1975–1979. doi: 10.1016/j.cub.2012.08.045

Kaplan, S. J. (1990). Visual metaphors in the representation of communication technology. *Critical Studies in Mass Communication, 7,* 37–47.

Katz, J. (1984). Why providers don't disclose uncertainty. *Hastings Center Report, 14,*35–44. doi:10.2307/3560848

Katz, J. N. (1995). *The invention of heterosexuality.* Chicago, IL: University of Chicago Press.

Keister, J., & Butts, G. (Writers). (2004). Gender swap [Television series episode]. In M. Chan (Executive producer), *Super surgery.* Silver Spring, MD: Discovery Communications.

Kenagy, G. (2005). Transgender health: Findings from two needs assessment studies in Philadelphia. *Health & Social Work, 30*(1), 19–26.

Kenney, R. (2008). The real gender-bender: The curious case of the coverage of the Steve Stanton story. *The Florida Communication Journal, 37,* 1–11.

Kerbel, M. R. (1998). *Edited for television: CNN, ANC, and American presidential politics* (2nd ed.). Boulder, CO: Westview.

Kerbel, M. R. (1999). *Remote and controlled: Media politics in a cynical age* (2nd ed.). Boulder, CO: Westview.

Kerry, S. (2009). "There's genderqueers on the starboard bow": The pregnant male in *Star Trek. Journal of Popular Culture, 42*(4), 699–714. doi: 10.1111/j.1540-5931.2009.00703.x

Killermann, S. (2012a, February). Sexual orientation for the genderqueer person. Retrieved from http://itspronouncedmetrosexual.com/2012/02/sexual-orientation-for-the-genderqueer/

Killermann, S. (2012b, May). What does the asterisk in "trans*" stand for? Retrieved from http://itspronouncedmetrosexual.com/2012/05/what-does-the-asterisk-in-trans-stand-for/.

Killermann, S. (2013, January). Comprehensive list of LGBTQ+ term definitions. *It's Pronounced Metrosexual* Retrieved from http://itspronouncedmetrosexual.com/2013/01/a-comprehensive-list-of-lgbtq-term-definitions/

Kimmel, D., Rose, T., & David, S. (Eds.). (2006). *Lesbian, gay, bisexual, and transgender aging: Research and clinical perspectives.* New York, NY: Columbia University Press.

Kirby, E. L., & Krone K. J. (2002). The policy exists but you can't really use it: Communication and the structuration of work/life policies. *Journal of Applied Communication Research, 30,* 50–77. doi: 10.1080/00909880216577

Knobloch, L. K., & Knobloch-Fedders, L. M. (2010). The role of relational uncertainty in depressive symptoms and relationship quality: An actor-partner interdependence model. *Journal of Social and Personal Relationships, 27,* 137–159. doi: 0.1177/0265407509348809.

Knobloch, L. K., & Theiss, J. A. (2010). An actor-partner interdependence model of relational turbulence: Cognitions and emotions. *Journal of Social and Personal Relationships, 27,* 595–619. doi: 10.1177/0265407510368967.

Knobloch, L. K., & Theiss, J. A. (2012). Experiences of U.S. military couples during the post-deployment transition: Applying the relational turbulence model. *Journal of Social and Personal Relationships, 29,* 423–450. doi: 10.1177/0265407511431186

Kosenko, K. A. (2010). Meanings and dilemmas of sexual safety and communication for transgender individuals. *Health Communication, 25,* 131–141. doi:10.1080/10410230903544928

Kosenko, K. A. (2011). The safer sex communication of transgender adults: Processes and problems. *Journal of Communication, 61,* 476–495. doi:10.1111/j.1460-2466.2011.01556.x

Kosenko, K., Rintamaki, L., Raney, S., & Maness, K. (2013). Transgender patient perceptions of stigma in health care contexts. *Medical Care, 51,* 819–822. doi:10.1097/MLR.0b013e31829fa90d

Kosilek, M. L. (2011). *Grace's daughter* [Smashwords edition]. Retrieved from Smashwords.com

Kosilek v. Spencer, 889 F. Supp. 2d 190 (D. Mass., 2012).

Kosilek v. Spencer, No. 12-2194 (1st. Cir. 2014).

Kraidy, M. (2009). Reality television, gender, and authenticity in Saudi Arabia. *Journal of Communication, 59*(2), 345–366. doi:10.1111/j.1460-2466.2009.01419.x

Kramer, M. W. (1995). A longitudinal study of superior-subordinate communication during job transfers. *Human Communication Research, 22,* 39–64. doi: 10.1111/j.1468-2958.1995.tb00361.x

Kramer, M. W. (2010). *Organizational socialization: Joining and leaving organizations.* Malden, MA: Polity.

Kramer, M. W. (2011). A study of voluntary organizational membership: The assimilation process in a community choir. *Western Journal of Communication, 75,* 52–74. doi: 10.1080/10570314.2010.536962

Kramer, M. W., & Noland, T. L. (1999). Communication during job promotions: A case of ongoing assimilation. *Journal of Applied Communication Research, 27,* 335–355. doi: 10.1080/00909889909365544

Kulick, D. (2000). Gay and lesbian language. *Annual Review of Anthropology 2000, 29,* 243–285.

Kuper, L. E., Wright, L., & Mustanski, B. (2014). Stud identity among female-born youth of color: Joint conceptualizations of gender variance and same-sex sexuality. *Journal of Homosexuality, 61*(5), 714–731. doi:10.1080/00918369.2014.870443

Labossiere, R. (2007, June 21). Media image of transgendered evolves. *Seattle Times.* Retrieved from http://seattletimes.com/html/living/2003755693_transgender21.html

Ladin, J. (2012). *Through the door of life: A Jewish journey between genders.* Madison: University of Wisconsin Press.

Lakoff, G., & Johnson, M. (2003). *Metaphors we live by.* Chicago, IL: University of Chicago Press.

Lambda Legal Defense and Education Fund. (1999, February 10). Lambda Legal opposes the death penalty. Retrieved from http://www.lambdalegal.org/sites/default/files/publications/downloads/fs_lambda-legal-oppose-death-penalty_1.pdf

Landau, J. (2009). Straightening out (the politics of) same-sex parenting: Representing gay families in U.S. print news stories and photographs. *Critical Studies in Media Communication, 26*(1), 80–100. doi:10.1080/15295030802684018

Landau, J. (2012). Reproducing and transgressing masculinity: A rhetorical analysis of women interacting with digital photographs of Thomas Beatie. *Women's Studies in Communication, 35*(2), 178–203. doi:10.1080/07491409.2012.724527

Lannutti, P. J. (2013). Same-sex marriage and privacy management: Examining couples' communication with family members. *Journal of Family Communication, 13,* 60–75. doi:10.1080/15267431.2012.742088

Lengel, L. (2004). Performing in/outside Islam: Music and gendered cultural politics in the Middle East and North Africa. *Text & Performance Quarterly, 24*(3/4), 212–232. doi:10.1080/1046293042000312742

Lenning, E. (2009). When trans translates into tolerance-or was it monstrous? Transsexual and transgender identity in liberal humanist discourse. *International Journal of Social Inquiry, 2*(2), 39–54.

Lennon, E., & Mistler, B. J. (2014). Cisgenderism. *TSQ: Transgender Studies Quarterly, 1*(1–2), 63–64. doi:10.1215/23289252-2399623

Lester, P. M. (2014). *Visual communication images with messages* (6th ed.). Boston, MA: Cengage Learning.

Lev, A. I. (2004). *Transgender emergence: Therapeutic guidelines for working with gender-variant people and their families.* New York, NY: Routledge.

Lev, A. I. (2005). Disordering gender identity: Gender identity disorder in the *DSM IV-TR.* In D. Karasic & J. Drescher (Eds.), *Sexual and gender diagnoses of the Diagnostic and Statistical Manual (DSM): A reevaluation* (pp. 35–70). Binghamton, NY: The Haworth Press.

Lev, A. I. (2013). *Transgender emergence: Therapeutic guidelines for working with gender-variant people and their families* (2nd ed.). New York, NY: Routledge.

Levinson, W., Roter, D., Mullooly, J., Dull, V., & Frankel, R. (1997). Physician-patient communication: The relationship with malpractice claims among primary care physicians and surgeons. *Journal of the American Medical Association, 277,* 553–559. doi:10.1001/jama.1997.03540310051034

Levitt, H. M., & Ippolito, M. R. (2013). Being transgender: Navigating minority stressors and developing authentic self-presentation. *Psychology of Women Quarterly, 38*(1), 46–64. doi:10.1177/0361684313501644

Levy, D. L., & Lo, J. R. (2013). Transgender, transsexual, and gender queer individuals with a Christian upbringing: The process of resolving conflict between gender identity and faith. *Journal of Religion & Spirituality in Social Work: Social Thought, 32*(1), 60–83. doi:10.1080/15426432.2013.749079

Lewis, P. (2013, August 13). Bradley Manning supervisor "ignored photo of Army private dressed as woman." *The Guardian.* Retrieved from http://www.theguardian.com/world/2013/aug/13/bradley-manning-email-dra-photo-sentencing

Lieberfeld, D., & Sanders, J. (1998). Keeping the characters straight: Comedy and identity in *Some Like It Hot. Journal of Popular Film and Television, 26*(3), 128–135. doi: 10.1080/01956059809602783.

Lin, D. C. (2006). Sissies online: Taiwanese male queers performing sissinesses in cyberspaces. *Inter-Asia Cultural Studies, 7*(2), 270–288. doi:0.1080/14649370600673938

Lindlof, T. R., & Taylor, B. C. (2002). *Qualitative communication research methods* (2nd ed.). Thousand Oaks, CA: Sage.

Livingston, A. L., & Campbell, P. O. (forthcoming). Critical trans solidarity [Review essay]. *Women's Studies Quarterly, 43.*

Lombardi, E. (2001). Enhancing transgender health care. *American Journal of Public Health, 91,* 869–872. doi:10.2105/AJPH.91.6.869

Lombardi, E. (2007). Substance use treatment experiences of transgender/transsexual men and women. *Journal of GLBT Health, 3,* 37–47. doi:10.1300/J463v03n02_05

Lombardi, E., Wilchins, R., Priesing, D., & Malouf, D. (2001). Gender violence: Transgender experiences with violence and discrimination. *Journal of Homosexuality, 42,* 89–101. doi:10.1300/J082v42n01_05

Lynch, J. (2005). Institution and imprimatur: Institutional rhetoric and the failure of the Catholic Church's pastoral letter on homosexuality. *Rhetoric & Public Affairs, 8*(3), 383–403. doi:10.1353/rap.2005.0064

Macdonald, M. (2006). Muslim women and the veil. *Feminist Media Studies, 6*(1), 7–23. doi:10.1080/14680770500471004

Macdonald, M. (2009). Politicizing the personal: Women's voices in British television documentaries. In S. Thornham, C. Bassett, & P. Marris (Eds.), *Media studies: A reader* (3rd ed., pp. 656–670). New York: New York University Press.

Mackie, V. (2008). How to be a girl: Mainstream media portrayals of transgendered lives in Japan. *Asian Studies Review, 32,* 411–423. doi: 10.1080/10357820802298538

Maddux, K. (2011). The Foursquare Gospel of Aimee Semple McPherson. *Rhetoric & Public Affairs, 14*(2), 291–326. doi:10.1353/rap.2010.0227

Madlock, P. E., & Chory, R. M. (2014). Socialization as a predictor of employee outcomes. *Communication Studies, 65,* 56–71. doi: 10.1080/10510974.2013.811429

Magnet, S., & Rodgers, T. (2012). Stripping for the state. *Feminist Media Studies, 12*(1), 101–118. doi:10.1080/14680777.2011.558352

Manning, C. (2013, August 22). "I am Chelsea": Read Manning's Full Statement. *The Today Show.* Retrieved from http://www.today.com/news/i-am-chelsea-read-mannings-full-statement-6C10974052

Marcel, M. (2008). *From scapegoat to citizen: Effects of transgender activism on news coverage of the murder of F. C. Martinez.* Paper presented at the National Communication Association, San Diego, CA. Retrieved from http://citation.allacademic.com/meta/p260620_index.html

Martin, L., Schonlau, M., Haas, A., Rosenfeld, L., Derose, K., Buka, S., & Rudd, R. (2011). Patient activation and advocacy: Which literacy skills matter most? *Journal of Health Communication, 16,* 177–190. doi:10.1080/10810730.2011.604705

Maurey, Y. (2009). Dana International and the politics of nostalgia. *Popular Music, 28*(1), 85–103. doi:10.1017/S0261143008001608

Maykut, P., & Morehouse, R. (1994). *Beginning qualitative research: A philosophical and practical guide.* Bristol, PA: Falmer Press.

Maza, C. (2013, August 29). CNN has no excuse for continuing to call Chelsea Manning a man. *LBGTQ Nation.* Retrieved from http://www.lgbtqnation.com/2013/08/cnn- has-no-excuse-for-continuing-to-call-chelsea-manning-a-man/

McAvan, E. (2011). Rhetorics of disgust and indeterminacy in transphobic acts of violence. In *Homofiles: Theory, sexuality, and graduate studies.* Battis, J. (Ed.). Lanham, MD: Lexington Books.

McCormack, L., Treiman, K., Rupert, D., Williams-Piehota, P., Nadler, E., Arora, N., & Street, R. (2011). Measuring patient-centered communication in cancer care: A literature review and the development of a systematic approach. *Social Science & Medicine, 72,* 1085–1095. doi:10.1016/j.socscimed.2011.01.020

McCroskey, J. C., Richmond, V. P., Sallinen, A., Fayer, J. M., Barraclough, R. A., & Sallinen-Kuparinen, A. (1995). A cross-cultural and multi-behavioral analysis of the relationship between nonverbal immediacy and teacher evaluation. *Communication Education, 44,* 281–291. doi:10.1080/03634529509379019

McCroskey, J. C., Valencic, K. M., & Richmond, V. P. (2004). Toward a general model of instructional communication. *Communication Quarterly, 52,* 197–210. doi:10.1080/01463370409370192

McCubbin, H. I., Joy, C. B., Cauble, A.E., Comeau, J. K., Patterson, J. M., & Needle, R. H. (1980). Family stress and coping: A decade review. *Journal of Marriage and Family, 42,* 855–871. http://www.jstor.org/stable/351829

McDonough, K. (2013, August 22). Media willfully misgender Chelsea Manning. *Salon.* Retrieved from http://www.salon.com/2013/08/22/media_willfully_misgender_chelsea_manning/

McGrath, K. (2013). Teaching sex, gender, transsexual, and transgender concepts. *Communication Teacher, 28*, 1–6. doi:10.1080/17404622.2013.865764

McKinnon, S. L. (2009). Citizenship and the performance of credibility: Audiencing gender-based asylum seekers in U.S. immigration courts. *Text & Performance Quarterly, 29*, 205–221. doi: 10.1080/10462930903017182

McKinnon, S. L. (2011). Positioned in/by the state: Incorporation, exclusion, and the appropriation of women's gender-based claims to political asylum in the United States. *Quarterly Journal of Speech, 97*, 178–200. doi:10.1080/00335630.2011.560176

McKinnon, S. L. (2014). Public access, privacy, and queer politics: An interview with Nathan Fuller. *QED: A Journal in GLBTQ Worldmaking, 1*(1), 148–161. doi:10.14321/qed.1.1.0148

McLaren, R. M., Solomon, D. H., & Priem, J. S. (2012). The effect of relationship characteristics and relational communication on experiences of hurt from romantic partners. *Journal of Communication, 62*, 950–971. doi: 10.1111/j.1460-2466.2012.01678.x

McLelland, M. (2000). Is there a Japanese "gay" identity"? *Culture, Health & Sexuality, 2*(4), 459–472. doi:10.1080/13691050050174459

McLelland, M., & Suganuma, K. (2009). Sexual minorities and human rights in Japan: An historical perspective. *The International Journal of Human Rights, 13*(2–3), 329–343. doi:10.1080/13642980902758176

McWilliam, C., & Freeman, T. (2006). The fourth component: Incorporating prevention and health promotion. In M. Stewart, J. Brown, & T. Freeman (Eds.), *Patient-centered medicine: Transforming the clinical method* (pp. 101–106). Oxford: Radcliffe Medical Press.

Meiners, E. R. (2011). Building and abolition democracy; or, the fight against public fear, private benefits, and prison expansion. In S.J. Hartnett (Ed.), *Challenging the prison-industrial complex: Activism, arts, and educational alternatives* (pp. 15–40). Urbana, IL: University of Illinois Press.

Methodist court defrocks lesbian minister. (2005, November 1). *USA Today*, p. 03a.

Meyer, J. C. (2000). Humor as a double-edged sword: Four functions of humor in communication. *Communication Theory, 10*(3), 310–331. doi: 10.1111/j.1468–2885.2000.tb00194.x

Meyer, M. D. E. (2003). Looking toward the interSEXions: Examining bisexual and transgender identity formation from a dialectical theoretical perspective. In J. Alexander & K. Yescavage (Eds.), *Bisexuality and transgenderism: InterSEXions of the others*. Binghampton, NY: Harrington Park Press.

Meyer, M. D. E. (2004). "We're too afraid of these imaginary tensions": Student organizing in lesbian, gay, bisexual and transgender campus communities. *Communication Studies, 55*(4), 499–514. doi:10.1080/10510970409388635

Meyerowitz, J. (1998). Sex change and the popular press. *GLQ: A Journal of Lesbian & Gay Studies, 4*(2), 159–188. doi: 10.1215/10642684-4-2-159

Meyerowitz, J. (2004). *How sex changed: A history of transsexuality in the United States*. Boston, MA: Harvard University Press.

Miller, J. A. (1993). *The psychoses, the seminar of Jacques Lacan*. (Seminar III, Chapter 1). Retrieved from http://www.lacanonline.com/index/2010/05/reading-seminar-iii-chapter-i-introduction-to-the-question-of-the-psychoses/

Minter, S. P. (2006). Do transsexuals dream of gay rights? In Currah, P., Juang, R.M., & Minter, S. P. (Eds.), *Transgender rights* (pp. 141–70). Minneapolis: University of Minnesota Press.

Mitchell, W. J. T. (1994). *Picture theory: Essays on verbal and visual representation*. Chicago, IL: University of Chicago Press.

Mitra, R., & Gajjala, R. (2008). Queer blogging in Indian digital diasporas: A dialogic encounter. *Journal of Communication Inquiry, 32*(4), 400–423. doi:10.1177/0196859908321003

Mocarski, R., Butler, S., Emmons, B., & Smallwood, R. (2013). "A different kind of man": Mediated transgendered subjectivity, Chaz Bono on *Dancing with the Stars. Journal of Communication Inquiry, 37*(3), 249–264. doi:10.1177/0196859913489572

Mohanty, C. T. (2003). *Feminism without borders: Decolonizing theory, practicing solidarity*. Durham, NC: Duke University Press.

Mollenkott, V. R. (2001). *Omnigender: A trans-religious approach*. Cleveland, OH: Pilgrim Press.

Molloy, P. M. (2013, November 20). Charges dropped in transgender woman Islan Nettles' murder: What now? *Huffington Post*. Retrieved from http://www.huffingtonpost.com/parker-marie-molloy/charges-dropped-islan-nettles-murder_b_4309549.html

Molloy, P. M. (2014, March 18). RuPaul stokes anger with use of transphobic slur. *Advocate*. Retrieved from http://www.advocate.com/politics/transgender/2014/03/18/rupaul-stokes-anger-use-transphobic-slur

Moon, D. G. (2008). Concepts of "culture": Implications for intercultural communication research. In M. K. Asante, Y. Miike, & J. Yin (Eds.), *The global intercultural communication reader* (pp. 11–26). New York, NY: Routledge.

Moon, D. G. (2013). Critical reflections on culture and critical intercultural communication. In T. K. Nakayama & R. T. Halualani (Eds.), *The handbook of critical intercultural communication* (pp. 34–52). Malden, MA: Wiley-Blackwell.

Moran, L. J. (2009). A queer case of judicial diversity: Sexuality, law, and judicial studies. In N. Giffney & M. O'Rourke (Eds.), *The Ashgate research companion to queer theory* (pp. 295–310). Burlington, VT: Ashgate Publishing Company.

Moretti, F. (2007). *Graphs, maps, trees: Abstract models for literary history*. New York, NY: Verso.

Morgan, S. W., & Stevens, P. E. (2008). Transgender identity development as represented by a group of female-to-male transgendered adults. *Issues in Mental Health Nursing, 29*(6), 585–599. doi:10.1080/01612840802048782

Morris III, C. E. (2004). My old Kentucky homo: Lincoln and the politics of queer public memory. In K. R. Phillips (Ed.), *Framing public memory* (pp. 89–114). Tuscaloosa, AL: University of Alabama Press.

Morris III, C. E. (2005). Passing by proxy: Collusive and convulsive silence in the trial of Leopold and Loeb. *Quarterly Journal of Speech, 91*, 264–290. doi: 10.1080/00335630500350350

Morris III, C. E. (Ed.). (2007). *Queering public address: Sexualities in American historical discourse*. Columbia: University of South Carolina Press.

Morris III, C. E., & Nakayama, T. K. (2014). Leaking Chelsea Manning. *QED: A Journal in GLBTQ Worldmaking, 1*, (1), vii–viii. doi:10.14321/qed.1.1.0vii

Morrison, E. G. (2010). Transgender as ingroup or outgroup? Lesbian, gay, and bisexual viewers respond to a transgender character in daytime television. *Journal of Homosexuality, 57*(5), 650–665. doi: 10.1080/00918361003712103

Morton, C. (1994). Feminist theory and the displaced music curriculum: Beyond the add and stir Projects. *Philosophy of Music Education Review, 2*, 106–121.

Motschenbacher, H., & Stegu, M. (2013). Queer linguistic approaches to discourse. *Discourse & Society, 13*(5), 519–535. doi: 10.1177/0957926513486069

Mulvey, L. (1975). Visual pleasure and narrative cinema. *Screen, 16*(3), 6–18. doi: http://dx.doi.org/10.1093/screen/16.3.6

Muñoz, J. E. (2009). *Cruising utopia: The then and there of queer futurity*. New York: New York University Press.

Murray, R. (2013). Private Manning will be called Chelsea, at least by some media outlets. *GLAAD*. Retrieved from http://www.glaad.org/blog/private-manning-will-be-called-chelsea-least-some-media-outlets

Nagy, M. E., & Theiss, J. A. (2013). Applying the relational turbulence model to the empty-nest transition: Sources of relationship change, relational uncertainty, and interference from partners. *Journal of Family Communication, 13*(4), 280–300. doi: 10.1080/15267431.2013.823430

Namaste, V. K. (2000). *Invisible lives: The erasure of transsexual and transgendered people*. Chicago, IL: The University of Chicago Press.

Nemoto, T., Bodeker, B., & Iwamoto, M. (2011). Social support, exposure to violence and transphobia, and correlates of depression among male-to-female transgender women with a history of sex work. *American Journal of Public Health, 101*, 1980–1988. doi:10.2105/AJPH.2010.197285

Nichols, B. (1983). The voice of documentary. *Film Quarterly, 36*(3), 17–30. doi: 10.2307/3697347

Nichols, J. (2013). The biggest transgender moments of 2013: Chelsea Manning, Fallon Fox, Laverne Cox and More. The *Huffington Post*. Retrieved from http://www.huffingtonpost.com/2013/12/26/biggest-transgender-moments-2013_n_4455775.html

Nichols, J. (2014, April 16). Monica Jones, transgender woman, convicted of manifesting prostitution. *Huffington Post*. Retried from http://www.huffingtonpost.com/2014/04/16/monica-jones-transgender_n_5159638.html?utm_hp_ref=politics&ir=Politics

NLGJA encourages journalists to be fair and accurate about manning's plans to live as a woman. (2013). *National Lesbian & Gay Journalists Association*. Retrieved from http://www.nlgja.org/article/nlgja-encourages-journalists-fair-accurate

Nora, P. (1989). Between memory and history: Les lieux de mémoire. *Representations, 26*, 7–24. doi: 10.2307/2928520

Norwood, K. (2012). Transitioning meanings? Family members' communicative struggles surrounding transgender identity. *Journal of Family Communication, 12*, 75–92. doi:10.1080/15267431.2010.509283

Norwood, K. (2013a). Grieving gender: Trans-identities, transition, and ambiguous loss. *Communication Monographs, 80*(1), 24–45. doi:10.1080/03637751.2012.739705

Norwood, K. (2013b). Meaning matters: Framing trans identity in the context of family relationships. *Journal of GLBT Family Studies, 9*, 152–178. doi:10.1080/1550428X.2013.765262

NPR Staff. (2014, April 28). Cake or death? Gâteau, s'il vous plaît! *NPR*. Retrieved from http://www.npr.org/2014/04/28/306526660/cake-or-death-g-teau-sil-vous-pla-t

Nuru, A. K. (2014). Between layers: Understanding the communicative negotiation of conflicting identities by transgender individuals. *Communication Studies, 65*(3), 281–297. doi:10.1080/10510974.2013.833527

Nuttbrock, L., Hwahng, S., Bockting, W., Rosenblum, A., Mason, M., Macri, M., & Becker, J. (2010). Psychiatric impact of gender-related abuse across the life-course of male-to-female transgender persons. *Journal of Sex Research, 47*, 12–23. doi:10.1080/0022449090306225

Obedin-Maliver, J., Goldsmith, E., Stewart, L., White, W., Tran, E., Brenman, S., & Lunn, M. (2011). Lesbian, gay, bisexual, and transgender-related content in undergraduate medical education. *Journal of the American Medical Association, 306*, 971–977. doi:10.1001/jama.2011.1255

Oberacker, J. (2007). Sex assignment surgery and the discourse of public television: The case of NOVA's *Sex Unknown*. *Television & New Media, 8*(1), 25–48. doi: 10.1177/1527476406296262

O'Connor, P., & Kellerman, S. (2009, November 24). Everyone's here and frightfully gay [Web log message]. Retrieved from http://www.grammarphobia.com/blog/2009/11/everyones-here-and-frightfully-gay.html

Ogden, J., Fuks, K., Gardner, M., Johnson, S., McLean, M., Martin, P., & Shah, R. (2002). Doctors' expressions of uncertainty and patient confidence. *Patient Education and Counseling, 8*, 171–177. doi:10.1016/S0738-3991(02)00020-4

Olson, L. (2014, February 25). Why commemorate the life and legacy of Audre Lorde today? *The Feminist Wire*. Retrieved from http://thefeministwire.com/2014/02/audre-lorde-commemorate/

Olson, L. C., Finnegan, C. A., & Hope, D. S. (Eds.). (2008). *Visual rhetoric: A reader in communication and American Culture*. Thousand Oaks, CA: Sage.

O'Neil, M. (1999). The gender gap argument: Exploring the disparity of sentencing women to death. *New England Journal of Civil and Criminal Confinement, 25*, 213–244.

Ono, K. A., & Sloop, J. M. (1992). Commitment to *telos*—a sustained critical rhetoric. *Communication Monographs, 59*, 49–60. doi:10.1080/03637759209376248

Patel, A. R. (2010). India's *hijras*: The case for transgender rights. *George Washington International Law Review, 42*(4), 835–863.

Patterson, R. [Producer & Director], & Hackett, E. [Executive producer]. (2007). *My secret female body* [Documentary]. London, England: British Broadcasting Corporation.

Patton, T. O., & Snyder-Yuly, J. (2012). Roles, rules, and rebellions: Creating the carnivalesque through the judges' behaviors on *America's Next Top Model*. *Communication Studies, 63*(3), 364–384. doi:10.1080/10510974.2012.678923

Pearlman, S. F. (2006). Terms of connection: Mother-talk about female-to-male transgender children. *Journal of GLBT Family Studies, 2*(3–4), 93–122. doi: 10.1300/J461v02n03_06

Peeples, J. (2013). Imaging toxins. *Environmental Communication: A Journal of Nature and Culture, 7*(2), 191–210.

Perlata E. (2013, August 23). *NPR* issues new guidance on Manning's gender identity. NPR. Retrieved from http://www.npr.org/blogs/thetwo-way/2013/08/23/214941331/npr-issues-new-guidance-on-mannings-gender-identity

Petronio, S. (2002). *Boundaries of privacy: Dialectics of disclosure*. Albany: State University of New York Press.

Phillips, J. (2006). *Transgender on screen*. New York, NY: Palgrave Macmillan.

Phillips, K. R. (Ed.). (2004). *Framing public memory*. Tuscaloosa: University of Alabama Press.

Pieper, L.P. (2013). Mike Penner "or" Christine Daniels: The U.S. media and the fractured representation of a transgender sportswriter. *Sport in Society*: 1–16. doi: 10.1080/17430437.2013.854472

Preston, J. [Producer & Director]. (2008). *Sex change soldier* [Documentary]. New York, NY: Time Warner Cable, Ltd.

Pritchard, E. D., (2009). This is not an empty-headed man in a dress: Literacy misused, reread and rewritten in Soulopoliz. *Southern Communication Journal, 74*(3), 278–299. doi:10.1080/10417940903061094

Prosser, J. (1998). *Second skins: The body narratives of transsexuality*. New York, NY: Columbia University Press.

Radia, K., & Martinez, L. (2011, December, 11). Bradley Manning defense reveals alter ego named "Breanna Manning." *ABC News*. Retrieved from http://abcnews.go.com/blogs/politics/2011/12/bradley-manning-defense-reveals-alter-ego-named-brianna-manning/

Ramirez-Valles, J., Kuhns, L., & Manjarrez, D. (2014). *Tal como somos/Just as we are*: An educational film to reduce stigma toward gay and bisexual men, transgender individuals, and persons living with HIV/AIDS. *Journal of Health Communication, 19*, 478–492. doi:10.1080/10810730.2013.821555

Rand, E. J. (2013). Queer critical rhetoric bites back. *Western Journal of Communication, 77*, 533–537. doi:10.1080/10570314.2013.799285

Rawson, K. J. (2009). Accessing transgender// desiring queer(er?) archival logics. *Archivaria, 68*, 123–140.

Rawson, K. J. (2014). Transgender worldmaking in cyberspace: Historical activism on the internet. *QED: A Journal in GLBTQ Worldmaking, 1*(2), 38–60. doi:10.14321/qed.1.2.0038

Rawson, K. J., & Williams, C. (2014). Transgender*: The rhetorical landscape of a term. *Present Tense: A Journal of Rhetoric in Society, 3*, 1–9. Retrieved from http://www.presenttensejournal.org/volume-3/transgender-the-rhetorical-landscape-of-a-term/

Reddy, M. S. (2014). *The rainbow effect: Exploring the implications of queer representation in film and television on social change*. Claremont McKenna College Senior Thesis. Retrieved from http://scholarship.claremont.edu/cmc_theses/953/

Redfern, J., & Sinclair, B. (2014). Improving health encounters and communication with transgender patients. *Journal of Communication in Healthcare, 7*, 25–40. doi:10.1179/1753807614Y.0000000045

Reed, B., Rhodes, S., Schofield, P., & Wylie, K. (2009). Gender variance in the UK: Prevalence, incidence, growth, and geographic distribution. Gender Identity Research and Education Society (GIRES). Available at www.gires.org.uk

Reed, J. (2009). Reading gender politics on *The L Word*: The Moira/Max transitions. *Journal of Popular Film & Television, 37*(4), 169–178. doi: 10.1080/01956050903227944

Riggs, D. W. (2014). What makes a man? Thomas Beatie, embodiment, and "mundane transphobia." *Feminism & psychology, 24*(2), 157–171. doi: 10.1177/0959353514526221

Riley, E., Sithathan, G., Clemson, L., & Diamond, M. (2011). The needs of gender-variant children and their parents: A parent survey. *International Journal of Sexual Health, 23*(3), 181–195. doi:10.1080/19317611.2011.593932

Ringo, P. (2002). Media roles in female-to-male transsexual and transgender identity formation. *International Journal of Transgenderism, 6*(3). Retrieved from http://www.symposion.com/ijt/ijtvo06no03_01.htm

Ritchie, L. D., & Fitzpatrick, M. A. (1990). Family communication patterns: Measuring intrapersonal perceptions of interpersonal relationships. *Communication Research, 17*(4), 523–544. doi: 10.1177/009365090017004007

Riverdale, J. (n.d.). My physical evolution on testosterone. *Gender Outlaw*. Retrieved from http://genderoutlaw.wordpress.com/evolution/

Riverdale, J. (2007a, November 7). First talk with my family doctor. *Gender Outlaw*. Retrieved from http://genderoutlaw.wordpress.com/2007/11/07/first-talk-with-my-family-doctor/

Riverdale, J. (2007b, December 14). My appointment with Dr. Preece. *Gender Outlaw*. Retrieved from http://genderoutlaw.wordpress.com/2007/12/14/my-appointment-with-dr-preece/

Riverdale, J. (2008a, February 26). Loren Cameron - Body Alchemy, Transsexual Portraits. *Gender Outlaw*. Retrieved from http://genderoutlaw.wordpress.com/2008/02/26/body-alchemy-transsexual-portraits-by-loren-cameron/

Riverdale, J. (2008b, April 3). First shot of testosterone! *Gender Outlaw*. Retrieved from http://genderoutlaw.wordpress.com/2008/04/03/first-shot-of-testosterone/

Riverdale, J. (2008c, June 18). Vitamins to combat testosterone side effects. *Gender Outlaw*. Retrieved from http://genderoutlaw.wordpress.com/2008/06/18/vitamins-to-combat-testosterone-side-effects/

Riverdale, J. (2009). *FTM transition - One year on testosterone*. Retrieved from https://www.youtube.com/watch?v=3itvXY4bj6E

Robson, R. (1998). *Sappho goes to law school: Fragments in lesbian legal theory*. New York, NY: Columbia University Press.

Roen, K. (2001). Transgender theory and embodiment: The risk of racial marginalization. *Journal of Gender Studies, 10*(3), 253–263. doi:10.1080/19317611.2011.593932

Roen, K., Blakar, R., & Nafstad, H. (2011). "Disappearing" transsexuals? Norwegian trans-discourses, visibility, and diversity. *Psykologisk tidsskrift, 1*, 28–33.

Rosedale, M. (2007). Loneliness: An exploration of meaning. *Journal of the American Psychiatric Nurses Association, 13*, (201). doi:10.1177/107839030706617

Rosser, B., Oakes, J., Bockting, W., & Miner, M. (2007). Capturing the social demographics of hidden sexual minorities: An Internet study of the transgender population in the United States. *Sexuality Research and Social Policy, 4*, 50–64. doi:10.1525/srsp.2007.4.2.50

Roter, D., & Hall, J. (2006). *Doctors talking with patients/Patients talking with doctors: Improving communication in medical visits*. Westport, CT: Praeger Publishers.

Roter, D., & Hall, J. (2011). How medical interaction shapes and reflects the physician-patient relationship. In T. Thompson, R. Parrott, & J. Nussbaum (Eds.), *The Routledge handbook of health communication* (pp. 55–68). New York, NY: Routledge.

Roy, A. (2006). Regenerating masculinity in the construction of Hindu nationalist identity: A case study of Shiv Sean. *Communication Studies, 57*(2), 135–152. doi:10.1080/10510970600666792

Roy, A., & Hammers, M. L. (2014). Swami Vivekananda's rhetoric of spiritual masculinity: Transforming effeminate Bengalis into virile men. *Western Journal of Communication. 78*, 545–562. doi:10.1080/10570314.2014.914567

Royle, S. A. (2001). *A geography of islands*. London: Routledge.

Rozin, P., Haidt, J., & McCauley, C. R. (2008). Disgust. In Lewis, M., J. M. Haviland-Jones, & Lisa F. Barrett (Eds.), *Handbook of emotions* (3rd ed., pp. 757–776). New York, NY: The Guilford Press.

Rubin, G. (2006). Of catamites and kings: Reflections on butch, gender, and boundaries. In S. Stryker and S. Whittle (Eds.). *The transgender studies reader*. (471–481) New York, NY: Routledge.

Rubin, H. S. (1999). Trans studies: Between a metaphysics of presence and absence. In K. More & S. Whittle (Eds.), *Reclaiming genders: Transsexual grammars at the fin de siècle*. (173–192). London: Cassel.

Saltzburg, S., & Davis, T. S. (2010). Co-authoring gender-queer youth identities: Discursive tellings and retellings. *Journal of Ethnic & Cultural Diversity in Social Work, 19*(2), 87–108. doi:10.1080/15313200903124028

Sanger, T. (2008). Trans govermentality: The production and regulation of gendered subjectivities. *Journal of Gender Studies, 17*(1), 41–53. doi:10.1080/09589230701838396

Scanlon, K., Travers, R., Coleman, T., Bauer, G., & Boyce, M. (2010, Nov. 12). Ontario's trans communities and suicide: Transphobia is bad for our health. *Trans PULSE E-Bulletin, 1*(2).

Schilt, K. (2006). Just one of the guys? How transmen make gender visible at work. *Gender & Society, 20*(4), 465–490. doi:10.1177/0891243206288077

Schilt, K. (2010). *Just one of the guys?: Transgender men and the persistence of gender inequality.* Chicago, IL: University of Chicago Press.

Schilt, K., & Westbrook, L. (2009). Doing gender, doing heteronormativity: 'Gender normals,' transgender people, and the social maintenance of heterosexuality. *Gender & Society, 23*(4), 440–464. doi: 10.1177/0891243209340034

Schurman, K. (2009, January 28). Stats show popularity of digital cameras. *About.com Digital Cameras.* Retrieved from http://cameras.about.com/b/2009/01/28/stats-show-popularity-of-digital-cameras.htm

Sears, B., & Mallory, C. (2011). Update: Economic motives for adopting LGBT-related workplace policies. *The Williams Institute.* Retrieved from http://williamsinstitute.law.ucla.edu/research/workplace/economic-motives-for-adopting-lgbt-related- workplace-policies/

Segrin, C. (2012). Loneliness and poor health within families. *Journal of Social and Personal Relationships, 29*(5), 597–611. doi: 10.1177/0265407512443434

Sentence of death or life imprisonment for capital felonies; further proceedings to determine sentence. § 921.141, Fla. Stat. (2013).

Serano, J. (2007). *Whipping girl: A transsexual woman on sexism and the scapegoating of femininity.* Emeryville, CA: Seal Press.

Shapiro, A. (1999). Unequal before the law: Men, women, and the death penalty. *Journal of Gender, Social Policy & the Law, 8,* 428–470. Retrieved from http://digitalcommons.wcl.american.edu/jgspl/vol8/iss2/4/

Shapiro, E. (2003). "Trans"cending barriers: Transgender organizing on the Internet. *Journal of Gay and Lesbian Social Services, 16*(3/4), 165–179. doi:10.1300/J041v16n03_11

Sheer, V., & Cline, R. (1995). Testing a model of perceived information adequacy and uncertainty reduction in physician-patient interactions. *Journal of Applied Communication Research, 23,* 44–59. doi:10.1080/00909889509365413

Shepherd, J. E. (2012, April 30). The music and meaning of "Paris Is Burning." *NPR.* Retrieved from http://www.npr.org/blogs/therecord/2012/04/23/151218475/the-music-and-meaning-of-paris-is-burning

Sheridan, V. (2009). *The complete guide to transgender in the workplace.* Santa Barbara, CA: Praeger.

Shippee, N. D. (2011). Gay, straight, and who I am: Interpreting passing within the frames for everyday life. *Deviant Behavior, 32,* 115–157. doi: 10.1080/01639621003748514

Sidelinger, R. J. (2010). College student involvement: An examination of student characteristics and perceived instructor communication behaviors in the classroom. *Communication Studies, 61,* 87–103. doi:10.1080/10510970903400311

Siebler, K. (2010). Transqueer representation and how we educate. *Journal of LGBT Youth, 7,* 320–345. doi: 10.1080/19359705.2012.632751

Siegel, R. B. (1998). The racial rhetorics of colorblind constitutionalism: The case of *Hopwood v. Texas.* In R. Post & M. Rogan (Eds.), *Race and representation: Affirmative Action* (pp. 29–72). New York, NY: Zone Books.

Siles, I. (2012). The rise of blogging: Articulation as a dynamic of technological stabilization. *New Media & Society, 14*(5), 781–797. doi:10.1177/1461444811425222

Siminoff, L. A., & Step, M. M. (2011). A comprehensive observational coding scheme for analyzing instrumental, affective, and relational communication in health care contexts. *Journal of Health Communication, 16,* 178–197. doi:10.1080/10810730.2010.535109

Singh, N. P. (2004). *Black is a country: Race and the unfinished struggle for democracy.* Cambridge, MA: Harvard University Press.

Sinnott, M. (2000). The semiotics of transgendered sexual identity in the Thai print media: Imagery and discourse of the sexual other. *Culture, Health & Sexuality, 2*(4), 425–440. doi:10.1080/13691050050174431

Sjöberg, J. (2012). Transgendered saints and harlots: Reproduction of popular Brazilian transgender stereotypes through performance on stage, screen, and in everyday life. In K. Ross (Ed.), *The Handbook of Gender, Sex, and Media* (pp. 344–361). Chichester, West Sussex: Wiley & Sons.

Skidmore, E. (2011). Constructing the "good transsexual": Christine Jorgensen, whiteness, and heteronormativity in the mid-Twentieth-century press. *Feminist Studies, 2*(37), 270–300.

Slagle, R. A. (2003). Queer criticism and sexual normativity: The case of Pee-wee Herman. *Journal of Homosexuality, 45*(2–4), 129–146. doi:10.1300/J082v45n02_06

Slatore, C., Hansen, L., Ganzini, L., Press, N., Osborne, M., Chesnutt, M., & Mularski, R. (2012). Communication by nurses in the intensive care unit: Qualitative analysis of domains of patient-centered care. *American Journal of Critical Care, 21*, 410–418. doi:10.4037/ajcc2012124

Sloop, J. (2000). Disciplining the transgendered: Brandon Teena, public representation, and normativity. *Western Journal of Communication, 64*(2), 165–189. doi: 10.1080/10570310009374670

Sloop, J. M. (2004). *Disciplining gender: Rhetorics of sex identity in contemporary U.S. culture.* Amherst: University of Massachusetts Press.

Sloop, J. M. (2006). Critical studies in gender/sexuality and media. In B. J. Dow & J. T. Wood (Eds.), *The Sage handbook of gender and communication* (pp. 319–333). Thousand Oaks, CA: Sage.

Sloop, J. M. (2007). Lucy Lobdell's queer circumstances. In C. E. Morris III (Ed.), *Queering public address: Sexualities in American historical discourse* (pp. 149–173). Columbia: University of South Carolina Press.

Social Security Administration. (2013, September 30). RM 10212.200 Changing numident data for reasons other than name change. *Program Operations Manual System.* Retrieved from https://secure.ssa.gov/poms.nsf/lnx/0110212200

Solomon, D. H., & Knobloch, L. K. (2004). A model of relational turbulence: The role of intimacy, relational uncertainty, and interference from partners in appraisals of irritations. *Journal of Social and Personal Relationships, 21*(6), 795–816. doi: 10.1177/0265407504047838

Solomon, D. H., Weber, K., & Steuber, K. R. (2010). Turbulence in relational transitions. In S. Smith & S. Wilson (Eds.), *New directions in interpersonal research* (pp. 115–134). Thousand Oaks, CA: Sage.

Sontag, S. (2003). *Regarding the pain of others.* London: Penguin.

Spack, N. P., Edwards-Leeper, L., Feldman, H. A., Leibowitz, S., Mandel, F., Diamond, D. A., & Vance, S. R. (2012). Children and adolescents with gender identity disorder referred to a pediatric medical center. *Pediatrics, 129*(3), 418–425. doi:10.1542/peds.2011-0907

Spade, D. (2006). Introduction. In D. M. Bassichis, *It's war in here: A report on the treatment of transgender and intersex people in New York State men's prisons* (pp. 3–4). Retrieved from http://srlp.org/files/warinhere.pdf

Spade, D. (2011). *Normal life: Administrative violence, critical trans politics, and the limits of law.* Brooklyn, NY: South End Press.

Spade, D. (2012). Their laws will never make us safer. In R. Conrad & D. Spade (Eds.), *Against equality: Prisons will not protect you* (pp. 1–12). Lewiston, ME: AE Press.

Spade, D., & Wills, C. (2014). Sex, gender, and war in an age of multicultural imperialism. *QED: A Journal in GLBTQ Worldmaking, 1*(1), 5–29. doi:10.14321/qed.1.1.0005

Spear, M., & Hagan, K. (2008). Photography and plastic surgery: Part 1. *Plastic Surgical Nursing, 28*(2), 66–68.

Spencer, L. G. (2013). Presiding Bishop Katharine Jeffers Schori and possibilities for a progressive civility. *Southern Communication Journal, 78*(5), 447–465. doi:10.1080/1041794X.2013.847480

Spencer, L. G. (2014). Performing transgender identity in *The Little Mermaid*: From Andersen to Disney. *Communication Studies, 65*(1), 112–127. doi:10.1080/10510974.2013.832691

Spencer, L. G. (2015). Sacralizing the politics of visibility: Coming out, and spirituality, and gay clergy. In A. R. Martinez & L. J. Miller (Eds.), *Gender in a transitional era: Changes and challenges*, (pp. 117-131) Lanham, MD: Lexington Books.

Spencer, L. G., & Barnett, J. T. (2013). Touring homophobia: Understanding the Soulforce Equality Ride as a toxic tour. *Southern Communication Journal, 78*(1), 25–41. doi:10.1080/1041794X.2012.717683

Sperber, J., Landers, S., & Lawrence, S. (2005). Access to health care for transgendered persons: Results of a needs assessment in Boston. *International Journal of Transgenderism, 8*, 75–91.

Squires, C., & Brouwer, D. (2002). In/discernible bodies: The politics of passing in dominant and marginal media. *Critical Studies in Media Communication, 19*(3), 283–310.

Stanley, E. A. (2014). Gender self-determination. *TSQ: Transgender Studies Quarterly, 1*(1–2), 89–91. doi:10.1215/23289252-2399695

Steinbock, E. (2014). On the affective force of "Nasty Love." *Journal of Homosexuality, 61*(5), 749–765. doi:10.1080/00918369.2014.870446

Step, M., Rose, J., Albert, J., Cheruvu, V., & Siminoff, L. (2009). Modeling patient-centered communication: Oncologist relational communication and patient communication involvement in breast cancer adjuvant therapy decision-making. *Patient Education and Counseling, 77*, 369–378. doi:10.1016/j.pec.2009.09.010

Stephens, E. (2014). Normal. *TSQ: Transgender Studies Quarterly, 1*(1–2), 141–145. doi:10.1215/23289252-2399848

Sterk, H. M. (1989). How rhetoric becomes real: Religious sources of gender identity. *Journal of Communication & Religion, 12*(2), 24–33.

Sterk, H. M. (1993). Womanly spiritual space within a patriarchal place. *Women & Language, 16*(1), 27–32.

Sterk, H. M. (2010). Faith, feminism and scholarship: The *Journal of Communication and Religion*, 1999–2009. *Journal of Communication & Religion, 33*, 206–216.

Steuber, K. R., & Solomon, D. H. (2008). Relational uncertainty, partner interference, and infertility: A qualitative study of discourse within online forums. *Journal of Social and Personal Relationships, 25*, 831–855.

Stewart, M. (1995). Effective physician-patient communication and health outcomes: A review. *Canadian Medical Association Journal, 152*, 1423–1433.

Stewart, M., Brown, J. B., Weston, W. W., McWilliam, C. L., & Freeman, T. R. (1995). *Patient-centered medicine: Transforming the clinical method.* Thousand Oaks, CA: Sage.

Stone, S. (1991). The empire strikes back: A posttranssexual manifesto. In J. Epstein & K. Straub (Eds.), *Body guards: The cultural politics of gender ambiguity*, (pp. 280-304). New York, NY: Routledge.

Stotzer, R. (2009). Violence against transgender people: A review of United States data. *Aggression and Violent Behavior, 14*, 170–179. doi:10.1016/j.avb.2009.01.006

Straayer, C. (1996). *Deviant eyes, deviant bodies: Sexual re-orientations in film and video.* New York, NY: Columbia University Press.

Strauss, A., & Corbin, J. (1998). *Basics of qualitative research techniques and procedures for developing grounded theory.* Newbury Park, CA: Sage.

Stryker, S. (1994). My words to Victor Frankenstein above the village of Chamounix: Performing transgender rage. *GLQ: A Journal of Lesbian and Gay Studies, 1*(3), 237–254.

Stryker, S. (2004). Transgender studies: Queer theory's evil twin. *GLQ: A Journal of Lesbian and Gay Studies, 10*, 212–215. doi: 10.1215/10642684-10-2-212

Stryker, S. (2006). (De)subjugated knowledges: An introduction to transgender studies. In S. Stryker & S. Whittle (Eds.), *The transgender studies reader* (pp. 1–17). New York, NY: Routledge.

Stryker, S. (2008). *Transgender history.* Berkeley, CA: Seal Press.

Stryker, S., & Currah, P. (2014). Introduction. *TSQ: Transgender Studies Quarterly, 1*(1–2), 1–18. doi:10.1215/23289252-2398540

Stryker, S., Currah, P., & Moore, L. J. (2008). Introduction: Trans-, trans, or transgender? *WSQ: Women's Studies Quarterly, 36*(3 - 4), 11–22. doi:10.1353/wsq.0.0112

Suess, A., Espineira, K., & Walters, P. C. (2014). Depathologization. *TSQ: Transgender Studies Quarterly, 1*(1–2), 73–76. doi:10.1215/23289252-2399650

Sullivan, N. (2005). Integrity, mayhem, and the question of self-demand amputation. *Continuum: Journal of Media & Culture Studies, 19*(3), 325–333. doi: 10.1080/10304310500176487

Sundén, J. (2001). What happened to difference in cyberspace? The (re)turn of the she-cyborg. *Feminist Media Studies, 1*(2), 215–232. doi:10.1080/14680770120062141

Tady, M. (2012). Being transgender in America. *Extra!* Retrieved from http://www.fair.org/index.php?page=4558

Tanis, J. E. (2003). *Trans-gendered: Theology, ministry, and communities of faith.* Cleveland, OH: Pilgrim Press.

Tarzwell, S. (2006). The gender lines are marked with razor wire: Addressing state prison policies and practices for the management of transgender prisoners. *Columbia Human Rights Law Review, 38*, 167–581.

Taylor, M. (2004). *Peter (A Young English Girl):* Visualizing transgender masculinities. *Camera Obscura, 19*(2), iv–45. doi:10.1215/02705346-19-2_56-1

Testosterone Hormone Replacement for Transsexuals (HRT). (n.d.). *Female to Male.* Retrieved from http://www.femaletomale.org/ftm-transitioning-guide/testosterone-hrt/

Thoreson, R. (2013). Beyond equality: The post-apartheid counternarrative of trans and intersex movements in South Africa. *African Affairs, 112*(449), 646–665. doi:10.1093/afraf/adt043

Thorne, A. (2004). Putting the person into social identity. *Human Development, 47*, 361–365. doi: 10.1159/000081038

Thornton, D. J. (2013). The rhetoric of civil rights photographs: James Meredith's March Against Fear. *Rhetoric & Public Affairs, 16*(3), 457–487. doi:10.1353/rap.2013.0023

Threadgold, T. (1997). *Feminist poetics: Poiesis, performance, histories.* New York, NY: Routledge.

Tigert, L. M., & Tirabassi, M. C. (Eds.). (2004). *Transgendering faith: Identity, sexuality, and spirituality.* Cleveland, OH: Pilgrim Press.

Tomasulo, F. P. (1996). Masculine/feminine: The "new masculinity" in *Tootsie* (1982). *Velvet Light Trap, 38*, 4–13. Retrieved from http://utpress.utexas.edu/index.php/journals/the-velvet-light-trap

Tompkins, A. B. (2014). "There's no chasing involved": Cis/trans relationships, "tranny chasers," and the future of sex-positive trans politics. *Journal of Homosexuality, 61*(5), 766–780. doi:10.1080/00918369.2014.870448

Tooley, M. (2009, September 22). More transsexual United Methodist ministers? *Juicy Ecumenism.* Retrieved from http://juicyecumenism.com/2009/09/22/more-transsexual-united-methodist-ministers/United Methodist News Service.

Towle, E. B., & Morgan, L.M (2002). Romancing the transgender native: Rethinking the use of the third gender concept. *GLQ: A Journal of Lesbian and Gay Studies, 8*(4), 469–497.

The TransAdvocate. (2014). *Glossary.* Retrieved from http://www.transadvocate.com/glossary#sthash.WDu7wS7n.dpuf.

Transas City. (n.d.). Should transpeople or gay men be happy with Neil Patrick Harris in *Hedwig?* Retrieved from http://transascity.org/should-transpeople-or-gay-men-be-happy-with-neil-patrick-harris-in-hedwig/

Transgender Archives. (2014). Retrieved from http://transgenderarchives.uvic.ca/

Transgender Equality Network Ireland (2014). *Glossary of trans terms.* Retrieved from http://www.teni.ie/glossary_of_trans_terms.

Transgender Law Center. (2012). *Organizing for transgender health care: A guide for community clinic organizing and advocacy.* Retrieved from http://www.thecentersd.org/pdf/health-advocacy/organizing-for-transgender.pdf

Transgender Law Center (2013). Journalists: Commit to fair and accurate coverage of transgender people, including Pvt. Chelsea Manning. Retrieved from http://transgenderlawcenter.org/archives/8910

TransJustice. (2005). Trans Day of Action for Social and Economic Justice: Statement by TransJustice. In INCITE! Women of Color Against Violence (Ed.), *The Color of violence: The INCITE! anthology* (pp. 227–228). Brooklyn, NY: South End Press.

Ulm, B. [Writer], & Grassie, J. [Executive producer]. (2004). *Sex change: Her to him* [Documentary]. Silver Spring, MD: Discovery Communications.

Valentine, D. (2007). *Imagining transgender: An ethnography of a category*. Durham, NC: Duke University Press.

Valerio, M. W. (2006). *The testosterone files*. Berkeley, CA: Seal Press.

Van Maanen, J., & Schein, E. G. (1979). Toward a theory of organizational socialization. In B. M. Staw (Ed.), *Research in organizational behavior* (pp. 209–264). Greenwich, CT: JAI Press, Inc.

Van Manen, M. (1990). *Researching lived experience: Human science for an action sensitive pedagogy*. New York: New York University Press.

Venetis, M., Robinson, J., Turkiewicz, K., & Allen, M. (2009). An evidence base for patient-centered cancer care: A meta-analysis of studies of observed communication between cancer specialists and their patients. *Patient Education and Counseling, 77,* 379–383. doi:10.1016/j.pec.2009.09.015

Vidal-Ortiz, S. (2014). Whiteness. *TSQ: Transgender Studies Quarterly, 1*(1–2), 264–266. doi:10.1215/23289252-2400217

Vitulli, E. (2010). Racialized criminality and the imprisoned trans body: Adjudicating access to gender-related medical treatment in prisons. *Social Justice, 37*(1), 53–68.

Volcano, D. L. (2000). *Sublime mutations*. Tübingen: Konkursbuch Verlag.

Wanzer, M., Booth-Butterfield, M., & Gruber, K. (2004). Perceptions of health care providers' communication: Relationships between patient-centered communication and satisfaction. *Health Communication, 16,* 363–384. doi:10.1207/S15327027HC1603_6

Waugh, T. (1997). Walking on tippy toes: Lesbian and gay liberation documentary of the post-Stonewall period 1969–84. In C. Holmlund & C. Fuchs (Eds.), *Between the sheets, in the streets: Queer, lesbian, gay documentary* (pp. 107–124). Minneapolis: University of Minnesota Press.

Warner, M. (2002). *Publics and counterpublics*. Brooklyn, NY: Zone Books.

Webb, J. (2009). *Understanding representation*. Thousand Oaks, CA: Sage.

Weber, K. M., & Solomon, D. H. (2008). Locating relationships and communication issues among stressors associated with breast cancer. *Health Communication, 23,* 548–559. doi: 10.1080/10410230802465233

Weekley, D. E. (2009, August 30). *My book report*. Portland, OR. Retrieved from http://www.epworthumc-pdx.org/messages/page/2/

Weekley, D. E. (2011). *In from the wilderness: She-r-man*. Eugene, OR: Pickwick Publications.

Weekley, D. E. (2013, January 30). In a time of transition. *Sherman's Wilderness*. Retrieved from http://www.shermanswilderness.org/in-a-time-of-transition/

West, I. (2008). Debbie Mayne's trans/scripts: Performative repertoires in law and everyday life. *Communication and Critical/Cultural Studies, 5,* 245–263. doi: 10.1080/14791420802206841

West, I. (2010). PISSAR's critically queer and disabled politics. *Communication and Critical/Cultural Studies, 7*(2), 156–175. doi:10.1080/14791421003759174

West, I. (2013). *Transforming citizenships: Transgender articulations of the law*. New York, NY: New York University Press.

Westbrook, L., & Schilt, K. (2014). Doing gender, determining gender: Transgender people, gender panics, and the maintenance of the sex/gender/sexuality system. *Gender & Society, 28*(1), 32–57. doi: 10.1177/0891243209340034

Whitley, C. T. (2013). Trans-kin undoing and redoing gender: Negotiating relational identity among friends and family of transgender persons. *Sociological Perspectives, 56*(4), 597–621. doi:10.1525/sop.2013.56.4.597

Wickman, J. (2003). Masculinity and female bodies. *Nora-Nordic Journal of Women's Studies, 11*(1), 40–54. doi:10.1080/08038740307272

Wideman, Q. (2014). Intersections: Young, black, and queer. [Web log article]. Retrieved from http://www.thenubianmessage.com/2014/09/09/black-gay/

Wight, J. (2014). Saving Private Manning? On erasure and the queer in the I am Bradley Manning campaign. *QED: A Journal in GLBTQ Worldmaking, 1*(1), 118–129. doi:10.14321/qed.1.1.0118

Wilcox, A. (2003). Branding Teena: (Mis)representations in the media. *Sexualities, 6*(3), 407–425. doi: 10.1177/136346070363009

Williams, C. (n.d). Tracking transgender: The historical truth. Retrieved from http://www.cristanwilliams.com/b/tracking-transgender-the-historical-truth/

Williams, C. (2014). Transgender. *TSQ: Transgender Studies Quarterly, 1*(1–2), 232–234. doi:10.1215/23289252-2400136

Willoughby, B. B., Malik, N. M., & Lindahl, K. M. (2006). Parental reactions to their sons' sexual orientation disclosures: The roles of family cohesion, adaptability, and parenting style. *Psychology of Men & Masculinity, 7*(1), 14–26.

Willoughby, B. L. B., Doty, N. D., & Malik, N. M. (2008). Parental reactions to their child's sexual orientation disclosure: A family stress perspective. *Parenting: Science and Practice, 8*, 70–91. doi:10.1080/15295190701830680

Wiltshire, J., Cronin, K., Sarto, G., & Brown, R. (2006). Self-advocacy during the medical encounter: Use of health information and racial/ethnic differences. *Medical Care, 44*, 100–109.

Winter, S., & Conway, L. (2011). How many trans* people are there? A 2011 update incorporating new data. Retrieved from http://web.hku.hk/~sjwinter/TransgenderASIA/

Wise, D. (2010). News about news in a presidential primary campaign: Press metacoverage on evening news, political talk, and political comedy programs. *Atlantic Journal of Communication, 18*, 127–143. doi: 10.1080/15456871003742070

Wiseman, M., & Davidson, S. (2011). Problems with binary gender discourse: Using context to promote flexibility and connection in gender identity. *Clinical Child Psychology and Psychiatry, 17*(4), 528–537. doi:10.1177/1359104511424991

Witt, P. L., & Wheeless, L. R. (2001). An experimental study of teachers' verbal and nonverbal immediacy and students' affective and cognitive learning. *Communication Education, 50*, 327–342. doi:10.1080/03634520109379259

Witt, P. L., Wheeless, L. R., & Allen, M. (2004). A meta-analytical review of the relationship between teacher immediacy and student learning. *Communication Monographs, 71*, 184–207. doi:10.1080/036452042000228054

Witt, P. L., Schrodt, P., Wheeless, V. E., & Bryand, M. C. (2014). Students' intent to persist in college: Moderating the negative effects of receiver apprehension with instructor credibility and nonverbal immediacy. *Communication Studies, 65*, 330–352. doi:10.1080/10510974.2013.811428

Woloshyn, T. A. (2013). Patients rebuilt: Dr. Auguste Rollier's heliotherapeutic portraits, c.1903–1944. *Medical Humanities, 39*(1), 38–46. doi:10.1136/medhum-2012-010281

Wong, Y. (2012). Islam, sexuality, and the marginal positioning of pengkids and their girlfriends in Malaysia. *Journal of Lesbian Studies, 16*(4), 435–448. doi:10.1080/10894160.2012.681267

Wood, R. (1986). *Hollywood from Vietnam to Reagan*. New York, NY: Columbia University Press.

Wyss, S. (2004). "This was my hell": The violence experienced by gender non-conforming youth in U.S. high schools. *International Journal of Qualitative Studies in Education, 17*, 709–730. doi:10.1080/0951839042000253676

Xavier, J. M., & Simmons, R. (2000). The Washington trans needs assessment survey. Retrieved from www.glaa.org/archive

Xavier, J. M., Bobbin, M., Singer, B., & Budd, E. (2005). A needs assessment of transgendered people of color living in Washington, DC. *International Journal of Transgenderism, 8*(2–3), 31–47. doi: 10.1300/J485v08n02_04

Yarhouse, M. A., & Carrs, T. L. (2012). MTF transgender Christians' experiences: A qualitative study. *Journal of LGBT Issues in Counseling, 6*(1), 18–33. doi:10.1080/15538605.2012.649405

Yep, G. A. (2013). Queering/quaring/kauering/crippin'/transing 'other bodies' in intercultural communication. *Journal of International and Intercultural Communication, 6*(2), 118–126. doi 10.1080/17513057.2013.777087

Yep, G. A. (in press). Toward thick(er) intersectionalities: Theorizing, researching, and activating the complexities of communication and identities. In K. Sorrells & S. Sekimoto (Eds.), *Globalizing intercultural communication: A reader*. Thousand Oaks, CA: Sage.

Zamboni, B. D. (2006). Therapeutic considerations in working with the family, friends, and partners of transgendered individuals. *The Family Journal, 14*(3), 174–179. doi: 10.1177/1066480705285251

Zarefsky, D. (2004). Presidential rhetoric and the power of definition. *Presidential Studies Quarterly, 34*(3), 607–619. doi:10.1111/j.1741-5705.2004.00214.x

Zukic, N. (2008). Webbing sexual/textual agency in autobiographical narratives of pleasure. *Text & Performance Quarterly, 28*(4), 396–414. doi:10.1080/10462930802352003

Index

About the Contributors

Mary Alice Adams (Ph.D., University of Alabama) is a visiting assistant professor in the Department of Media, Journalism, and Film at Miami University. Her research interests include the examination of mediated visual rhetoric in the production and dissemination of culture and the critical analysis of stereotypes in the popular media.

Jace Allen (B.A., University of Montana) is a graduate student in the Communication Studies Department at San Francisco State University. His research focuses on sexuality and communication, representations of non-normative sexual identities in video games, new media, and sexual identity in cross-cultural settings with a focus on Asia and the U.S.

Joshua Trey Barnett (M.A., Indiana University) is a Ph.D. student in the Department of Communication and Fellow at the Global Change and Sustainability Center at the University of Utah. His essays on gender and sexuality have appeared in the *Journal of Leisure Research,* the *Southern Communication Journal*, and *Speaker & Gavel.*

E. Tristan Booth (Ph.D., Arizona State University) is a communication scholar with an emphasis in rhetoric, focusing on the rhetorical strategies of individuals whose gendered, sexed, and sexual identities are marginalized in society. His work has examined the rhetorical strategies employed by transsexual gay men as they navigate medical protocols, the conceptualization of the term *man* in 20th and 21st century U.S. discourse, and the impact of liminal social identities on an episode of *Queer Eye for the Straight Guy* featuring a transsexual man. He is a full-time instructor for the Hugh Downs School of Human Communication at Arizona State University.

Peter Odell Campbell (Ph.D., University of Illinois at Urbana-Champaign) is an assistant professor in the Department of English at the University of Pittsburgh. His work focuses on arguments about race and sexuality in U.S. law and screen media. Peter's writing can be found in *Monster Culture in the 21st Century, Women's Studies Quarterly,* and the *Quarterly Journal of Speech.*

Jamie C. Capuzza (Ph.D., The Ohio State University) is a professor of Communication at the University of Mount Union and director of the Gender Studies program. Her teaching and research interests lie in the areas of gender communication, social movement rhetorics, and global feminisms. Jamie's work appears in *Communication Education, Newspaper Research Journal,* and *The International Journal of Transgenderism.*

Jenny Dixon (Ph.D., University of Missouri) is an assistant professor in the Communication Arts Department and the Coordinator of the Gender and Sexuality Studies minor at Marymount Manhattan College. Her work is featured in the *Journal of Applied Communication Research, Research on Aging,* and *Communication Quarterly.* Jenny's research focuses on the navigation of public and private identities communicated in workplace settings. Specifically, her current research focuses on work and family balance for employees of non-traditional family structures (LGBTQ, polyamorous, non-married, etc.).

Thomas R. Dunn (Ph.D., University of Pittsburgh) is a rhetorical critic, a public address scholar, and an assistant professor of Communication Studies at Colorado State University. His research examines the intersection of queer culture, politics, and rhetoric with a focus on public memory, visual rhetoric, and the rhetoric of the built environment. He is particularly interested in how gay, lesbian, bisexual, transgender, and queer people and communities use the past to argue for contemporary social, political, and cultural change.

matthew heinz (Ph.D., University of Nebraska-Lincoln) is Dean of the Faculty of Social and Applied Sciences and a professor in the School of Communication and Culture at Royal Roads University in Victoria, British Columbia. His work focuses on the intersections of language, gender, and culture. He recently led a transgender needs assessment for Vancouver Island and published a discourse analysis of online transmasculine discourses. heinz held faculty positions at Bowling Green State University and the University of North Dakota.

Cory Holding (Ph.D., University of Illinois) is an assistant professor in the Department of English at the University of Pittsburgh. Her research focuses on the rhetoric of gesture, particularly as gesture relates to persuasion, embodiment, and communicative transmission, as well as the theory and practice of writing pedagogy in contexts of incarceration. Her work appears in *Rhetorica, College Communication and Composition, 9th Letter*, and several textbooks and edited volumes.

Kami Kosenko (Ph.D., University of Illinois at Urbana-Champaign) is an associate professor in the Department of Communication at North Carolina State University whose research focuses on the experiences of stigmatized individuals and groups. She has published in various journals, including the *Journal of Communication, Communication Monographs*, and *Human Communication Research*.

Pamela J. Lannutti (Ph.D., University of Georgia) is an associate professor of Communication and Director of the Graduate Program in Professional and Business Communication at La Salle University. She studies communication in personal relationships, especially in same-sex relationships. She has published her research in various journals, including the *Journal of Family Communication, Journal of Social and Personal Relationships*, and *Journal of Homosexuality*.

Paul Martin Lester (Ph.D., Indiana University) worked as a photojournalist for the *Times-Picayune* in New Orleans. After completing his graduate degrees, Lester was named editor of *Journalism & Communication Monographs* in 2011. From 2006 until 2011, he was editor of the *Visual Communication Quarterly*. Lester has given speeches, presentations, and workshops throughout the United States and in Australia, Canada, Finland, the Netherlands, Northern Ireland, South Africa, Spain, Sweden, and Turkey.

Kathleen Maness is a graduate student at the University of North Carolina at Wilmington pursuing a degree in Social Work.

Lucy J. Miller (Ph.D., Texas A&M University) is a lecturer in the Department of Communication at Texas A&M University. Her research focuses on media representations of marginalized groups.

Kristen M. Norwood (Ph.D., University of Iowa) is an assistant professor in the Department of English and Communication at Fontbonne University. Her teaching and research interests lie in the areas of interpersonal, family, and gender communication. Her work has examined connections between relationships, identity, and cultural discourses in the contexts of transgender identity, adoption, and motherhood.

Lance Rintamaki (Ph.D., University of Illinois at Urbana-Champaign) is an associate professor in the Department of Communication, SUNY Buffalo whose work centers on the intersection of communication theory and health behavior outcomes. His work appears in journals such as *AIDS Patient Care and STDs*, the *Journal of Health Communication*, and *Health Communication*.

Sage E. Russo (B.A., San Francisco State University) is a graduate student and forensics coach in the Communication Studies Department at San Francisco State University. In addition to her work in performance studies, her current research explores the development of a parenting method to inspire individuality, diversity appreciation, and sex positivity within parental communication.

Leland G. Spencer, IV (Ph.D., University of Georgia) is an assistant professor in the Integrative Studies Department at Miami University in Hamilton, Ohio. Leland's research interests are in rhetorics of religion, gender, and sexuality. Leland's research has appeared in *Communication Studies*, the *Southern Communication Journal*, and *Speaker & Gavel.*

Gust A. Yep (Ph.D., University of Southern California) is a professor of Communication Studies, Core Graduate Faculty of Sexuality Studies, and Faculty in the Ed.D. Program in Educational Leadership at San Francisco State University. His research focuses on communication at the intersections of culture, gender, sexuality, and health. In addition to three books, he has published over seventy articles in (inter)disciplinary journals and anthologies. He is the recipient of the 2006 NCA Randy Majors Memorial Award for "Outstanding Lesbian, Gay, Bisexual, and Transgender Scholarship in Communication" and the 2011 San Francisco State University Distinguished Faculty Award for Professional Achievement.